Remembering
the Women

Women's Stories from Scripture for Sundays and Festivals

REMEMBERING
THE WOMEN

Compiled and annotated by
J. FRANK HENDERSON

Foreword by
MARJORIE PROCTER-SMITH

Essays by
JEAN CAMPBELL, OSH, RUTH FOX, OSB
and EILEEN SCHULLER, OSU

Art by
LUBA LUKOVA

A GENEALOGY OF JESUS CHRIST

A genealogy of Jesus Christ, the son of Miriam, the daughter of Anna:
Sarah was the mother of Isaac,
And Rebekah was the mother of Jacob,
Leah was the mother of Judah,
Tamar was the mother of Perez.
The names of the mothers of Hezron, Ram, Amminadab,
        Nahshon and Salmon have been lost.
Rahab was the mother of Boaz,
        and Ruth was the mother of Obed.
Obed's wife, whose name is unknown, bore Jesse.
The wife of Jesse was the mother of David.
Bathsheba was the mother of Solomon,
Naamah, the Ammonite, was the mother of Rehoboam.
Maacah was the mother of Abijam and the grandmother of Asa.
Azubah was the mother of Jehoshaphat.
The name of Jehoram's mother is unknown.
Athaliah was the mother of Ahaziah,
Zibiah of Beersheba, the mother of Joash.
Jecoliah of Jerusalem bore Uzziah,
Jerusha bore Jotham; Ahaz's mother is unknown.
Abi was the mother of Hezekiah,
Hephzibah was the mother of Manasseh,
Meshullemeth was the mother of Amon,
Jedidah was the mother of Josiah.
Zebidah was the mother of Jehoiakim,
        Nehushta was the mother of Jehoiachin,
Hamutal was the mother of Zedekiah.
Then the deportation to Babylon took place.
After the deportation to Babylon
the names of the mothers go unrecorded.
These are their sons:
Jechoniah, Shealtiel, Zerubbabel,
Abiud, Eliakim, Azor and Zadok,
Achim, Eliud, Eleazar,
Matthan, Jacob and Joseph, the husband of Miriam.
Of her was born Jesus who is called Christ.
The sum of generations is therefore: fourteen from Sarah to David's mother;
        fourteen from Bathsheba to the Babylonian deportation;
        and fourteen from the Babylonian deportation to Miriam, the mother of Christ.

Acknowledgments

"A Genealogy of Jesus Christ" was compiled by Ann Patrick Ware of The Women's Liturgy Group of New York, who has graciously put this text in the public domain for all to use.

The scripture quotations, except the psalms and the canticles, and unless otherwise noted, are emended from the New Revised Standard Version of the Bible © 1993 and 1989 by the Division of Christian Education of the National Council of the Churches of Christ in the U.S.A. Used and emended with permission. All rights reserved. The English translation of the psalms and canticles is from the *Liturgical Psalter* © 1995 International Committee on English in the Liturgy, Inc. All rights reserved. "The Feminine as Omitted, Optional or Alternative Story: A Feminist Review of the Episcopal Eucharistic Lectionary" is © Jean Campbell, OSH. It first appeared in the *Proceedings of the North American Academy of Liturgy,* 1990. Used with permission. "Women in the Bible and the Lectionary" by Ruth Fox, OSB, first appeared in the May/June 1996 issue of *Liturgy 90* © 1996 LTP. All rights reserved. "Women in the Lectionary," by Eileen Schuller, OSU, first appeared in the *National Bulletin on Liturgy,* Volume 27, Number 157, Summer 1994 © Concacan Inc., 1994. All rights reserved. Used with permission of the Canadian Conference of Catholic Bishops, Ottawa, Canada.

Text © 1999 J. Frank Henderson. All rights reserved.

REMEMBERING THE WOMEN: WOMEN'S STORIES FROM SCRIPTURE FOR SUNDAYS AND FESTIVALS © 1999 Archdiocese of Chicago: Liturgy Training Publications, 1800 North Hermitage Avenue, Chicago IL 60622-1101; 1-800-933-1800; orders@ltp.org; fax 1-800-933-7094. All rights reserved.

Visit our website at www.ltp.org

03 02 01 00   5 4 3 2

This book was edited by David Philippart and designed by M. Urgo. The production editor was Bryan Cones. Typesetting was done by Karen Mitchell in Bembo. The illustrations and hand-lettering are by Luba Lukova. Printed in the United States of America by Quebecor Printing.

Library of Congress Cataloging-in-Publication Data
Remembering the women: women's stories from scripture for Sundays and
   festivals /compiled and annotated by J. Frank Henderson; foreword by
   Marjorie Procter-Smith; essays by Jean Campbell, Ruth Fox, and Eileen
   Schuller; art by Luba Lukova.
      p.   cm.
   ISBN 1-56854-174-0
   1. Women in the Bible. 2. Bible — Liturgical lessons, English. I.
Henderson, Frank (J. Frank) II. Campbell, Jean, OSH. III. Fox, Ruth, OSB.
IV. Schuller, Eileen M., 1946–   .
BS575.R46   1998
220.9'2'082 — dc21   98-37931
                                                          CIP

WOMEN

LITURGY
TRAINING
PUBLICATIONS

CONTENTS

ILLUSTRATIONS

FOREWORD: TELLING STORIES

Then they remembered his words, and returning from the tomb, they told all this to the eleven and to all the others. Now it was Mary Magdalene, Joanna, Mary the mother of James, and the other women with them who told this to the apostles. But these words seemed to them an idle tale, and they did not believe them.

Luke 24:8–11

We make our lives out of stories: the stories we hear, the stories we are told, the stories we create about ourselves, our people, our world. When the church makes a lectionary, when it chooses which stories to tell and which stories to leave out, it gives to us — or withholds from us — the stories we need in order to make our lives. The Bible itself withholds more women's stories than it offers. More often than not, we women live on the margins of the texts, in the spaces between the words of men, in the silences and the oblique glances. The story hurries past us, or moves over or around us; we are the object, perhaps, but rarely the subject. The acted-upon, sometimes, but almost never the actor.

And yet, we are not absent altogether either. We are not completely silent, never simply acquiescent. Beneath, behind, in the margins, we breathe and struggle and resist and call out to the reader to see us, to hear us, to attend to the message we bear and to believe.

Because church lectionary systems focus on the central actors and the major themes of the Bible, they deepen the silencing and increase the marginalizing of women that starts in the biblical text itself. Without access to these stories, however ambiguous, the church is poorer. We don't have all the stories we need to make our lives, as individuals and as churches. And all of us, women and men, may begin to believe that women have always been silent in and marginal to the story of God's relationship with people, and that the present and future can only either continue this pattern from the past or make a dramatic and wrenching break with it. To come to a clearer sense of our future as a church, we need all the stories we can gather, the painful and difficult ones as well as the beautiful and inspiring ones. Only when we have all the stories can we the church begin to see ourselves as a whole people.

This book offers us the resources for such a clearer seeing. This is not a radical break with our heritage and our history; it is an amplification and an enrichment of it. Working from the Roman lectionary (the official lectionary of the Roman Catholic Church) and the Revised Common Lectionary (widely used by most mainline Protestant churches), Frank Henderson opens a way to incorporate more of the biblical stories of women into our common life. By locating biblical women's stories in the larger interpretive context of the lectionary (with its collection of readings) and the Christian year (with its progression of Christ-centered commemorations), this anthology enables communities to hear these stories not as peripheral and occasional but as central and essential to our self-understanding and our ongoing relationship with God.

Whose stories do we encounter in this expanded and enriched set of readings? Women heroes, omitted or marginalized in other lectionaries, appear here: Jael and Deborah; Rahab the prostitute; Rebekah, Rachel and Leah; the women disciples of Jesus and the prophet daughters of Philip. The woman-centered story of Ruth and Naomi receives fuller treatment, as does the story of the pre-eminent woman disciple, Mary of Magdala. During the Easter season, when the readings focus on the origins of the church, the story of our beginnings is expanded to recognize the many women leaders of the early church, whose names are sadly little known to us: Phoebe, Prisca, Chloe, Nympha, Mary, Junia, Tryphena and Tryphosa. The music of their names, all that survives for us of their stories, invites us to listen harder for their message of resurrection and not to dismiss these stories, however brief, as nothing but "idle tales."

Other stories are here, too, hard ones to hear. The painful story of the conflict between Sarai and Hagar, and Sarai's banishing of Hagar and her child Ishmael, are here, inviting our sorrowful contemplation. Jephthah's daughter and the Levite's concubine, poignantly nameless, appear to ask that we remember the suffering of countless others of their sisters, and ours. Delilah is here too, and Potiphar's wife. Not all the stories are happy ones.

But joyful or tragic, exemplary or appalling, they are our stories. This anthology invites us into the stories, and challenges us to make use of them, because finally a book is only the raw material from which the communities that hear the stories must make their own stories. Like the biblical stories, our stories too will be complex and contradictory, and full of promise and despair, loss and hope. Without these stories, all of them, the ones included in the lectionary and the ones that hide beneath and behind those stories, we do not know who we are. These are not idle tales, and their inclusion in the church's proclamation invites a deeper hearing of the Word of God. While they are not idle tales, they are in a sense unfinished until we take them up, struggle with them (how can we claim that the story of the rape of Tamar is "the Word of God"?) and make them our own.

Marjorie Procter-Smith

INTRODUCTION

This book is a collection of more than 250 women's scriptures from both Testaments of the Bible. What are "women's scriptures"? Here, the term means:
- biblical passages that tell about women, both named and anonymous
- biblical passages that use feminine images such as childbirth
- biblical passages that use feminine images of God
- biblical passages that refer to the feminine figure of holy Wisdom.

Some of these pericopes are found in the Roman lectionary or the Revised Common Lectionary; many are not. The pericopes are arranged here to be read throughout the year on Sundays and festivals (solemnities, feasts and memorials) following the same principles used in the construction of the two official lectionaries. (More on these principles for selecting and arranging texts is found below.)

This book is not itself a lectionary. In part it is a guide to the women's scriptures included in the lectionaries now in use. This book seeks to highlight the inclusion of these passages in the lectionaries, as well as encourage fresh preaching on them. In part this book is a companion to the liturgical year, an anthology setting out the riches of women's scriptures that otherwise might go unread because they are not included in the lectionaries. This book may be used:
- by individuals for personal reflection
- by small groups for study, prayer and discussion
- by preachers seeking to draw on women's biblical experience
- by church musicians seeking to compose or find and appreciate liturgical music based on women's biblical experiences
- by catechists, to supplement the study of the lectionary
- by groups praying in rites or on occasions that do not have prescribed scripture passages.

Depending on a particular denomination's regulations about its lectionary, a passage in this book that is also found in that church's lectionary either must, should or may be used in Sunday worship. The index beginning on page 375 indicates which texts in this book appear in the Roman lectionary (RL) and the Revised Common Lectionary (RCL). In denominations that recommend but do not prescribe lectionary readings, the passages here may be used in addition to other pericopes, however they are chosen.

INTERPRETING THESE TEXTS

The mere collecting of texts under the heading of "women's scriptures" and their use as suggested above are not in themselves going to help the church understand itself as a community of men *and* women. Nor will these things alone help Christian women and men live in appropriate relationship to one another, or empower women—and men, too—to enter more deeply into worship and thus be readied for witness and for mission. Rather, these stories need to be pondered and interpreted in ways that give life and lead to liberation. In this regard it is important to appreciate that the pericopes presented here have already undergone two stages of interpretation.

First, these "women's scriptures" most likely were originally written and edited by men, and preserved and used in societies that were male-oriented. They were incorporated into the biblical text because communities found them valuable and understood them in ways that were helpful to those whose responsibilities including teaching and preaching. The stories communicated messages that were considered significant in particular times and places.

Second, the very act of selecting them for this collection interprets them in a new way: They are taken out of their original literary contexts and juxtaposed to each other. Assigning them to particular Sundays, seasons and festivals contributes to this layer of interpretation. And finally, added titles and brief introductions overtly interpret these texts. These elements of interpretation are not intended to provide a definitive exegesis — which is not only beyond the scope of this book but also simply impossible. Nor are they intended to limit interpretation by assigning meanings. Instead, the purpose of this book is to help bring fresh insight and promote new avenues of interpretation and application for those who ponder these scriptures.

Thus the last and most important stage of interpretation needs to be done by the individuals and communities that use these women's scriptures. What do they mean to you? What do they say to the church? How are they illuminating or empowering or challenging for you? For us? How do they affirm us? How do they challenge us?

In this process, readers may seek to learn especially from contemporary scripture scholars and theologians who focus on women's perspectives. These scholars have introduced and employed new approaches to biblical interpretation, have brought about a new appreciation for what is known of women in biblical times, and have given us new insights into the significance of biblical stories of women to the lives of women and the entire church today.

The modern literature on biblical stories of women and on women's approaches to biblical interpreration is vast — far too great to permit even a representative listing here. Two works, however, are recommended as places to start:

The Women's Bible Commentary, edited by Carol A. Newson and Sharon H. Ringe (London: SPCK and Louisville: Westminister/John Knox Press, 1992). This study provides a book-by-book survey of the Bible from the view of contemporary women's scholarship.

Biblical Women: Mirrors, Models, and Metaphors, by Elizabeth Huwiler (Cleveland: United Church Press, 1993). This book considers several different ways of approaching women's stories; it is a useful introduction to alternative methods of interpretation.

SCRIPTURES IN LECTIONARIES

The reading of scripture is central to Christian worship. The Roman Catholic, Anglican and many Protestant churches in North America today assign three biblical passages plus a psalm for each Sunday and festival of the year. These readings ("lections") are organized according to a three-year cycle and collected in a book called a lectionary. Roman Catholics use the Roman lectionary, and Anglicans and Protestants may use the Revised Common Lectionary. The Revised Common Lectionary is based on the Roman lectionary, but has distinctive readings on some days.

In the early 1980s a number of people noticed that women's stories appear relatively infrequently among the biblical readings of the lectionaries. Writers have discussed the relative invisibility of women in the lectionary, and hence in a major element of Sunday worship (see, for example, the essays by Joan Campbell, Ruth Fox and Eileen Schuller in this book, beginning on page 351).

In response to this criticism, the Revised Common Lectionary of 1992 included a greater number of women's stories than did its predecessor, the Common Lectionary of 1983. During part of the liturgical year (roughly May through November), alternative sets of first readings are offered; the first series contains many more women's stories than the other.

The 1981 edition of the Roman lectionary also included more women's stories from scripture than the 1970 edition; this was due to the addition of new readings rather than the substitution of certain readings for others, as had been done for the Revised Common Lectionary.

Both the Roman lectionary and the Revised Common Lectionary offer longer and shorter versions of some readings; some women's stories are omitted in the shorter versions.

The result of these differences in lectionary composition is that there is variation — at times considerable — in the number of women's stories from scripture proclaimed in Sunday worship from assembly to assembly. Many worshipers are probably unaware of this variation, and of the full scope of the women's stories contained in their lectionaries.

Not to include women's stories and references to women in the scripture passages proclaimed in Christian worship has consequences. It is to fail to acknowledge the place and contributions of women among the Jewish people and the Christian church through the centuries and today. It is to say that women's stories are not important for the church; and perhaps hence to suggest that women themselves are not important in the church. It is to keep women invisible and unempowered. It is to blot out the memory of women in the Christian community, and hence to impede the future of women in the Christian community.

And it affects men negatively, too. Not to include women's biblical stories and references in the liturgical readings denies men as well as women these riches. It is to imply that men's experience is normative for all human beings, and that there is nothing to learn from women. It is to tempt men to believe that their authority over creation and responsibility for society is absolute, and not to be shared with women. It is to leave men with an unhealthy and abridged understanding of themselves as well as of women.

For these reasons and more, the churches face the urgent task of recovering and proclaiming for all people the biblical stories of women.

ARRANGEMENT OF READINGS

The women's stories in this book are arranged according to the method of the lectionaries. This is described briefly here.

The Roman and Revised Common lectionaries assign passages to be proclaimed in the Sunday assembly according to a three-year cycle. In year A, the

Gospel according to Matthew predominates among the gospel readings; in year B, Mark; in year C, Luke. The gospel of John is used at various times in all three years.

For each Sunday and festival of each year of the three-year cycle there are three readings assigned. (Festivals — also called solemnities, feasts or memorials — are important days that do not fall regularly on Sunday but nonetheless call the Christian assembly together to give thanks and praise in common.) The first reading in each set of three is from the First Testament, except during the Easter season, when it is taken from the Acts of the Apostles in the Second. The second reading is from the letters of the Second Testament and the Book of Revelation. The third reading is always from the Christian gospels.

The liturgical calendar divides the days and weeks of the year into two categories. "Seasons" include the festivals of Christmas and Easter and the periods of time that prepare for and extend these celebrations; that is, Advent and Christmas season; Lent and Easter season. The readings assigned during these seasons are primarily related to the season. The rest of the year is called Ordinary Time in the Roman lectionary, and Sundays after Epiphany or Sundays after Pentecost in the Revised Common Lectionary. The Revised Common Lectionary also numbers these Sundays as Proper 1 through Proper 29. During this part of the year, the second and third readings are semi-continuous — that is, a particular biblical book is read bit by bit week after week.

In contrast, the first reading of the lectionaries is related to the third reading, all year. The Revised Common Lectionary also offers a second, optional series of first readings which may be used from Proper 4, known in the Roman calendar as the Ninth Sunday in Ordinary Time, through the end of the liturgical year (roughly from the end of May through late November); in this series the first readings are semi-continuous.

CHOICE OF READINGS

The first step in choosing passages for this anthology was to identify the women's stories from the Bible that are included in the Roman and Revised Common lectionaries. These are used here on the same Sunday or festival as in the particular lectionary. In some cases, the passage has been abridged to highlight the women's story. If a women's story is embedded in a long passage that includes other stories as well, only the women's story and closely related material are presented here; the index provides complete references.

The second step was to choose women's stories from either Testament for those Sundays and festivals that do not now have women's stories prescribed for them by either lectionary. The general principle of choosing readings to relate to the season or festival is retained.

In addition, four subsidiary principles were used in the selection of new women's stories. One principle was to select passages that are closely linked to the existing lectionary readings for a particular day; as much as possible they come from the same biblical books — sometimes even the same chapter — or are at least closely related material from other books. This principle has governed the choice of women's stories for the Sundays of Lent. Based on this principle also, the gospels for the second and third Sundays of Easter tell of women and the resurrection. The readings for the fourth through seventh Sundays of Easter tell of women in the life of the early church, and are taken mostly from the Acts of the Apostles.

A second principle was more imaginative: Women's stories were chosen based on theological or allusive relationships to the festival or season and the lectionary readings. This applies to the women's stories used on the first three Sundays of Advent, the festivals of Epiphany and the Baptism of Christ, Ash Wednesday, Passion (Palm) Sunday, Holy Thursday, Good Friday, Pentecost, Trinity Sunday and the last day of the liturgical year, known as Christ the King or Reign of Christ Sunday.

A third principle was to use passages that included feminine images of God, as in the readings for the Transfiguration for example (which is variously celebrated on the last Sunday after Epiphany or on the second Sunday of Lent).

A fourth principle was to use passages that refer to the feminine figure of holy Wisdom. This principle helped in the choice of readings for some of the mysteries of Jesus Christ: Christmas Day, Ascension, Trinity, Christ the King/Reign of Christ and Ash Wednesday.

After using these four principles in the second step, the third step was to add women's stories for the Sundays of Ordinary Time. When essentially the same women's story is told in all three synoptic gospels — as often happens — the lectionaries generally use that story only in one year of the three-year cycle. Here such stories are told in all three years. Women's stories in the gospels that are not used in the lectionaries (for festivals or the seasons of Advent, Christmastime, Lent and Eastertime) were placed approximately where they should be in the sequence of semi-continuous readings.

A variety of women's stories from the Hebrew scriptures that are not now included in the lectionaries were chosen for this book. These passages were chosen (a) to relate to other women's stories from the Hebrew scriptures that are already included in the lectionaries on adjoining Sundays; (b) to relate to gospel readings being used; and (c) where no other reading had already been assigned. Because a variety of principles has been used, both here and in the official lectionaries, these stories do not always appear in the order of the biblical narrative itself.

Where possible, the principles used by the Revised Common Lectionary for the semi-continuous reading of the Hebrew scriptures have been followed: The Pentateuch is favored for year A; the two books of Samuel, the two books of Kings and the wisdom books for year B; prophetic books for year C. It is impossible to follow this principle consistently, however.

An important area of expansion is the generous use of passages from the "women's books": Ruth, Esther, Judith and Susanna (Daniel, chapter 13). Ruth is used mostly in year B, and the others mostly in year C.

Some women's stories appear more than once; this is usually because they appear more than once in the lectionaries, or because a particular reading is assigned to different days by the Roman lectionary and Revised Common Lectionary. These variants have been retained here.

The psalms that follow the first reading as responsorial psalms in the lectionaries have not been considered in this project on a regular basis. Excerpts from certain psalms that include feminine images of God are presented beginning on page 345. Some of these are suggested for use among the women's stories offered for the Easter Vigil.

This collection of women's stories from scripture, and its arrangement in relation to the lectionaries, is of course not the only way such a project might be undertaken; some stories are still omitted, and the arrangement might follow other principles and take another shape. This work is therefore offered for critique and improvement. It is hoped that in due course it will contribute to the inclusion of more women's stories in the lectionaries.

TRANSLATION AND EMENDATION

The New Revised Standard Version (NRSV) of the Bible is the main source of the biblical passages used in this work — as it is in the Revised Common Lectionary and the translation of the Roman lectionary used in Canada. Psalms and some canticles have been taken from the recent translation by the International Commission on English in the Liturgy. In a very few passages, alternative translations suggested by other scholars have been used.

The language of the NRSV is inclusive with respect to human beings: The word "man" is not used to mean "person" and the phrase "brothers and sisters" is used rather than "brethren," for example.

In some instances, the biblical texts have been further emended according to the principles published in the *Lectionary for the Christian People* (New York: Pueblo, 1986) and more recently in *Readings for the Assembly* (Minneapolis: Augsburg Fortress, 1996). Both of these are the work of editors Gail Ramshaw and Gordon Lathrop, to whom we owe thanks. Further emendation includes replacing masculine pronouns for God with proper name designations, and using the term "the Judeans" instead of "the Jews," to avoid an anti-Semitic reading of the gospels. A few texts that posed special challenges were emended by consulting translations of the Bible other than the NRSV.

IN HER MEMORY

In the book *In Her Own Rite: Constructing Feminist Liturgical Tradition* (Nashville: Abingdon, 1990) Marjorie Procter-Smith wrote:

> At the beginning of the passion narratives of both Matthew and Mark, Jesus receives a Messianic anointing with precious oil by a woman disciple (Matthew 26:6 – 13; Mark 14:3 – 9). Over the protests of the male disciples, Jesus praises the woman's act, and promises that it will be told in her memory wherever the gospel is proclaimed. However, by the time that the gospels were written down, the woman's name had already been forgotten. It is important to note that the context and the content of the story are thoroughly liturgical — she performs a significant and readily recognizable liturgical act, that of anointing. And Jesus' promise to her is a liturgical one, involving proclamation and remembering. Yet there is no trace of this woman and her liturgical action in our liturgical commemorations of the passion of Jesus. Our lectionaries largely ignore her, our liturgies of anointing do not remember her, our sanctoral cycles confuse her with Mary of Bethany or Mary Magdalene. The church has not kept Jesus' promise to this woman.

May this book of readings begin to help us to remedy this failure of ours to keep Jesus' promise — not only to this woman, but to all the women of scripture. Though we may have forgotten their names, let us not forget their stories.

YEAR A

FIRST SUNDAY OF ADVENT

CREATION GROANS IN CHILDBIRTH

Both lectionaries use a passage from Romans 13 for the second reading. That passage tells us that the day of the Lord is near, and that we should wake up and prepare. This passage likens the sufferings of creation to the sufferings of a woman in labor to convey the idea of preparation for glorious new life.

I consider that the sufferings of this present time are not worth comparing with the glory about to be revealed to us. For the creation waits with eager longing for the revealing of the children of God; for the creation was subjected to futility, not of its own will but by the will of the one who subjected it, in hope that the creation itself will be set free from its bondage to decay and will obtain the freedom of the glory of the children of God. We know that the whole creation has been groaning in labor pains until now; and not only the creation, but we ourselves, who have the first fruits of the Spirit, groan inwardly while we wait for adoption, the redemption of our bodies. For in hope we were saved. Now hope that is seen is not hope. For who hopes for what is seen? But if we hope for what we do not see, we wait for it with patience.

Likewise the Spirit helps us in our weakness; for we do not know how to pray as we ought, but that very Spirit intercedes with sighs too deep for words.

Romans 8:18–26

SECOND SUNDAY OF ADVENT

TAMAR, FOREMOTHER OF JESUS, PURSUES HER LEGAL RIGHTS
Both lectionaries tell us this day about John the Baptist, the forerunner of Jesus. In this passage, Judah
refuses to give his youngest son to Tamar so that she may have children — her legal right. Tamar uses her
knowledge of Judah's actions and a disguise to gain what is rightfully hers under the Law — and thereby
becomes a foremother of Jesus.

Judah took a wife for Er his firstborn; her name was Tamar. But Er, Judah's first-born, was wicked in the sight of the LORD, and the LORD put him to death.

Then Judah said to Onan, "Go in to your brother's wife and perform the duty of a brother-in-law to her; raise up offspring for your brother." But since Onan knew that the offspring would not be his, he spilled his semen on the ground whenever he went in to his brother's wife, so that he would not give offspring to his brother. What he did was displeasing in the sight of the LORD, and God put Onan to death also.

Then Judah said to his daughter-in-law Tamar, "Remain a widow in your father's house until my son Shelah grows up" — for he feared that Shelah too would die, like his brothers. So Tamar went to live in her father's house.

In course of time the wife of Judah, Shua's daughter, died; when Judah's time of mourning was over, he went up to Timnah to his sheepshearers, he and his friend Hirah the Adullamite. When Tamar was told, "Your father-in-law is going up to Timnah to shear his sheep," she put off her widow's garments, put on a veil, wrapped herself up, and sat down at the entrance to Enaim, which is on the road to Timnah. She saw that Shelah was grown up, yet she had not been given to him in marriage.

When Judah saw her, he thought her to be a prostitute, for she had covered her face. He went over to her at the roadside and said, "Come, let me come in to you," for he did not know that she was his daughter-in-law. She said, "What will you give me, that you may come in to me?" He answered, "I will send you a kid from the flock." And she said, "Only if you give me a pledge, until you send it." He said, "What pledge shall I give you?" She replied, "Your signet and your cord, and the staff that is in your hand." So Judah gave them to her, and went in to her, and she conceived by him. Then she got up and went away, and taking off her veil she put on the garments of her widowhood.

Genesis 38:6–19

THIRD SUNDAY OF ADVENT

TAMAR, FOREMOTHER OF JESUS, IS VINDICATED

The lectionaries continue to tell about John the Baptist, the messenger who preaches, "Prepare the way." Here, after making false accusations against Tamar, Judah admits his fault. Tamar is vindicated. She bears twins, preparing the way for the coming of the Lord.

Judah sent a kid by his friend the Adullamite to recover the pledge from the woman, but he could not find her. He asked the townspeople, "Where is the temple prostitute who was at Enaim by the wayside?" But they said, "No prostitute has been here." So he returned to Judah, and said, "I have not found her; moreover the townspeople said, 'No prostitute has been here.'" Judah replied, "Let her keep the things as her own, otherwise we will be laughed at; you see, I sent this kid, and you could not find her."

About three months later Judah was told, "Your daughter-in-law Tamar has played the whore; moreover she is pregnant as a result of whoredom." And Judah said, "Bring her out, and let her be burned." As she was being brought out, she sent word to her father-in-law, "It was the owner of these who made me pregnant." And she said, "Take note, please, whose these are, the signet and the cord and the staff." Then Judah acknowledged them and said, "She is more in the right than I, since I did not give her to my son Shelah." And he did not lie with her again.

When the time of her delivery came, there were twins in her womb. While she was in labor, one put out a hand; and the midwife took and bound on his hand a crimson thread, saying "This one came out first." But just then he drew back his hand, and out came his brother; and she said, "What a breach you have made for yourself!" Therefore he was named Perez. Afterward his brother came out with the crimson thread on his hand; and he was named Zerah.

Genesis 38:20–30

SONG OF MARY: Responsory

Mary sings that God continues to rescue Israel, giving strength to Mary as to Tamar.

I acclaim the greatness of the Lord,
I delight in God my savior,
who regarded my humble state.
Truly from this day on
all ages will call me blest.

For God, wonderful in power,
has used that strength for me.
Holy the name of the Lord!
whose mercy embraces the faithful,
one generation to the next.

The mighty arm of God
scatters the proud in their conceit,
pulls tyrants from their thrones,
and raises up the humble.
The Lord fills the starving
and lets the rich go hungry.

God rescues lowly Israel,
recalling the promise of mercy,
the promise made to our ancestors,
to Abraham's heirs for ever.

Canticle of Luke 1:46–55 ICEL

FOURTH SUNDAY OF ADVENT

MARY IS WITH CHILD FROM THE HOLY SPIRIT
When Mary conceives by the Holy Spirit and not by a human father, a family that is not defined by a male head of household is born. Joseph's conventional expectations about marriage and fatherhood are turned upside down by God.

The birth of Jesus Christ took place in this way. When his mother Mary had been engaged to Joseph, but before they lived together, she was found to be with child from the Holy Spirit. Her husband Joseph, being a righteous man and unwilling to expose her to public disgrace, planned to dismiss her quietly. But just when he had resolved to do this, an angel of the Lord appeared to him in a dream and said, "Joseph, son of David, do not be afraid to take Mary as your wife, for the child conceived in her is from the Holy Spirit. She will bear a son, and you are to name him Jesus, for he will save his people from their sins." All this took place to fulfill what had been spoken by the Lord through the prophet:

"Look, the virgin shall conceive and bear a son,
and they shall name him Emmanuel,"

which means, "God is with us." When Joseph awoke from sleep, he did as the angel of the Lord commanded him; he took her as his wife, but had no marital relations with her until she had borne a son; and Joseph named him Jesus.

Matthew 1:18–25

THE NATIVITY OF CHRIST: VIGIL

FOREMOTHERS AND FOREFATHERS OF JESUS
This list of Jesus' ancestors includes four women: Tamar, Rahab, Ruth and Bathsheba, the wife of David.
The first three women (and the fourth's husband) acted in ways not understood by social convention in
order to be faithful to God's purpose. They are models for Jesus in that way.

An account of the genealogy of Jesus the Christ, the son of David, the son of Abraham.

Abraham was the father of Isaac, Isaac of Jacob, Jacob of Judah and his brothers, Judah of Perez and Zerah by Tamar, Perez of Hezron, Hezron of Aram, Aram of Aminadab, Aminidab of Nahshon, Nahshon of Salmon, Salmon of Boaz by Rahab, Boaz of Obed by Ruth, Obed of Jesse, and Jesse the father of King David.

David was the father of Solomon by the wife of Uriah, Solomon of Rehoboam, Rehoboam of Abijah, Abijah of Asaph, Asaph of Jehoshaphat, Jehoshaphat of Joram, Joram of Uzziah, Uzziah of Jotham, Jotham of Ahaz, Ahaz of Hezekiah, Hezekiah of Manasseh, Manasseh of Amos, Amos of Josiah, and Josiah the father of Jechoniah and his brothers, at the time of the deportation to Babylon.

After the deportation to Babylon: Jechoniah was the father of Salathiel, Salathiel of Zerubbabel, Zerubbabel of Abiud, Abiud of Eliakim, Eliakim of Azor, Azor of Zadok, Zadok of Achim, Achim of Eliud, Eliud of Eleazar, Eleazar of Matthan, Matthan of Jacob, and Jacob of Joseph the husband of Mary, of whom Jesus was born, who is called the Christ.

So all the generations from Abraham to David are fourteen generations; and from David to the deportation to Babylon, fourteen generations; and from the deportation to Babylon to the Christ, fourteen generations.

Matthew 1:1 – 17

THE NATIVITY OF CHRIST: DURING THE NIGHT

MARY GIVES BIRTH TO JESUS

Giving birth in a stable is a sign of how insignificant this family is in its society. The true meaning of the event is first revealed to other outcasts, the shepherds. God works through people like these.

In those days a decree went out from Emperor Augustus that all the world should be registered. This was the first registration and was taken while Quirinius was governor of Syria. All went to their own towns to be registered.

Joseph also went from the town of Nazareth in Galilee to Judea, to the city of David called Bethlehem, because he was descended from the house and family of David. He went to be registered with Mary, to whom he was engaged and who was expecting a child.

While they were there, the time came for her to deliver her child. And she gave birth to her firstborn son and wrapped him in bands of cloth, and laid him in a manger, because there was no place for them in the inn.

In that region there were shepherds living in the fields, keeping watch over their flock by night. Then an angel of the Lord stood before them, and the glory of the Lord shone around them, and they were terrified. But the angel said to them, "Do not be afraid; for see — I am bringing you good news of great joy for all the people: to you is born this day in the city of David a Savior, who is the Christ, the Lord. This will be a sign for you: you will find a child wrapped in bands of cloth and lying in a manger." And suddenly there was with the angel a multitude of the heavenly host, praising God and saying,

"Glory to God in the highest heaven,
and peace to God's people on earth."

When the angels had left them and gone into heaven, the shepherds said to one another, "Let us go now to Bethlehem and see this thing that has taken place, which the Lord has made known to us." So they went with haste and found Mary and Joseph, and the child lying in the manger.

Luke 2:1 – 16

Eve

THE NATIVITY OF CHRIST: DAWN

DAUGHTER ZION

On one level, Mary herself is daughter Zion, who is sought out and not forsaken. On another level, Mary is the one who brings the promised salvation to daughter Zion, Jerusalem.

Upon your walls, O Jerusalem,
  I have posted sentinels;
  all day and all night
  they shall never be silent.
You who remind the LORD,
  take no rest,
  and give God no rest
  until Jerusalem is established
  and renowned throughout the earth.
The LORD has sworn by right hand
  and by mighty arm;
I will not again give your grain
  to be food for your enemies,
and foreigners shall not drink the wine
  for which you have labored;
but those who garner it shall eat it
  and praise the LORD,
and those who gather it shall drink it
  in my holy courts.

Go through, go through the gates,
  prepare the way for the people;
build up, build up the highway,
  clear it of stones,
  lift up an ensign over the peoples.
The LORD has proclaimed
  to the end of the earth:
Say to daughter Zion,
  "See, your salvation comes;
  behold, God comes bearing the reward,
  preceded by the recompense."
They shall be called, "The Holy People,
  The Redeemed of the Lord";
and you shall be called, "Sought Out,
  A City Not Forsaken."

Isaiah 62:6 – 12

Mary was a thoughtful and reflective woman. She did indeed have much to ponder. What did she think about all this?

When the angels had left them and gone into heaven, the shepherds said to one another, "Let us go now to Bethlehem and see this thing that has taken place, which the Lord has made known to us." So they went with haste and found Mary and Joseph, and the child lying in the manger. When they saw this, they made known what had been told them about this child; and all who heard it were amazed at what the shepherds told them. But Mary treasured all these words and pondered them in her heart. The shepherds returned, glorifying and praising God for all they had heard and seen, as it had been told them.

Luke 2:15 – 20

THE NATIVITY OF CHRIST: DURING THE DAY

WISDOM MAKES HER DWELLING AMONG GOD'S PEOPLE
The lectionaries offer the prologue to the Gospel of John: "In the beginning was the word . . . the word dwelled among us." In this passage, we hear of divine Wisdom, a feminine figure who is with God from the beginning, co-creator with God who pitches her tent in the midst of her people.

Wisdom praises herself,
     and tells of her glory in the midst of her people.
In the assembly of the Most High she opens her mouth,
     and in the presence of God's hosts she tells of her glory:

"I came forth from the mouth of the Most High,
     and covered the earth like a mist.
I dwelt in the highest heavens,
     and my throne was in a pillar of cloud.
Alone I compassed the vault of heaven
     and traversed the depths of the abyss.
Over waves of the sea, over all the earth,
     and over every people and nation I have held sway.
Among all these I sought a resting place;
     in whose territory should I abide?

"Then the Creator of all things gave me a command,
     and my Creator chose the place for my tent.
God said, 'Make your dwelling in Jacob,
     and in Israel receive your inheritance.'
Before the ages, in the beginning, God created me,
     and for all the ages I shall not cease to be.
In the holy tent I ministered before God,
     and so I was established in Zion.
Thus in the beloved city God gave me a resting place,
     and in Jerusalem was my domain.
I took root in an honored people,
     in the portion of the Lord's heritage."

Sirach 24:1 – 12

THE HOLY FAMILY

SUNDAY AFTER CHRISTMAS DAY

HONOR MOTHER AND FATHER
Children are called to respect and honor mother as well as father.

For the Lord honors a father above his children,
    and confirms a mother's right over her children.
Those who honor their father atone for sins,
    and those who respect their mother are like those who lay up treasure.
Those who honor their father will have joy in their own children,
    and when they pray they will be heard.
Those who respect their father will have long life,
    and those who honor their mother obey the Lord;
    they will serve their parents as their masters.

Sirach 3:2–7

THE HOLY FAMILY FLEES TO EGYPT
A father is one who stands by the family and keeps it from harm, not one who rules over it or abandons it.

An angel of the Lord appeared to Joseph in a dream and said, "Get up, take the child and his mother, and flee to Egypt, and remain there until I tell you; for Herod is about to search for the child, to destroy him." Then Joseph got up, took the child and his mother by night, and went to Egypt, and remained there until the death of Herod. This was to fulfill what had been spoken by the Lord through the prophet, "Out of Egypt I have called my son."

When Herod saw that he had been tricked by the magi, he was infuriated, and he sent and killed all the children in and around Bethlehem who were two years old or under, according to the time that he had learned from the magi. Then was fulfilled what had been spoken through the prophet Jeremiah:
"A voice was heard in Ramah,
    wailing and loud lamentation.
Rachel weeping for her children;
    she refused to be consoled,
    because they are no more."

When Herod died, an angel of the Lord suddenly appeared in a dream to Joseph in Egypt and said, "Get up, take the child and his mother, and go to the land of Israel, for those who were seeking the child's life are dead." Then Joseph got up, took the child and his mother, and went to the land of Israel. But when he heard that Archelaus was ruling over Judea in place of his father Herod, Joseph was afraid to go there. And after being warned in a dream, he went away to the district of Galilee. There Joseph made his home in a town called Nazareth, so that what had been spoken through the prophets might be fulfilled, "He will be called a Nazarean."

Matthew 2:13–23

1 JANUARY: MARY, MOTHER OF JESUS
1 JANUARY: HOLY NAME OF JESUS

JESUS, BORN OF A WOMAN
Our adoption as children of God through Christ is effected through a woman, Mary.

When the fullness of time had come, God sent the Son, born of a woman, born under the law, in order to redeem those who were under the law, so that we might receive adoption as children. And because you are children, God has sent the Spirit of the Son into our hearts, crying, "Abba! Father!" So you are no longer a slave but a child, and if a child then also an heir, through God.

Galatians 4:4–7

MARY KNOWS JESUS' NAME
The name of Jesus was proclaimed to Mary by the angel before he was conceived. Mary is the bearer of this good news.

When the angels had left them and gone into heaven, the shepherds said to one another, "Let us go now to Bethlehem and see this thing that has taken place, which the Lord has made known to us." So they went with haste and found Mary and Joseph, and the child lying in the manger. When they saw this, they made known what had been told them about this child; and all who heard it were amazed at what the shepherds told them. But Mary treasured all these words and pondered them in her heart. The shepherds returned, glorifying and praising God for all they had heard and seen, as it had been told them.

After eight days had passed, it was time to circumcise the child; and he was called Jesus, the name given by the angel before he was conceived in the womb.

Luke 2:15–21

SECOND SUNDAY AFTER CHRISTMAS

WISDOM MAKES HER DWELLING AMONG GOD'S PEOPLE
The lectionaries offer the prologue to the Gospel of John: "In the beginning was the word . . . the word dwelled among us." In this passage, we hear of divine Wisdom, a feminine figure who is with God from the beginning, co-creator with God who pitches her tent in the midst of her people.

Wisdom praises herself,
    and tells of her glory in the midst of her people.
In the assembly of the Most High she opens her mouth,
    and in the presence of God's hosts she tells of her glory:

"I came forth from the mouth of the Most High,
    and covered the earth like a mist.
I dwelt in the highest heavens,
    and my throne was in a pillar of cloud.
Alone I compassed the vault of heaven
    and traversed the depths of the abyss.
Over waves of the sea, over all the earth,
    and over every people and nation I have held sway.
Among all these I sought a resting place;
    in whose territory should I abide?

"Then the Creator of all things gave me a command,
    and my Creator chose the place for my tent.
God said, 'Make your dwelling in Jacob,
    and in Israel receive your inheritance.'
Before the ages, in the beginning, God created me,
    and for all the ages I shall not cease to be.
In the holy tent I ministered before God,
    and so I was established in Zion.
Thus in the beloved city God gave me a resting place,
    and in Jerusalem was my domain.
I took root in an honored people,
    in the portion of the Lord's heritage."

Sirach 24:1 – 12

THE EPIPHANY OF CHRIST

When Epiphany falls on the Second Sunday after Christmas, the two sets of readings may be combined.

THE QUEEN OF SHEBA GIVES AND RECEIVES GIFTS

In the lectionaries, the first reading tells that kings and ordinary people will bring homage and gifts; the gospel is about the magi. This passage tells about the Queen of Sheba, who brought gifts to King Solomon and received his gifts in return.

When the queen of Sheba heard of the fame of Solomon (fame due to the name of the LORD), she came to test him with hard questions. She came to Jerusalem with a very great retinue, with camels bearing spices, and very much gold, and precious stones; and when she came to Solomon, she told him all that was on her mind. Solomon answered all her questions; there was nothing hidden from the king that he could not explain to her. When the queen of Sheba had observed all the wisdom of Solomon, the house that he had built, the food of his table, the seating of his officials, and the attendance of his servants, their clothing, his valets, and his burnt offerings that he offered at the house of the LORD, there was no more spirit in her.

So she said to the king, "The report was true that I heard in my own land of your accomplishments and of your wisdom, but I did not believe the reports until I came and my own eyes had seen it. Not even half had been told me; your wisdom and prosperity far surpass the report that I had heard. Happy are your wives! Happy are these your servants, who continually attend you and hear your wisdom! Blessed be the LORD your God, who has delight in you and set you on the throne of Israel! Because the LORD loved Israel forever, you have been made king to execute justice and righteousness." Then she gave the king one hundred twenty talents of gold, a great quantity of spices, and precious stones; never again did spices come in such quantity as that which the queen of Sheba gave to King Solomon.

Moreover, the fleet of Hiram, which carried gold from Ophir, brought from Ophir a great quantity of almug wood and precious stones. From the almug wood the king made supports for the house of the LORD, and for the king's house, lyres also and harps for the singers; no such almug wood has come or been seen to this day.

Meanwhile King Solomon gave to the queen of Sheba every desire that she expressed, as well as what he gave her out of Solomon's royal bounty. Then she returned to her own land, with her servants.

1 Kings 10:1–13

THE MAGI SEE THE CHILD WITH MARY HIS MOTHER

Mary's motherhood is honored; the magi offer gifts and pay homage.

In the time of King Herod, after Jesus was born in Bethlehem of Judea, magi from the East came to Jerusalem, asking, "Where is the child who has been born king of the Jews? For we observed his star at its rising, and have come to pay him homage." When King Herod heard this, he was frightened, and all Jerusalem with him; and

calling together all the chief priests and scribes of the people, he inquired of them where the Christ was to be born. They told him, "In Bethlehem of Judea; for so it has been written by the prophet:
'And you, Bethlehem, in the land of Judah,
      are by no means least among the rulers of Judah;
for from you shall come a ruler
      who is to shepherd my people Israel.'"

Then Herod secretly called for the magi and learned from them the exact time when the star had appeared. Then he sent them to Bethlehem, saying, "Go and search diligently for the child; and when you have found him, bring me word so that I may also go and pay him homage." When they had heard the king, they set out; and there, ahead of them, went the star that they had seen at its rising, until it stopped over the place where the child was. When they saw that the star had stopped, they were overwhelmed with joy. On entering the house, they saw the child with Mary his mother; and they knelt down and paid him homage. Then, opening their treasure chests, they offered him gifts of gold, frankincense, and myrrh. And having been warned in a dream not to return to Herod, they left for their own country by another road.

Matthew 2:1 – 12

THE BAPTISM OF CHRIST

FIRST SUNDAY AFTER THE EPIPHANY

JUDITH IS BLESSED

In the lectionaries, Jesus is described as God's beloved, with whom God is well pleased. In this story, Uzziah declares that Judith is blessed by God for her valor in saving her people. God's blessings are her reward.

Uzziah said to Judith, "O daughter, you are blessed by the Most High God above all other women on earth; and blessed be the Lord God, who created the heavens and the earth, who has guided you to cut off the head of the leader of our enemies. Your praise will never depart from the hearts of those who remember the power of God. May God grant this to be a perpetual honor to you, and may God reward you with blessings, because you risked your own life when our nation was brought low, and you averted our ruin, walking in the straight path before our God." And all the people said, "Amen. Amen."

Judith 13:18 – 20

SECOND SUNDAY IN ORDINARY TIME

SECOND SUNDAY AFTER THE EPIPHANY

THE WISE WOMAN OF TEKOA

The gospel story in the lectionaries tells of the beginning of the public ministry of Jesus. This passage tells of a wise woman who exercises a public ministry in Israel. She speaks in parables and she flatters, argues and scolds. She ultimately persuades King David to forgive his son Absalom.

Joab son of Zeruiah perceived that the king's mind was on Absalom. Joab sent to Tekoa and brought from there a wise woman. He said to her, "Pretend to be a mourner; put on mourning garments, do not anoint yourself with oil, but behave like a woman who has been mourning many days for the dead. Go to the king and speak to him as follows." And Joab put the words into her mouth.

When the woman of Tekoa came to the king, she fell on her face to the ground and did obeisance, and said, "Help, O king!" The king asked her, "What is your trouble?" She answered, "Alas, I am a widow; my husband is dead. Your servant had two sons, and they fought with one another in the field; there was no one to part them, and one struck the other and killed him. Now the whole family has risen against your servant. They say, 'Give up the man who struck his brother, so that we may kill him for the life of his brother whom he murdered, even if we destroy the heir as well.' Thus they would quench my one remaining ember, and leave to my husband neither name nor remnant on the face of the earth."

Then the king said to the woman, "Go to your house, and I will give orders concerning you." The woman of Tekoa said to the king, "On me be the guilt, my lord the king, and on my father's house; let the king and his throne be guiltless." The king said, "If anyone says anything to you, bring him to me, and he shall never touch you again." Then she said, "Please, may the king keep the LORD your God in mind, so that the avenger of blood may kill no more, and my son not be destroyed." He said, "As the LORD lives, not one hair of your son shall fall to the ground."

Then the woman said, "Please let your servant speak a word to my lord the king." He said, "Speak." The woman said, "Why then have you planned such a thing against the people of God? For in giving this decision the king convicts himself, inasmuch as the king does not bring his banished one home again. We must all die; we are like water spilled on the ground, which cannot be gathered up. But God will not take away a life, but will devise plans so as not to keep an outcast banished forever from the divine presence. Now I have come to say this to my lord the king because the people have made me afraid; your servant thought, 'I will speak to the king; it may be that the king will perform the request of his servant. For the king will hear, and deliver his servant from the hand of the one who would cut both me and my son off from the heritage of God.' Your servant thought, 'The word of my lord the king will set me at rest'; for my lord the king is like the angel of God, discerning good and evil. The LORD your God be with you!"

Then the king answered the woman, "Do not withhold from me anything I ask you." The woman said, "Let my lord the king speak." The king said, "Is the hand of Joab with you in all this?" The woman answered and said, "As surely as you live, my lord the king, one cannot turn right or left from anything that my lord the king has said. For it was your servant Joab who commanded me; it was he who put all these words into the mouth of your servant. In order to change the course of affairs your servant Joab did this. But my lord has wisdom like the wisdom of the angel of God to know all things that are on the earth."

Then the king said to Joab, "Very well, I grant this; go, bring back the young man Absalom."

2 Samuel 14:1 – 21

WOMEN WHO FOLLOWED JESUS
Jesus had faithful women disciples who remained with him at his death.

Many women were also keeping watch, looking on from a distance; they had followed Jesus from Galilee and had provided for him. Among them were Mary Magdalene, and Mary the mother of James and Joseph, and the mother of the sons of Zebedee.

Matthew 27:55 – 56

THIRD SUNDAY IN ORDINARY TIME

THIRD SUNDAY AFTER THE EPIPHANY

CHLOE IS CONCERNED ABOUT DIVISION

Chloe was a leader who worked for unity in the early church in Corinth. Concerned about quarrels in the community, she sent messengers to Paul about the matter.

I appeal to you, brothers and sisters, by the name of our Lord Jesus Christ, that all of you be in agreement and that there be no divisions among you, but that you be united in the same mind and the same purpose. For it has been reported to me by Chloe's people that there are quarrels among you, my brothers and sisters. What I mean is that each of you says, "I belong to Paul," or "I belong to Apollos," or "I belong to Christ." Has Christ been divided? Was Paul crucified for you? Or were you baptized in the name of Paul? I thank God that I baptized none of you except Crispus and Gaius, so that no one can say that you were baptized in my name. (I did baptize also the household of Stephanas; beyond that, I do not know whether I baptized anyone else.) For Christ did not send me to baptize but to proclaim the gospel, and not with eloquent wisdom, so that the cross of Christ might not be emptied of its power.

For the message about the cross is foolishness to those who are perishing, but to us who are being saved it is the power of God.

1 Corinthians 1:10 – 18

FOURTH SUNDAY IN ORDINARY TIME
FOURTH SUNDAY AFTER THE EPIPHANY

MIRIAM, PROPHET IN ISRAEL
For Micah, the leadership of Miriam and her brothers at the time of the Exodus is evidence of God's love and saving acts.

Hear what the LORD says:
Rise, plead your case before the mountains,
      and let the hills hear your voice.
Hear, you mountains, the controversy of the LORD,
      and you enduring foundations of the earth;
for the LORD has a controversy with the people,
      and the LORD will contend with Israel.

"O my people, what have I done to you?
      In what have I wearied you? Answer me!
For I brought you up from the land of Egypt,
      and redeemed you from the house of slavery;
and I sent before you Moses, Aaron, and Miriam.
O my people, remember now
      what King Balak of Moab devised
      what Balaam son of Beor answered him,
and what happened from Shittim to Gilgal,
      that you may know the saving acts of the LORD."

"With what shall I come before the LORD,
      and bow myself before God on high?
Shall I come before God with burnt offerings,
      with calves a year old?
Will the LORD be pleased with thousands of rams,
      with ten thousands of rivers of oil?
Shall I give my firstborn for my transgression,
      the fruit of my body for the sin of my soul?"
The LORD has told you, O mortal, what is good;
      and what does the LORD require of you
but to do justice, and to love kindness,
      and to walk humbly with your God?

Micah 6:1 – 8

FIFTH SUNDAY IN ORDINARY TIME
FIFTH SUNDAY AFTER THE EPIPHANY

MIRIAM CHALLENGES MOSES

In this mysterious passage, Miriam and Aaron challenge Moses for marrying outside of the clan and for superseding them as prophets of equal stature. Why is Miriam punished physically and Aaron merely scolded?

While they were at Hazeroth, Miriam and Aaron spoke against Moses because of the Cushite woman whom he had married (for he had indeed married a Cushite woman); and they said, "Has the LORD spoken only through Moses? Has he not spoken through us also?" And the LORD heard it. Now the man Moses was very humble, more so than anyone else on the face of the earth. Suddenly the LORD said to Moses, Aaron, and Miriam, "Come out, you three, to the tent of meeting." So the three of them came out. Then the LORD came down in a pillar of cloud, and stood at the entrance of the tent and called Aaron and Miriam; and they both came forward. And God said, "Hear my words:

When there are prophets among you,
    I the Lord make myself known to them in visions;
    I speak to them in dreams.
Not so with my servant Moses;
he is entrusted with all my house,
With him I speak face to face —
    clearly, not in riddles;
    and he beholds the form of the LORD.

Why then were you not afraid to speak against my servant Moses?" And the anger of the LORD was kindled against them, and God departed.

When the cloud went away from over the tent, Miriam had become leprous, as white as snow. And Aaron turned toward Miriam and saw that she was leprous. Then Aaron said to Moses, "Oh, my lord, do not punish us for a sin that we have so foolishly committed. Do not let her be like one stillborn, whose flesh is half consumed when it comes out of its mother's womb." And Moses cried to the LORD, "O God, please heal her." But the LORD said to Moses, "If her father had but spit in her face, would she not bear her shame for seven days? Let her be shut out of the camp for seven days, and after that she may be brought in again." So Miriam was shut out of the camp for seven days; and the people did not set out on the march until Miriam had been brought in again. After that the people set out from Hazeroth, and camped in the wilderness of Paran.

The Israelites, the whole congregation, came into the wilderness of Zin in the first month, and the people stayed in Kadesh. Miriam died there, and was buried there.

Numbers 12:1–16; 20:1

Sarah

SIXTH SUNDAY IN ORDINARY TIME

SIXTH SUNDAY AFTER THE EPIPHANY
PROPER 1: SUNDAY BETWEEN 11 AND 17 FEBRUARY

THE DAUGHTERS OF LOT

The daughters of Lot were saved by the actions of the visitors; divine intention prevails over human weakness. But how did these two women feel about being offered to the mob to be raped in order to protect the male visitors?

The two angels came to Sodom in the evening, and Lot was sitting in the gateway of Sodom. When Lot saw them, he rose to meet them, and bowed down with his face to the ground. He said, "Please, my lords, turn aside to your servant's house and spend the night, and wash your feet; then you can rise early and go on your way." They said, "No; we will spend the night in the square." But he urged them strongly; so they turned aside to him and entered his house; and he made them a feast, and baked unleavened bread, and they ate.

But before they lay down, the men of the city, the men of Sodom, both young and old, all the people to the last man, surrounded the house; and they called to Lot, "Where are the men who came to you tonight? Bring them out to us, so that we may know them." Lot went out of the door to the men, shut the door after him, and said, "I beg you, my brothers, do not act so wickedly. Look, I have two daughers who have not known a man; let me bring them out to you, and do to them as you please; only do nothing to these men, for they have come under the shelter of my roof."

But they replied, "Stand back!" And they said, "This fellow came here as an alien, and he should play the judge! Now we will deal worse with you than with them." Then they pressed hard against the man Lot, and came near the door to break it down. But the men inside reached out their hands and brought Lot into the house with them, and shut the door. And they struck with blindness the men who were at the door of the house, both small and great, so that they were unable to find the door.

Genesis 19:1 – 11

SEVENTH SUNDAY IN ORDINARY TIME

SEVENTH SUNDAY AFTER THE EPIPHANY
PROPER 2: SUNDAY BETWEEN 18 AND 24 FEBRUARY

THE WIFE OF LOT

Did Lot's wife look back in fear, out of curiosity, or out of compassion for her neighbors?

When morning dawned, the angels urged Lot, saying, "Get up, take your wife and your two daughters who are here, or else you will be consumed in the punishment of the city." But Lot lingered; so the men seized him and his wife and his two daughters by the hand, the LORD being merciful to him, and they brought Lot out and left him outside the city.

When they had brought them outside, they said, "Flee for your life; do not look back or stop anywhere in the Plain; flee to the hills, or else you will be consumed." And Lot said to them, "Oh, no, my lords; your servant has found favor with you, and you have shown me great kindness in saving my life; but I cannot flee to the hills, for fear the disaster will overtake me and I die. Look, that city is near enough to flee to, and it is a little one. Let me escape there — is it not a little one? — and my life will be saved?"

God said to Lot, "Very well, I grant you this favor too, and will not overthrow the city of which you have spoken. Hurry, escape there, for I can do nothing until you arrive there." Therefore the city was called Zoar. The sun had risen on the earth when Lot came to Zoar.

Then the LORD rained on Sodom and Gomorrah sulfur and fire from the LORD out of heaven; and God overthrew those cities, and all the Plain, and all the inhabitants of the cities, and what grew on the ground. But Lot's wife, behind him, looked back, and she became a pillar of salt.

Genesis 19:15–26

EIGHTH SUNDAY IN ORDINARY TIME

EIGHTH SUNDAY AFTER THE EPIPHANY
PROPER 3: SUNDAY BETWEEN 25 AND 29 FEBRUARY

DOES A WOMAN FORGET HER CHILD?
God's love for Israel is that of a nursing mother.

Sing for joy, O heavens, and exult, O earth;
    break forth, O mountains, into singing!
For the LORD has comforted the people,
    and will have compassion on God's suffering ones.

But Zion said, "The LORD has forsaken me,
    my Lord has forgotten me."
Can a woman forget her nursing child,
    or show no compassion for the child of her womb?
Even these may forget,
    yet I will not forget you.
See, I have inscribed you on the palms of my hands;
    your walls are continually before me.
Your builders outdo your destroyers,
    and those who laid you waste go away from you.
Lift up your eyes all around and see;
    they all gather, they come to you.
As I live, says the LORD,
    you shall put all of them on like an ornament,
    and like a bride you shall bind them on.

Isaiah 49:13–16a

YEAR A

TRANSFIGURATION SUNDAY

Some celebrate the Transfiguration on the Last Sunday after the Epiphany while others do so on the Second Sunday of Lent.

GOD, LIKE A NURSE WITH A BABY AT THE BREAST

In the gospel story of the Transfiguration, God is encountered on a high mountain as a voice from a bright cloud. In this story, Moses complains to God, who takes on the care of the people like a mother, a nurse and one who provides food.

Moses heard the people weeping throughout their families, all at the entrances of their tents. Then the LORD became very angry, and Moses was displeased. So Moses said to the LORD, "Why have you treated your servant so badly? Why have I not found favor in your sight, that you lay the burden of all this people on me? Did I conceive all this people? Did I give birth to them, that you should say to me, 'Carry them in your bosom, as a nurse carries a sucking child,' to the land that you promised on oath to their ancestors? Where am I to get meat to give to all this people? For they come weeping to me and say, 'Give us meat to eat!' I am not able to carry all this people alone, for they are too heavy for me. If this is the way you are going to treat me, put me to death at once — if I have found favor in your sight — and do not let me see my misery."

Numbers 11:10 – 15

ASH WEDNESDAY

The lectionaries' readings call us to prayer, fasting and almsgiving; and to reconciliation with God and neighbor. The first three passages here tell how women in different circumstances were to be treated according to the ancient Law. They challenge all to do justice to and for women in contemporary society.

THE TREATMENT OF WOMEN SLAVES

When a man sells his daughter as a slave, she shall not go out as the male slaves do. If she does not please her master, who designated her for himself, then he shall let her be redeemed; he shall have no right to sell her to a foreign people, since he has dealt unfairly with her. If he designates her for his son, he shall deal with her as with a daughter. If he takes another wife to himself, he shall not diminish the food, clothing, or marital rights of the first wife. And if he does not do these three things for her, she shall go out without debt, without payment of money.

Exodus 21:7 – 11

SLAVES, WOMEN AND MEN, ARE SET FREE IN THE SABBATH YEAR

If a member of your community, whether a Hebrew man or a Hebrew woman, is sold to you and works for you six years, in the seventh year you shall set that person free. And when you send a male slave out from you a free person; you shall not send him out empty-handed. Provide liberally out of your flock, your threshing floor, and your wine press, thus giving to him some of the bounty with which the LORD your God has blessed you. Remember that you were a slave in the land of Egypt, and the LORD your God redeemed you; for this reason I lay this command upon you today. But if he says to you, "I will not go out from you," because he loves you and your household, since he is well off with you, then you shall take an awl and thrust it through his earlobe into the door, and he shall be your slave forever.

You shall do the same with regard to your female slave.

Deuteronomy 15:12 – 17

THE TREATMENT OF WOMEN TAKEN IN WAR

When you go out to war against your enemies, and the LORD your God hands them over to you and you take them captive, suppose you see among the captives a beautiful woman whom you desire and want to marry, and so you bring her home to your house; she shall shave her head, pare her nails, discard her captive's garb, and shall remain in your house a full month, mourning for her father and mother; after that you may go in to her and be her husband, and she shall be your wife.

But if you are not satisfied with her, you shall let her go free and not sell her for money. You must not treat her as a slave, since you have dishonored her.

Deuteronomy 21:10 – 14

PRIZE WISDOM!
Lent is interpreted as a journey toward Wisdom, the feminine figure of divine presence.

Get wisdom; get insight: do not forget, nor turn away
  from the words of my mouth.
Do not forsake her, and she will keep you;
  love her, and she will guard you.
The beginning of wisdom is this: Get wisdom
  and whatever else you get, get insight.
Prize her highly, and she will exalt you;
  she will honor you if you embrace her.
She will place on your head a fair garland;
  she will bestow on you a beautiful crown.

Hear, my child, and accept my words,
  that the years of your life may be many.
I have taught you the way of wisdom;
  I have led you in the paths of uprightness.
When you walk, your step will not be hampered;
  and if you run, you will not stumble.
Keep hold to instruction; do not let go;
  guard her, for she is your life.

Proverbs 4:5 – 13

Four other passages give us examples of women at prayer. Mary, Hannah, Judith and Esther can be models for Lent.

MARY, MODEL OF PRAYER
Mary sings that God continues to rescue Israel, a fact which gives her strength.

I acclaim the greatness of the Lord,
I delight in God my savior,
who regarded my humble state.
Truly from this day on
all ages will call me blest.

For God, wonderful in power,
has used that strength for me.
Holy the name of the Lord!

whose mercy embraces the faithful,
one generation to the next.

The mighty arm of God
scatters the proud in their conceit,
pulls tyrants from their thrones,
and raises up the humble.
The Lord fills the starving
and lets the rich go hungry.

God rescues lowly Israel,
recalling the promise of mercy,
the promise made to our ancestors,
to Abraham's heirs for ever.

Canticle of Luke 1:46 – 55 ICEL

HANNAH, MODEL OF PRAYER
Hannah pours out her heart in joyful song. Her song is like the song of Mary.

I acclaim the LORD's greatness,
source of my strength.
I devour my foe,
I say to God with joy:
"You saved my life.
Only you are holy, LORD;
there is none but you,
no other rock like you."

God knows when deeds match words,
so make no arrogant claims.
The weapons of the strong are broken,
the defenseless gain strength.
The overfed now toil to eat,
while the hungry have their fill.

The childless bear many children,
but the fertile learn they are sterile.
The LORD commands death and life,
consigns to Sheol or raises up.

God deals out poverty and wealth,
casts down and lifts up,
raising the poor from squalor,
the needy from the trash heap,

to sit with the high and mighty,
taking their places of honor.

God owns the universe
and sets the earth within it.
God walks with the faithful
but silences the wicked in darkness;
their power does not prevail.

God's enemies will be broken,
heaven thunders against them.
The LORD will judge the earth,
and give power to the king,
victory to the anointed.

Canticle of 1 Samuel 2:1 – 10 ICEL

JUDITH, MODEL OF PRAYER
Judith prays that she can be the means by which God rescues the chosen people. God will protect the poor and downtrodden.

Judith cried out to the Lord with a loud voice, and said,
"O Lord God of my ancestor Simeon, to whom you gave a sword to take revenge on those strangers who had torn off a virgin's clothing to defile her, and exposed her thighs to put her to shame, and polluted her womb to disgrace her; for you said, 'It shall not be done' — yet they did it. So you gave up their rulers to be killed, and their bed, which was ashamed of the deceit they had practiced, was stained with blood, and you struck down slaves along with princes, and princes on their thrones. You gave up their wives for booty and their daughters to captivity, and all their booty to be divided among your beloved children who burned with zeal for you and abhorred the pollution of their blood and called on you for help — O God, my God, hear me also — a widow.
"For you have done these things and those that went before and those that followed. You have designed the things that are now, and those that are to come. What you had in mind has happened; the things you decided on presented themselves and said, 'Here we are!' For all your ways are prepared in advance, and your judgment is with foreknowledge.
"Here now are the Assyrians, a greatly increased force, priding themselves in their horses and riders, boasting in the strength of their foot soldiers, and trusting in shield and spear, in bow and sling. They do not know that you are the Lord who crushes wars; the Lord is your name. Break their strength by your might, and bring down their power in your anger; for they intend to defile your sanctuary, and to pollute the tabernacle where your glorious name resides, and to break off the horns of your altar with the sword. Look at their pride, and send your wrath upon their heads. Give to me, a widow, the strong hand to do what I plan. By the deceit of my

lips strike down the slave with the prince and the prince with his servant; crush their arrogance by the hand of a woman.

"For your strength does not depend on numbers, nor your might on the powerful. But you are the God of the lowly, helper of the oppressed, upholder of the weak, protecter of the forsaken, savior of those without hope."

Judith 9:1 – 11

ESTHER, MODEL OF PRAYER
Esther prays for the deliverance of her people. She asks for courage and eloquent speech that she may do her part.

Queen Esther prayed to the Lord God of Israel, and said: "O my Lord, you only are our ruler; help me, who am alone and have no helper but you, for my danger is in my hand. Ever since I was born I have heard in the tribe of my family that you, O Lord, took Israel out of all the nations, and our ancestors from among all their forebears, for an everlasting inheritance, and that you did for them all that you promised. And now we have sinned before you, and you have handed us over to our enemies because we glorified their gods. You are righteous, O Lord! And now they are not satisfied that we are in bitter slavery, but they have covenanted with their idols to abolish what your mouth has ordained, and to destroy your inheritance, to stop the mouths of those who praise you and to quench your altar and the glory of your house, to open the mouths of the nations for the praise of vain idols, and to magnify forever a mortal ruler.

"O Lord, do not surrender your scepter to what has no being; and do not let them laugh at our downfall; but turn their plan against them, and make an example of him who began this against us. Remember, O Lord; make yourself known in this time of our affliction, and give me courage, O Ruler of the gods and Master of all dominion! Put eloquent speech in my mouth before the lion, and turn his heart to hate the man who is fighting against us, so that there may be an end of him and those who agree with him. But save us by your hand, and help me, who am alone and have no helper but you, O Lord."

Esther 14:3 – 14

FIRST SUNDAY OF LENT

THE WOMAN AND MAN ATE OF THE TREE
While the man is passive, the woman actively seeks knowledge and tests the limits.

The LORD God took the man and put him in the garden of Eden to till it and keep it. And the LORD God commanded the man, "You may freely eat of every tree of the garden; but of the tree of the knowledge of good and evil you shall not eat, for in the day that you eat of it you shall die."

Now the serpent was more crafty than any other wild animal that the LORD God had made. He said to the woman, "Did God say, 'You shall not eat from any tree in the garden'?" The woman said to the serpent, "We may eat of the fruit of the trees in the garden; but God said, 'You shall not eat of the fruit of the tree that is in the middle of the garden, nor shall you touch it, or you shall die.'" But the serpent said to the woman, "You will not die, for God knows that when you eat of it your eyes will be opened, and you will be like God, knowing good and evil."

So when the woman saw that the tree was good for food, and that it was a delight to the eyes, and that the tree was to be desired to make one wise, she took of its fruit and ate; and she also gave some to her husband, who was with her, and he ate. Then the eyes of both were opened, and they knew that they were naked; and they sewed fig leaves together and made loincloths for themselves.

Genesis 2:15 – 17; 3:1 – 7

33

SECOND SUNDAY OF LENT

SARAI AND ABRAM IN CHALDEA, HARAN AND EGYPT

The lectionaries tell of God's call and promise to Abraham. This passage points out that Sarah and Abraham together left the land of their birth, shared the dangers and adventures of the journey, and came together into Canaan. God's promise to Abraham could not have been fulfilled without Sarah. How did Sarah feel about her husband's deceit in Egypt, and about being part of Pharoah's harem?

These are the descendants of Terah. Terah was the father of Abram, Nahor, and Haran; and Haran was the father of Lot. Haran died before his father Terah in the land of his birth, in Ur of the Chaldeans. Abram and Nahor took wives; the name of Abram's wife was Sarai, and the name of Nahor's wife was Milcah. She was the daughter of Haran the father of Milcah and Iscah. Now Sarai was barren; she had no child.

Terah took his son Abram and his grandson Lot son of Haran, and his daughter-in-law Sarai, his son Abram's wife, and they went out together from Ur of the Chaldeans to go into the land of Canaan; but when they came to Haran, they settled there. The days of Terah were two hundred five years; and Terah died in Haran.

Now there was a famine in the land. So Abram went down to Egypt to reside there as an alien, for the famine was severe in the land. When Abram was about to enter Egypt, he said to his wife Sarai, "I know well that you are a woman beautiful in appearance; and when the Egyptians see you, they will say, 'This is his wife'; then they will kill me, but they will let you live. Say you are my sister, so that it may go well with me because of you, and that my life may be spared on your account."

When Abram entered Egypt the Egyptians saw that the woman was very beautiful. When the officials of Pharoah saw Sarai, they praised her to Pharoah. And the woman was taken into Pharoah's house. And for her sake he dealt well with Abram; and he had sheep, oxen, male donkeys, male and female slaves, female donkeys, and camels.

But the LORD afflicted Pharoah and his house with great plagues because of Sarai, Abram's wife. So Pharoah called Abram, and said, "What is this you have done to me? Why did you not tell me that she was your wife? Why did you say, 'She is my sister,' so that I took her for my wife? Now then, here is your wife, take her, and be gone." And Pharoah gave his men orders concerning Abram; and they set him on the way, with Sarai his wife and all that he had.

Genesis 11:27 – 32; 12:10 – 20

When the Transfiguration is celebrated on this Sunday:

GOD, LIKE A NURSE WITH A BABY AT THE BREAST
In the gospel story of the Transfiguration, God is encountered on a high mountain as a voice from a bright cloud. This story presents other images: God is a mother, a wet-nurse, and one who raises food and cooks for her people.

Moses heard the people weeping throughout their families, all at the entrances of their tents. Then the LORD became very angry, and Moses was displeased. So Moses said to the LORD, "Why have you treated your servant so badly? Why have I not found favor in your sight, that you lay the burden of all this people on me? Did I conceive all this people? Did I give birth to them, that you should say to me, 'Carry them in your bosom, as a nurse carries a sucking child,' to the land that you promised on oath to their ancestors? Where am I to get meat to give to all this people? For they come weeping to me and say, 'Give us meat to eat!' I am not able to carry all this people alone, for they are too heavy for me. If this is the way you are going to treat me, put me to death at once — if I have found favor in your sight — and do not let me see my misery."

Numbers 11:10–15

Hagar

THIRD SUNDAY OF LENT

THE SAMARITAN WOMAN, WITNESS TO JESUS
This woman is the first person in the Gospel of John to engage in serious theological conversation with Jesus. By conversing with her, Jesus demonstrates that God's grace is offered to all. Through her words and witness, many come to faith; she is a true disciple.

Jesus came to a Samaritan city called Sychar, near the plot of ground that Jacob had given to his son Joseph. Jacob's well was there, and Jesus, tired out by his journey, was sitting by the well. It was about noon.

A Samaritan woman came to draw water, and Jesus said to her, "Give me a drink." (His disciples had gone to the city to buy food.) The Samaritan woman said to him, "How is it that you, a Jewish man, ask a drink of me, a woman of Samaria?" (Judeans do not share things in common with Samaritans.) Jesus answered her, "If you knew the gift of God, and who it is that is saying to you, 'Give me a drink,' you would have asked him, and he would have given you living water." The woman said to him, "Sir, you have no bucket, and the well is deep. Where do you get that living water? Are you greater than our ancestor Jacob, who gave us the well, and with his sons and his flocks drank from it?" Jesus said to her, "Everyone who drinks of this water will be thirsty again, but those who drink of the water that I will give them will never be thirsty. The water that I will give will become in them a spring of water gushing up to eternal life." The woman said to Jesus, "Sir, give me this water, so that I may never be thirsty or have to keep coming here to draw water."

Jesus said to her, "Go call your husband, and come back." The woman answered him, "I have no husband." Jesus said to her, "You are right in saying, 'I have no husband'; for you have had five husbands, and the one you have now is not your husband. What you have said is true!"

The woman said to Jesus, "Sir, I see that you are a prophet. Our ancestors worshiped on this mountain, but you say that the place where people must worship is in Jerusalem." Jesus said to her, "Woman, believe me, the hour is coming when you will worship the Father neither on this mountain nor in Jerusalem. You worship what you do not know; we worship what we know, for salvation is from the Jews. But the hour is coming, and is now here, when the true worshipers will worship the Father in spirit and truth, for the Father seeks such as these to worship God. God is spirit, and those who worship God must worship in spirit and truth." The woman said to him, "I know that Messiah is coming" (who is called Christ). "When he comes he will proclaim all things to us." Jesus said to her, "I am he, the one who is speaking to you."

Just then his disciples came. They were astonished that Jesus was speaking with a woman, but no one said, "What do you want?" or, "Why are you speaking with her?" Then the woman left her water jar and went back to the city. She said to the people, "Come and see a man who told me everything I have ever done! He cannot be the Christ, can he?" They left the city and were on their way to him.

Many Samaritans from that city believed in Jesus because of the woman's testimony. "He told me everything I have ever done." So when the Samaritans came to him, they asked him to stay with them; and Jesus stayed there two days. And many more believed because of his word. They said to the woman, "It is no longer because of what you said that we believe, for we have heard for ourselves, and we know that this is truly the Savior of the world."

John 4:5 – 30, 39 – 42

FOURTH SUNDAY OF LENT

MICHAL LOVES DAVID AND SAVES HIS LIFE
The lectionaries tell about Samuel anointing David as king. This passage tells of Michal's love for David and how she saves his life.

Now Saul's daughter Michal loved David. Saul was told, and the thing pleased him. Saul thought, "Let me give her to him that she may be a snare for him and that the hand of the Philistines may be against him." Therefore Saul said to David a second time, "You shall now be my son-in-law." Saul commanded his servants, "Speak to David in private and say, 'See, the king is delighted with you, and all his servants love you; now then, become the king's son-in-law.'"

David rose and went, along with his men, and killed one hundred of the Philistines; and David brought their foreskins, which were given in full number to the king, that he might become the king's son-in-law. Saul gave him his daughter Michal as a wife. But when Saul realized that the LORD was with David, and that Saul's daughter Michal loved him, Saul was still more afraid of David. So Saul was David's enemy from that time forward.

Saul sent messengers to David's house to keep watch over him, planning to kill him in the morning. David's wife Michal told him, "If you do not save your life tonight, tomorrow you will be killed." So Michal let David down through the window; he fled away and escaped. Michal took an idol and laid it on the bed; she put a net of goats' hair on its head, and covered it with the clothes. When Saul sent messagers to take David, she said, "He is sick." Then Saul sent the messengers to see David for themselves. He said, "Bring him up to me in the bed, that I may kill him." When the messengers came in, the idol was in the bed, with the covering of goats' hair on its head. Saul said to Michal, "Why have you deceived me like this, and let my enemy go, so that he has escaped?" Michal answered Saul, "David said to me, 'Let me go; why should I kill you?'"

1 Samuel 18:20 – 22, 27 – 29; 19:11 – 17

FIFTH SUNDAY OF LENT

THE FAITH OF MARTHA AND MARY
The bold faith of Martha and Mary leads them to bring their grief and loss to Jesus, and their unfailing love.
These are marks of true discipleship.

A certain man was ill, Lazarus of Bethany, the village of Mary and her sister Martha. Mary was the one who anointed the Lord with perfume and wiped his feet with her hair; her brother Lazarus was ill. So the sisters sent a message to Jesus, "Lord, he whom you love is ill." But when Jesus heard it he said, "This illness does not lead to death; rather it is for God's glory, so that the Son of God may be glorified through it." Accordingly, though Jesus loved Martha and her sister and Lazarus, after having heard that Lazarus was ill, he stayed two days longer in the place where he was.

Then after this Jesus said to the disciples, "Let us go to Judea again." The disciples said to him, "Rabbi, the Judeans were just now trying to stone you, and are you going there again?" Jesus answered, "Are there not twelve hours of daylight? Those who walk during the day do not stumble, because they see the light of this world. But those who walk at night stumble, because the light is not in them."

After saying this, Jesus told them, "Our friend Lazarus has fallen asleep, but I am going there to awaken him." The disciples said to him, "Lord, if he has fallen asleep, he will be all right." Jesus, however, had been speaking about his death, but they thought that he was referring merely to sleep. Then Jesus told them plainly, "Lazarus is dead. For your sake I am glad I was not there, so that you may believe. But let us go to him." Thomas, who was called the Twin, said to his fellow disciples, "Let us also go, that we may die with him."

When Jesus arrived, he found that Lazarus had already been in the tomb four days. Now Bethany was near Jerusalem, some two miles away, and many of the Judeans had come to Martha and Mary to console them about their brother. When Martha heard that Jesus was coming, she went and met him, while Mary stayed at home. Martha said to Jesus, "Lord, if you had been here, my brother would not have died. But even now I know that God will give you whatever you ask." Jesus said to her, "Your brother will rise again." Martha said to him, "I know that he will rise again in the resurrection on the last day." Jesus said to her, "I am the resurrection and the life. Those who believe in me, even though they die, will live, and everyone who lives and believes in me will never die. Do you believe this?" She said to him, "Yes, Lord, I believe that you are the Christ, the Son of God, the one coming into the world."

When Martha had said this, she went back and called her sister Mary, and told her privately, "The Teacher is here and is calling for you." And when Mary heard this, she got up quickly and went to him. Now Jesus had not yet come to the village, but was still at the place where Martha had met him. The Judeans who were with her in the house, consoling her, saw Mary get up quickly and go out. They followed her because they thought that she was going to the tomb to weep there.

When Mary came where Jesus was and saw him, she knelt at his feet and said to him, "Lord, if you had been here, my brother would not have died." When Jesus saw her weeping, and the Judeans who came with her also weeping, he was greatly disturbed in spirit and deeply moved. Jesus said, "Where have you laid him?" They said to him, "Lord, come and see." Jesus began to weep. So the Judeans said, "See how he loved him!" But some of them said, "Could not he who opened the eyes of the blind man have kept this man from dying?"

Then Jesus, again greatly disturbed, came to the tomb. It was a cave, and a stone was lying against it. Jesus said, "Take away the stone." Martha, the sister of the dead man, said to him, "Lord, already there is a stench because he has been dead four days." Jesus said to her, "Did I not tell you that if you believed, you would see the glory of God?" So they took away the stone. And Jesus looked upward and said, "Father, I thank you for having heard me. I knew that you always hear me, but I have said this for the sake of the crowd standing here, so that they may believe that you sent me." When he had said this, he cried with a loud voice, "Lazarus, come out!" The dead man came out, his hands and feet bound with strips of cloth, and his face wrapped in a cloth. Jesus said to them, "Unbind him, and let him go."

Many of the Judeans therefore, who had come with Mary and had seen what Jesus did, believed in him.

John 11:1–45

PASSION (PALM) SUNDAY

THE RAPE OF DINAH

The lectionaries tell of the passion and death of Jesus; this passage tells of the suffering of Dinah and her brothers' response. Although she is the main character, Dinah is not given a voice by the writer. What do you think Dinah would say?

Dinah the daughter of Leah, whom she had borne to Jacob, went out to visit the women of the region. When Shechem son of Hamor the Hivite, prince of the region, saw her, he seized her and lay with her by force. And his soul was drawn to Dinah daughter of Jacob; he loved the girl, and spoke tenderly to her. So Shechem spoke to his father Hamor, saying, "Get me this girl to be my wife."

Now Jacob heard that Shechem had defiled his daughter Dinah; but his sons were with his cattle in the field, so Jacob held his peace until they came. And Hamor the father of Shechem went out to Jacob to speak with him, just as the sons of Jacob came in from the field. When they heard of it, the men were indignant and very angry, because he had committed an outrage in Israel by lying with Jacob's daugher Dinah, for such a thing ought not to be done.

Two of the sons of Jacob, Simeon and Levi, Dinah's brothers, took their swords and came against the city unawares, and killed all the males. They killed Hamor and his son Shechem with the sword, and took Dinah out of Shechem's house, and went away. And the other sons of Jacob came upon the slain, and plundered the city, because their sister had been defiled. They took their flocks and their herds, their donkeys, and whatever was in the city and in the field. All their wealth, all their little ones and their wives, all that was in the houses, they captured and made their prey.

Then Jacob said to Simeon and Levi, "You have brought trouble on me by making me odious to the inhabitants of the land, the Canaanites and the Perizzites; my numbers are few, and if they gather themselves against me and attack me, I shall be destroyed, both I and my household." But they said, "Should our sister be treated like a whore?"

Genesis 34:1 – 7, 25 – 31

THE WOMAN ANOINTS JESUS

The passion narrative in the gospel of Matthew begins with the story of the woman who anointed Jesus. Omitted by the lectionaries, that passage is given here. Anointing the dead is an act of charity often performed by women; the woman anoints Jesus' head as the prophet Samuel anointed David king.

While Jesus was at Bethany in the house of Simon the leper, a woman came to him with an alabaster jar of very costly ointment, and she poured it on his head as he sat at the table. But when the disciples saw it, they were angry and said, "Why this waste? For this ointment could have been sold for a large sum, and the money given to the poor."

But Jesus, aware of this, said to them, "Why do you trouble the woman? She has performed a good service for me. For you always have the poor with you, but you will not always have me. By pouring this ointment on my body she has prepared me for burial. Truly I tell you, wherever this good news is proclaimed in the whole world, what she has done will be told in remembrance of her."

Matthew 26:6 – 13

WOMEN IN THE PASSION ACCORDING TO MATTHEW
Both the Roman lectionary and Revised Common Lectionary assign most of chapters 26 and 27 of Matthew's gospel for this Sunday. Excerpts that tell women's stories are given here.

TWO SERVANT GIRLS CONFRONT PETER
These women of Jerusalem are familiar enough with Jesus and his followers to recognize Peter.

Peter was sitting outside in the courtyard. A servant-girl came to him and said, "You also were with Jesus the Galilean." But he denied it before all of them, saying, "I do not know what you are talking about." When Peter went out to the porch, another servant-girl saw him and she said to the bystanders, "This man was with Jesus of Nazareth." Again he denied it with an oath, "I do not know the man." After a little while the bystanders came up and said to Peter, "Certainly you are also one of them, for your accent betrays you." Then he began to curse, and he swore an oath, "I do not know the man!" At that moment the cock crowed. Then Peter remembered what Jesus had said: "Before the cock crows, you will deny me three times." And he went out and wept bitterly.

Matthew 26:69 – 75

THE WIFE OF PILATE
Only Matthew presents the story of the governor's wife interceding on Jesus' behalf during the trial. She knows of his righteousness by a revelation in a dream. Pilate ignores his wife's advice, to his shame.

At the festival the governor was accustomed to release a prisoner for the crowd, anyone whom they wanted. At that time they had a notorious prisoner, called Jesus Barabbas. So after they had gathered, Pilate said to them, "Whom do you want me to release for you, Jesus Barabbas or Jesus who is called the Christ?" For he realized that it was out of jealousy that they had handed him over.

While he was sitting on the judgment seat, Pilate's wife sent word to him, "Have nothing to do with that innocent man, for today I have suffered a great deal because of a dream about him." Now the chief priests and the elders persuaded the crowds to ask for Barabbas and to have Jesus killed. The governor again said to them, "Which of the two do you want me to release for you?" And they said,

"Barabbas." Pilate said to them, "Then what should I do with Jesus who is called the Christ?" All of them said, "Let him be crucified!"

Matthew 27:15 – 22

WOMEN KEPT WATCH
The women at the cross and tomb stand in contrast with the apostles, who fled. Sitting opposite the grave, they do not merely observe the place of burial; they hold a vigil.

Many women were also keeping watch, looking on from a distance; they had followed Jesus from Galilee and had provided for him. Among them were Mary Magdalene, and Mary the mother of James and Joseph, and the mother of the sons of Zebedee.

When it was evening, there came a rich man from Arimathea, named Joseph, who was also a disciple of Jesus. He went to Pilate and asked for the body of Jesus; then Pilate ordered it to be given to him. So Joseph took the body and wrapped it in a clean linen cloth and laid it in his own new tomb, which he had hewn in the rock. He then rolled a great stone to the door of the tomb and went away. Mary Magdalene and the other Mary were there, sitting opposite the tomb.

Matthew 27:55 – 61

HOLY THURSDAY

The spirit of the LORD came upon Jephthah, and he passed through Gilead and Manasseh. He passed on to Mizpah of Gilead, and from Mizpah of Gilead he passed on to the Ammonites. And Jephthah made a vow to the LORD, and said, "If you will give the Ammonites into my hand, then whoever comes out of the doors of my house to meet me, when I return victorious from the Ammonites, shall be the LORD's to be offered up by me as a burnt offering." So Jephthah crossed over to the Ammonites to fight against them; and the LORD gave them into his hand. Jephthah inflicted a massive defeat on them from Aroer to the neighborhood of Minnith, twenty towns, and as far as Abel-keramin. So the Ammonites were subdued before the people of Israel.

Then Jephthah came to his home at Mizpah; and there was his daughter coming out to meet him with timbrels and with dancing. She was his only child; he had no son or daughter except her. When he saw here, he tore his clothes, and said, "Alas, my daughter! You have brought me very low; you have become the cause of greater trouble to me. For I have opened my mouth to the LORD, and I cannot take back my vow."

She said to him, "My father, if you have opened your mouth to the LORD, do to me according to what has gone out of your mouth, now that the LORD has given you vengeance against your enemies, the Ammonites." And she said to her father, "Let this thing be done for me: Grant me two months, so that I may go and wander on the mountains, and bewail my virginity, my companions and I." "Go," he said and sent her away for two months.

So she departed, she and her companions, and bewailed her virginity on the mountains. At the end of two months, she returned to her father, who did with her according to the vow he had made. She had never slept with a man. So there arose an Israelite custom that for four days every year the daughters of Israel would go out to lament the daughter of Jephthah the Gileadite.

Judges 11:29–40

David sent and wooed Abigail, to make her his wife. When David's servants came to Abigail at Carmel, they said to her, "David has sent us to you to take you to him as his wife." She rose and bowed down, with her face to the ground, and said,

"Behold your handmaiden is a servant to wash the feet of the servants of my lord." Abigail got up hurriedly and rode away on a donkey; her five maids attended her. She went after the messengers of David and became his wife.

1 Samuel 25:39c – 42

WIDOWS WHO WASH THE FEET OF THE SAINTS

The ministry of widows in the early church included prayer and service, such as washing the feet of the members of the community, as Jesus washed his disciples' feet. Widows probably washed other women's feet.

Let a widow be put on the list if she is not less than sixty years old and has been married only once; she must be well attested for her good works, as one who has brought up children, shown hospitality, washed the saints' feet, helped the afflicted, and devoted herself to doing good in every way.

1 Timothy 5:9 – 10

GOOD FRIDAY

The lectionaries tell of the passion and death of Jesus. Jesus' agony on the cross is a kind of childbirth, leading to new life. These passages tell of death in childbirth. The death of Jesus is also related here to Israel's loss of the ark, which in other writings is sometimes viewed as a fruitful womb.

THE DEATH OF RACHEL IN CHILDBIRTH

God appeared to Jacob again when he came from Paddan-aram, and he befriended Jacob. God said to him, "Your name is Jacob; no longer shall you be called Jacob, but Israel shall be your name." So he was called Israel. God said to him, "I am God Almighty; be fruitful and multiply; a nation and a company of nations shall come from you, and kings shall spring from you. The land that I gave to Abraham and Isaac I will give to you, and I will give the land to your offspring after you." Then God went up from him at the place where he had spoken with him. Jacob set up a pillar on the place where he had spoken with God, a pillar of stone; and Jacob poured out a drink offering on it, and poured oil on it. So Jacob called the place where God had spoken with him Bethel.

Then they journeyed from Bethel; and when they were still some distance from Ephrath, Rachel was in childbirth, and she had hard labor. When she was in her hard labor, the midwife said to her, "Do not be afraid; for now you will have another son." As her soul was departing (for she died), she named him Ben-oni; but his father called him Benjamin. So Rachel died, and she was buried on the way to Ephrath (that is, Bethlehem), and Jacob set up a pillar at her grave; it is the pillar of Rachel's tomb, which is there to this day.

Genesis 35:9–20

LOSS OF THE ARK AND THE DEATH OF THE WIFE OF PHINEHAS IN CHILDBIRTH

The ark of the covenant, Israel's symbol of Immanuel, God-with-us, is captured in battle. The story also shows that women, even when not engaged in violence, suffer the brunt of its consequences.

The word of Samuel came to all Israel.

In those days the Philistines mustered for war against Israel, and Israel went out to battle against them; they encamped at Ebenezer, and the Philistines encamped at Aphek. The Philistines drew up in line against Israel, and when the battle was joined, Israel was defeated by the Philistines, who killed about four thousand men on the field of battle.

When the troops came to the camp, the elders of Israel said, "Why has the LORD put us to rout today before the Philistines? Let us bring the ark of the covenant of the LORD here from Shiloh, so that God may come among us and save us from the power of our enemies." So the people sent to Shiloh, and brought from there the ark of the covenant of the LORD of hosts, who is enthroned on the cherubim. The two sons of Eli, Hophni and Phinehas, were there with the ark of the covenant of God.

When the ark of the covenant of the LORD came into the camp, all Israel gave a mighty shout, so that the earth resounded. When the Philistines heard the noise of the shouting, they said, "What does this great shouting in the camp of the Hebrews mean?" When they learned that the ark of the LORD had come to the camp, the Philistines were afraid; for they said, "Gods have come into the camp." They also said, "Woe to us! For nothing like this has happened before. Woe to us! Who can deliver us from the power of these mighty gods? These are the gods who struck the Egyptians with every sort of plague in the wilderness. Take courage, and be men, O Philistines, in order not to become slaves to the Hebrews as they have been to you; be men and fight."

So the Philistines fought; Israel was defeated, and they fled, everyone to his home. There was a very great slaughter, for there fell of Israel thirty thousand foot soldiers. The ark of God was captured, and the two sons of Eli, Hophni and Phinehas, died.

A man of Benjamin ran from the battle line, and came to Shiloh the same day, with his clothes torn and with earth upon his head. When he arrived, Eli was sitting upon his seat by the road watching, for his heart trembled for the ark of God. When the man came into the city and told the news, all the city cried out. When Eli heard the sound of the outcry, he said, "What is this uproar?" Then the man came quickly and told Eli. Now Eli was ninety-eight years old and his eyes were set, so that he could not see. The man said to Eli, "I have just come from the battle; I fled from the battle today." He said, "How did it go, my son?" The messenger replied, "Israel has fled before the Philistines, and there has also been a great slaughter among the troops; your two sons also, Hophni and Phinehas, are dead, and the ark of God has been captured." When he mentioned the ark of God, Eli fell over backward from his seat by the side of the gate; and his neck was broken and he died, for he was an old man, and heavy. He had judged Israel forty years.

Now his daughter-in-law, the wife of Phinehas, was pregnant, about to give birth. When she heard the news that the ark of God was captured, and that her father-in-law and her husband were dead, she bowed and gave birth; for her labor pains overwhelmed her. As she was about to die, the women attending her said to her, "Do not be afraid, for you have borne a son." But she did not answer or give heed. She named the child Ichabod, meaning, "The glory has departed from Israel," because the ark of God had been captured and because of her father-in-law and her husband. She said, "The glory has departed from Israel, for the ark of God has been captured."

1 Samuel 4:1 – 22

Mary and Martha demonstrate discipleship: They welcome Jesus, bring others to table with him, and share in his death. Mary's anointing is an act of loving extravangance.

Six days before the Passover Jesus came to Bethany, the home of Lazarus, whom he had raised from the dead. There they gave a dinner for Jesus. Martha served, and Lazarus was one of those at the table with him. Mary took a pound of costly perfume made of pure nard, anointed Jesus' feet, and wiped them with her hair. The house was filled with the fragrance of the perfume. But Judas Iscariot, one of his disciples (the one who was about to betray him), said, "Why was this perfume not sold for three hundred denarii and the money given to the poor." (He said this not because he cared about the poor, but because he was a thief; he kept the common purse and used to steal what was put into it.) Jesus said, "Leave her alone. She bought it so that she might keep it for the day of my burial. You always have the poor with you, but you do not always have me."

John 12:1 – 8

WOMEN IN THE PASSION ACCORDING TO JOHN

Both the Roman lectionary and Revised Common Lectionary assign chapters 18 and 19 of John's gospel to this day. Excerpts that tell women's stories are given here.

THE SERVANT WOMAN CONFRONTS PETER

While Jesus affirms his identity to the high priest, Peter denies his connection to Jesus after being challenged by a woman who knows the truth.

Simon Peter and another disciple followed Jesus. Since that disciple was known to the high priest, he went with Jesus into the courtyard of the high priest, but Peter was standing outside at the gate. So the other disciple, who was known to the high priest, went out, spoke to the woman who guarded the gate, and brought Peter in. The woman said to Peter, "You are not also one of this man's disciples, are you?" He said, "I am not."

Now Simon Peter was standing and warming himself. They asked him, "You are not also one of his disciples, are you?" He denied it and said, "I am not." One of the slaves of the high priest, a relative of the man whose ear Peter had cut off, asked, "Did I not see you in the garden with him?" Again Peter denied it, and at that moment the cock crowed.

John 18:15 – 17, 25 – 27

JESUS AND HIS MOTHER

Jesus' death is witnessed by his mother and other faithful women followers. Jesus' creation of a new family of God is symbolized when the disciple takes Jesus' mother into his own home.

Standing near the cross of Jesus were his mother, and his mother's sister, Mary the wife of Clopas, and Mary Magdalene. When Jesus saw his mother and the disciple whom he loved standing beside her, he said to his mother, "Woman, here is your son." Then Jesus said to the disciple, "Here is your mother." And from that hour the disciple took her into his own home.

John 19:25–27

Lot's Wife

EASTER VIGIL

MALE AND FEMALE, CREATED IN GOD'S IMAGE
Of all creatures, only humankind is made in the image of God. Together women and men mirror the divine image.

God said, "Let us make humankind in our image, according to our likeness; and let them have dominion over the fish of the sea, and over the birds of the air, and over the cattle, and over all the wild animals of the earth, and over every creeping thing that creeps upon the earth."

So God created humankind in the divine image,
in the image of God humankind was created,
male and female God created them.

God blessed them, and God said to them, "Be fruitful and multiply, and fill the earth and subdue it; and have dominion over the fish of the sea and over the birds of the air and over every living thing that moves upon the earth." God said, "See, I have given you every plant yielding seed that is upon the face of all the earth, and every tree with seed in its fruit; you shall have them for food. And to every beast of the earth, and to every bird of the air, and to everything that creeps on the earth, everything that has the breath of life, I have given every green plant for food." And it was so.

God saw everything that had been made, and indeed, it was very good. And there was evening and there was morning, the sixth day.

Thus the heavens and the earth were finished, and all their multitude. And on the seventh day God finished the work which God had done, and God rested on the seventh day from all the work that had been done. So God blessed the seventh day and hallowed it, because on it God rested from all the work that God had done in creation.

Genesis 1:26 — 2:3

SONG OF HANNAH: Responsory
Hannah pours out her heart in joyful song.

I acclaim the LORD's greatness,
source of my strength.
I devour my foe,
I say to God with joy:
"You saved my life.
Only you are holy, LORD;
there is none but you,
no other rock like you."

God knows when deeds match words,
so make no arrogant claims.
The weapons of the strong are broken,
the defenseless gain strength.
The overfed now toil to eat,
while the hungry have their fill.

The childless bear many children,
but the fertile learn they are sterile.

Canticle of 1 Samuel 2:1 – 5 ICEL

HAGAR AND ISHMAEL ARE DRIVEN OUT INTO THE DESERT
Sarah exercises her authority, though her actions are cruel. Hagar looks after her son with God's help; later, she exercises her authority by finding a wife for him.

Isaac grew and was weaned; and Abraham made a great feast on the day that Isaac was weaned. But Sarah saw the son of Hagar the Egyptian, whom she had borne to Abraham, playing with her son Isaac. So she said to Abraham, "Cast out this slave woman with her son; for the son of the slave woman shall not inherit along with my son Isaac."

The matter was very distressing to Abraham on account of his son. But God said to Abraham, "Do not be distressed because of the boy and because of your slave woman; whatever Sarah says to you, do as she tells you, for it is through Isaac that offspring shall be named for you. As for the son of the slave woman, I will make a nation of him also, because he is your offspring." So Abraham rose early in the morning, and took bread and a skin of water, and gave it to Hagar, putting it on her shoulder, along with the child, and sent her away. And she departed, and wandered about in the wilderness of Beer-sheba.

When the water in the skin was gone, Hagar cast the child under one of the bushes. Then she went and sat down opposite him a good way off, about the distance of a bowshot; for she said, "Do not let me look on the death of the child." And as Hagar sat opposite him, she lifted up her voice and wept. And God heard the voice of the boy; and the angel of God called to Hagar from heaven, and said to her, "What troubles you, Hagar? Do not be afraid; for God has heard the voice of the boy where he is. Come, lift up the boy and hold him fast with your hand, for I will make a great nation of him." Then God opened her eyes and she saw a well of water. Hagar went, and filled the skin with water, and gave the boy a drink.

God was with the boy, and he grew up; he lived in the wilderness, and became an expert with the bow. He lived in the wilderness of Paran; and his mother got a wife for him from the land of Egypt.

Genesis 21:8 – 21

The LORD commands death and life,
consigns to Sheol or raises up.

God deals out poverty and wealth,
casts down and lifts up,
raising the poor from squalor,
the needy from the trash heap,
to sit with the high and mighty,
taking their places of honor.

God owns the universe
and sets the earth within it.
God walks with the faithful
but silences the wicked in darkness;
their power does not prevail.

God's enemies will be broken,
heaven thunders against them.
The LORD will judge the earth,
and give power to the king,
victory to the anointed.

Canticle of 1 Samuel 2:6 – 10 ICEL

GOD'S PROMISE TO SARAH

The Roman lectionary tells the story of the binding of Isaac and of God's promise. In this passage God blesses Sarah and says that God's promise will come through her.

God said to Abraham, "As for Sarai your wife, you shall not call her Sarai, but Sarah shall be her name. I will bless her, and moreover I will give you a son by her. I will bless her, and she shall give rise to nations; kings of people shall come from her." Then Abraham fell on his face and laughed, and said to himself, "Can a child be born to a man who is a hundred years old? Can Sarah, who is ninety years old, bear a child?"

And Abraham said to God, "O that Ishmael might live in your sight!" God said, "No, but your wife Sarah shall bear you a son, and you shall name him Isaac. I will establish my covenant with him as an everlasting covenant for his offspring after him. As for Ishmael, I have heard you; I will bless him and make him fruitful and exceedingly numerous; he shall be the father of twelve princes, and I will make him a great nation. But my covenant I will establish with Isaac, whom Sarah shall bear to you at this season next year." And when he had finished talking with him, God went up from Abraham.

Genesis 17:15 – 22

All you sheltered by the Most High,
who live in Almighty God's shadow,
say to the Lord, "My refuge, my fortress,
my God in whom I trust!"

God will free you from hunters' snares,
will save you from deadly plague,
will cover you like a nesting bird.
God's wings will shelter you.

"I deliver all who cling to me,
raise the ones who know my name,
answer those who call me,
stand with those in trouble.
These I rescue and honor,
satisfy with long life,
and show my power to save."

Psalm 91:1 – 2, 3 – 4, 14 – 16 ICEL

THE HEBREW MIDWIVES, PHARAOH'S DAUGHTER, MOSES' MOTHER

Pharaoh seeks to destroy the Hebrews by having their newborn sons murdered, but the midwives foil his cruel plan. Moses' sister and mother help Pharaoh's daughter reclaim him from the Nile.

A new king arose over Egypt, who did not know Joseph. He said to his people, "Look, the Israelite people are more numerous and more powerful than we. Come, let us deal shrewdly with them, or they will increase and, in the event of war, join our enemies and fight against us and escape from the land." Therefore they set taskmasters over them to oppress them with forced labor. They built supply cities, Pithom and Rameses, for Pharaoh. But the more they were oppressed, the more they multiplied and spread, so that the Egyptians came to dread the Israelites. The Egyptians became ruthless in imposing tasks on the Israelites, and made their lives bitter with hard service in mortar and brick and in every kind of field labor. They were ruthless in all the tasks that they imposed on them.

The king of Egypt said to the Hebrew midwives, one of whom was named Shiphrah and the other Puah, "When you act as midwives to the Hebrew women, and see them on the birthstool, if it is a boy, kill him; but it if is a girl, she shall live." But the midwives feared God; they did not do as the king of Egypt commanded them, but they let the boys live. So the king of Egypt summoned the midwives and said to them, "Why have you done this, and allowed the boys to live?" The midwives said to Pharaoh, "Because the Hebrew women are not like the Egyptian women; for they are vigorous and give birth before the midwife comes to them." So God dealt well with the midwives; and the people multiplied and became very strong. And because the midwives feared God, they were given families. Then Pharaoh commanded all his people, "Every boy that is born to the Hebrews you shall throw into the Nile, but you shall let every girl live."

Now a man from the house of Levi went and married a Levite woman. The woman conceived and bore a son; and when she saw that he was a fine baby, she hid him three months. When she could hide him no longer she got a papyrus basket for him, and plastered it with bitumen and pitch; she put the child in it and placed it among the reeds on the bank of the river. His sister stood at a distance, to see what would happen to him.

The daughter of Pharaoh came down to bathe at the river, while her attendants walked beside the river. She saw the basket among the reeds and sent her maid to bring it. When she opened it, she saw the child. He was crying, and she took pity on him. "This must be one of the Hebrews' children," she said. Then his sister said to Pharaoh's daughter, "Shall I go and get you a nurse from the Hebrew women to nurse the child for you?" Pharaoh's daughter said to her, "Yes." So the girl went and called the child's mother. Pharaoh's daughter said to her, "Take this child and nurse it for me, and I will give you your wages." So the woman took the child and nursed it. When the child grew up, she brought him to Pharaoh's daughter, and she took him as her son. She named him Moses, "because," she said, "I drew him out of the water."

Exodus 1:8 — 2:10

SONG OF DEBORAH (1): Responsory
This passage speaks of Deborah, a prophet in Israel.

"Hear, O kings; give ear, O princes;
　　to the LORD I will sing,
　　I will make melody to the LORD, the God of Israel.

"LORD, when you sent out from Seir,
　　when you marched from the region of Edom,
the earth trembled,
　　and the heavens poured,
　　the clouds indeed poured water.
The peasantry prospered in Israel,
　　they grew fat on plunder,
because you arose, Deborah,
　　arose as a mother in Israel.
When new gods were chosen,
　　then war was in the gates.
Was shield or spear to be seen
　　among forty thousand in Israel?

My heart goes out to the commanders of Israel
>who offered themselves willing among the people.
>Bless the LORD.

Judges 5:3 – 4, 7 – 9

WISDOM BRINGS HER PEOPLE OUT OF EGYPT
The Exodus from Egypt is attributed to the action of holy Wisdom; it was she who brought about the deliverance of the people of Israel and led them through the desert.

A holy people and blameless race
wisdom delivered from a nation of oppressors.

She entered the soul of a servant of the Lord,
and withstood dread kings with wonders and signs.
She gave to holy people the reward of their labors;
she guided them along a marvelous way,
and became a shelter to them by day,
and a starry flame through the night.

She brought them over the Red Sea,
and led them through deep water;
but she drowned their enemies,
and cast them up from the depth of the sea.
Therefore the righteous plundered the ungodly;
they sang hymns, O Lord, to your holy name,
and praised with one accord your defending hand;
for wisdom opened the mouths of those who were mute,
and made the tongues of infants speak clearly.

Wisdom prospered their works by the hand of a holy prophet.
They journeyed through an uninhabited wilderness,
and pitched their tents in untrodden places.
They withstood their enemies and fought off their foes.

When they were thirsty, they called upon you
and water was given them out of flinty rock,
and from hard stone a remedy for their thirst.
For through the very things by which their enemies were punished,
they themselves received benefit in their need.

Wisdom of Solomon 10:15 – 21; 11:1 – 5

Hear my just claim, God,
give me your full attention.
My prayer deserves an answer,
for I speak the truth.
Decide in my favor,
you always see what is right.

I call to you, God,
for you answer me.
Give me your attention,
hear me out.

Show me your wonderful love,
save the victims
of those who resist you.

Keep a loving eye on me.
Guard me under your wings,
hide me from those who attack,
from predators who surround me.
They close their heart,
they mouth contempt.

Psalm 17:1 – 2, 6 – 7, 8 – 10 ICEL

THE PROPHET MIRIAM

For Micah, the leadership of Miriam and her brothers at the time of the Exodus is evidence of God's love and saving acts.

Hear what the LORD says:
Rise, plead your case before the mountains,
     and let the hills hear your voice.
Hear, you mountains, the controversy of the LORD,
     and you enduring foundations of the earth;
for the LORD has a controversy with the people,
     and the LORD will contend with Israel.

"O my people, what have I done to you?
     In what have I wearied you? Answer me!
For I brought you up from the land of Egypt,
     and redeemed you from the house of slavery;
and I sent before you Moses, Aaron, and Miriam.

O my people, remember now
> what King Balak of Moab devised
> what Balaam son of Beor answered him,

and what happened from Shittim to Gilgal,
> that you may know the saving acts of the LORD."

"With what shall I come before the LORD,
> and bow myself before God on high?

Shall I come before God with burnt offerings,
> with calves a year old?

Will the LORD be pleased with thousands of rams,
> with ten thousands of rivers of oil?

Shall I give my firstborn for my transgression,
> the fruit of my body for the sin of my soul?"

The LORD has told you, O mortal, what is good;
> and what does the LORD require of you

but to do justice, and to love kindness,
> and to walk humbly with your God?

Micah 6:1–8

SONG OF MIRIAM: Responsory
The first reading of the lectionaries proclaims that daughters shall prophesy. This passage tells of Miriam, a prophet in Israel.

When the horses of Pharaoh with his chariots and his chariot drivers went into the sea, the Lord brought back the waters of the sea upon them; but the Israelites walked through the sea on dry ground.

Then the prophet Miriam, Aaron's sister, took a tambourine in her hand; and all the women went out after her with tambourines and with dancing.

And Miriam sang to them:

"Sing to the Lord, for God has triumphed gloriously;
horse and rider God has thrown into the sea."

Exodus 15:19–21

FIVE SISTERS CONFRONT MOSES
The sisters confront Moses and the other leaders to challenge the established pattern of inheritance that excluded women. God takes their side.

The daughters of Zelophehad came forward. Zelophehad was son of Hepher son of Gilead son of Machir son of Manasseh son of Joseph, a member of the Manassite clans. The names of his daughters were: Mahlah, Noah, Hoglah, Milcah, and Tirzah. They stood before Moses, Eleazar the priest, the leaders, and all the congregation, at the entrance of the tent of meeting, and they said, "Our father died in the wilderness;

he was not among the company of those who gathered themselves together against the LORD in the company of Korah, but died for his own sin; and he had no sons. Why should the name of our father be taken away from his clan because he had no son? Give to us a possession among our father's brothers."

Moses brought their case before the LORD. And the LORD spoke to Moses, saying: The daughters of Zelophehad are right in what they are saying; you shall indeed let them possess an inheritance among their father's brothers and pass the inheritance of their father on to them. You shall also say to the Israelites, "If a man dies, and has no son, then you shall pass his inheritance on to his daughter. If he has no daughter, then you shall give his inheritance to his brothers. If he has no brothers, then you shall give his inheritance to his father's brothers. And if his father has no brothers, then you shall give his inheritance to the nearest kinsman of his clan, and he shall possess it. It shall be for the Israelites a statute and ordinance, as the LORD commanded Moses."

Numbers 27:1–11

SONG OF DEBORAH (2): Responsory

"Tell of it, you who ride on white donkeys,
    you who sit on rich carpets
    and you who walk by the way.
To the sound of musicans at the watering places,
    there they repeat the triumphs of the Lord,
    the triumphs of his peasantry in Israel.

"Then down to the gates marched the people of the Lord.

"Awake, awake, Deborah!
    Awake, awake, utter a song!
Arise, Barak, lead away your captives,
    O son of Abinoam."

Judges 5:10–12

ISRAEL, GOD'S SPOUSE

God is Israel's creator and redeemer, and is also Israel's faithful, steadfast spouse. The covenant of peace will not be removed.

For your Maker is your husband,
    the LORD of hosts is the Creator's name;
the Holy One of Israel is your Redeemer,
    the one called the God of the whole earth.
For the LORD has called you
    like a wife forsaken and grieved in spirit,

like the wife of a man's youth when she is cast off,
     says your God.

For a brief moment I abandoned you,
     but with great compassion I will gather you.
In overflowing wrath for a moment
     I hid my face from you,
but with everlasting love I will have compassion on you,
     says the LORD, your Redeemer.

This is like the days of Noah to me:
     Just as I swore that the waters of Noah
     would never again go over the earth,
so I have sworn that I will not be angry with you
     and will not rebuke you.
For the mountains may depart
     and the hills be removed,
but my steadfast love shall not depart from you
     and my covenant of peace shall not be removed,
     says the LORD, who has compassion on you.

O afflicted one, storm-tossed, and not comforted,
     I am about to set your stones in antimony,
     and lay your foundations with sapphires.
I will make your pinnacles of rubies,
     your gates of jewels,
     and all your wall of precious stones.

All your children shall be taught by the LORD,
     and great shall be the prosperity of your children.
In righteousness you shall be established;
     you shall be far from oppression, for you shall not fear;
     and from terror, for it shall not come near you.

Isaiah 54:5 – 14

GOD AS A SHELTERING MOTHER: Responsory

Hear me, God! I cry out,
listen to my prayer.
I call from far away,
for my courage fails.
Lead me to a mountain height
where I can be safe.

You are my refuge,
a tower of strength against my foes.
Welcome me into your home,
under your wings for ever.

God, you surely hear my vows;
give me the blessings of those who honor your name.

I sing your name always,
each day fulfilling my vows.

Psalm 61:2 – 3, 4 – 5, 6, 9 ICEL

DOES A MOTHER FORGET HER CHILD?
God's love for Israel is that of a nursing mother.

Sing for joy, O heavens, and exult, O earth;
      break forth, O mountains, into singing!
For the LORD has comforted the people,
      and will have compassion on God's suffering ones.

But Zion said, "The LORD has forsaken me,
      my Lord has forgotten me."
Can a woman forget her nursing child,
      or show no compassion for the child of her womb?
Even these may forget,
      yet I will not forget you.
See, I have inscribed you on the palms of my hands;
      your walls are continually before me.
Your builders outdo your destroyers,
      and those who laid you waste go away from you.
Lift up your eyes all around and see;
      they all gather, they come to you.
As I live, says the LORD,
      you shall put all of them on like an ornament,
      and like a bride you shall bind them on.

Isaiah 49:13 – 16a

GOD AS SHELTERING MOTHER: Responsory

Care for me, God, take care of me,
I have nowhere else to hide.
Shadow me with your wings
until all danger passes.

I have decided, O God,
my decision is firm:
to you I will sing my praise.
Awake, my soul, to song!

Awake, my harp and lyre,
so I can wake up the dawn!
I will lift my voice in praise,
sing of you, Lord, to all nations.
For your love reaches heaven's edge,
your unfailing love, the skies.

O God, rise high above the heavens!
Spread your glory across the earth!

Psalm 57:2, 8 – 9, 10 – 12 ICEL

THE PROPHET HULDAH
This story tells of Huldah, prophet in Israel. She authenticates the newly rediscovered book of the Law and the community believes.

The priest Hilkiah, Akikam, Achbor, Shaphan, and Asaiah went to the prophetess Huldah the wife of Shullum son of Tikvah, son of Harhas, keeper of the wardrobe; she resided in Jerusalem in the Second Quarter, where they consulted her. She declared to them, "Thus says the LORD, the God of Israel: Tell the man who sent you to me, Thus says the LORD, I will indeed bring disaster on this place and on its inhabitants — all the words of the book that the king of Judah has read. Because they have abandoned me and have made offerings to other gods, so that they have provoked me to anger with all the work of their hands, therefore my wrath will be kindled against this place and it will not be quenched.

"But as to the king of Judah, who sent you to inquire of the LORD, thus shall you say to him, Thus says the LORD, the God of Israel: Regarding the words that you have heard, because your heart was penitent, and you humbled yourself before the LORD, when you heard how I spoke against this place, and against its inhabitants, that they should become a desolation and a curse, and because you have torn your clothes and wept before me, I also have heard you, says the LORD. Therefore, I will gather you to your ancestors, and you shall be gathered to your place in peace; your eyes shall not see all the disasters that I will bring on this place." They took the message back to the king.

2 Kings 22:14 – 20

THE SONG OF JUDITH (1): Responsory
Judith sings a song of triumph, for God has foiled the enemy through her hand.

Judith began this thanksgiving before all Israel, and all the people loudly sang this song of praise. And Judith said:

Begin a song to my God with tambourines,
    sing to my Lord with cymbals.
Raise a new psalm;
    exalt and call upon God's name.
For the Lord is a God who crushes wars
    and sets up camp among the chosen people;
    God delivered me from the hands of my pursuers.
The Assyrian came down from the mountains of the north;
    they came with myriads of warriors;
their numbers blocked up the wadis,
    and their cavalry covered the hills.
The boasted that they would burn up my territory,
    and kill my youth with the sword,
and dash my infants to the ground,
    and seize my children as booty,
    and take my virgins as spoil.

But the Lord Almighty has foiled them
    by the hand of a woman.

Judith 15:14 — 16:5

SUSANNA: FALSELY ACCUSED AND VINDICATED
Two lustful and wicked judges try to trap Susanna, a righteous woman who trusts in God and cries out to defend herself. Although she is first unjustly convicted, her innocence is later proven and her trust in God confirmed. Justice triumphs, due to Susanna's faith and Daniel's integrity.

There was a man living in Babylon whose name was Joakim. He married the daughter of Hilkiah, named Susanna, a very beautiful woman and one who feared the Lord. Her parents were righteous, and had trained their daughter according to the law of Moses. Joakim was very rich, and had a fine garden adjoining his house; the Jews used to come to him because he was the most honored of them all.

That year two elders from the people were appointed as judges. Concerning them the Lord has said, "Wickedness came forth from Babylon, from elders who were judges, who were supposed to govern the people." These men were frequently at Joakim's house, and all who had a case to be tried came to them there.

When the people left at noon, Susanna would go into her husband's garden to walk. Every day the two elders used to see her, going in and walking about, and they began to lust for her. They suppressed their consciences and turned away their eyes from looking to heaven or remembering their duty to administer justice. Both were overwhelmed with passion for her, but they did not tell each other of their distress, for they were ashamed to disclose their lustful desire to seduce her. Day after day they watched eagerly to see her.

One day they said to each other, "Let us go home, for it is time for lunch." So they both left and parted from each other. But turning back, they met again, and when each pressed the other for the reason, they confessed their lust. Then together they arranged for a time when they could find her alone.

Once, while they were watching for an opportune day, she went in as before with only two maids, and wished to bathe in the garden, for it was a hot day. No one was there except the two elders, who had hidden themselves and were watching her. She said to her maids, "Bring me olive oil and ointments, and shut the garden doors so that I can bathe." They did as she told them; they shut the doors of the garden and went out by the side doors to bring what they had been commanded; they did not see the elders, because they were hiding.

When the maids had gone out, the two elders got up and ran to her. They said, "Look, the garden doors are shut, and no one can see us. We are burning with desire for you; so give your consent, and lie with us. If you refuse, we will testify against you that a young man was with you, and this was why you sent your maids away."

Susanna groaned and said, "I am completely trapped. For if I do this, it will mean death for me; if I do not, I cannot escape your hands. I choose not to do it; I will fall into your hands, rather than sin in the sight of the Lord."

Then Susanna cried out with a loud voice, and the two elders shouted against her. And one of them ran and opened the garden doors. When the people in the house heard the shouting in the garden, they rushed in at the side door to see what had happened to her. And when the leaders told their story, the servants felt very much ashamed, for nothing like this had ever been said about Susanna.

The next day, when the people gathered at the house of her husband Joakim, the two elders came, full of their wicked plot to have Susanna put to death. In the presence of the people they said, "Send for Susanna daughter of Hilkiah, the wife of Joakim." So they sent for her. And she came with her parents, her children, and all her relatives.

Now Susanna was a woman of great refinement and beautiful in appearance. As she was veiled, the scoundrals ordered her to be unveiled, so that they might feast their eyes on her beauty. Those who were with her and all who saw her were weeping.

Then the two elders stood up before the people and laid their hands on her head. Through her tears she looked up toward heaven, for her heart trusted in the Lord. The elders said, "While we were walking in the garden alone, this woman came in with two maids, shut the garden doors, and dismissed the maids. Then a young man, who was hiding there, came to her and lay with her. We were in a corner of the garden, and when we saw this wickedness we ran to them. Although we saw them embracing, we could not hold the man, because he was stronger than we, and he opened the doors and got away. We did, however, seize this woman and asked who the young man was, but she would not tell us. These things we testify."

Because they were elders of the people and judges, the assembly believed them and condemned her to death.

Then Susanna cried out with a loud voice, and said, "O eternal God, you know what is secret and are aware of all things before they come to be; you know that these men have given false evidence against me. And now I am to die, though I have done none of the wicked things that they have charged against me."

The Lord heard Susanna's cry. Just as she was being led off to execution, God stirred up the holy spirit of a young lad named Daniel, and he shouted with a loud voice, "I want no part in shedding this woman's blood!"

All the people turned to him and asked, "What is this you are saying?" Taking his stand among them he said, "Are you such fools, O Israelites, as to condemn a daughter of Israel without examination and without learning the facts? Return to court, for these men have given false evidence against her."

So all the people hurried back. And the rest of the elders said to Daniel, "Come, sit among us and inform us, for God has given you the standing of an elder." Daniel said to them, "Separate them far from each other, and I will examine them."

When they were separated from each other, he summoned one of them and said to him, "You old relic of wicked days, your sins have now come home, which you have committed in the past, pronouncing unjust judgments, condemning the innocent and acquitting the guilty, though the Lord said, 'You shall not put an innocent and righteous person to death.' Now then, if you really saw this woman, tell me this: Under what tree did you see them being intimate with each other?" He answered, "Under a mastic tree." And Daniel said, "Very well! This lie has cost you your head, for the angel of God has received the sentence from God and will immediately cut you in two."

Then, putting him to one side, he ordered them to bring the other. And he said to him, "You offspring of Canaan and not of Judah, beauty has beguiled you and lust has perverted your heart. This is how you have been treating the daughters of Israel, and they were intimate with you through fear; but a daughter of Judah would not tolerate your wickedness. Now then, tell me: Under what tree did you catch them being intimate with each other?" He answered, "Under an evergreen oak." Daniel said to him, "Very well! This lie has cost you also your heart, for the angel of God is waiting with the sword to split you in two, so as to destroy you both."

Then the whole assembly raised a great shout and blessed God, who saves those who hope in God. And they took action against the two elders, because out of their own mouths Daniel had convicted them of bearing false witness; they did to them as they had wickedly planned to do to their neighbor. Acting in accordance with the law of Moses, they put them to death. Thus innocent blood was spared that day.

Hilkiah and his wife praised God for their daughter Susanna, and so did her husband Joakim and all her relatives, because she was found innocent of a shameful deed. And from that day onward Daniel had a great reputation among the people.

Daniel 13:1–64

For their mighty one did not fall by the hands of the young men,
>nor did the sons of the Titans strike him down,
>nor did tall giants set upon him;
but Judith daughter of Merari
>with the beauty of her countenance undid them.

For Judith put away her widow's clothing
>to exalt the oppressed in Israel.
She anointed her face with perfume;
>she fastened her hair with a tiara
>and put on a linen gown to beguile him.
Her sandal ravished his eyes,
>her beauty captivated his mind,
>and the sword severed his neck.
The Persians trembled at her boldness,
>the Medes were daunted at her daring.
Then my oppressed people shouted;
>my weak people cried out, and the enemy trembled;
>they lifted up their voices, and the enemy were turned back.
Sons of slave girls pierced them through
>and wounded them like the children of fugitives;
>they perished before the army of my Lord.

I will sing to my God a new song.
O Lord, you are great and glorious,
>wonderful in strength, invincible.
Let all your creatures serve you,
>for you spoke, and they were made.
You sent forth your spirit, and it formed them;
>there is none that can resist your voice.
For the mountains shall be shaken to their foundations with the waters;
>before your glance the rocks shall melt like wax.
But to those who fear you
>you show mercy.

Judith 16:5 – 16:15

THE ONE WHO KNOWS ALL THINGS KNOWS HER
Holy Wisdom — a feminine figure in the Bible — here is identified with strength, understanding, riches and the word of God.

Hear the commandments of life, O Israel;
>give ear, and learn wisdom!

Why is it, O Israel, why is it that you are in the land of your enemies,
        that you are growing old in a foreign country,
that you are defiled with the dead,
        that you are counted among those in Hades?
You have forsaken the fountain of wisdom.
If you had walked in the way of God,
        you would be living in peace forever.
Learn where there is wisdom,
        where there is strength,
        where there is understanding,
so that you may at the same time discern
        where there is length of days, and life,
where there is light for the eyes, and peace.

Who has found her place?
        And who has entered her storehouses?
The one who knows all things knows her,
        she was found by God's understanding.
The one who prepared the earth for all time
filled it with four-footed creatures;
the one who sends forth the light, and it goes;
        it was called, and it obeyed God, trembling;
the stars shone in their watches and were glad;
        they were called, and they said, "Here we are!"
        They shone with gladness for God who made them.

This is our God;
        no other can be compared to our God,
who found the whole way to knowledge,
        and gave her to servant Jacob
        and to beloved Israel.
Afterward she appeared on earth and lived with humankind.

She is the book of the commandments of God,
        the law that endures forever.
All who hold her fast will live,
        and those who forsake her will die.
Turn, O Jacob, and take her;
        walk toward the shining of her light.
Do not give your glory to another,
        or your advantages to an alien people.
Happy are we, O Israel,
        for we know what is pleasing to God.

Baruch 3:9 – 15, 32 — 4:4

Have mercy, tender God,
forget that I defied you.
Wash away my sin,
cleanse me from my guilt.

You love those centered in truth;
teach me your hidden wisdom.
Wash me with fresh water,
wash me bright as snow.

Creator, reshape my heart,
God, steady my spirit.
Do not cast me aside
stripped of your holy spirit.

Help me, stop my tears,
and I will sing your goodness.
Lord, give me words
and I will shout your praise.

Psalm 51:3−4, 8−9, 12−13, 16−17 ICEL

NO LONGER MALE OR FEMALE

*Is this a vision of the time of salvation, or of the garden of Eden, when the man and the woman were equal?
Equality of women and men in Christ has yet to be realized.*

In Christ Jesus you are all children of God through faith. As many of you as were
baptized into Christ have clothed yourselves with Christ. There is no longer Jew or
Greek, there is no longer slave or free, there is no longer male and female; for all of
you are one in Christ Jesus.

Galatians 3:26−28

JESUS APPEARS TO THE WOMEN

*The lectionaries tell of Jesus appearing to his disciples as they hid in the upper room. This passage tells of
the risen Christ appearing to two of the women disciples in the garden. They are the first to worship him,
and Jesus commissions them to carry the good news to the men.*

After the sabbath, as the first day of the week was dawning, Mary Magdalene and
the other Mary went to see the tomb. And suddenly there was a great earthquake;
for an angel of the Lord, descending from heaven, came and rolled back the stone
and sat on it. Its appearance was like lightning, and its clothing white as snow. For
fear of the angel the guards shook and became like dead men. But the angel said to

the women, "Do not be afraid; I know that you are looking for Jesus was was crucified. He is not here; for he has been raised, as he said. Come, see the place where he lay. Then go quickly and tell the disciples, 'He has been raised from the dead, and indeed he is going ahead of you to Galilee; there you will see him.' This is my message for you." Suddenly Jesus met them and said, "Greetings!" And they came to him, took hold of his feet, and worshiped him. Then Jesus said to them, "Do not be afraid; go and tell my brothers to go to Galilee; there they will see me."

Matthew 28:1 – 10

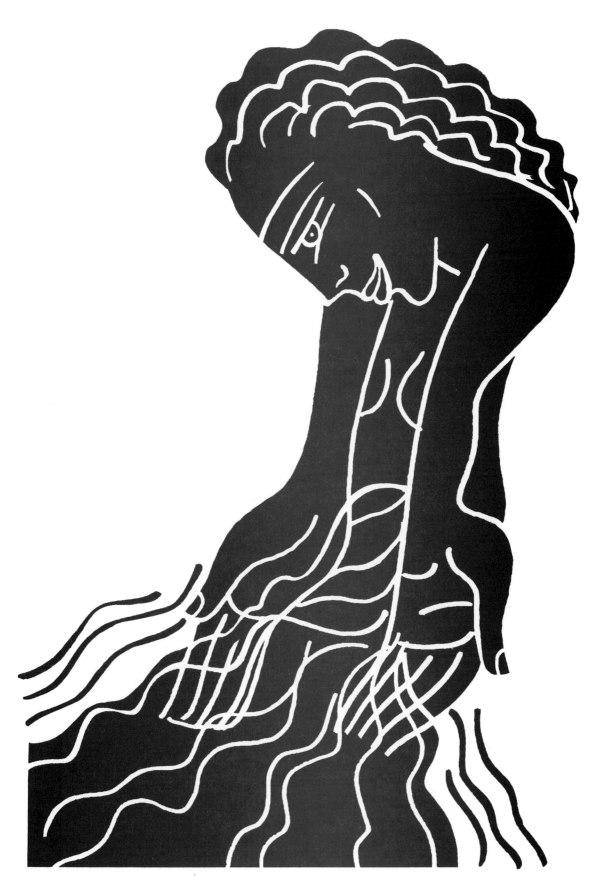

Rebekah

EASTER SUNDAY

JESUS APPEARS TO MARY MAGDALENE

Mary Magdalene, the first witness of the empty tomb, runs to report the news. She is unable to fully communicate what has happened: It is a novel and earth-shattering event. Her sorrow is soon transformed to joy. The risen Christ commissions the faithful disciple Mary Magdalene as "apostle to the apostles."

Early on the first day of the week, while it was still dark, Mary Magdalene came to the tomb and saw that the stone had been removed from the tomb. So she ran and went to Simon Peter and the other disciple, the one whom Jesus loved, and said to them, "They have taken the Lord out of the tomb, and we do not know where they have laid him." Then Peter and the other disciple set out and went toward the tomb. The two were running together, but the other disciple outran Peter and reached the tomb first. He bent down to look in and saw the linen wrappings lying there, but he did not go in. Then Simon Peter came, following him, and went into the tomb. He saw the linen wrappings lying there, and the cloth that had been on Jesus' head, not lying with the linen wrappings but rolled up in a place by itself. Then the other disciple, who reached the tomb first, also went in, and he saw and believed; for as yet they did not understand the scripture, that he must rise from the dead. Then the disciples returned to their homes.

But Mary stood weeping outside the tomb. As she wept, she bent over to look into the tomb; and she saw two angels in white, sitting where the body of Jesus had been lying, one at the head and the other at the feet. They said to her, "Woman, why are you weeping?" She said to them, "They have taken away my Lord, and I do not know where they have laid him."

When she had said this, she turned around and saw Jesus standing there, but she did not know that it was Jesus. Jesus said to her, "Woman, why are you weeping? Whom are you looking for?" Supposing him to be the gardener, she said to him, "Sir, if you have carried him away, tell me where you have laid him, and I will take him away." Jesus said, "Mary!" She turned and said to him in Hebrew, "Rabbouni!" (which means Teacher). Jesus said to her, "Do not hold on to me, because I have not yet ascended to the Father. But go to my brothers and say to them, 'I am ascending to my Father and your Father, to my God and your God.'" Mary Magdalene went and announced to the disciples, "I have seen the Lord"; and she told them that Jesus had said these things to her.

John 20:1 – 18

SECOND SUNDAY OF EASTER

JESUS APPEARS TO THE WOMEN

The lectionaries tell of Jesus appearing to his male disciples as they hid in the upper room. This passage tells of the risen Christ appearing to two of the women disciples in the garden. They are the first to worship him, and Jesus commissions them to carry the good news to the men.

After the sabbath, as the first day of the week was dawning, Mary Magdalene and the other Mary went to see the tomb. And suddenly there was a great earthquake; for an angel of the Lord, descending from heaven, came and rolled back the stone and sat on it. Its appearance was like lightning, and its clothing white as snow. For fear of the angel the guards shook and became like dead men. But the angel said to the women, "Do not be afraid; I know that you are looking for Jesus who was crucified. He is not here; for he has been raised, as he said. Come, see the place where he lay. Then go quickly and tell the disciples, 'He has been raised from the dead, and indeed he is going ahead of you to Galilee; there you will see him.' This is my message for you." Suddenly Jesus met them and said, "Greetings!" And they came to him, took hold of his feet, and worshiped him. Then Jesus said to them, "Do not be afraid; go and tell my brothers to go to Galilee; there they will see me."

Matthew 28:1–10

THIRD SUNDAY OF EASTER

JESUS APPEARS TO MARY MAGDALENE

The lectionaries tell of the encounter with Jesus on the road to Emmaus. This passage continues the story of the women disciples and the risen Christ.

Early on the first day of the week, while it was still dark, Mary Magdalene came to the tomb and saw that the stone had been removed from the tomb. So she ran and went to Simon Peter and the other disciple, the one whom Jesus loved, and said to them, "They have taken the Lord out of the tomb, and we do not know where they have laid him."

John 20:1–2

FOURTH SUNDAY OF EASTER

For the remainder of the Easter season, the lectionaries tell stories of the early church from the Acts of the Apostles. Stories of women leaders and members of the early church are presented here.

MARY AND RHODA

Mary is wealthy; her home is large enough for a gathering of believers, and she has a maid named Rhoda. When Rhoda announces that Peter is at the gate, those gathered don't believe her because she is "merely" a slave. Her insistence overcomes their doubt, but as with the women at the tomb, her preaching of the good news is rejected because of who she is.

King Herod laid violent hands upon some who belonged to the church. He had James, the brother of John, killed with the sword. After he saw that it pleased the Judeans, he proceeded to arrest Peter also. (This was during the festival of Unleavened Bread.) When he had seized Peter, he put him in prison and handed him over to four squads of soldiers to guard him, intending to bring him out to the people after the Passover. While Peter was kept in prison, the church prayed fervently to God for him.

The very night before Herod was going to bring him out, Peter, bound with two chains, was sleeping between two soldiers, while guards in front of the door were keeping watch over the prison. Suddenly an angel of the Lord appeared and a light shone in the cell. It tapped Peter on the side and woke him, saying, "Get up quickly." And the chains fell off his wrists. The angel said to him, "Fasten your belt and put on your sandals." Peter did so. Then it said to Peter, "Wrap your cloak around you and follow me." Peter went out and followed the angel; he did not realize that what was happening with the angel's help was real; he thought he was seeing a vision. After they had passed the first and the second guard, they came before the iron gate leading into the city. It opened for them of its own accord, and they went outside and walked along a lane, when suddenly the angel left him. Then Peter came to himself and said, "Now I am sure that the Lord has sent an angel and rescued me from the hands of Herod and from all that the Judeans were expecting."

As soon as Peter realized this, he went to the house of Mary, the mother of John whose other name was Mark, where many had gathered and were praying. When he knocked at the outer gate, a maid named Rhoda came to answer. On recognizing Peter's voice, she was so overjoyed that, instead of opening the gate, she ran in and announced that Peter was standing at the gate. They said to her, "You are out of your mind!" But she insisted that it was so. They said, "It is an angel." Meanwhile Peter continued knocking; and when they opened the gate, they saw him and were amazed. Peter motioned to them with his hand to be silent, and described for them how the Lord had brought him out of the prison. And he added, "Tell this to James and to the believers." Then Peter left and went to another place.

Acts of the Apostles 12:1–17

FIFTH SUNDAY OF EASTER

THE FOUR SISTERS WHO WERE PROPHETS
Women are full participants in the churches of Tyre and Caesarea. Prophetic ministry, like that of the four women in Caesarea, is a sign of the Spirit at work in the church — and a ministry suitable to women.

We looked up the disciples at Tyre and stayed there for seven days. Through the Spirit they told Paul not to go on to Jerusalem. When our days there were ended, we left and proceeded on our journey; and all of them, with women and children, escorted us outside the city. There we knelt down on the beach and prayed and said farewell to one another. Then we went on board the ship, and they returned home.

When we had finished the voyage from Tyre, we arrived at Ptolemais; and we greeted the believers and stayed with them for one day. The next day we left and came to Caesarea; and we went into the house of Philip the evangelist, one of the seven, and stayed with him. He had four unmarried daughters who had the gift of prophecy. While we were staying there for several days, a prophet named Agabus came down from Judea. He came to us and took Paul's belt, bound his own feet and hands with it, and said, "Thus says the Holy Spirit, 'This is the way the Judeans in Jerusalem will bind the man who owns this belt and will hand him over to the Gentiles.'" When we heard this, we and the people there urged him not to go up to Jerusalem. Then Paul answered, "What are you doing, weeping and breaking my heart? For I am ready not only to be bound but even to die in Jerusalem for the name of the Lord Jesus." Since he would not be persuaded, we remained silent except to say, "The Lord's will be done."

Acts of the Apostles 21:4 – 14

SIXTH SUNDAY OF EASTER

NYMPHA AND HER HOUSE CHURCH
Another local church meets in the house of Nympha. She provides hospitality and most likely leadership for her community.

Give my greetings to the brothers and sisters in Laodicea, and to Nympha and the church in her house. And when this letter has been read among you, have it read also in the church of the Laodiceans; and see that you read also the letter from Laodicea. And say to Archippus, "See that you complete the task that you have received in the Lord."

I, Paul, write this greeting with my own hand. Remember my chains. Grace be with you.

Colossians 4:15 – 18

THE ASCENSION OF CHRIST

THE MYSTERY OF WISDOM

Christ at his ascension can be likened to the feminine figure of divine presence, holy Wisdom. Wisdom is also an image of the Spirit that will soon be poured out.

All wisdom is from the Lord,
>and with God it remains forever.
The sand of the sea, the drops of rain,
>and the days of eternity — who can count them?
The height of heaven, the breadth of the earth,
>the abyss and wisdom — who can search them out?
Wisdom was created before all other things,
>and prudent understanding from eternity.
The root of wisdom — to whom has it been revealed?
>Her subtleties — who knows them?
There is but one who is wise, greatly to be feared,
>seated upon the throne — the Lord.
It is God who created her;
>God saw her and took her measure;
>God poured her out upon all created works,
upon all the living according to God's gift;
>God lavished her upon those who love God.

Sirach 1:1 – 10

SEVENTH SUNDAY OF EASTER

When the Ascension is celebrated on the Seventh Sunday of Easter, the two sets of readings may be combined.

WOMEN DISCIPLES AND MARY

After Jesus' ascension, a group of believers, men and women, gather in the upper room to pray. The men are all identified by name, but the only woman named is Mary. Why do we not know the other women's names?

When the apostles had come together to wait for the Holy Spirit, they asked Jesus, "Lord, is this the time when you will restore dominion to Israel?" Jesus replied, "It is not for you to know the times or periods that the Father has set by his own authority. But you will receive power when the Holy Spirit has come upon you; and you will be my witnesses in Jerusalem, in all Judea and Samaria, and to the ends of the earth."

When Jesus had said this, as they were watching, he was lifted up, and a cloud took him out of their sight. While he was going and they were gazing up toward heaven, suddenly two men in white robes stood by them. They said, "O Galileans, why do you stand looking up toward heaven? This Jesus, who has been taken up from you into heaven, will come in the same way as you saw him go into heaven."

Then they returned to Jesusalem from the mount called Olivet, which is near Jerusalem, a sabbath day's journey away. When they had entered the city, they went to the room upstairs where they were staying, Peter, and John, and James, and Andrew, Philip and Thomas, Bartholomew and Matthew, James son of Alphaeus, and Simon the Zealot, and Judas son of James.

All these were constantly devoting themselves to prayer, together with certain women, including Mary the mother of Jesus, as well as his brothers.

Acts of the Apostles 1:6–14

PENTECOST

DAUGHTERS AND MAIDSERVANTS SHALL PROPHESY
When the Holy Spirit descends on the church at Pentecost, women and men are empowered to prophesy, as had been foretold.

When the day of Pentecost had come, the twelve were all together in one place. And suddenly from heaven there came a sound like the rush of a violent wind, and it filled the entire house where they were sitting. Divided tongues, as of fire, appeared among them, and tongues rested on each of them. All of them were filled with the Holy Spirit and began to speak in other languages, as the Spirit gave them ability.

Peter, standing with the eleven, raised his voice and addressed the crowd, "O you Jewish people and all who live in Jerusalem, let this be known to you, and listen to what I say. Indeed, these are not drunk, as you suppose, for it is only nine o'clock in the morning. No, this is what was spoken through the prophet Joel:

'In the last days it will be, God declares,
that I will pour out my Spirit upon all flesh,
   and your sons and your daughters shall prophesy,
and your youth shall see visions,
   and your elders shall dream dreams.
Even upon my menservants and maidservants,
   in those days I will pour out my Spirit;
   and they shall prophesy.'"

Acts of the Apostles 2:1 – 4, 14 – 18

DAUGHTERS AND MAIDSERVANTS SHALL PROPHESY
In the reading included above, Peter quotes this passage from the book of the prophet Joel.

You shall eat in plenty and be satisfied,
   and praise the name of the LORD your God,
   who has dealt wondrously with you.
And my people shall never again be put to shame.
You shall know that I am in the midst of Israel,
   and that I, the LORD, am your God and there is no other.
And my people shall never again
   be put to shame.

Then afterward
    I will pour out my spirit on all flesh;
your sons and your daughters shall prophesy,
        your elders shall dream dreams,
        and your youth shall see visions.
Even on the menservants and maidservants
        in those days, I will pour out my spirit.

Joel 2:26–29

THE PROPHET MIRIAM

The first reading of the lectionaries proclaims that daughters shall prophesy. This passage tells of Miriam, a prophet in Israel.

When the horses of Pharaoh with his chariots and his chariot drivers went into the sea, the Lord brought back the waters of the sea upon them; but the Israelites walked through the sea on dry ground.

Then the prophet Miriam, Aaron's sister, took a tambourine in her hand; and all the women went out after her with tambourines and with dancing.

And Miriam sang to them:
"Sing to the Lord, for God has triumphed gloriously;
horse and rider God has thrown into the sea."

Exodus 15:19–21

SERVANT WOMEN CHALLENGE PETER

This passage tells of two women who speak prophetically to Peter.

Peter was sitting outside in the courtyard. A servant-girl came to him and said, "You also were with Jesus the Galilean." But he denied it before all of them, saying, "I do not know what you are talking about." When Peter went out to the porch, another servant-girl saw him, and she said to the bystanders, "This man was with Jesus of Nazareth." Again he denied it with an oath, "I do not know the man." After a little while the bystanders came up and said to Peter, "Certainly you are also one of them, for your accent betrays you." Then he began to curse, and he swore an oath, I do not know the man!" At that moment the cock crowed. Then Peter remembered what Jesus had said: "Before the cock crows, you will deny me three times." And he went out and wept bitterly.

Matthew 26:69–75

Leah and Rachel

TRINITY SUNDAY

FIRST SUNDAY AFTER PENTECOST

MALE AND FEMALE, CREATED IN GOD'S IMAGE
Of all creatures, only humankind is made in God's image. Both women and men mirror the divine image.

God said, "Let us make humankind in our image, according to our likeness; and let them have dominion over the fish of the sea, and over the birds of the air, and over the cattle, and over all the wild animals of the earth, and over every creeping thing that creeps upon the earth."

So God created humankind in the divine image,
in the image of God humankind was created,
male and female God created them.

God blessed them, and God said to them, "Be fruitful and multiply, and fill the earth and subdue it; and have dominion over the fish of the sea and over the birds of the air and over every living thing that moves upon the earth." God said, "See, I have given you every plant yielding seed that is upon the face of all the earth, and every tree with seed in its fruit; you shall have them for food. And to every beast of the earth, and to every bird of the air, and to everything that creeps on the earth, everything that has the breath of life, I have given every green plant for food." And it was so.

God saw everything that had been made, and indeed, it was very good. And there was evening and there was morning, the sixth day.

Thus the heavens and the earth were finished, and all their multitude. And on the seventh day God finished the work which God had done, and God rested on the seventh day from all the work that had been done. So God blessed the seventh day and hallowed it, because on it God rested from all the work that God had done in creation.

Genesis 1:26 — 2:3

GOD AS CHILDBEARER
This passage provides an image of God as a mother who faithfully carries and cares for her children.

Listen to me, O house of Jacob,
all the remnant of the house of Israel,
who have been borne by me from your birth,
carried from the womb;
even to your old age I am she
even when you turn gray I will carry you.
I have made, and I will bear;
I will carry and will save.

Isaiah 46:3 – 4

PRISCA AND AQUILA

Paul's letters often conclude with names of members of the early church, followed by doxologies or blessings. In this passage Prisca is named; she and her husband are leaders in the church.

The churches of Asia send greetings. Aquila and Prisca, together with the church in their house, greet you warmly in the Lord. All the brothers and sisters send greetings. Greet one another with a holy kiss.

I, Paul, write this greeting with my own hand. Let anyone be accursed who has no love for the Lord. Our Lord, come! The grace of the Lord Jesus be with you. My love be with all of you in Christ Jesus.

1 Corinthians 16:19–24

NINTH SUNDAY IN ORDINARY TIME

SECOND SUNDAY AFTER PENTECOST
PROPER 4: SUNDAY BETWEEN 29 MAY AND 4 JUNE

THE WIFE AND DAUGHTERS-IN-LAW OF NOAH

Four human couples took refuge in the ark and survived the flood. The wife and three daughters-in-law of Noah are significant figures in this story, but they are not named. Why?

These are the descendants of Noah. Noah was a righteous man, blameless in his generation; Noah walked with God. And Noah had three sons, Shem, Ham, and Japheth.

Now the earth was corrupt in God's sight, and the earth was filled with violence. And God saw that the earth was corrupt; for all flesh had corrupted its ways upon the earth. And God said to Noah, "I have determined to make an end of all flesh, for the earth is filled with violence because of them; now I am going to destroy them along with the earth.

"Make yourself an ark of cypress wood, make rooms in the ark, and cover it inside and out with pitch. This is how you are to make it: the length of the ark three hundred cubits, its width fifty cubits, and its height thirty cubits. Make a roof for the ark, and finish it to a cubit above, and put the door of the ark in its side; make it with lower, second, and third decks.

"For my part, I am going to bring a flood of waters on the earth, to destroy from under heaven all flesh in which is the breath of life; everything that is on the earth shall die. But I will establish my covenant with you; and you shall come into the ark, you, your sons, your wife, and your sons' wives with you. And of every living thing, of all flesh, you shall bring two of every kind into the ark, to keep them alive with you; they shall be male and female.

"Of the birds according to their kinds, and of the animals according to their kinds, of every creeping thing of the group according to its kind, two of every kind shall come in to you, to keep them alive. Also take with you every kind of food that is eaten, and store it up; and it shall serve as food for you and for them." Noah did this; he did all that God commanded him.

And the waters swelled on the earth for one hundred fifty days.

In the second month, on the twenty-seventh day of the month, the earth was dry. Then God said to Noah, "Go out of the ark, you and your wife, and your sons and your sons' wives with you. Bring out with you every living thing that is with you of all flesh — birds and animals and every creeping thing that creeps on the earth — so that they may abound on the earth, and be fruitful and multiply on the earth." So Noah went out with his sons and his wife and his sons' wives. And every animal, every creeping thing, and every bird, everything that moves on the earth, went out of the ark by families.

Genesis 6:9 – 22; 7:24; 8:14 – 19

THE MOTHER OF THE WIFE OF PETER

The matron of Peter's household is among the first to be healed by Jesus and she responds with generous hospitality. Her willing response is in contrast to Peter's later denial of Jesus. Her house becomes the place where Jesus heals others later that evening.

When Jesus entered Peter's house, he saw Peter's mother-in-law lying in bed with a fever; Jesus touched her hand, and the fever left her, and she got up and began to serve him.

That evening they brought to him many who were possessed with demons, and he cast out the spirits with a word, and cured all who were sick. This was to fulfill what had been spoken through the prophet Isaiah, "He took our infirmities and bore our diseases."

Matthew 8:14 – 17

TENTH SUNDAY IN ORDINARY TIME

THIRD SUNDAY AFTER PENTECOST
PROPER 5: SUNDAY BETWEEN 5 JUNE AND 11 JUNE

SARAI AND ABRAM SET OUT FOR THE LAND OF CANAAN
Sarai shared the hardship and adventure of the migration from Haran to Canaan.

The LORD said to Abram, "Go from your country and your kindred and your father's house to the land that I will show you. I will make of you a great nation, and I will bless you, and make your name great, so that you will be a blessing. I will bless those who bless you, and the one who curses you I will curse; and in you all the families of the earth shall be blessed."

So Abram went, as the LORD had told him; and Lot went with him. Abram was seventy-five years old when he departed from Haran. Abram took his wife Sarai and his brother's son Lot, and all the possessions that they had gathered, and the persons whom they had acquired in Haran; and they set forth to go to the land of Canaan. When they had come to the land of Canaan, Abram passed through the land to the place at Shechem, to the oak of Moreh. At that time the Canaanites were in the land.

Then the LORD appeared to Abram, and said, "To your offspring I will give this land." So he built there an altar to the LORD, who had appeared to him. From there he moved on to the hill country on the east of Bethel, and pitched his tent, with Bethel on the west and Ai on the east; and there he built an altar to the LORD and invoked the name of the LORD. And Abram journeyed on by stages toward the Negeb.

Genesis 12:1 – 9

THE FAITH OF SARAH AND ABRAHAM
The age and infertility of Abraham and Sarah, usually blamed only on Sarah, was no obstacle to their faith in God.

The promise that Abraham would inherit the world did not come to him or to his descendants through the law but through the righteousness of faith. If it is the adherents of the law who are to be the heirs, faith is null and the promise is void. For the law brings wrath; but where there is no law, neither is there violation.

For this reason it depends on faith, in order that the promise may rest on grace and be guaranteed to all his descendants, not only to the adherents of the law but also to those who share the faith of Abraham (for he is the ancestor of all of us, as it is written, "I have made you the father of many nations") — in the presence of the God in whom he believed, who gives life to the dead and calls into existence the things that do not exist. Hoping against hope, he believed that he would become "the father of many nations," according to what was said, "So numerous shall your descendants be." He did not weaken in faith when he considered his own body, which was already as good as dead (for he was about a hundred years old), or when he considered the barrenness of Sarah's womb. No distrust made him waver concerning the promise of God, but he grew strong in his faith as he gave glory to God, being fully convinced that God was able to do what God had promised. There Abraham's faith "was reckoned to him as righteousness." Now the words, "It is reckoned to him," were written not for his sake alone, but for ours also. It will be reckoned to us who believe in him who raised Jesus our Lord from the dead, who was handed over to death for our trespasses and was raised for our justification.

Romans 4:13 – 25

THE OFFICIAL'S DAUGHTER AND THE WOMAN WITH HEMORRHAGES

A twelve-year-old girl is important enough to Jesus that he interrupts his teaching to go to her. The older woman violates social propriety by touching Jesus' cloak, but he commends her faith and she is healed.

While Jesus was speaking, suddenly a leader of the synagogue came in and knelt before him, saying, "My daughter has just died; but come and lay your hand on her, and she will live." And Jesus got up and followed him, with his disciples.

Then suddenly a woman who had been suffering from hemorrhages for twelve years came up behind him and touched the fringe of his cloak, for she said to herself, "If I only touch his cloak, I will be made well." Jesus turned, and seeing her he said, "Take heart, daughter; your faith has made you well." And instantly the woman was made well.

When Jesus came to the leader's house and saw the flute players and the crowd making a commotion, he said, "Go away; for the girl is not dead but sleeping." And they laughed at him. But when the crowd had been put outside, Jesus went in and took her by the hand, and the girl got up. And the report of this spread throughout that district.

Matthew 9:18 – 26

ELEVENTH SUNDAY IN ORDINARY TIME

FOURTH SUNDAY AFTER PENTECOST
PROPER 6: SUNDAY BETWEEN 12 AND 18 JUNE

SARAH IS PROMISED A SON AND BEARS ISAAC

Sarah's laughs, first with wry humor when the visitors promise her a child, and later with joy when she gives birth to Isaac. Her laughter and her child are gifts from God.

The LORD appeared to Abraham by the oaks of Mamre, as he sat at the entrance of his tent in the heat of the day. Abraham looked up and saw three men standing near him. When he saw them, he ran from the tent entrance to meet them, and bowed down to the ground. He said, "My lord, if I find favor with you, do not pass by your servant. Let a little water be brought, and wash your feet, and rest yourselves under the tree. Let me bring a little bread, that you may refresh yourselves, and after that you may pass on — since you have come to your servant." So they said, "Do as you have said."

And Abraham hastened into the tent to Sarah, and said, "Make ready quickly three measures of choice flour, knead it, and make cakes." Abraham ran to the herd, and took a calf, tender and good, and gave it to the servant, who hastened to prepare it. Then he took curds and milk and the calf that he had prepared, and set it before them; and he stood by them under the tree while they ate.

They said to him, "Where is your wife Sarah?" And Abraham said, "There, in the tent." Then one said, "I will surely return to you in due season, and your wife Sarah shall have a son." And Sarah was listening at the tent entrance behind him. Now Abraham and Sarah were old, advanced in age; it had ceased to be with Sarah after the manner of women.

So Sarah laughed to herself, saying, "After I have grown old and my husband is old, shall I have pleasure?" The LORD said to Abraham, "Why did Sarah laugh, and say, 'Shall I indeed bear a child, now that I am old?' Is anything too wonderful for the LORD? At the set time I will return to you, in due season, and Sarah shall have a son." But Sarah denied, saying, "I did not laugh"; for she was afraid. God said, "Oh yes, you did laugh."

The LORD dealt with Sarah as had been said, and the LORD did for Sarah as had been promised. Sarah conceived and bore Abraham a son in his old age, at the time of which God had spoken to him. Abraham gave the name Isaac to his son whom Sarah bore him. And Abraham circumcised his son Isaac when he was eight days old, as God had commanded him. Abraham was a hundred years old when his son Isaac was born to him. Now Sarah said, "God has brought laughter for me; everyone who hears will laugh with me." And she said, "Who would ever have said to Abraham that Sarah would nurse children? Yet I have borne him a son in his old age."

Genesis 18:1 – 15; 21:1 – 7

TWELFTH SUNDAY IN ORDINARY TIME

FIFTH SUNDAY AFTER PENTECOST
PROPER 7: SUNDAY BETWEEN 19 AND 25 JUNE

HAGAR AND ISHMAEL ARE SENT OUT INTO THE DESERT
Sarah exercises authority, though her actions are cruel. Hagar looks after her son even in difficult circum-stances; later, she exercises her authority by finding a wife for him.

Isaac grew and was weaned; and Abraham made a great feast on the day that Isaac was weaned. But Sarah saw the son of Hagar the Egyptian, whom she had borne to Abraham, playing with her son Isaac. So she said to Abraham, "Cast out this slave woman with her son; for the son of the slave woman shall not inherit along with my son Isaac."

The matter was very distressing to Abraham on account of his son. But God said to Abraham, "Do not be distressed because of the boy and because of your slave woman; whatever Sarah says to you, do as she tells you, for it is through Isaac that offspring shall be named for you. As for the son of the slave woman, I will make a nation of him also, because he is your offspring." So Abraham rose early in the morning, and took bread and a skin of water, and gave it to Hagar, putting it on her shoulder, along with the child, and sent her away. And she departed, and wandered about in the wilderness of Beer-sheba.

When the water in the skin was gone, Hagar cast the child under one of the bushes. Then she went and sat down opposite him a good way off, about the distance of a bowshot; for she said, "Do not let me look on the death of the child." And as Hagar sat opposite him, she lifted up her voice and wept. And God heard the voice of the boy; and the angel of God called to Hagar from heaven, and said to her, "What troubles you, Hagar? Do not be afraid; for God has heard the voice of the boy where he is. Come, lift up the boy and hold him fast with your hand, for I will make a great nation of him." Then God opened her eyes and she saw a well of water. Hagar went, and filled the skin with water, and gave the boy a drink.

God was with the boy, and he grew up; he lived in the wilderness, and became an expert with the bow. He lived in the wilderness of Paran; and his mother got a wife for him from the land of Egypt.

Genesis 21:8 – 21

THIRTEENTH SUNDAY IN ORDINARY TIME

SIXTH SUNDAY AFTER PENTECOST
PROPER 8: SUNDAY BETWEEN 26 JUNE AND 2 JULY

THE WOMAN OF SHUNEM

The Shunammite woman offers generous hospitality to the prophet with no thought for reward. Even so, she and her elderly husband are given a child to support them in their old age.

One day Elisha was passing through Shunem, where a wealthy woman lived, who urged him to have a meal. So whenever he passed that way, he would stop there for a meal. She said to her husband, "Look, I am sure that this man who regularly passes our way is a holy man of God. Let us make a small roof chamber with walls, and put there for him a bed, a table, a chair, and a lamp, so that he can stay there whenever he comes to us."

One day when Elisha came there, he went up to the chamber and lay down there. He said to his servant Gehazi, "Call the Shunammite woman." When Gehazi had called her, she stood before him. Elisha said to Gehazi, "Say to her, Since you have taken all this trouble for us, what may be done for you? Would you have a word spoken on your behalf to the king or to the commander of the army?" She answered, "I live among my own people."

Elisha said, "What then may be done for her?" Gehazi answered, "Well, she has no son, and her husband is old." He said, "Call her." When he had called her, she stood at the door. He said, "At this season, in due time, you shall embrace a son." She replied, "No, my lord, O man of God; do not deceive your servant."

The woman conceived and bore a son at that season, in due time, as Elisha had declared to her.

2 Kings 4:8 – 17

FOURTEENTH SUNDAY IN ORDINARY TIME

SEVENTH SUNDAY AFTER PENTECOST
PROPER 9: SUNDAY BETWEEN 3 AND 9 JULY

REBEKAH MARRIES ISAAC

Rebekah is generous and industrious, and Abraham's servant hopes she is the one. She is not forced into marriage, though; her family asks if she agrees.

Abraham's servant said to Rebekah's family, "The LORD has greatly blessed my master, and he has become wealthy; God has given him flocks and herds, silver and gold, male and female slaves, camels and donkeys. And Sarah my master's wife bore a son to my master when she was old; and Abraham has given him all that he has. My master made me swear, saying, 'You shall not take a wife for my son from the daughters of the Canaanites, in whose land I live; but you shall go to my father's house, to my kindred, and get a wife for my son.'

"I came today to the spring, and said, 'O LORD, the God of my master Abraham, if now you will only make successful the way I am going! I am standing here by the spring of water; let the young woman who comes out to draw, to whom I shall say, "Please give me a little water from your jar to drink," and who will say to me, "Drink, and I will draw for your camels also" — let her be the woman whom the LORD has appointed for my master's son.'

"Before I had finished speaking in my heart, there was Rebekah coming out with her water jar on her shoulder; and she went down to the spring, and drew. I said to her, 'Please let me drink.' She quickly let down her jar from her shoulder, and said, 'Drink, and I will also water your camels.' So I drank, and she also watered the camels.

"Then I asked her, 'Whose daughter are you?' Rebekah said, 'The daughter of Bethuel, Nahor's son, whom Milcah bore to him.' So I put the ring on her nose, and the bracelets on her arms. Then I bowed my head and worshiped the LORD, and blessed the LORD, the God of my master Abraham, who had led me by the right way to obtain the daughter of my master's kinsman for his son. Now then, if you will deal loyally and truly with my master, tell me; and if not, tell me, so that I may turn either to the right hand or to the left."

And they called Rebekah and said to her, "Will you go with this man?" She said, "I will." So they sent away their sister Rebekah and her nurse along with Abraham's servant and his men. And they blessed Rebekah and said to her:

"May you, our sister, become thousands of myriads;
    may your offspring gain possession of the gates of their foes."

Then Rebekah and her maids rose up, mounted the camels, and followed the man; thus the servant took Rebekah, and went his way.

Now Isaac had come from Beer-lahai-roi, and was settled in the Negeb. Isaac went out in the evening to walk in the field; and looking up, he saw camels coming. And Rebekah looked up, and when she saw Isaac, she slipped quickly from the camel, and said to the servant, "Who is the man over there, walking in the field to meet us?" The servant said, "It is my master." So she took her veil and covered herself. And the servant told Isaac all the things that he had done. Then Isaac brought her into his mother Sarah's tent. He took Rebekah, and she became his wife; and he loved her. So Isaac was comforted after his mother's death.

Genesis 24:34 – 38, 42 – 49, 58 – 67

DAUGHTER ZION
The city of Jerusalem is imagined as God's daughter, who will live in peace in God's broad dominion.

Rejoice greatly, O daughter Zion!
    Shout aloud, O daughter Jerusalem!
Lo, your ruler comes to you,
    triumphant and victorious;
humble and riding on a donkey,
    on a colt, the foal of a donkey.
I will cut off the chariot from Ephraim
    and the war horse from Jerusalem;
and the battle bow shall be cut off,
    and I shall command peace to the nations;
my dominion shall be from sea to sea,
    and from the River to the ends of the earth.

Zechariah 9:9 – 12

JESUS AS HOLY WISDOM
Jesus assumes the role of holy Wisdom, a traditional feminine image of the divine presence.

At that time Jesus said, "To what will I compare this generation? It is like children sitting in the marketplace and calling to one another,

    'We played the flute for you, and you did not dance;
      we wailed, and you did not mourn.'

"For John came neither eating nor drinking, and they say, 'He has a demon'; the Son of Man came eating and drinking, and they say, 'Look, a glutton and a drunkard, a friend of tax collectors and sinners!' Yet wisdom is vindicated by her deeds."

At that time Jesus said, "I thank you, Father, Lord of heaven and earth, because you have hidden these things from the wise and the intelligent and have revealed them to infants; yes, Father, for such was your gracious will. All things have been handed over to me by the Father, and no one knows the Father except the Son and anyone to whom the Son chooses to reveal him.

"Come to me, all you that are weary and are carrying heavy burdens, and I will give you rest. Take my yoke upon you, and learn from me; for I am gentle and humble in heart, and you will find rest for your souls. For my yoke is easy, and my burden is light."

Matthew 11:16 – 19, 25 – 30

FIFTEENTH SUNDAY IN ORDINARY TIME

EIGHTH SUNDAY AFTER PENTECOST
PROPER 10: SUNDAY BETWEEN 10 AND 16 JULY

REBEKAH BEARS ESAU AND JACOB

The movements of the twins within her womb make Rebekah's pregnancy uncomfortable and difficult. She asks God what this means, and God tells her.

These are the descendents of Isaac, Abraham's son: Abraham was the father of Isaac, and Isaac was forty years old when he married Rebekah, daughter of Bethuel the Aramean of Paddan-aram, sister of Laban the Aramean. Isaac prayed to the LORD for his wife, because she was barren; and the LORD granted his prayer, and his wife Rebekah conceived.

The children struggled together within her; and she said, "If it is to be this way, why do I live?" So Rebekah went to inquire of the LORD. And the LORD said to her,

"Two nations are in your womb,
  and two peoples born of you shall be divided;
the one shall be stronger than the other,
  the elder shall serve the younger."

When Rebekah's time to give birth was at hand, there were twins in her womb. The first came out red, all his body like a hairy mantle; so they named him Esau. Afterward his brother came out, with his hand gripping Esau's heel; so he was named Jacob. Isaac was sixty years old when she bore them.

When the boys grew up, Esau was a skillful hunter, a man of the field, while Jacob was a quiet man, living in tents. Isaac loved Esau, because he was fond of game; but Rebekah loved Jacob.

Once when Jacob was cooking a stew, Esau came in from the field, and he was famished. Esau said to Jacob, "Let me eat some of that red stuff, for I am famished." (Therefore he was called Edom.) Jacob said, "First sell me your birthright." Esau said, "I am about to die; of what use is a birthright to me?" Jacob said, "Swear to me first." So Esau swore to him, and sold his birthright to Jacob. Then Jacob gave Esau bread and lentil stew, and he ate and drank, and rose and went his way. Thus Esau despised his birthright.

Genesis 25:19 – 34

SIXTEENTH SUNDAY IN ORDINARY TIME

NINTH SUNDAY AFTER PENTECOST
PROPER 11: SUNDAY BETWEEN 17 AND 23 JULY

REBEKAH THE TRICKSTER

Rebekah takes the initiative in tricking Isaac into giving the elder son's blessing to the younger, whom she favors. Rebekah's clever scheme is an example of God's purposes being accomplished by unexpected means.

When Isaac was old and his eyes were dim so that he could not see, he called his elder son Esau and said to him, "My son"; and he answered, "Here I am." Isaac said, "See, I am old; I do not know the day of my death. Now then, take your weapons, your quiver and your bow, and go out to the field, and hunt game for me. Then prepare for me savory food, such as I like, and bring it to me to eat, so that I may bless you before I die."

Now Rebekah was listening when Isaac spoke to his son Esau. So when Esau went to the field to hunt for game and bring it, Rebekah said to her son Jacob, "I heard your father say to your brother Esau, 'Bring me game, and prepare for me savory food to eat, that I may bless you before the LORD before I die.' Now therefore, my son, obey my word as I command you. Go to the flock, and get me two choice kids, so that I may prepare from them savory food for your father, such as he likes; and you shall take it to your father to eat, so that he may bless you before he dies."

But Jacob said to his mother Rebekah, "Look, my brother Esau is a hairy man, and I am a man of smooth skin. Perhaps my father will feel me, and I shall seem to be mocking him, and bring a curse on myself and not a blessing." His mother said to him, "Let your curse be on me, my son; only obey my word, and go, get them for me."

So Jacob went and got them and brought them to his mother; and his mother prepared savory food, such as his father loved. Then Rebekah took the best garments of her elder son Esau, which were with her in the house, and put them on her younger son Jacob; and she put the skins of the kids on his hands and on the smooth part of his neck. Then she handed the savory food, and the bread that she had prepared, to her son Jacob.

Genesis 27:1–17

The Roman lectionary assigns the first of the following readings to this Sunday, while the Revised Common Lectionary assigns it to the next Sunday.

THE WOMAN WHO MIXED YEAST INTO THE DOUGH

Jesus teaches in parables, assuming wisdom's role. In one of his parables, a woman is making bread. By her expertise and effort, a small amount of yeast leavens all the flour, and yields the bread of life.

Jesus put before them another parable: "The dominion of heaven is like a mustard seed that someone took and sowed in his field; it is the smallest of all the seeds, but when it has grown it is the greatest of shrubs and becomes a tree, so that the birds of the air come and make nests in its branches."

Jesus told them another parable: "The dominion of heaven is like yeast that a woman took and mixed in with three measures of flour until all of it was leavened."

Matthew 13:31–33

The Revised Common Lectionary assigns the next reading to this Sunday, while the Roman lectionary assigns it to the following Sunday.

JESUS' MOTHER AND BROTHERS AND SISTERS

Because Jesus and his mother, brothers and sisters are fellow townspeople, the people cannot accept his wisdom and healing power.

Jesus came to his hometown and began to teach the people in their synagogue, so that they were astounded and said, "Where did this man get this wisdom and these deeds of power? Is not this the carpenter's son? Is not his mother called Mary? And are not his brothers James and Joseph and Simon and Judas? And are not all his sisters with us? Where then did this man get all this?" And they took offense at him. But Jesus said to them, "Prophets are not without honor except in their own country and in their own house." And he did not do many deeds of power there, because of their unbelief.

Matthew 13:54–58

SEVENTEENTH SUNDAY IN ORDINARY TIME

TENTH SUNDAY AFTER PENTECOST
PROPER 12: SUNDAY BETWEEN 24 AND 30 JULY

LEAH AND RACHEL, WIVES OF JACOB

Jacob does not love Leah, who was foisted on him by her father's trickery. How does Laban's deception affect the relationships among Leah, her sister Rachel, and their husband Jacob? How does Leah feel?

Laban said to Jacob, "Because you are my kinsman, should you therefore serve me for nothing? Tell me, what shall your wages be?" Now Laban had two daughters; the name of the elder was Leah, and the name of the younger was Rachel. Leah's eyes were lovely, and Rachel was graceful and beautiful. Jacob loved Rachel; so he said, "I will serve you seven years for your younger daugher Rachel." Laban said, "It is better that I give her to you than that I should give her to any other man; stay with me." So Jacob served seven years for Rachel, and they seemed to him but a few days because of the love he had for her.

Then Jacob said to Laban, "Give me my wife that I may go in to her, for my time is completed." So Laban gathered together all the people of the place, and made a feast. But in the evening he took his daughter Leah and brought her to Jacob; and he went in to her. (Laban gave his maid Zilpah to his daughter Leah to be her maid.) When morning came it was Leah!

And Jacob said to Laban, "What is this you have done to me? Did I not serve with you for Rachel? Why then have you deceived me?" Laban said, "This is not done in our country — giving the younger before the firstborn. Complete the week of this one, and we will give you the other also in return for serving me another seven years." Jacob did so, and completed her week; then Laban gave him his daughter Rachel as a wife.

Genesis 29:15 – 28

The Revised Common Lectionary assigns this reading here, while the Roman lectionary assigns it to the preceding Sunday.

THE WOMAN WHO MIXED YEAST INTO THE DOUGH

Jesus teaches in parables, assuming wisdom's role. In one of his parables, a woman is making bread. By her expertise and effort, a small amount of yeast leavens all the flour, and yields the bread of life.

Jesus put before them another parable: "The dominion of heaven is like a mustard seed that someone took and sowed in his field; it is the smallest of all the seeds, but when it has grown it is the greatest of shrubs and becomes a tree, so that the birds of the air come and make nests in its branches."

Jesus told them another parable: "The dominion of heaven is like yeast that a woman took and mixed in with three measures of flour until all of it was leavened."

Matthew 13:31 – 33

The Roman lectionary assigns this reading to this Sunday, while the Revised Common Lectionary assigns it to the preceding Sunday.

JESUS' MOTHER AND BROTHERS AND SISTERS

Because Jesus and his mother, brothers and sisters are fellow townspeople, the people cannot accept his wisdom and healing power.

Jesus came to his hometown and began to teach the people in their synagogue, so that they were astounded and said, "Where did this man get this wisdom and these deeds of power? Is not this the carpenter's son? Is not his mother called Mary? And are not his brothers James and Joseph and Simon and Judas? And are not all his sisters with us? Where then did this man get all this?" And they took offense at him. But Jesus said to them, "Prophets are not without honor except in their own country and in their own house." And he did not do many deeds of power there, because of their unbelief.

Matthew 13:54–58

EIGHTEENTH SUNDAY IN ORDINARY TIME

ELEVENTH SUNDAY AFTER PENTECOST
PROPER 13: SUNDAY BETWEEN 31 JULY AND 6 AUGUST

POTIPHAR'S WIFE TRIES TO SEDUCE JOSEPH

Joseph shows the characteristics of holy Wisdom, a feminine image. When he resists Potiphar's wife and her adulterous intent, she cunningly has Joseph imprisoned.

Joseph was handsome and good-looking. And after a time his master Potiphar's wife cast her eyes on Joseph and said, "Lie with me." But he refused and said to his master's wife, "Look, with me here, my master has no concern about anything in the house, and he has put everything that he has in my hand. He is not greater in this house than I am, nor has he kept back anything from me except yourself, because you are his wife. How then could I do this great wickedness, and sin against God?"

And although she spoke to Joseph day after day, he would not consent to lie beside her or to be with her. One day, however, when he went into the house to do his work and while no one else was in the house, she caught hold of his garment, saying, "Lie with me!" But he left his garment in her hand, and fled and ran outside. When she saw that he had left his garment in her hand and had fled outside, she called out to the members of the household and said to them, "See, my husband has brought among us a Hebrew to insult us! He came in to me to lie with me, and I cried out with a loud voice; and when he heard me raise my voice and cry out, he left his garment beside me, and fled outside." Then she kept his garment by her until his master came home, and she told him the same story, saying, "The Hebrew servant, whom you have brought among us, came in to me to insult me; but as soon as I raised my voice and cried out, he left his garment beside me, and fled outside."

When his master heard the words that his wife spoke to him, saying, "This is the way your servant treated me," he became enraged. And Joseph's master took him and put him into the prison, the place where the king's prisoners were confined.

Genesis 39:6c – 20

HERODIAS AND HER DAUGHTER

This powerful and unscrupulous woman uses her daughter as a tool to eliminate John, who has spoken the truth about her unlawful union.

Herod the ruler heard reports about Jesus; and he said to his servants, "This is John the Baptist; he has been raised from the dead, and for this reason these powers are at work in him." For Herod had arrested John, bound him, and put him in prison on account of Herodias, his brother Philip's wife, because John had been telling him, "It is not lawful for you to have her." Though Herod wanted to put John to death, he feared the crowd, because they regarded him as a prophet. But when Herod's birthday came, the daughter of Herodias danced before the company, and she pleased Herod so much that he promised on oath to grant her whatever she might ask. Prompted by her mother, she said, "Give me the head of John the Baptist here on a platter." The king was grieved, yet out of regard for his oath and for the guests, he commanded it to be given; he sent and had John beheaded in the prison. The head was brought on a platter and given to the girl, who brought it to her mother. John's disciples came and took the body and buried it; then they went and told Jesus.

Matthew 14:1 – 12

Tamar

NINETEENTH SUNDAY IN ORDINARY TIME

TWELFTH SUNDAY AFTER PENTECOST
PROPER 14: SUNDAY BETWEEN 7 AND 13 AUGUST

THE DEATH AND BURIAL OF SARAH

Abraham mourned and wept upon the death of Sarah. The place of Sarah's burial at Hebron is still remembered today.

Sarah lived one hundred twenty-seven years; this was the length of Sarah's life. And Sarah died at Kiriath-arba (that is Hebron) in the land of Canaan; and Abraham went in to mourn for Sarah and to weep for her. Abraham rose up from beside his dead, and said to the Hittites, "I am a stranger and an alien residing among you; give me property among you for a burying place, so that I may bury my dead out of my sight."

The Hittites answered Abraham, "Hear us, my lord; you are a mighty prince among us. Bury your dead in the choicest of our burial places; none of us will withhold from you any burial ground for burying your dead."

So the field of Ephron in Machpelah, which was to the east of Mamre, the field with the cave that was in it and all the trees that were in the field, throughout its whole area, passed to Abraham as a possession in the presence of the Hittites, in the presence of all who went in at the gate of his city.

After this Abraham buried Sarah his wife in the cave of the field of Machpelah facing Mamre (that is, Hebron) in the land of Canaan. The field and the cave that is in it passed from the Hittites into Abraham's possession as a burying place.

Genesis 23:1 – 6, 17 – 20

TWENTIETH SUNDAY IN ORDINARY TIME

THIRTEENTH SUNDAY AFTER PENTECOST
PROPER 15: SUNDAY BETWEEN 14 AND 20 AUGUST

ASENATH MARRIES JOSEPH

An Egyptian noblewoman is given to Joseph to be his wife. How does she feel about marrying this foreigner, the king's favorite?

Pharaoh said to his servants, "Can we find anyone else like this—one in whom is the spirit of God?" So Pharaoh said to Joseph, "Since God has shown you all this, there is no one so discerning and wise as you. You shall be over my house, and all my people shall order themselves as you command; only with regard to the throne will I be greater than you." And Pharaoh said to Joseph, "See, I have set you over all the land of Egypt."

Removing his signet ring from his hand, Pharaoh put it on Joseph's hand; he arrayed him in garments of fine linen, and put a gold chain around his neck. He had him ride in the chariot of his second-in-command; and they cried out in front of him, "Bow the knee!" Thus he set him over all the land of Egypt. Moreover Pharaoh said to Joseph, "I am Pharaoh, and without your consent no one shall lift up hand or foot in all the land of Egypt."

Pharaoh gave Joseph the name Zaphenath-paneah; and he gave him Asenath daughter of Potiphera, priest of On, as his wife. Thus Joseph gained authority over the land of Egypt.

Genesis 41:38–45

THE CANAANITE WOMAN

This woman's love for her daughter and faith in Jesus inspire her to noisy persistence in seeking Jesus' help. Her clever argument leads Jesus to do as she asks.

Jesus went away to the district of Tyre and Sidon. Just then a Canaanite woman from that region came out and started shouting, "Have mercy on me, Lord, Son of David; my daughter is tormented by a demon." But Jesus did not answer her at all. And his disciples came and urged him, saying "Send her away, for she keeps shouting after us." Jesus answered, "I was sent only to the lost sheep of the house of Israel." But she came and knelt before him, saying, "Lord help me." Jesus answered, "It is not fair to take the children's food and throw it to the dogs." She said, "Yes, Lord, yet even the dogs eat the crumbs that fall from their master's table." Then Jesus answered her, "Woman, great is your faith! Let it be done for you as you wish." And her daughter was healed instantly.

Matthew 15:21–28

TWENTY-FIRST SUNDAY IN ORDINARY TIME

FOURTEENTH SUNDAY AFTER PENTECOST
PROPER 16: SUNDAY BETWEEN 21 AND 27 AUGUST

THE HEBREW MIDWIVES, PHARAOH'S DAUGHTER,
THE SISTER AND MOTHER OF MOSES

Pharaoh seeks to destroy the Hebrews by having their newborn sons murdered, but the midwives foil his cruel plan. Moses' sister and mother help Pharaoh's daughter reclaim him from the Nile.

A new king arose over Egypt, who did not know Joseph. He said to his people, "Look, the Israelite people are more numerous and more powerful than we. Come, let us deal shrewdly with them, or they will increase and, in the event of war, join our enemies and fight against us and escape from the land." Therefore they set taskmasters over them to oppress them with forced labor. They built supply cities, Pithom and Rameses, for Pharaoh. But the more they were oppressed, the more they multiplied and spread, so that the Egyptians came to dread the Israelites. The Egyptians became ruthless in imposing tasks on the Israelites, and made their lives bitter with hard service in mortar and brick and in every kind of field labor. They were ruthless in all the tasks that they imposed on them.

The king of Egypt said to the Hebrew midwives, one of whom was named Shiphrah and the other Puah, "When you act as midwives to the Hebrew women, and see them on the birthstool, if it is a boy, kill him; but it if is a girl, she shall live." But the midwives feared God; they did not do as the king of Egypt commanded them, but they let the boys live. So the king of Egypt summoned the midwives and said to them, "Why have you done this, and allowed the boys to live?" The midwives said to Pharaoh, "Because the Hebrew women are not like the Egyptian women; for they are vigorous and give birth before the midwife comes to them." So God dealt well with the midwives; and the people multiplied and became very strong. And because the midwives feared God, they were given families. Then Pharaoh commanded all his people, "Every boy that is born to the Hebrews you shall throw into the Nile, but you shall let every girl live."

Now a man from the house of Levi went and married a Levite woman. The woman conceived and bore a son; and when she saw that he was a fine baby, she hid him three months. When she could hide him no longer she got a papyrus basket for him, and plastered it with bitumen and pitch; she put the child in it and placed it among the reeds on the bank of the river. His sister stood at a distance, to see what would happen to him.

The daughter of Pharaoh came down to bathe at the river, while her attendants walked beside the river. She saw the basket among the reeds and sent her maid to bring it. When she opened it, she saw the child. He was crying, and she took pity on him. "This must be one of the Hebrews' children," she said. Then his sister said to Pharaoh's daughter, "Shall I go and get you a nurse from the Hebrew women to nurse the child for you?" Pharaoh's daughter said to her, "Yes." So the girl went and called the child's mother. Pharaoh's daughter said to her, "Take this child and nurse it for me, and I will give you your wages." So the woman took the child and nursed it. When the child grew up, she brought him to Pharaoh's daughter, and she took him as her son. She named him Moses, "Because," she said, "I drew him out of the water."

Exodus 1:8 — 2:10

SARAH WHO BORE YOU

Sarah is named as mother of the chosen people. Just as God acted through Sarah and Abraham in the past, so God will again bring deliverance and salvation.

Listen to me, you that pursue righteousness,
　　　　you that seek the LORD.
Look to the rock from which you were hewn,
　　　　and to the quarry from which you were dug.
Look to Abraham your father
　　　　and to Sarah who bore you;
for Abraham was but one when I called him,
　　　　but I blessed him and made him many.
For the LORD will comfort Zion:
　　　　comfort all its waste places,
and will make its wilderness like Eden,
　　　　its desert like the garden of the LORD;
joy and gladness will be found in Zion,
　　　　thanksgiving and the voice of song.

Listen to me, my people,
　　　　and give heed to me, my nation;
for a teaching will go out from me,
　　　　and my justice for a light to the peoples.
I will bring near my deliverance swiftly,
　　　　my salvation has gone out
　　　　and my arms will rule the peoples;
the coastlands wait for me,
　　　　and for my arm they hope.
Lift up your eyes to the heavens,
　　　　and look at the earth beneath;
for the heavens will vanish like smoke,
　　　　the earth will wear out like a garment,
　　　　and those who live on it will die like gnats;
but my salvation will be forever,
　　　　and my deliverance will never be ended.

Isaiah 51:1 – 6

TWENTY-SECOND SUNDAY IN ORDINARY TIME

FIFTEENTH SUNDAY AFTER PENTECOST
PROPER 17: SUNDAY BETWEEN 28 AUGUST AND 3 SEPTEMBER

LEAH BEARS CHILDREN
Leah, though unloved by her husband, becomes the mother of several of the heads of the twelve tribes. She chooses the names of her children based on her own experiences.

When the LORD saw that Leah was unloved, he opened her womb; but Rachel was barren. Leah conceived and bore a son, and she named him Reuben; for she said, "Because the LORD has looked on my affliction; surely now my husband will love me." She conceived again and bore a son, and said, "Because the LORD has heard that I am hated, God has given me this son also"; and she named him Simeon. Again she conceived and bore a son, and said, "Now this time my husband will be joined to me, because I have borne him three sons"; therefore he was named Levi. She conceived again and bore a son, and said, "This time I will praise the LORD"; therefore she named him Judah; then she ceased bearing.

Genesis 29:31 – 35

TWENTY-THIRD SUNDAY IN ORDINARY TIME

SIXTEENTH SUNDAY AFTER PENTECOST
PROPER 18: SUNDAY BETWEEN 4 AND 10 SEPTEMBER

RACHEL AND BILHAH, LEAH AND ZILPAH

Rachel blames her husband and Jacob blames God for their infertility. The servants Bilhah and Zilpah are given to Jacob, and Rachel and Leah name the children as their own. How did Bilhah and Zilpah feel about being "given" to Jacob?

When Rachel saw that she bore Jacob no children, she envied her sister; and she said to Jacob, "Give me children, or I shall die!" Jacob became very angry with Rachel and said, "Am I in the place of God, who has withheld from you the fruit of the womb?" Then she said, "Here is my maid Bilhah; go in to her, that she may bear upon my knees and that I too may have children through her." So she gave him her maid Bilhah as a wife; and Jacob went in to her. And Bilhah conceived and bore Jacob a son.

Then Rachel said, "God has judged me, and has also heard my voice and given me a son"; therefore she named him Dan. Rachel's maid Bilhah conceived again and bore Jacob a second son. Then Rachel said, "With mighty wrestlings I have wrestled with my sister, and have prevailed"; so she named him Napthali.

When Leah saw that she had ceased bearing children, she took her maid Zilpah and gave her to Jacob as a wife. Then Leah's maid Zilpah bore Jacob a son. And Leah said, "Good fortune!" so she named him Gad. Leah's maid Zilpah bore Jacob a second son. And Leah said, "Happy am I! For the women will call me happy"; so she named him Asher.

Genesis 30:1 – 13

YEAR A

TWENTY-FOURTH SUNDAY IN ORDINARY TIME

SEVENTEENTH SUNDAY AFTER PENTECOST
PROPER 19: SUNDAY BETWEEN 11 AND 17 SEPTEMBER

LEAH BEARS MORE CHILDREN, AND RACHEL BEARS JOSEPH
The competition between Leah and Rachel continues. Leah has three more children, and Rachel has her first child, Joseph.

In the days of wheat harvest Reuben went and found mandrakes in the field, and brought them to his mother Leah. Then Rachel said to Leah, "Please give me some of your son's mandrakes." But Leah said to Rachel, "Is it a small matter that you have taken away my husband? Would you take away my son's mandrakes also?" Rachel said, "Then he may lie with you tonight for your son's mandrakes."

When Jacob came from the field in the evening, Leah went out to meet him, and said, "You must come in to me; for I have hired you with my son's mandrakes." So he lay with her that night. And God heeded Leah, and she conceived and bore Jacob a fifth son. Leah said, "God has given me my hire because I gave my maid to my husband"; so she named him Issachar. And Leah conceived again, and she bore Jacob a sixth son. Then Leah said, "God has endowed me with a good dowry; now my husband will honor me, because I have borne him six sons"; so she named him Zebulun. Afterward she bore a daughter, and named her Dinah.

Then God remembered Rachel, and God heeded her and opened her womb. She conceived and bore a son, and said, "God has taken away my reproach"; and she named him Joseph, saying, "May the LORD add to me another son!"

Genesis 30:14–24

YEAR A

TWENTY-FIFTH SUNDAY IN ORDINARY TIME

EIGHTEENTH SUNDAY AFTER PENTECOST
PROPER 20: SUNDAY BETWEEN 18 AND 24 SEPTEMBER

MOTHER OF ZEBEDEE'S SONS

Jesus reproaches this mother's ambition for her sons. She becomes a disciple and later will be among the faithful women who observe Jesus' crucifixion.

While Jesus was going up to Jerusalem, he took the twelve disciples aside by themselves, and said to them on the way, "See we are going up to Jerusalem, and the Son of Man will be handed over to the chief priests and scribes, and they will condemn him to death; then they will hand him over to the Gentiles to be mocked and flogged and crucified; and on the third day he will be raised."

Then the mother of the sons of Zebedee came to Jesus with her sons, and kneeling before him, she asked a favor of him. And Jesus said to her, "What do you want?" She said to him, "Declare that these two sons of mine will sit, one at your right hand and one at your left, in your kingdom." But Jesus answered, "You do not know what you are asking. Are you able to drink the cup that I am about to drink?" They said to him, "We are able." Jesus said to them, "You will indeed drink my cup, but to sit at my right hand and at my left, this is not mine to grant, but it is for those for whom it has been prepared by my Father."

When the ten heard it, they were angry with the two brothers. But Jesus called them to him and said, "You know that the rulers of the Gentiles lord it over them, and their great ones are tyrants over them. It will not be so among you; but whoever wishes to be great among you must be your servant, and whoever wishes to be first among you must be your slave; just as the Son of Man came not to be served but to serve, and to give his life a ransom for many."

Matthew 20:17–28

TWENTY-SIXTH SUNDAY IN ORDINARY TIME

NINTEENTH SUNDAY AFTER PENTECOST
PROPER 21: SUNDAY BETWEEN 25 SEPTEMBER AND 1 OCTOBER

RACHEL THE SCHEMER

Why did Rachel steal her father's household gods — to acquire the power he attributed to them? Later she pretends to be menstruating; was she protected by Laban's consideration, or his fear of this womanly function?

Now Laban had gone to shear his sheep, and Rachel stole her father's household gods. And Jacob deceived Laban the Aramean, in that he did not tell him that he intended to flee. So he fled with all that he had; starting out he crossed the Euphrates, and set his face toward the hill country of Gilead.

On the third day Laban was told that Jacob had fled. So he took his kinsfolk with him and pursued him for seven days until he caught up with him in the hill country of Gilead. But God came to Laban the Aramean in a dream by night, and said to him, "Take heed that you say not a word to Jacob, either good or bad."

Laban overtook Jacob. Now Jacob had pitched his tent in the hill country, and Laban with his kinsfolk camped in the hill country of Gilead. Laban said to Jacob, "What have you done? You have deceived me, and carried away my daughters like captives of the sword. Why did you flee secretly and deceive me and not tell me? I would have sent you away with mirth and songs, with tambourine and lyre. And why did you not permit me to kiss my sons and my daughters farewell? What you have done is foolish. It is in my power to do you harm; but the God of your father spoke to me last night, saying 'Take heed that you speak to Jacob neither good nor bad.' Even though you had to go because you longed greatly for your father's house, why did you steal my gods?"

Jacob answered Laban, "Because I was afraid, for I thought that you would take your daughters from me by force. But anyone with whom you find your gods shall not live. In the presence of our kinsfolk point out what I have that is yours, and take it." Now Jacob did not know that Rachel had stolen the gods. So Laban went into Jacob's tent, and into Leah's tent, and into the tent of the two maids, but he did not find them.

And he went out of Leah's tent, and entered Rachel's. Now Rachel had taken the household gods and put them in the camel's saddle, and sat on them. Laban felt all about in the tent, but did not find them. And she said to her father, "Let not my lord be angry that I cannot rise before you, for the way of women is upon me." So he searched, but did not find the household gods.

Genesis 31:19 – 35

JESUS AS MOTHER HEN

Jesus compares himself to a mother hen, an image of attentive concern. His public lament for Jerusalem resembles that of Rachel — and is traditionally a woman's role.

At that time, Jesus said, "Jerusalem, Jerusalem, the city that kills the prophets and stones those who are sent to it! How often have I desired to gather your children together as a hen gathers her brood under her wings, and you were not willing! See, your house is left to you, desolate. For I tell you, you will not see me again until you say, 'Blessed is the one who comes in the name of the Lord.'"

Matthew 23:37 – 39

TWENTY-SEVENTH SUNDAY IN ORDINARY TIME

TWENTIETH SUNDAY AFTER PENTECOST
PROPER 22: SUNDAY BETWEEN 2 AND 8 OCTOBER

HONOR MOTHER AND FATHER, DO NOT COVET YOUR NEIGHBOR'S WIFE
Both mother and father are to be honored. The neighbor's wife and female slave, however, are viewed as a man's property. What do you make of this?

God spoke all these words: I am the LORD your God, who brought you out of the land of Egypt, out of the house of slavery; you shall have no other gods before me.

You shall not make for yourself an idol, whether in the form of anything that is in heaven above, or that is on the earth beneath, or that is in the water under the earth.

You shall not make wrongful use of the name of the LORD your God, for the LORD will not acquit anyone who misuses the divine name.

Remember the sabbath day, and keep it holy. Six days you shall labor and do all your work.

Honor your father and your mother, so that your days may be long in the land that the LORD your God is giving you.

You shall not murder.

You shall not commit adultery.

You shall not steal.

You shall not bear false witness against your neighbor.

You shall not covet your neighbor's house; you shall not covet your neighbor's wife, or male or female slave, or ox, or donkey, or anything that belongs to your neighbor.

When all the people witnessed the thunder and lightning, the sound of the trumpet, and the mountains smoking, they were afraid and trembled and stood at a distance, and said to Moses, "You speak to us, and we will listen; but do not let God speak to us, or we will die." Moses said to the people, "Do not be afraid; for God has come only to test you and to put the fear of God upon you so that you do not sin."

Exodus 20:1–4, 7–9, 12–20

JAEL SAVES HER PEOPLE AND IS PRAISED BY DEBORAH
In time of war, Jael performed an act of violence that resulted in victory for Israel. She is remembered for her bravery and cunning.

Sisera had fled away on foot to the tent of Jael wife of Heber the Kenite; for there was peace between King Jabin of Hazor and the clan of Heber the Kenite. Jael came out to meet Sisera, and said to him, "Turn aside, my lord, turn aside to me; have no fear." So he turned aside to her into the tent, and she covered him with a rug. Then he said to her, "Please give me a little water to drink; for I am thirsty." So Jael opened a skin of milk and gave him a drink and covered him. He said to her, "Stand at the entrance of the tent, and if anybody comes and asks you, 'Is anyone here?' say, 'No.'"

But Jael wife of Heber took a tent peg, and took a hammer in her hand, and went softly to him and drove the peg into his temple, until it went down into the ground — he was lying fast asleep from weariness — and he died. Then, as Barak came in pursuit of Sisera, Jael went out to meet him, and said to him, "Come, and I will show you the man whom you are seeking." So he went into her tent; and there was Sisera lying dead, with the tent peg in his temple.

Then Deborah and Barak son of Abinoam sang on that day, saying:

> "Most blessed of women be Jael,
>> the wife of Heber the Kenite,
>> of tent-dwelling women most blessed.
> He asked water and she gave him milk,
>> she brought him curds in a lordly bowl.
> She put her hand to the tent peg
>> and her right hand to the workmen's mallet;
> she struck Sisera a blow,
>> she crushed his head,
>> she shattered and pierced his temple.
> He sank, he fell,
>> he lay still at her feet;
> at her feet he sank, he fell;
>> where he sank, there he fell dead.

> "So perish all your enemies, O LORD!
>> But may your friends be like the sun as it rises in its might."

Judges 4:17 – 22; 5:1, 24 – 27, 31

TWENTY-EIGHTH SUNDAY IN ORDINARY TIME

TWENTY-FIRST SUNDAY AFTER PENTECOST

PROPER 23: SUNDAY BETWEEN 9 AND 15 OCTOBER

EUODIA AND SYNTYCHE

These two women, together with Lydia, are leaders of the church at Philippi. Though they disagree on some issue, Paul recognizes them as co-workers with each other and with him.

My brothers and sisters, whom I love and long for, my joy and crown, stand firm in the Lord in this way, my beloved.

I urge Euodia and I urge Syntyche to be of the same mind in the Lord. Yes, and I ask you also, my loyal companions, help these women, for they have struggled beside me in the work of the gospel, together with Clement and the rest of my co-workers, whose names are in the book of life.

Rejoice in the Lord always; again I will say, Rejoice. Let your gentleness be known to everyone. The Lord is near. Do not worry about anything, but in everything by prayer and supplication with thanksgiving let your requests be made known to God. And the peace of God, which surpasses all understanding, will guard your hearts and your minds in Christ Jesus.

Philippians 4:1–7

TWENTY-NINTH SUNDAY IN ORDINARY TIME

TWENTY-SECOND SUNDAY AFTER PENTECOST
PROPER 24: SUNDAY BETWEEN 16 AND 22 OCTOBER

FIVE SISTERS CONFRONT MOSES
The sisters confront Moses and the other leaders to challenge the established pattern of inheritance that excluded women. God takes their side.

The daughters of Zelophehad came forward. Zelophehad was son of Hepher son of Gilead son of Machir son of Manasseh son of Joseph, a member of the Manassite clans. The names of his daughters were: Mahlah, Noah, Hoglah, Milcah, and Tirzah. They stood before Moses, Eleazar the priest, the leaders, and all the congregation, at the entrance of the tent of meeting, and they said, "Our father died in the wilderness; he was not among the company of those who gathered themselves together against the LORD in the company of Korah, but died for his own sin; and he had no sons. Why should the name of our father be taken away from his clan because he had no son? Give to us a possession among our father's brothers."

Moses brought their case before the LORD. And the LORD spoke to Moses, saying: The daughters of Zelophehad are right in what they are saying; you shall indeed let them possess an inheritance among their father's brothers and pass the inheritance of their father on to them. You shall also say to the Israelites, "If a man dies, and has no son, then you shall pass his inheritance on to his daughter. If he has no daughter, then you shall give his inheritance to his brothers. If he has no brothers, then you shall give his inheritance to his father's brothers. And if his father has no brothers, then you shall give his inheritance to the nearest kinsman of his clan, and he shall possess it. It shall be for the Israelites a statute and ordinance, as the LORD commanded Moses."

Numbers 27:1–11

THIRTIETH SUNDAY IN ORDINARY TIME

TWENTY-THIRD SUNDAY AFTER PENTECOST
PROPER 25: SUNDAY BETWEEN 23 AND 29 OCTOBER

YOU SHALL NOT ABUSE ANY WIDOW
Widows and others who are insignificant and unprotected in society are to be cared for by individuals and the people as a whole.

You shall not wrong or oppress a resident alien, for you were aliens in the land of Egypt. You shall not abuse any widow or orphan. If you do abuse them, when they cry out to me, I will surely heed their cry; my wrath will burn, and I will kill you with the sword, and your wives shall become widows and your children orphans.

If you lend money to my people, to the poor among you, you shall not deal with them as a creditor; you shall not exact interest from them. If you take your neighbor's cloak in pawn, you shall restore it before the sun goes down; for it may be your neighbor's only clothing to use as cover; in what else shall that person sleep? And if your neighbor cries out to me, I will listen, for I am compassionate.

Exodus 22:21–27

ACHSAH, LANDOWNER IN THE NEGEB
Achsah negotiates and becomes a landowner in her own right (though she has no choice in marriage). Her property is particularly valuable because it includes two springs.

Caleb said, "Whoever attacks Kiriath-sepher and takes it, to him I will give my daugher Achsah as wife." Othniel son of Kenaz, the brother of Caleb, took it; and Caleb gave Othniel his daughter Achsah as wife. When she came to him, she urged him to ask her father for a field. As she dismounted from her donkey, Caleb said to her, "What do you wish?" She said to him, "Give me a present; since you have set me in the land of the Negeb, give me springs of water as well." So Caleb gave her the upper springs and the lower springs.

Joshua 15:16–19

THIRTY-FIRST SUNDAY IN ORDINARY TIME

TWENTY-FOURTH SUNDAY AFTER PENTECOST

PROPER 26: SUNDAY BETWEEN 30 OCTOBER AND 5 NOVEMBER

DELILAH

For a bribe, Delilah acts with persistence and cunning to find out how to render Samson powerless.

Samson fell in love with a woman in the valley of Sorek, whose name was Delilah. The lords of the Philistines came to her and said to her, "Coax him, and find out what makes his strength so great, and how we may overpower him, so that we may bind him in order to subdue him; and we will each give you eleven hundred pieces of silver."

So Delilah said to Samson, "Please tell me what makes your strength so great, and how you could be bound, so that one could subdue you." Samson said to her, "If they bind me with seven fresh bowstrings that are not dried out, then I shall become weak, and be like anyone else." Then the lords of the Philistines brought her seven fresh bowstrings that had not dried out, and she bound him with them. While men were lying in wait in an inner chamber, she said to him, "The Philistines are upon you, Samson!" But he snapped the bowstrings, as a strand of fiber snaps when it touches the fire. So the secret of his strength was not known.

Then Delilah said to Samson, "You have mocked me and told me lies; please tell me how you could be bound." He said to her, "If they bind me with new ropes that have not been used, then I shall become weak, and be like anyone else." So Delilah took new ropes and bound him with them, and said to him, "The Philistines are upon you, Samson!" (The men lying in wait were in an inner chamber.) But he snapped the ropes off his arms like a thread.

Then Delilah said to Samson, "Until now you have mocked me and told me lies; tell me how you could be bound." He said to her, "If you weave the seven locks of my head with the web and make it tight with the pin, then I shall become weak, and be like anyone else." So while he slept, Delilah took the seven locks of his head and wove them into the web, and made them tight with the pin. Then she said to him, "The Philistines are upon you, Samson!" But he woke from his sleep, and pulled away the pin, the loom, and the web.

Then she said to him, "How can you say, 'I love you,' when your heart is not with me? You have mocked me three times now and have not told me what makes your strength so great." Finally, after she had nagged him with her words day after day, and pestered him, he was tired to death. So he told her his whole secret, and said to her, "A razor has never come upon my head; for I have been a nazirite to God from my mother's womb. If my head were shaved, then my strength would leave me; I would become weak, and be like anyone else."

When Delilah realized that he had told her his whole secret, she sent and called the lords of the Philistines, saying, "This time come up, for he has told his whole secret to me." Then the lords of the Philistines came up to her, and brought the money in their hands. She let him fall asleep on her lap, and she called a man, and had him shave off the seven locks of his head. He began to weaken, and his strength left him.

Then she said, "The Philistines are upon you, Samson!" When he awoke from his sleep, he thought, "I will go out as at other times, and shake myself free." But he did not know that the Lord had left him. So the Philistines seized him and gouged out his eyes. They brought him down to Gaza and bound him with bronze shackles; and he ground at the mill in the prison. But the hair of his head began to grow again after it had been shaved.

Judges 16:4–22

Miriam

THIRTY-SECOND SUNDAY IN ORDINARY TIME

TWENTY-FIFTH SUNDAY AFTER PENTECOST
PROPER 27: SUNDAY BETWEEN 6 AND 12 NOVEMBER

WISDOM MAKES HERSELF KNOWN

The feminine figure of Wisdom makes herself known to those who seek her and seeks those who are worthy of her. This passage is linked in the lectionaries to the gospel story of the wise and foolish bridesmaids.

Wisdom is radiant and unfading,
and she is easily discerned by those who love her,
and is found by those who seek her.
She hastens to make herself known to those who desire her.
One who rises early to see her will have no difficulty,
for she will be found sitting at the gate.
To fix one's thought on her is perfect understanding,
and one who is vigilant on her account will soon be free from care,
because she goes about seeking those worthy of her,
and she graciously appears to them in their paths,
and meets them in every thought.

Wisdom of Solomon 6:12 – 16

THE TEN BRIDESMAIDS

In times of God's apparent absence, some are faithful and others are not. The wise women stay alert and prepared. They are rewarded for their forethought and faithfulness.

Jesus said, "The dominion of heaven will be like this. Ten bridesmaids took their lamps and went to meet the bridegroom. Five of them were foolish, and five were wise. When the foolish took their lamps, they took no oil with them; but the wise took flasks of oil with their lamps. As the bridegroom was delayed, all of them became drowsy and slept. But at midnight there was a shout, "Look! Here is the bridegroom! Come out to meet him.' Then all those bridesmaids got up and trimmed their lamps. The foolish said to the wise, "Give us some of your oil, for our lamps are going out." But the wise replied, 'No! there will not be enough for you and for us; you had better go to the dealers and buy some for yourselves.' And while they went to buy it, the bridegroom came, and those who were ready went with him into the wedding banquet; and the door was shut. Later the other bridesmaids came also, saying, 'Sir, sir, open to us.' But he replied, 'Truly I tell you, I do not know you.' Keep awake therefore, for you know neither the day nor the hour."

Matthew 25:1 – 13

THIRTY-THIRD SUNDAY IN ORDINARY TIME

TWENTY-SIXTH SUNDAY AFTER PENTECOST

PROPER 28: SUNDAY BETWEEN 13 AND 19 NOVEMBER

DEBORAH IS JUDGE OVER ISRAEL

Deborah is prophet and judge over Israel. She hears and interprets God's will, and gives military orders to Barak her general.

The Israelites again did what was evil in the sight of the LORD, after Ehud died. So the LORD sold them into the hand of King Jabin of Canaan, who reigned in Hazor; the commander of his army was Sisera, who lived in Harosheth-ha-goiim. Then the Israelites cried out to the LORD for help; for Sisera had nine hundred chariots of iron, and had oppressed the Israelites cruelly twenty years.

At that time Deborah, a prophetess, wife of Lappidoth, was judging Israel. She used to sit under the palm of Deborah between Ramah and Bethel in the hill country of Ephraim; and the Israelites came up to her for judgment. She sent and summoned Barak son of Abinoam from Kedish in Naphtali, and said to him, "The LORD, the God of Israel, commands you, 'Go, take position at Mount Tabor, bringing ten thousand from the tribe of Naphtali and the tribe of Zebulun. I will draw out Sisera, the general of Jabin's army, to meet you by the Wadi Kishon with his chariots and his troops; and I will give him into your hand.'"

Judges 4:1–7

THE WOMAN OF WORTH

The capable woman is a competent businesswoman and provident householder. She carries out her responsibilities with wisdom and diligence, generosity and kindness. She is worthy of praise.

A capable wife who can find?
> She is far more precious than jewels.
The heart of her husband trusts in her,
> and he will have no lack of gain.
She does him good, and not harm,
> all the days of her life.
She seeks wool and flax,
> and works with willing hands.
She is like the ships of the merchant,
> she brings her food from far away.
She rises while it is still night
> and provides food for her household
> and tasks for her servant girls.

She considers a field and buys it;
>with the fruit of her hands she plants a vineyard.
She girds herself with strength,
>and makes her arms strong.
She perceives that her merchandise is profitable.
>Her lamp does not go out at night.
She puts her hands to the distaff,
>and her hands hold the spindle.
She opens her hand to the poor,
>and reaches out her hands to the needy.
She is not afraid for her household when it snows,
>for all her household are clothed in crimson.
She makes herself coverings;
>her clothing is fine linen and purple.
Her husband is known in the city gates,
>taking his seat among the elders of the land.
She makes linen garments and sells them;
>she supplies the merchant with sashes.
Strength and dignity are her clothing,
>and she laughs at the time to come.
She opens her mouth with wisdom,
>and the teaching of kindness is on her tongue.
She looks well to the ways of her household,
>and does not eat the bread of idleness.
Her children rise up and call her happy;
>her husband too, and he praises her:
"Many women have done excellently,
>but you surpass them all."
Charm is deceitful, and beauty is vain,
>but a woman who fears the LORD is to be praised.
Give her a share in the fruit of her hands,
>and let her works praise her in the city gates.

Proverbs 31:10 – 31

CHRIST THE KING

REIGN OF CHRIST
PROPER 29: SUNDAY BETWEEN 20 AND 26 NOVEMBER

WISDOM TEACHES HER CHILDREN
The relationship of Wisdom and her children is an image of Christ's reign.

Wisdom teaches her children
    and gives help to those who seek her.
Whoever loves her loves life,
    and those who seek her from early morning are filled with joy.
Whoever holds her fast inherits glory,
    and the Lord blesses the place she enters.
Those who serve her minister to the Holy One;
    the Lord loves those who love her.
Those who obey her will judge the nations,
    and all who listen to her will live secure.
If they remain faithful, they will inherit her;
    their descendants will also obtain her.
For at first she will walk with them on tortuous paths;
    she will bring fear and dread upon them,
and will torment them by her discipline
    until she trusts them,
and she will test them with her ordinances.
Then she will come straight back to them again and gladden them,
    and will reveal her secrets to them.

Sirach 4:11–18

IN REMEMBRANCE OF HER
Jesus ministered to women and accepted their ministry to him. One characteristic of Christ's reign is that women's faithful love is remembered and honored.

While Jesus was at Bethany in the house of Simon the leper, a woman came to him with an alabaster jar of very costly ointment, and she poured it on his head as he sat at the table. But when the disciples saw it, they were angry and said, "Why this waste? For this ointment could have been sold for a large sum, and the money given to the poor." But Jesus, aware of this, said to them, "Why do you trouble the woman? She has performed a good service for me. For you always have the poor with you, but you will not always have me. By pouring this ointment on my body she has prepared me for burial. Truly I tell you, wherever this good news is proclaimed in the whole world, what she has done will be told in remembrance of her."

Matthew 26:6–13

YEAR B

FIRST SUNDAY OF ADVENT

A GREAT SIGN: A WOMAN IN CHILDBIRTH

The second reading of the lectionaries speaks of the need to be strengthened for the coming day of our Lord Jesus Christ. This passage uses the image of a woman in the agony of giving birth to suggest the struggle of the end times.

A great portent appeared in heaven: a woman clothed with the sun, with the moon under her feet, and on her head a crown of twelve stars. She was pregnant and was crying out in birthpangs, in the agony of giving birth. Then another portent appeared in heaven: a great red dragon, with seven heads and ten horns, and seven diadems on his heads. Its tail swept down a third of the stars of heaven and threw them to the earth. Then the dragon stood before the woman who was about to bear a child, so that it might devour her child as soon as it was born. And she gave birth to a son, a male child, who is to rule all the nations with a rod of iron.

Revelation 12:1 – 5a

SECOND SUNDAY OF ADVENT

RAHAB, FOREMOTHER OF JESUS, SAVES THE ISRAELITE SCOUTS

The gospel reading of the lectionaries tells of John the Baptist and his call to prepare the way of the Lord. In this passage Rahab saves the messengers from capture, thereby helping Israel prepare the way to enter the promised land. For offering hospitality and protection to Joshua's spies, Rahab is remembered as a savior. And even though she is a marginal person — a woman, a prostitute, a foreigner — she understands well the God of the Israelites.

Joshua son of Nun sent two men secretly from Shittim as spies, saying, "Go, view the land, especially Jericho." So they went, and entered the house of a prostitute whose name was Rahab, and spent the night there. The king of Jericho was told, "Some Israelites have come here tonight to search out the land." Then the king of Jericho sent orders to Rahab, "Bring out the men who have come to you, who entered your house, for they have come only to search out the whole land."

But the woman took the two men and hid them. Then Rahab said, "True, the men came to me, but I did not know where they came from. And when it was time to close the gate at dark, the men went out. Where the men went I do not know. Pursue them quickly, for you can overtake them." She had, however, brought them up to the roof and hidden them with the stalks of flax that she had laid out on the roof. So the men pursued them on the way to the Jordan as far as the fords. As soon as the pursuers had gone out, the gate was shut.

Before they went to sleep, Rahab came up to them on the roof and said to the men: "I know that the LORD has given you the land, and that dread of you has fallen on us, and that all the inhabitants of the land melt in fear before you. For we have heard how the LORD dried up the water of the Red Sea before you when you came out of Egypt, and what you did to the two kings of the Amorites that were beyond the Jordan, to Sihon and Og, whom you utterly destroyed. As soon as we heard it, our hearts melted, and there was no courage left in any of us because of you. The LORD your God is indeed God in heaven above and on earth below. Now then, since I have dealt kindly with you, swear to me by the LORD that you in turn will deal kindly with my family. Give me a sign of good faith that you will spare my father and mother, my brothers and sisters, and all who belong to them, and deliver our lives from death." The men said to her, "Our life for yours! If you do not tell this business of ours, then we will deal kindly and faithfully with you when the LORD gives us the land."

Then Rahab let them down by a rope through the window, for her house was on the outer side of the city wall and she resided within the wall itself. She said to them, "Go toward the hill country, so that the pursuers may not come upon you. Hide yourselves there three days, until the pursuers have returned; than afterward you may go your way."

The men said to Rahab, "We will be released from this oath that you have made us swear to you if we invade the land and you do not tie this crimson cord in the window through which you let us down, and you do not gather into your house your father and mother, your brothers and sisters, and all your family. If any of you go out of the doors of your house into the street, they shall be responsible for their own death, and we shall be innocent; but if a hand is laid upon any who are with you in the house, we shall bear the responsibility for their death. But if you tell this business of ours, then we shall be released from this oath that you made us swear to you." Rahab said, "According to your words, so be it." She sent them away and they departed. Then she tied the crimson cord in the window.

Joshua 2:1 – 21

THIRD SUNDAY OF ADVENT

RAHAB, FOREMOTHER OF JESUS, IS SAVED
The lectionaries continue to tell of John the Baptist and his call to make straight the way of the Lord.
Rahab makes straight the way of the Lord's people. Jericho is destroyed, but she and her family are saved.
Yet how many women like her were killed in Jericho — and in other holy wars?

"The city Jericho and all that is in it shall be devoted to the LORD for destruction. Only Rahab the prostitute and all who are with her in her house shall live because she hid the messengers we sent. As for you, keep away from the things devoted to destruction, so as not to covet and take any of the devoted things and make the camp of Israel an object for destruction, bringing trouble upon it. But all silver and gold, and vessels of bronze and iron, are sacred to the LORD; they shall go into the treasury of the LORD."

So the people shouted, and the trumpets were blown. As soon as the people heard the sound of the trumpets, they raised a great shout, and the wall fell down flat; so the people charged straight ahead into the city and captured it. Then they devoted to destruction by the edge of the sword all in the city, both men and women, young and old, oxen, sheep, and donkeys.

Joshua said to the two men who had spied out the land, "Go into the prostitute's house, and bring the woman out of it and all who belong to her, as you swore to her." So the young men who had been spies went in and brought Rahab out, along with her father, her mother, her brothers and sisters, and all who belonged to her — they brought all her kindred out — and set them outside the camp of Israel.

They burned down the city, and everything in it; only the silver and gold, and the vessels of bronze and iron, they put into the treasury of the house of the LORD. But Rahab the prostitute, with her family and all who belonged to her, Joshua spared. Her family has lived in Israel ever since. For she hid the messengers whom Joshua sent to spy out Jericho.

Joshua 6:17 – 25

SONG OF MARY: Responsory
Mary sings that God continues to rescue Israel, as in the days of Rahab.

I acclaim the greatness of the Lord,
I delight in God my savior,
who regarded my humble state.
Truly from this day on
all ages will call me blest.

For God, wonderful in power,
has used that strength for me.
Holy the name of the Lord!

whose mercy embraces the faithful,
one generation to the next.

The mighty arm of God
scatters the proud in their conceit,
pulls tyrants from their thrones,
and raises up the humble.
The Lord fills the starving
and lets the rich go hungry.

God rescues lowly Israel,
recalling the promise of mercy,
the promise made to our ancestors,
to Abraham's heirs for ever.

Canticle of Luke 1:46–55 ICEL

Ruth and Naomi

FOURTH SUNDAY OF ADVENT

MARY CONVERSES WITH THE ANGEL

Mary has direct access to the heavenly world. She considers what the angel says and asks reasonable questions before she accepts God's invitation. Mary is a model for all believers.

In the sixth month the angel Gabriel was sent by God to a town in Galilee called Nazareth, to a virgin engaged to a man whose name was Joseph, of the house of David. The virgin's name was Mary. And the angel came to her and said, "Greetings, favored one! The Lord is with you." But she was much perplexed by these words and pondered what sort of greeting this might be. The angel said to her, "Do not be afraid, Mary, for you have found favor with God. And now, you will conceive in your womb and bear a son, and you will name him Jesus. He will be great, and will be called the Son of the Most High, and the Lord God will give to him the throne of his ancestor David. He will reign over the house of Jacob forever, and of his dominion there will be no end."

Mary said to the angel, "How can this be, since I am a virgin?" The angel said to her, "The Holy Spirit will come upon you, and the power of the Most High will overshadow you; therefore the child to be born will be holy; he will be called Son of God. And now, your relative Elizabeth in her old age has also conceived a son; and this is the sixth month for her who was said to be barren. For nothing will be impossible with God."

Then Mary said, "Here am I, the servant of the Lord; let it be with me according to your word." Then the angel departed from her.

Luke 1:26–38

THE NATIVITY OF CHRIST: VIGIL

FOREMOTHERS AND FOREFATHERS OF JESUS
This list of Jesus' ancestors includes four women: Tamar, Rahab, Ruth and Bathsheba, the wife of David.
The first three women (and the fourth's husband) acted in ways not understood by social convention in
order to be faithful to God's purpose. They are models for Jesus in that way.

An account of the genealogy of Jesus the Christ, the son of David, the son of Abraham.

Abraham was the father of Isaac, Isaac of Jacob, Jacob of Judah and his brothers, Judah of Perez and Zerah by Tamar, Perez of Hezron, Hezron of Aram, Aram of Aminadab, Aminidab of Nahshon, Nahshon of Salmon, Salmon of Boaz by Rahab, Boaz of Obed by Ruth, Obed of Jesse, and Jesse the father of King David.

David was the father of Solomon by the wife of Uriah, Solomon of Rehoboam, Rehoboam of Abijah, Abijah of Asaph, Asaph of Jehoshaphat, Jehoshaphat of Joram, Joram of Uzziah, Uzziah of Jotham, Jotham of Ahaz, Ahaz of Hezekiah, Hezekiah of Manasseh, Manasseh of Amos, Amos of Josiah, and Josiah the father of Jechoniah and his brothers, at the time of the deportation to Babylon.

After the deportation to Babylon: Jechoniah was the father of Salathiel, Salathiel of Zerubbabel, Zerubbabel of Abiud, Abiud of Eliakim, Eliakim of Azor, Azor of Zadok, Zadok of Achim, Achim of Eliud, Eliud of Eleazar, Eleazar of Matthan, Matthan of Jacob, and Jacob of Joseph the husband of Mary, of whom Jesus was born, who is called the Christ.

So all the generations from Abraham to David are fourteen generations; and from David to the deportation to Babylon, fourteen generations; and from the deportation to Babylon to the Christ, fourteen generations.

Matthew 1:1–17

THE NATIVITY OF CHRIST: DURING THE NIGHT

MARY GIVES BIRTH TO JESUS

Giving birth in a stable is a sign of how insignificant this family is in its society. The true meaning of the event is first revealed to other outcasts, the shepherds. God works through people like these.

In those days a decree went out from Emperor Augustus that all the world should be registered. This was the first registration and was taken while Quirinius was governor of Syria. All went to their own towns to be registered.

Joseph also went from the town of Nazareth in Galilee to Judea, to the city of David called Bethlehem, because he was descended from the house and family of David. He went to be registered with Mary, to whom he was engaged and who was expecting a child.

While they were there, the time came for her to deliver her child. And she gave birth to her firstborn son and wrapped him in bands of cloth, and laid him in a manger, because there was no place for them in the inn.

In that region there were shepherds living in the fields, keeping watch over their flock by night. Then an angel of the Lord stood before them, and the glory of the Lord shone around them, and they were terrified. But the angel said to them, "Do not be afraid; for see — I am bringing you good news of great joy for all the people: to you is born this day in the city of David a Savior, who is the Christ, the Lord. This will be a sign for you: you will find a child wrapped in bands of cloth and lying in a manger." And suddenly there was with the angel a multitude of the heavenly host, praising God and saying,

"Glory to God in the highest heaven,
and peace to God's people on earth."

When the angels had left them and gone into heaven, the shepherds said to one another, "Let us go now to Bethlehem and see this thing that has taken place, which the Lord has made known to us." So they went with haste and found Mary and Joseph, and the child lying in the manger.

Luke 2:1 – 16

THE NATIVITY OF CHRIST: DAWN

DAUGHTER ZION
On one level, Mary herself is daughter Zion, who is sought out and not forsaken. On another level, Mary
is the one who brings the promised salvation to daughter Zion, Jerusalem.

Upon your walls, O Jerusalem,
    I have posted sentinels;
    all day and all night
    they shall never be silent.
You who remind the LORD,
    take no rest,
    and give God no rest
    until Jerusalem is established
    and renowned throughout the earth.
The LORD has sworn by right hand
    and by mighty arm;
I will not again give your grain
    to be food for your enemies,
and foreigners shall not drink the wine
    for which you have labored;
but those who garner it shall eat it
    and praise the LORD,
and those who gather it shall drink it
    in my holy courts.

Go through, go through the gates,
    prepare the way for the people;
build up, build up the highway,
    clear it of stones,
    lift up an ensign over the peoples.
The LORD has proclaimed
    to the end of the earth:
Say to daughter Zion,
    "See, your salvation comes;
    behold, God comes bearing the reward,
    preceded by the recompense."
They shall be called, "The Holy People,
    The Redeemed of the Lord";
and you shall be called, "Sought Out,
    A City Not Forsaken."

Isaiah 62:6 – 12

Mary was a thoughtful and reflective woman. She did indeed have much to ponder. What did she think about all this?

When the angels had left them and gone into heaven, the shepherds said to one another, "Let us go now to Bethlehem and see this thing that has taken place, which the Lord has made known to us." So they went with haste and found Mary and Joseph, and the child lying in the manger. When they saw this, they made known what had been told them about this child; and all who heard it were amazed at what the shepherds told them. But Mary treasured all these words and pondered them in her heart. The shepherds returned, glorifying and praising God for all they had heard and seen, as it had been told them.

Luke 2:15 – 20

THE NATIVITY OF CHRIST: DURING THE DAY

WISDOM MAKES HER DWELLING AMONG GOD'S PEOPLE
The lectionaries offer the prologue to the Gospel of John: "In the beginning was the word . . . the word dwelled among us." In this passage, we hear of divine Wisdom, a feminine figure who is with God from the beginning, co-creator with God who pitches her tent in the midst of her people.

Wisdom praises herself,
     and tells of her glory in the midst of her people.
In the assembly of the Most High she opens her mouth,
     and in the presence of God's hosts she tells of her glory:

"I came forth from the mouth of the Most High,
     and covered the earth like a mist.
I dwelt in the highest heavens,
     and my throne was in a pillar of cloud.
Alone I compassed the vault of heaven
     and traversed the depths of the abyss.
Over waves of the sea, over all the earth,
     and over every people and nation I have held sway.
Among all these I sought a resting place;
     in whose territory should I abide?

"Then the Creator of all things gave me a command,
     and my Creator chose the place for my tent.
God said, 'Make your dwelling in Jacob,
     and in Israel receive your inheritance.'
Before the ages, in the beginning, God created me,
     and for all the ages I shall not cease to be.
In the holy tent I ministered before God,
     and so I was established in Zion.
Thus in the beloved city God gave me a resting place,
     and in Jerusalem was my domain.
I took root in an honored people,
     in the portion of the Lord's heritage."

Sirach 24:1 – 12

THE HOLY FAMILY

SUNDAY AFTER CHRISTMAS DAY

SARAH CONCEIVES AND BEARS ISAAC
God's promise to Abraham could not be fulfilled without Sarah, whom God blesses. This parallels the story
of Mary, whose cooperation God invited.

The word of the LORD came to Abram in a vision, "Do not be afraid, Abram, I am your shield; your reward shall be very great." But Abram said, "O LORD God, what will you give me, for I continue childless, and the heir of my house is Eliezer of Damascus?" And Abram said, "You have given me no offspring, and so a slave born in my house is to be my heir." But the word of the LORD came to him, "This man shall not be your heir; no one but your very own issue shall be your heir." God brought him outside and said, "Look toward heaven and count the stars, if you are able to count them." Then God said to Abram, "So shall your descendants be." And Abram believed the LORD; and the LORD reckoned it to him as righteousness.

God said to Abram, "As for me, this is my covenant with you: You shall be the ancestor of a multitude of nations. No longer shall your name be Abram, but your name shall be Abraham; for I have made you the ancestor of a multitude of nations.

God said to Abraham, "As for Sarai your wife, you shall not call her Sarai, but Sarah shall be her name. I will bless her, and moreover I will give you a son by her. I will bless her, and she shall give rise to nations; kings of peoples shall come from her."

The LORD dealt with Sarah as had been said, and the LORD did for Sarah as had been promised. Sarah conceived and bore Abraham a son in his old age, at the time of which God had spoken to him. Abraham gave the name Isaac to his son whom Sarah bore him. And Abraham circumcised his son Isaac when he was eight days old, as God had commanded him. Abraham was a hundred years old when his son Isaac was born to him. Now Sarah said, "God has brought laughter for me; everyone who hears will laugh with me." And she said, "Who would ever have said to Abraham that Sarah would nurse children? Yet I have borne him a son in his old age."

Genesis 15:1 – 6; 17:3b – 5, 15 – 16; 21:1 – 7

THE FAITH OF SARAH AND RAHAB
Sarah and Rahab are named as models of faith, together with Abraham.

By faith Abraham obeyed when he was called to set out for a place that he was to receive as an inheritance; and he set out, not knowing where he was going.

By faith Sarah received power to conceive, even when she was past the age, since she considered faithful the one who had promised. Therefore from one person, and this one as good as dead, descendants were born, "as many as the stars of heaven and as the innumerable grains of sand by the seashore."

By faith Rahab the prostitute did not perish with those who were disobedient, because she had received the spies in peace.

Hebrews 11:8, 11–12, 31

THE HOLY FAMILY WITH SIMEON AND ANNA

Simeon predicts that Mary will suffer as her son is opposed and rejected. Anna is a woman of prayer, one who recognizes God's work in the baby. She is called a prophet.

When the time came for their purification according to the law of Moses, Mary and Joseph brought Jesus up to Jerusalem to present him to the Lord (as it is written in the law of the Lord, "Every firstborn male shall be designated as holy to the Lord"), and they offered a sacrifice according to what is stated in the law of the Lord, "A pair of turtledoves or two young pigeons."

Now there was a person in Jerusalem named Simeon, who was righteous and devout, looking forward to the consolation of Israel, and the Holy Spirit rested on him. It had been revealed to him by the Holy Spirit that he would not see death before he had seen the Lord's Anointed One. Guided by the Spirit, Simeon came into the temple; and when the parents brought in the child Jesus, to do for him what was customary under the law, Simeon took Jesus in his arms and praised God, saying,

"Lord, let your servant
now die in peace,
for you kept your promise.
With my own eyes
I see the salvation
you prepared for all peoples:
a light of revelation for the Gentiles
and glory to your people Israel."

And the child's father and mother were amazed at what was being said about Jesus. Then Simeon blessed them and said to his mother Mary, "This child is destined for the falling and the rising of many in Israel, and to be a sign that will be opposed so that the inner thoughts of many will be revealed—and a sword will pierce your own soul too."

There was also a prophet, Anna the daughter of Phanuel, of the tribe of Asher. She was of a great age, having lived with her husband seven years after her marriage, then as a widow to the age of eighty-four. She never left the temple but worshiped there with fasting and prayer night and day. At that moment she came, and began to praise God and to speak about the child to all who were looking for the redemption of Jerusalem.

When they had finished everything required by the law of the Lord, they returned to Galilee, to their own town of Nazareth. The child grew and became strong, filled with wisdom; and the favor of God was upon him.

Luke 2:22–40 (Canticle of Luke 2:29–32 ICEL)

1 JANUARY: MARY, MOTHER OF JESUS
1 JANUARY: HOLY NAME OF JESUS

JESUS, BORN OF A WOMAN
Our adoption as children of God through Christ is effected through a woman, Mary.

When the fullness of time had come, God sent the Son, born of a woman, born under the law, in order to redeem those who were under the law, so that we might receive adoption as children. And because you are children, God has sent the Spirit of the Son into our hearts, crying, "Abba! Father!" So you are no longer a slave but a child, and if a child then also an heir, through God.

Galatians 4:4 – 7

MARY KNOWS JESUS' NAME
The name of Jesus was proclaimed to Mary by the angel before he was conceived. Mary is the bearer of this good news.

When the angels had left them and gone into heaven, the shepherds said to one another, "Let us go now to Bethlehem and see this thing that has taken place, which the Lord has made known to us." So they went with haste and found Mary and Joseph, and the child lying in the manger. When they saw this, they made known what had been told them about this child; and all who heard it were amazed at what the shepherds told them. But Mary treasured all these words and pondered them in her heart. The shepherds returned, glorifying and praising God for all they had heard and seen, as it had been told them.

After eight days had passed, it was time to circumcise the child; and he was called Jesus, the name given by the angel before he was conceived in the womb.

Luke 2:15 – 21

SECOND SUNDAY AFTER CHRISTMAS

WISDOM MAKES HER DWELLING AMONG GOD'S PEOPLE
The lectionaries offer the prologue to the Gospel of John: "In the beginning was the word . . . the word dwelled among us." In this passage, we hear of divine Wisdom, a feminine figure who is with God from the beginning, co-creator with God who pitches her tent in the midst of her people.

Wisdom praises herself,
    and tells of her glory in the midst of her people.
In the assembly of the Most High she opens her mouth,
    and in the presence of God's hosts she tells of her glory:

"I came forth from the mouth of the Most High,
    and covered the earth like a mist.
I dwelt in the highest heavens,
    and my throne was in a pillar of cloud.
Alone I compassed the vault of heaven
    and traversed the depths of the abyss.
Over waves of the sea, over all the earth,
    and over every people and nation I have held sway.
Among all these I sought a resting place;
    in whose territory should I abide?

"Then the Creator of all things gave me a command,
    and my Creator chose the place for my tent.
God said, 'Make your dwelling in Jacob,
    and in Israel receive your inheritance.'
Before the ages, in the beginning, God created me,
    and for all the ages I shall not cease to be.
In the holy tent I ministered before God,
    and so I was established in Zion.
Thus in the beloved city God gave me a resting place,
    and in Jerusalem was my domain.
I took root in an honored people,
    in the portion of the Lord's heritage."

Sirach 24:1 – 12

THE EPIPHANY OF CHRIST

When Epiphany falls on the Second Sunday after Christmas, the two sets of readings may be combined.

THE QUEEN OF SHEBA GIVES AND RECEIVES GIFTS

In the lectionaries, the first reading tells that kings and ordinary people will bring homage and gifts; the gospel is about the magi. This passage tells about the Queen of Sheba, who brought gifts to King Solomon and received his gifts in return.

When the queen of Sheba heard of the fame of Solomon (fame due to the name of the LORD), she came to test him with hard questions. She came to Jerusalem with a very great retinue, with camels bearing spices, and very much gold, and precious stones; and when she came to Solomon, she told him all that was on her mind. Solomon answered all her questions; there was nothing hidden from the king that he could not explain to her. When the queen of Sheba had observed all the wisdom of Solomon, the house that he had built, the food of his table, the seating of his officials, and the attendance of his servants, their clothing, his valets, and his burnt offerings that he offered at the house of the LORD, there was no more spirit in her.

So she said to the king, "The report was true that I heard in my own land of your accomplishments and of your wisdom, but I did not believe the reports until I came and my own eyes had seen it. Not even half had been told me; your wisdom and prosperity far surpass the report that I had heard. Happy are your wives! Happy are these your servants, who continually attend you and hear your wisdom! Blessed be the LORD your God, who has delight in you and set you on the throne of Israel! Because the LORD loved Israel forever, you have been made king to execute justice and righteousness." Then she gave the king one hundred twenty talents of gold, a great quantity of spices, and precious stones; never again did spices come in such quantity as that which the queen of Sheba gave to King Solomon.

Moreover, the fleet of Hiram, which carried gold from Ophir, brought from Ophir a great quantity of almug wood and precious stones. From the almug wood the king made supports for the house of the LORD, and for the king's house, lyres also and harps for the singers; no such almug wood has come or been seen to this day.

Meanwhile King Solomon gave to the queen of Sheba every desire that she expressed, as well as what he gave her out of Solomon's royal bounty. Then she returned to her own land, with her servants.

1 Kings 10:1 – 13

In the time of King Herod, after Jesus was born in Bethlehem of Judea, magi from the East came to Jerusalem, asking, "Where is the child who has been born king of the Jews? For we observed his star at its rising, and have come to pay him homage." When King Herod heard this, he was frightened, and all Jerusalem with him; and calling together all the chief priests and scribes of the people, he inquired of them where the Christ was to be born. They told him, "In Bethlehem of Judea; for so it has been written by the prophet:

'And you, Bethlehem, in the land of Judah,
      are by no means least among the rulers of Judah;
for from you shall come a ruler
      who is to shepherd my people Israel.'"

Then Herod secretly called for the magi and learned from them the exact time when the star had appeared. Then he sent them to Bethlehem, saying, "Go and search diligently for the child; and when you have found him, bring me word so that I may also go and pay him homage." When they had heard the king, they set out; and there, ahead of them, went the star that they had seen at its rising, until it stopped over the place where the child was. When they saw that the star had stopped, they were overwhelmed with joy. On entering the house, they saw the child with Mary his mother; and they knelt down and paid him homage. Then, opening their treasure chests, they offered him gifts of gold, frankincense, and myrrh. And having been warned in a dream not to return to Herod, they left for their own country by another road.

Matthew 2:1 – 12

THE BAPTISM OF CHRIST

FIRST SUNDAY AFTER THE EPIPHANY

REBEKAH IS BLESSED

In the gospel reading of the lectionaries, Jesus is described as God's beloved, with whom God is well pleased. In this story Rebekah too is beloved of God. She gives her consent to become Isaac's wife and her family blesses her.

Abraham's servant brought out jewelry of silver and of gold, and garments, and gave them to Rebekah; he also gave to her brother and to her mother costly ornaments. Then he and the men who were with him ate and drank, and they spent the night there. When they rose in the morning, he said, "Send me back to my master." Rebekah's brother and her mother said, "Let the girl remain with us a while, at least ten days; after that she may go." But he said to them, "Do not delay me, since the LORD has made my journey successful; let me go that I may go to my master."

They said, "We will call the girl, and ask her." And they called Rebekah, and said to her, "Will you go with this man?" She said, "I will." So they sent away their sister Rebekah and her nurse along with Abraham's servant and his men.

And they blessed Rebekah and said to her,

"May you, our sister, become thousands of myriads;
may your offspring gain possession of the gates of their foes."

Then Rebekah and her maids rose up, mounted the camels, and followed the man; thus the servant took Rebekah, and went his way.

Genesis 24:53 – 61

SECOND SUNDAY IN ORDINARY TIME
SECOND SUNDAY AFTER THE EPIPHANY

THE WISE WOMAN OF ABEL

The gospel story in the lectionaries tells of the beginning of the public ministry of Jesus. This passage tells of a wise woman who exercises a public ministry in Israel. Even in this society where most public power is in the hands of men, wise women still exercise authority. Her dramatic response to Joab saves her city.

A scoundrel named Sheba son of Bichri, a Benjaminite, sounded the trumpet and cried out,

"We have no portion in David,
no share in the son of Jesse!
Everyone to your tents, O Israel!"

So all the people of Israel withdrew from David and followed Sheba son of Bichri; but the people of Judah followed their king steadfastly from the Jordan to Jerusalem.

Sheba passed through all the tribes of Israel to Abel of Beth-maacah; and all the Bichrites assembled, and followed him inside. Joab's forces came and besieged him in Abel of Beth-maacah; they threw up a siege-ramp against the city, and it stood against the rampart. Joab's forces were battering the wall to break it down.

Then a wise woman called from the city, "Listen! Listen! Tell Joab, 'Come here, I want to speak to you.'" He came near her; and the woman said, "Are you Joab?" He answered, "I am." Then she said to him, "Listen to the words of your servant." He answered, "I am listening." Then she said, "They used to say in the old days, 'Let them inquire at Abel'; and so they would settle a matter. I am one of those who are peaceable and faithful in Israel; you seek to destroy a city that is a mother in Israel; why will you swallow up the heritage of the LORD?"

Joab answered, "Far be it from me, far be it, that I should swallow up or destroy! That is not the case! But a man of the hill country of Ephraim, called Sheba son of Bichri, has lifted up his hand against King David; give him up alone, and I will withdraw from the city."

The woman said to Joab, "His head shall be thrown over the wall to you." Then the woman went to all the people with her wise plan. And they cut off the head of Sheba son of Bichri, and threw it out to Joab. So he blew the trumpet, and they dispersed from the city, and all went to their homes, while Joab returned to Jerusalem to the king.

2 Samuel 20:1 – 2, 14 – 22

These passages tell of women disciples of Jesus. These faithful women are a link between Jesus' ministry in Galilee and his death and burial; they will be the first to experience the Easter event.

There were women looking on from a distance; among them were Mary Magdalene, and Mary the mother of James the younger and of Joses, and Salome. These used to follow Jesus and provided for him when he was in Galilee; and there were many other women who had come up with him to Jerusalem.

Mark 15:40–41

Jesus went on through cities and villages, proclaiming and bringing the good news of the dominion of God. The twelve were with Jesus, as well as some women who had been cured of evil spirits and infirmities: Mary, called Magdalene, from whom seven demons had gone out, and Joanna, the wife of Herod's steward Chuza, and Susanna, and many others, who provided for them out of their resources.

Luke 8:1–3

Judith

THIRD SUNDAY IN ORDINARY TIME
THIRD SUNDAY AFTER THE EPIPHANY

GOD AS A WOMAN IN LABOR

After an invitation to praise God, the canticle's imagery paints God as a warrior and then as a woman in labor. In the end there will be peace and justice.

Sing the LORD a new song.
Let the sea with its creatures,
the coastland and its people
fill the world with praise.

Let every village and town,
from Kedar on the plain
to Sela in the hills,
take up the joyful song.
Sing glory to the LORD,
give praise across the world.

The LORD strides like a hero
who rouses fury
with a great battle cry
and charges against the enemy.
"I have kept quiet too long,
too long held back.
Like a woman in labor
I now scream and cry out:

"I will lay waste mountains and hills
and stunt all their greenery.
I will dry up rivers and pools
and create an arid wasteland.

"I will lead the blind safely
along strange roads.
I will make their darkness light,
their winding ways straight.
I will do all this,
I will not fail them."

Canticle of Isaiah 42:10 – 16 ICEL

FOURTH SUNDAY IN ORDINARY TIME
FOURTH SUNDAY AFTER THE EPIPHANY

GOD AS MIDWIFE
God is a midwife who assists as the chosen people are reborn from mother Zion.

Hear the word of the LORD,
  you who tremble at God's word:
Your own people who hate you
  and reject you for my name's sake
have said, "Let the LORD be glorified,
  so that we may see your joy";
  but it is they who shall be put to shame.

Listen, an uproar from the city!
  A voice from the temple!
The voice of the LORD,
  dealing retribution to God's enemies!

Before she was in labor
  she gave birth;
before her pain came upon her
  she delivered a son.

Who has heard of such a thing?
  Who has seen such things?
Shall a land be born in one day?
  Shall a nation be delivered in one moment?
Yet as soon as Zion was in labor
  she delivered her children.
Shall I open the womb and not deliver?
  says the LORD;
shall I, the one who delivers, shut the womb?
  says your God.

Isaiah 66:5 – 9

FIFTH SUNDAY IN ORDINARY TIME

FIFTH SUNDAY AFTER THE EPIPHANY

ISRAEL, GOD'S SPOUSE

God is not only Israel's creator and redeemer, but also Israel's faithful, steadfast spouse. The covenant of peace will be renewed, and God will be the teacher of Israel's children.

For your Maker is your husband,
    the LORD of hosts is the Creator's name;
the Holy One of Israel is your Redeemer,
    the one called the God of the whole earth.
For the LORD has called you
    like a wife forsaken and grieved in spirit,
like the wife of a man's youth when she is cast off,
    says your God.

For a brief moment I abandoned you,
    but with great compassion I will gather you.
In overflowing wrath for a moment
    I hid my face from you,
but with everlasting love I will have compassion on you,
    says the LORD, your Redeemer.

This is like the days of Noah to me:
    Just as I swore that the waters of Noah
    would never again go over the earth,
so I have sworn that I will not be angry with you
    and will not rebuke you.
For the mountains may depart
    and the hills be removed,
but my steadfast love shall not depart from you
    and my covenant of peace shall not be removed,
    says the LORD, who has compassion on you.

O afflicted one, storm-tossed, and not comforted,
    I am about to set your stones in antimony,
    and lay your foundations with sapphires.
I will make your pinnacles of rubies,
    your gates of jewels,
    and all your wall of precious stones.

All your children shall be taught by the LORD,
    and great shall be the prosperity of your children.

in righteousness you shall be established;
> you shall be far from oppression, for you shall not fear;
> and from terror, for it shall not come near you.

Isaiah 54:5 – 14

THE MOTHER OF THE WIFE OF SIMON

Jesus went into this woman's room, took her hand and raised her up. Healed, she served all of them. The word used for her service was also used for the service that the angels rendered to Jesus in the desert. The woman's house becomes the center for Jesus' healing ministry to the whole city.

Jesus left the synagogue and entered the house of Simon and Andrew, with James and John. Now Simon's mother-in-law was in bed with a fever, and they told Jesus about her at once. Jesus came and took her by the hand and lifted her up. Then the fever left her, and she began to serve them.

That evening, at sundown, they brought to Jesus all who were sick or possessed with demons. And the whole city was gathered around the door. And Jesus cured many who were sick with various diseases, and cast out many demons; and he would not permit the demons to speak, because they knew him.

Mark 1:29 – 34

SIXTH SUNDAY IN ORDINARY TIME

SIXTH SUNDAY AFTER THE EPIPHANY
PROPER 1: SUNDAY BETWEEN 11 AND 17 FEBRUARY

THE ISRAELITE SLAVE GIRL ADVISES NAAMAN
The Israelite slave girl who serves Naaman's wife does not rejoice at Naaman's ailment, but in mercy brings the good news of the prophet Elisha who can heal him.

Naaman, commander of the army of the king of Aram, was a great man and in high favor with his master, because by him the LORD had given victory to Aram. The man, though a mighty warrior, suffered from leprosy. Now the Arameans on one of their raids had taken a young girl captive from the land of Israel, and she served Naaman's wife. She said to her mistress, "If only my lord were with the prophet who is in Samaria! He would cure him of his leprosy." So Naaman went in and told his lord just what the girl from the land of Israel had said. And the king of Aram said, "Go then, and I will send along a letter to the king of Israel."

Naaman went, taking with him ten talents of silver, six thousand shekels of gold, and ten sets of garments. He brought the letter to the king of Israel, which read, "When this letter reaches you, know that I have sent to you my servant Naaman, that you may cure him of his leprosy." When the king of Israel read the letter, he tore his clothes and said, "Am I God, to give death or life, that this man sends word to me to cure a man of his leprosy. Just look and see how he is trying to pick a quarrel with me."

But when Elisha the man of God heard that the king of Israel had torn his clothes, he sent a message to the king, "Why have you torn your clothes? Let him come to me, that he may learn that there is a prophet in Israel." So Naaman came with his horses and chariots, and halted at the entrance of Elisha's house.

Elisha sent a messenger to him, saying, "Go, wash in the Jordan seven times, and your flesh shall be restored and you shall be clean." But Naaman became angry and went away, saying, "I thought that for me he would surely come out, and stand and call on the name of the LORD his God, and would wave his hand over the spot, and cure the leprosy! Are not Abana and Pharpar, the rivers of Damascus, better than all the waters of Israel? Could I not wash in them, and be clean?" He turned and went away in a rage. But his servants approached and said to him, "Dear master, if the prophet had commanded you to do something difficult, would you not have done it? How much more, when all he said to you was, 'Wash, and be clean'?" So he went down and immersed himself seven times in the Jordan, according to the word of the man of God; his flesh was restored like the flesh of a young boy, and he was clean.

2 Kings 5:1 – 14

SEVENTH SUNDAY IN ORDINARY TIME

SEVENTH SUNDAY AFTER THE EPIPHANY
PROPER 2: SUNDAY BETWEEN 18 AND 24 FEBRUARY

ABIGAIL MEETS DAVID AND SAVES HER HUSBAND
Abigail protects her husband from the consequences of his foolishness and rudeness. She prevents violence by soft words and gifts to David and his men.

One of the young men told Abigail, Nabal's wife, "David sent messengers out of the wilderness to salute our master; and he shouted insults at them. Yet the men were very good to us, and we suffered no harm, and we never missed anything when we were in the fields, as long as we were with them; they were a wall to us both by night and by day, all the while we were with them keeping the sheep. Now therefore know this and consider what you should do; for evil has been decided against our master and against all his house; he is so ill-natured that no one can speak to him."

Then Abigail hurried and took two hundred loaves, two skins of wine, five sheep ready dressed, five measures of parched grain, one hundred clusters of raisins, and two hundred cakes of figs. She loaded them on donkeys and said to her young men, "Go on ahead of me; I am coming after you." But she did not tell her husband Nabal. As she rode on the donkey and came down under cover of the mountain, David and his men came down toward her; and she met them. Now David had said, "Surely it was in vain that I protected all that this fellow has in the wilderness, so that nothing was missed of all that belonged to him; but he has returned me evil for good. God do so to David and more also, if by morning I leave so much as one male of all who belong to him."

When Abigail saw David, she hurried and alighted from the donkey, fell before David on her face, bowing to the ground. She fell at his feet and said, "Upon me alone, my lord, be the guilt; please let your servant speak in your ears, and hear the words of your servant. My lord, do not take seriously this ill-natured fellow, Nabal; for as his name is, so is he; Nabal is his name, and folly is with him; but I, your servant, did not see the young men of my lord, whom you sent.

"Now then, my lord, as the LORD lives, and as you yourself live, since the LORD has restrained you from bloodguilt and from taking vengence with your own hands, now let your enemies and those who seek to do evil to my lord be like Nabal. And now let this present that your servant has brought to my lord be given to the young men who follow my lord. Please forgive the trespass of your servant; for the LORD will certainly make my lord a sure house, because my lord is fighting the battles of the LORD; and evil shall not be found in you so long as you live. If anyone should rise up to pursue you and to seek your life, the life of my lord shall be bound in the bundle of the living under the care of the LORD your God; but the lives of your enemies he shall sling out as from the hollow of a sling. When the LORD has done to my lord according to all the good that God has spoken concerning you, and has appointed you prince over Israel, my lord shall have no cause of grief, or pangs of conscience, for having shed blood without cause or for having saved himself. And when the LORD has dealt well with my lord, then remember your servant."

1 Samuel 25:14 – 31

EIGHTH SUNDAY IN ORDINARY TIME

EIGHTH SUNDAY AFTER THE EPIPHANY
PROPER 3: SUNDAY BETWEEN 25 AND 29 FEBRUARY

ISRAEL, GOD'S SPOUSE

God professes love for Israel, and Israel is invited to renew its love for God. They will be like a married couple, living in mutuality and tenderness.

Thus says the LORD:
Therefore, I will now allure you,
     and bring you into the wilderness,
     and speak tenderly to you.
From there I will give you your vineyards,
     and make the Valley of Achor a door of hope.
There you shall respond as in the days of your youth,
     as at the time when you came out of the land of Egypt.
On that day, says the LORD, you will call me, "My husband," and no longer will you call me, "My Baal." For I will remove the names of the Baals from your mouth, and they shall be mentioned by name no more. I will make for you a covenant on that day with the wild animals, the birds of the air, and the creeping things of the ground; and I will abolish the bow, the sword, and war from the land; and I will make you lie down in safety. And I will take you for my wife forever; I will take you for my wife in righteousness and in justice, in steadfast love, and in mercy. I will take you for my wife in faithfulness; and you shall know the LORD.

Hosea 2:14–20

TRANSFIGURATION SUNDAY

Some celebrate the Transfiguration on the Last Sunday after the Epiphany while others celebrate it on the Second Sunday of Lent.

GOD AS A PROVIDER OF FOOD, WATER AND CLOTHING

In the gospel story of the Transfiguration, God is encountered on a high mountain as a voice from a bright cloud. This story offers a complementary image: God provides food, drink and clothing, tasks often accomplished by women.

"You, O God, came down also upon Mount Sinai, and spoke with them from heaven, and gave them right ordinances and true laws, good statutes and commandments, and you made known your holy sabbath to them and gave them commandments and statutes and a law through your servant Moses. For their hunger you gave them bread from heaven, and for their thirst you brought water for them out of the rock, and you told them to go in to possess the land that you swore to give them.

"But they and our ancestors acted presumptuously and stiffened their necks and did not obey your commandments; they refused to obey, and were not mindful of the wonders that you performed among them; but they stiffened their necks and determined to return to their slavery in Egypt. But you are a God ready to forgive, gracious and merciful, slow to anger and abounding in steadfast love, and you did not forsake them. Even when they had cast an image of a calf for themselves and said, 'This is your God who brought you up out of Egypt,' and had committed great blasphemies, you in your great mercies did not forsake them in the wilderness; the pillar of cloud that led them in the way did not leave them by day, nor the pillar of fire by night that gave them light on the way by which they should go. You gave your good spirit to instruct them, and did not withhold your manna from their mouths, and gave them water for their thirst. Forty years you sustained them in the wilderness so that they lacked nothing; their clothes did not wear out and their feet did not swell."

Nehemiah 9:13–21

ASH WEDNESDAY

The lectionaries' readings call us to prayer, fasting and almsgiving; and to reconciliation with God and neighbor. The first three passages here tell how women in different circumstances were to be treated according to the ancient Law. They challenge all to do justice to and for women in contemporary society.

THE TREATMENT OF WOMEN SLAVES

When a man sells his daughter as a slave, she shall not go out as the male slaves do. If she does not please her master, who designated her for himself, then he shall let her be redeemed; he shall have no right to sell her to a foreign people, since he has dealt unfairly with her. If he designates her for his son, he shall deal with her as with a daughter. If he takes another wife to himself, he shall not diminish the food, clothing, or marital rights of the first wife. And if he does not do these three things for her, she shall go out without debt, without payment of money.

Exodus 21:7 – 11

SLAVES, WOMEN AND MEN, ARE SET FREE IN THE SABBATH YEAR

If a member of your community, whether a Hebrew man or a Hebrew woman, is sold to you and works for you six years, in the seventh year you shall set that person free. And when you send a male slave out from you a free person; you shall not send him out empty-handed. Provide liberally out of your flock, your threshing floor, and your wine press, thus giving to him some of the bounty with which the LORD your God has blessed you. Remember that you were a slave in the land of Egypt, and the LORD your God redeemed you; for this reason I lay this command upon you today. But if he says to you, "I will not go out from you," because he loves you and your household, since he is well off with you, then you shall take an awl and thrust it through his earlobe into the door, and he shall be your slave forever.

You shall do the same with regard to your female slave.

Deuteronomy 15:12 – 17

THE TREATMENT OF WOMEN TAKEN IN WAR

When you go out to war against your enemies, and the LORD your God hands them over to you and you take them captive, suppose you see among the captives a beautiful woman whom you desire and want to marry, and so you bring her home to your house; she shall shave her head, pare her nails, discard her captive's garb, and shall remain in your house a full month, mourning for her father and mother; after that you may go in to her and be her husband, and she shall be your wife. But if you are not satisfied with her, you shall let her go free and not sell her for money. You must not treat her as a slave, since you have dishonored her.

Deuteronomy 21:10 – 14

PRIZE WISDOM!
Lent is interpreted as a journey toward Wisdom, the feminine figure of divine presence.

Get wisdom; get insight: do not forget, nor turn away
     from the words of my mouth.
Do not forsake her, and she will keep you;
     love her, and she will guard you.
The beginning of wisdom is this: Get wisdom
     and whatever else you get, get insight.
Prize her highly, and she will exalt you;
     she will honor you if you embrace her.
She will place on your head a fair garland;
     she will bestow on you a beautiful crown.

Hear, my child, and accept my words,
     that the years of your life may be many.
I have taught you the way of wisdom;
     I have led you in the paths of uprightness.
When you walk, your step will not be hampered;
     and if you run, you will not stumble.
Keep hold to instruction; do not let go;
     guard her, for she is your life.

Proverbs 4:5 – 13

Four other passages give us examples of women at prayer. Mary, Hannah, Judith and Esther can be models for Lent.

MARY, MODEL OF PRAYER
Mary sings that God continues to rescue Israel, a fact which gives her strength.

I acclaim the greatness of the Lord,
I delight in God my savior,
who regarded my humble state.
Truly from this day on
all ages will call me blest.

For God, wonderful in power,
has used that strength for me.
Holy the name of the Lord!

whose mercy embraces the faithful,
one generation to the next.

The mighty arm of God
scatters the proud in their conceit,
pulls tyrants from their thrones,
and raises up the humble.
The Lord fills the starving
and lets the rich go hungry.

God rescues lowly Israel,
recalling the promise of mercy,
the promise made to our ancestors,
to Abraham's heirs for ever.

Canticle of Luke 1:46 – 55 ICEL

HANNAH, MODEL OF PRAYER
Hannah pours out her heart in joyful song. Her song is like the song of Mary.

I acclaim the LORD's greatness,
source of my strength.
I devour my foe,
I say to God with joy:
"You saved my life.
Only you are holy, LORD;
there is none but you,
no other rock like you."

God knows when deeds match words,
so make no arrogant claims.
The weapons of the strong are broken,
the defenseless gain strength.
The overfed now toil to eat,
while the hungry have their fill.

The childless bear many children,
but the fertile learn they are sterile.
The LORD commands death and life,
consigns to Sheol or raises up.

God deals out poverty and wealth,
casts down and lifts up,
raising the poor from squalor,
the needy from the trash heap,

to sit with the high and mighty,
taking their places of honor.

God owns the universe
and sets the earth within it.
God walks with the faithful
but silences the wicked in darkness;
their power does not prevail.

God's enemies will be broken,
heaven thunders against them.
The Lord will judge the earth,
and give power to the king,
victory to the anointed.

> Canticle of 1 Samuel 2:1–10 ICEL

JUDITH, MODEL OF PRAYER

Judith prays that she can be the means by which God rescues the chosen people. God will protect the poor and downtrodden.

Judith cried out to the Lord with a loud voice, and said,

"O Lord God of my ancestor Simeon, to whom you gave a sword to take revenge on those strangers who had torn off a virgin's clothing to defile her, and exposed her thighs to put her to shame, and polluted her womb to disgrace her; for you said, 'It shall not be done' — yet they did it. So you gave up their rulers to be killed, and their bed, which was ashamed of the deceit they had practiced, was stained with blood, and you struck down slaves along with princes, and princes on their thrones. You gave up their wives for booty and their daughters to captivity, and all their booty to be divided among your beloved children who burned with zeal for you and abhorred the pollution of their blood and called on you for help — O God, my God, hear me also — a widow.

"For you have done these things and those that went before and those that followed. You have designed the things that are now, and those that are to come. What you had in mind has happened; the things you decided on presented themselves and said, 'Here we are!' For all your ways are prepared in advance, and your judgment is with foreknowledge.

"Here now are the Assyrians, a greatly increased force, priding themselves in their horses and riders, boasting in the strength of their foot soldiers, and trusting in shield and spear, in bow and sling. They do not know that you are the Lord who crushes wars; the Lord is your name. Break their strength by your might, and bring down their power in your anger; for they intend to defile your sanctuary, and to pollute the tabernacle where your glorious name resides, and to break off the horns of your altar with the sword. Look at their pride, and send your wrath upon their heads. Give to me, a widow, the strong hand to do what I plan. By the deceit of my lips strike down the slave with the prince and the prince with his servant; crush their arrogance by the hand of a woman.

"For your strength does not depend on numbers, nor your might on the powerful. But you are the God of the lowly, helper of the oppressed, upholder of the weak, protecter of the forsaken, savior of those without hope."

Judith 9:1 – 11

ESTHER, MODEL OF PRAYER

Esther prays for the deliverance of her people. She asks for courage and eloquent speech that she may do her part.

Queen Esther prayed to the Lord God of Israel, and said: "O my Lord, you only are our ruler; help me, who am alone and have no helper but you, for my danger is in my hand. Ever since I was born I have heard in the tribe of my family that you, O Lord, took Israel out of all the nations, and our ancestors from among all their forebears, for an everlasting inheritance, and that you did for them all that you promised. And now we have sinned before you, and you have handed us over to our enemies because we glorified their gods. You are righteous, O Lord! And now they are not satisfied that we are in bitter slavery, but they have covenanted with their idols to abolish what your mouth has ordained, and to destroy your inheritance, to stop the mouths of those who praise you and to quench your altar and the glory of your house, to open the mouths of the nations for the praise of vain idols, and to magnify forever a mortal ruler.

"O Lord, do not surrender your scepter to what has no being; and do not let them laugh at our downfall; but turn their plan against them, and make an example of him who began this against us. Remember, O Lord; make yourself known in this time of our affliction, and give me courage, O Ruler of the gods and Master of all dominion! Put eloquent speech in my mouth before the lion, and turn his heart to hate the man who is fighting against us, so that there may be an end of him and those who agree with him. But save us by your hand, and help me, who am alone and have no helper but you, O Lord."

Esther 14:3 – 14

FIRST SUNDAY OF LENT

THE WIFE AND DAUGHTERS-IN-LAW OF NOAH

The lectionaries tell of God making covenant with Noah and his sons. This passage tells of Noah's wife and daughters-in-law and all the animals and birds coming out of the ark. Why aren't we told the names of Noah's wife and daughters-in-law?

God said to Noah, "Go out of the ark, you and your wife, and your sons and your sons' wives with you. Bring out with you every living thing that is with you of all flesh — birds and animals and every creeping thing that creeps on the earth — so that they may abound on the earth, and be fruitful and multiply on the earth." So Noah went out with his sons and his wife and his sons' wives. And every animal, every creeping thing, and every bird, everything that moves on the earth, went out of the ark by families.

Then Noah built an altar to the LORD, and took of every clean animal and of every clean bird, and offered burnt offerings on the altar. and when the LORD smelled the pleasing odor, the LORD said with sincerity, "I will never again curse the ground because of humankind, for the inclination of the human heart is evil from youth; nor will I ever again destroy every living creature as I have done.

As long as the earth endures,
    seedtime and harvest, cold and heat,
summer and winter, day and night,
    shall not cease."

Genesis 8:15 – 21

SECOND SUNDAY OF LENT

GOD'S PROMISE TO SARAH
The Roman lectionary tells the story of the binding of Isaac and of God's promise. In this passage God blesses Sarah and says that God's promise will come through her.

God said to Abraham, "As for Sarai your wife, you shall not call her Sarai, but Sarah shall be her name. I will bless her, and moreover I will give you a son by her. I will bless her, and she shall give rise to nations; kings of people shall come from her." Then Abraham fell on his face and laughed, and said to himself, "Can a child be born to a man who is a hundred years old? Can Sarah, who is ninety years old, bear a child?"

And Abraham said to God, "O that Ishmael might live in your sight!" God said, "No, but your wife Sarah shall bear you a son, and you shall name him Isaac. I will establish my covenant with him as an everlasting covenant for his offspring after him. As for Ishmael, I have heard you; I will bless him and make him fruitful and exceedingly numerous; he shall be the father of twelve princes, and I will make him a great nation. But my covenant I will establish with Isaac, whom Sarah shall bear to you at this season next year." And when he had finished talking with him, God went up from Abraham.

Genesis 17:15 – 22

SARAH WILL GIVE RISE TO NATIONS
The Revised Common Lectionary assigns this passage, which gives less attention to Sarah.

When Abram was ninety-nine years old, the LORD appeared to Abram, and said to him, "I am God Almighty; walk before me, and be blameless. And I will make my covenant between me and you, and will make you exceedingly numerous." Then Abram fell on his face; and God said to him, "As for me, this is my covenant with you: You shall be the ancestor of a multitude of nations. No longer shall your name be Abram, but your name shall be Abraham; for I have made you the ancestor of a multitude of nations. I will make you exceedingly fruitful; and I will make nations of you, and kings shall come from you. I will establish my covenant between me and you, and your offspring after you throughout their generations, for an everlasting covenant, to be God to you and to your offspring after you.

God said to Abraham, "As for Sarai your wife, you shall not call her Sarai, but Sarah shall be her name. I will bless her, and moreover I will give you a son by her. I will bless her, and she shall give rise to nations; kings of peoples shall come from her."

Genesis 17:1 – 7, 15 – 16

If the Transfiguration is celebrated on this Sunday:

GOD AS A PROVIDER OF FOOD, WATER AND CLOTHING

In the gospel story of the Transfiguration, God is encountered on a high mountain as a voice from a bright cloud. This story offers a complementary image: God provides food, drink and clothing, tasks often accomplished by women.

"You, O God, came down also upon Mount Sinai, and spoke with them from heaven, and gave them right ordinances and true laws, good statutes and commandments, and you made known your holy sabbath to them and gave them commandments and statutes and a law through your servant Moses. For their hunger you gave them bread from heaven, and for their thirst you brought water for them out of the rock, and you told them to go in to possess the land that you swore to give them.

"But they and our ancestors acted presumptuously and stiffened their necks and did not obey your commandments; they refused to obey, and were not mindful of the wonders that you performed among them; but they stiffened their necks and determined to return to their slavery in Egypt. But you are a God ready to forgive, gracious and merciful, slow to anger and abounding in steadfast love, and you did not forsake them. Even when they had cast an image of a calf for themselves and said, 'This is your God who brought you up out of Egypt,' and had committed great blasphemies, you in your great mercies did not forsake them in the wilderness; the pillar of cloud that led them in the way did not leave them by day, nor the pillar of fire by night that gave them light on the way by which they should go. You gave your good spirit to instruct them, and did not withhold your manna from their mouths, and gave them water for their thirst. Forty years you sustained them in the wilderness so that they lacked nothing; their clothes did not wear out and their feet did not swell."

Nehemiah 9:13–21

THIRD SUNDAY OF LENT

HONOR MOTHER AND FATHER, DO NOT COVET YOUR NEIGHBOR'S WIFE
Both mother and father are to be honored. The neighbor's wife and female slave, however, are viewed as a man's property. What do you make of this?

God spoke all these words: I am the LORD your God, who brought you out of the land of Egypt, out of the house of slavery; you shall have no other gods before me.

You shall not make for yourself an idol, whether in the form of anything that is in heaven above, or that is on the earth beneath, or that is in the water under the earth.

You shall not make wrongful use of the name of the LORD your God, for the LORD will not acquit anyone who misuses the divine name.

Remember the sabbath day, and keep it holy. Six days you shall labor and do all your work.

Honor your father and your mother, so that your days may be long in the land that the LORD your God is giving you.

You shall not murder.

You shall not commit adultery.

You shall not steal.

You shall not bear false witness against your neighbor.

You shall not covet your neighbor's house; you shall not covet your neighbor's wife, or male or female slave, or ox, or donkey, or anything that belongs to your neighbor.

When all the people witnessed the thunder and lightning, the sound of the trumpet, and the mountains smoking, they were afraid and trembled and stood at a distance, and said to Moses, "You speak to us, and we will listen; but do not let God speak to us, or we will die." Moses said to the people, "Do not be afraid; for God has come only to test you and to put the fear of God upon you so that you do not sin."

Exodus 20:1–4, 7–9, 12–20

haman

Esther

FOURTH SUNDAY OF LENT

ESTHER SAVES HER PEOPLE

The Roman lectionary tells how Cyrus, king of Persia, became an agent of God's promise of redemption. This passage tells how Esther saved her people in Persia. She defeated Haman's plot and obtained justice for the Jews from the king.

On that day King Ahasuerus gave to Queen Esther the house of Haman, the enemy of the Jews; and Mordecai came before the king, for Esther had told what he was to her. Then the king took off his signet ring, which he had taken from Haman, and gave it to Mordecai. So Esther set Mordecai over the house of Haman.

Then Esther spoke again to the king; she fell at his feet, weeping and pleading with him to avert the evil design of Haman the Agagite and the plot that he had devised against the Jews. The king held out the golden scepter to Esther, and Esther rose and stood before the king. She said, "If it pleases the king, and if I have won his favor, and if the things seem right before the king, and I have his approval, let an order be written to revoke the letters devised by Haman son of Hammedatha the Agagite, which he wrote giving orders to destroy the Jews who are in all the provinces of the king. For how can I bear to see the calamity that is coming on my people? Or how can I bear to see the destruction of my kindred?"

Then King Ahasuerus said to Queen Esther and to the Jew Mordecai, "See, I have given Esther the house of Haman, and they have hanged him on the gallows, because he plotted to lay hands on the Jews. You may write as you please with regard to the Jews, in the name of the king, and seal it with the king's ring; for an edict written in the name of the king and sealed with the king's ring cannot be revoked."

Esther 8:1 – 8

WOMEN HELP CONSTRUCT THE TENT OF MEETING IN THE DESERT

The Revised Common Lectionary tells the story of the bronze serpent erected by Moses in the desert. This passage tells how women contribute to the construction of the tabernacle in the desert. Women give with willing spirit, generosity and skill.

All the congregation of the Israelites withdrew from the presence of Moses. And they came, everyone whose heart was stirred, and everyone whose spirit was willing, and brought the LORD's offering to be used for the tent of meeting, and for all its service, and for the sacred vestments. So they came, both men and women; all who were of a willing heart brought brooches and earrings and signet rings and pendants, all sorts of gold objects, everyone bringing an offering of gold to the LORD. And everyone who possessed blue or purple or crimson yarn of fine linen or goats' hair or tanned rams' skins or fine leather, brought them. Everyone who could make an offering of silver or bronze brought it as the LORD's offering; and everyone who possessed acacia wood of any use in the work, brought it.

All the skillful women spun with their hands, and brought what they had spun in blue and purple and crimson yarns and fine linen; all the women whose hearts moved them to use their skill spun the goats' hair. And the leaders brought onyx stones and gems to be set in the ephod and the breastpiece, and spices and oil for the light, and for the anointing oil, and for the fragrant incense. All the Israelite men and women whose hearts made them willing to bring anything for the work that the LORD had commanded by Moses to be done, brought it as a freewill offering to the LORD.

Exodus 35:20 – 29

FIFTH SUNDAY OF LENT

RACHEL WEEPS

The lectionaries tell of a new covenant. This passage recalls Rachel lamenting her children and promises hope: Her children will be restored.

Thus says the LORD:
A voice is heard in Ramah,
      lamentation and bitter weeping.
Rachel is weeping for her children;
      she refuses to be comforted for her children,
      because they are no more.
Thus says the LORD:
Keep your voice from weeping,
      and your eyes from tears;
for there is a reward for your work, says the LORD:
      they shall come back from the land of the enemy;
there is hope for your future, says the LORD:
      your children shall come back to their own country.

Jeremiah 31:15 – 17

PASSION (PALM) SUNDAY

THE RAPE OF TAMAR

The lectionaries tell of the passion and death of Jesus. This passage tells of the suffering of Tamar. What happened to Tamar continues to occur: rape and incest followed by hatred. Society fails to prosecute the males involved.

David's son Absalom had a beautiful sister whose name was Tamar; and David's son Amnon fell in love with her. Amnon was so tormented that he made himself ill because of his sister Tamar, for she was a virgin and it seemed impossible to Amnon to do anything to her. But Amnon had a friend whose name was Jonadab, the son of David's brother Shimeah; and Jonadab was a very crafty man. Jonadab said to Amnon, "O son of the king, why are you so haggard morning after morning? Will you not tell me?" Amnon said to Jonadab, "I love Tamar, my brother Absalom's sister." Jonadab said to him, "Lie down on your bed, and pretend to be ill; and when your father comes to see you, say to him, 'Let my sister Tamar come and give me something to eat, and prepare the food in my sight, so that I may see it and eat it from her hand.'" So Amnon lay down, and pretended to be ill; and when the king came to see him, Amnon said to the king, "Please let my sister Tamar come and make a couple of cakes in my sight, so that I may eat from her hand."

Then David sent home to Tamar, saying, "Go to your brother Amnon's house, and prepare food for him." So Tamar went to her brother Amnon's house, where he was lying down. She took dough, kneaded it, made cakes in his sight, and baked the cakes. Then she took the pan and set them out before him, but he refused to eat. Amnon said, "Send out everyone from me." So everyone went out from him. Then Amnon said to Tamar, "Bring the food into the chamber, so that I may eat from your hand." So Tamar took the cakes she had made, and brought them into the chamber to Amnon her brother.

But when she brought them near him to eat, he took hold of her, and said to her. "Come lie with me, my sister." She answered him, "No, my brother, do not force me; for such a thing is not done in Israel; do not do anything so vile! As for me, where could I carry my shame? And as for you, you would be as one of the scoundrels in Israel. Now therefore, I beg you, speak to the king; for he will not withhold me from you." But he would not listen to her; and being stronger than Tamar, he forced her and lay with her.

Then Amnon was seized with a very great loathing for her; indeed, his loathing was even greater than the lust he had felt for her. Amnon said to Tamar, "Get out!" But she said to him, "No, my brother; for this wrong in sending me away is greater than the other that you did to me." But he would not listen to her. He called the young man who served him and said, "Put this woman out of my presence, and bolt the door after her." (Now she was wearing a long robe with sleeves; for this is how the virgin daughters of the king were clothed in earlier times.) So his servant put her out and bolted the door after her. But Tamar put ashes on her head, and tore the long robe that she was wearing; she put her hand on her head, and went away, crying aloud as she went.

Her brother Absalom said to her, "Has Amnon your brother been with you? Be quiet for now, my sister; he is your brother; do not take this to heart." So Tamar remained, a desolate woman, in her brother Absalom's house. When King David heard of all these things, he became very angry, but he would not punish his son Amnon, because he loved him; for he was his firstborn. But Absalom spoke to Amnon neither good nor bad; for Absalom hated Amnon, because he had raped his sister Tamar.

2 Samuel 13:1 – 22

WOMEN IN THE PASSION ACCORDING TO MARK

Both the Roman lectionary and Revised Common Lectionary appoint chapters 14 and 15 of Mark's gospel for this Sunday. Excerpts that tell women's stories are given here.

THE WOMAN ANOINTS JESUS

An unnamed woman gives a royal anointing to Jesus, at the same time preparing his body for burial. It is an example of loving compassion to one in need.

While Jesus was at Bethany in the house of Simon the leper, as he sat at the table, a woman came with an alabaster jar of very costly ointment of nard, and she broke open the jar and poured the ointment on his head. But some were there who said to one another in anger, "Why was the ointment wasted in this way? For this ointment could have been sold for more than three hundred denarii, and the money given to the poor." And they scolded her.

But Jesus said, "Let her alone; why do you trouble her? She has performed a good service for me. For you always have the poor with you, and you can show kindness to them whenever you wish; but you will not always have me. She has done what she could; she has anointed my body beforehand for its burial. Truly I tell you, wherever the good news is proclaimed in the whole world, what she has done will be told in remembrance of her."

Mark 14:3 – 9

THE SERVANT GIRL CONFRONTS PETER

While Jesus is questioned about his true identity by the high priest, Peter faces similar questions from the high priest's servants and others. The unnamed woman seeks the truth; Peter denies the truth.

While Peter was below in the courtyard, one of the servant-girls of the high priest came by. When she saw Peter warming himself, she stared at him and said, "You also were with Jesus, the man from Nazareth." But he denied it, saying, "I do not know or understand what you are talking about." And he went out into the fore-court. Then the cock crowed.

And the servant-girl, on seeing him, began again to say to the bystanders, "This man is one of them." But again he denied it. Then after a little while the bystanders again said to Peter, "Certainly you are one of them; for you are a Galilean." But he began to curse, and he swore an oath, "I do not know this man you are talking about."

At that moment the cock crowed for the second time. Then Peter remembered that Jesus had said to him, "Before the cock crows twice, you will deny me three times." And he broke down and wept.

Mark 14:66 – 72

THE WOMEN KEEP WATCH
The faithful women prove themselves to be more devoted disciples of Jesus than the Twelve.

There were women looking on from a distance; among them were Mary Magdalene, and Mary the mother of James the younger and of Joses, and Salome. These used to follow Jesus and provided for him when he was in Galilee; and there were many other women who had come up with him to Jerusalem.

Mark 15:40 – 41

HOLY THURSDAY

MEMORIAL FEAST FOR THE DAUGHTER OF JEPHTHAH

In the lectionaries, the first reading tells of the establishment of the memorial feast of Passover, and the second reading tells of the institution of the eucharist as a memorial. This passage tells of the death of the daughter of Jephthah and the memorial feast kept by the women in her honor.

The spirit of the LORD came upon Jephthah, and he passed through Gilead and Manasseh. He passed on to Mizpah of Gilead, and from Mizpah of Gilead he passed on to the Ammonites. And Jephthah made a vow to the LORD, and said, "If you will give the Ammonites into my hand, then whoever comes out of the doors of my house to meet me, when I return victorious from the Ammonites, shall be the LORD's to be offered up by me as a burnt offering." So Jephthah crossed over to the Ammonites to fight against them; and the LORD gave them into his hand. Jephthah inflicted a massive defeat on them from Aroer to the neighborhood of Minnith, twenty towns, and as far as Abel-keramin. So the Ammonites were subdued before the people of Israel.

Then Jephthah came to his home at Mizpah; and there was his daughter coming out to meet him with timbrels and with dancing. She was his only child; he had no son or daughter except her. When he saw here, he tore his clothes, and said, "Alas, my daughter! You have brought me very low; you have become the cause of greater trouble to me. For I have opened my mouth to the LORD, and I cannot take back my vow."

She said to him, "My father, if you have opened your mouth to the LORD, do to me according to what has gone out of your mouth, now that the LORD has given you vengeance against your enemies, the Ammonites." And she said to her father, "Let this thing be done for me: Grant me two months, so that I may go and wander on the mountains, and bewail my virginity, my companions and I." "Go," he said and sent her away for two months.

So she departed, she and her companions, and bewailed her virginity on the mountains. At the end of two months, she returned to her father, who did with her according to the vow he had made. She had never slept with a man. So there arose an Israelite custom that for four days every year the daughters of Israel would go out to lament the daughter of Jephthah the Gileadite.

Judges 11:29 – 40

ABIGAIL, WASHER OF FEET

The gospel reading of the lectionaries tells how Jesus washed the feet of his disciples. This passage tells of Abigail, who washed the feet of David's servants as a gesture of hospitality and in response to being invited to marry King David.

David sent and wooed Abigail, to make her his wife. When David's servants came to Abigail at Carmel, they said to her, "David has sent us to you to take you to him as his wife." She rose and bowed down, with her face to the ground, and said,

"Behold your handmaiden is a servant to wash the feet of the servants of my lord." Abigail got up hurriedly and rode away on a donkey; her five maids attended her. She went after the messengers of David and became his wife.

1 Samuel 25:39c – 42

WIDOWS WHO WASH THE FEET OF THE SAINTS

The ministry of widows in the early church included prayer and service, such as washing the feet of the members of the community, as Jesus washed his disciples' feet. Widows probably washed other women's feet.

Let a widow be put on the list if she is not less than sixty years old and has been married only once; she must be well attested for her good works, as one who has brought up children, shown hospitality, washed the saints' feet, helped the afflicted, and devoted herself to doing good in every way.

1 Timothy 5:9 – 10

GOOD FRIDAY

The lectionaries tell of the passion and death of Jesus. Jesus' agony on the cross is a kind of childbirth, leading to new life. These passages tell of death in childbirth. The death of Jesus is also related here to Israel's loss of the ark, which in other writings is sometimes viewed as a fruitful womb.

THE DEATH OF RACHEL IN CHILDBIRTH

God appeared to Jacob again when he came from Paddan-aram, and he befriended Jacob. God said to him, "Your name is Jacob; no longer shall you be called Jacob, but Israel shall be your name." So he was called Israel. God said to him, "I am God Almighty; be fruitful and multiply; a nation and a company of nations shall come from you, and kings shall spring from you. The land that I gave to Abraham and Isaac I will give to you, and I will give the land to your offspring after you." Then God went up from him at the place where he had spoken with him. Jacob set up a pillar on the place where he had spoken with God, a pillar of stone; and Jacob poured out a drink offering on it, and poured oil on it. So Jacob called the place where God had spoken with him Bethel.

Then they journeyed from Bethel; and when they were still some distance from Ephrath, Rachel was in childbirth, and she had hard labor. When she was in her hard labor, the midwife said to her, "Do not be afraid; for now you will have another son." As her soul was departing (for she died), she named him Ben-oni; but his father called him Benjamin. So Rachel died, and she was buried on the way to Ephrath (that is, Bethlehem), and Jacob set up a pillar at her grave; it is the pillar of Rachel's tomb, which is there to this day.

Genesis 35:9–20

LOSS OF THE ARK AND THE DEATH OF THE WIFE
OF PHINEHAS IN CHILDBIRTH
The ark of the covenant, Israel's symbol of Immanuel, God-with-us, is captured in battle. The story also shows that women, even when not engaged in violence, suffer the brunt of its consequences.

The word of Samuel came to all Israel.

In those days the Philistines mustered for war against Israel, and Israel went out to battle against them; they encamped at Ebenezer, and the Philistines encamped at Aphek. The Philistines drew up in line against Israel, and when the battle was joined, Israel was defeated by the Philistines, who killed about four thousand men on the field of battle.

When the troops came to the camp, the elders of Israel said, "Why has the LORD put us to rout today before the Philistines? Let us bring the ark of the covenant of the LORD here from Shiloh, so that God may come among us and save us from the power of our enemies." So the people sent to Shiloh, and brought from there the ark of the covenant of the LORD of hosts, who is enthroned on the cherubim. The two sons of Eli, Hophni and Phinehas, were there with the ark of the covenant of God.

When the ark of the covenant of the LORD came into the camp, all Israel gave a mighty shout, so that the earth resounded. When the Philistines heard the noise of the shouting, they said, "What does this great shouting in the camp of the Hebrews mean?" When they learned that the ark of the LORD had come to the camp, the Philistines were afraid; for they said, "Gods have come into the camp." They also said, "Woe to us! For nothing like this has happened before. Woe to us! Who can deliver us from the power of these mighty gods? These are the gods who struck the Egyptians with every sort of plague in the wilderness. Take courage, and be men, O Philistines, in order not to become slaves to the Hebrews as they have been to you; be men and fight."

So the Philistines fought; Israel was defeated, and they fled, everyone to his home. There was a very great slaughter, for there fell of Israel thirty thousand foot soldiers. The ark of God was captured, and the two sons of Eli, Hophni and Phinehas, died.

A man of Benjamin ran from the battle line, and came to Shiloh the same day, with his clothes torn and with earth upon his head. When he arrived, Eli was sitting upon his seat by the road watching, for his heart trembled for the ark of God. When the man came into the city and told the news, all the city cried out. When Eli heard the sound of the outcry, he said, "What is this uproar?" Then the man came quickly and told Eli. Now Eli was ninety-eight years old and his eyes were set, so that he could not see. The man said to Eli, "I have just come from the battle; I fled from the battle today." He said, "How did it go, my son?" The messenger replied, "Israel has fled before the Philistines, and there has also been a great slaughter among the troops; your two sons also, Hophni and Phinehas, are dead, and the ark of God has been captured." When he mentioned the ark of God, Eli fell over backward from his seat by the side of the gate; and his neck was broken and he died, for he was an old man, and heavy. He had judged Israel forty years.

Now his daughter-in-law, the wife of Phinehas, was pregnant, about to give birth. When she heard the news that the ark of God was captured, and that her father-in-law and her husband were dead, she bowed and gave birth; for her labor pains overwhelmed her. As she was about to die, the women attending her said to her, "Do not be afraid, for you have borne a son." But she did not answer or give heed. She named the child Ichabod, meaning, "The glory has departed from Israel," because the ark of God had been captured and because of her father-in-law and her husband. She said, "The glory has departed from Israel, for the ark of God has been captured."

1 Samuel 4:1 – 22

MARY OF BETHANY ANOINTS JESUS
Mary and Martha demonstrate discipleship: They welcome Jesus, bring others to table with him, and share in his death. Mary's anointing is an act of loving extravangance.

Six days before the Passover Jesus came to Bethany, the home of Lazarus, whom he had raised from the dead. There they gave a dinner for Jesus. Martha served, and Lazarus was one of those at the table with him. Mary took a pound of costly perfume made of pure nard, anointed Jesus' feet, and wiped them with her hair. The house was filled with the fragrance of the perfume. But Judas Iscariot, one of his disciples (the one who was about to betray him), said, "Why was this perfume not sold for three hundred denarii and the money given to the poor." (He said this not because he cared about the poor, but because he was a thief; he kept the common purse and used to steal what was put into it.) Jesus said, "Leave her alone. She bought it so that she might keep it for the day of my burial. You always have the poor with you, but you do not always have me."

John 12:1–8

WOMEN IN THE PASSION ACCORDING TO JOHN
Both the Roman lectionary and Revised Common Lectionary assign chapters 18 and 19 of John's gospel to this day. Excerpts that tell women's stories are given here.

THE SERVANT WOMAN CONFRONTS PETER
While Jesus affirms his identity to the high priest, Peter denies his connection to Jesus after being challenged by a woman who knows the truth.

Simon Peter and another disciple followed Jesus. Since that disciple was known to the high priest, he went with Jesus into the courtyard of the high priest, but Peter was standing outside at the gate. So the other disciple, who was known to the high priest, went out, spoke to the woman who guarded the gate, and brought Peter in. The woman said to Peter, "You are not also one of this man's disciples, are you?" He said, "I am not."

Now Simon Peter was standing and warming himself. They asked him, "You are not also one of his disciples, are you?" He denied it and said, "I am not." One of the slaves of the high priest, a relative of the man whose ear Peter had cut off, asked, "Did I not see you in the garden with him?" Again Peter denied it, and at that moment the cock crowed.

John 18:15–17, 25–27

JESUS AND HIS MOTHER
Jesus' death is witnessed by his mother and other faithful women followers. Jesus' creation of a new family of God is symbolized when the disciple takes Jesus' mother into his own home.

Standing near the cross of Jesus were his mother, and his mother's sister, Mary the wife of Clopas, and Mary Magdalene. When Jesus saw his mother and the disciple whom he loved standing beside her, he said to his mother, "Woman, here is your son." Then Jesus said to the disciple, "Here is your mother." And from that hour the disciple took her into his own home.

John 19:25–27

EASTER VIGIL

JESUS APPEARS TO THE WOMEN

The lectionaries tell about Jesus appearing to his disciples after the resurrection. This passage tells about the women disciples at the empty tomb. Ending the passage with a reference to the women's fear is a literary device that invites readers to witness to Jesus in their own time and place.

When the sabbath was over, Mary Magdalene, and Mary the mother of James, and Salome bought spices, so that they might go and anoint Jesus. And very early on the first day of the week, when the sun had risen, they went to the tomb. They had been saying to one another, "Who will roll away the stone for us from the entrance to the tomb?" When they looked up, they saw that the stone, which was very large, had already been rolled back. As they entered the tomb, they saw a youth, dressed in a white robe, sitting on the right side; and they were alarmed. But the youth said to them, "Do not be alarmed; you are looking for Jesus of Nazareth, who was crucified. He has been raised; he is not here. Look, there is the place they laid him. But go, tell his disciples and Peter that he is going ahead of you to Galilee; there you will see him, just as he told you." So they went out and fled from the tomb, for terror and amazement had seized them; and they said nothing to anyone, for they were afraid.

Mark 16:1 – 8

Further readings for the Easter Vigil appear on pages 52 – 70, Easter Vigil, Year A.

EASTER SUNDAY

JESUS APPEARS TO MARY MAGDALENE
Mary Magdalene, the first witness of the empty tomb, runs to report the news. She is unable to fully communicate what has happened: It is a novel and earth-shattering event. Her sorrow is soon transformed to joy. The risen Christ commissions the faithful disciple Mary Magdalene as "apostle to the apostles."

Early on the first day of the week, while it was still dark, Mary Magdalene came to the tomb and saw that the stone had been removed from the tomb. So she ran and went to Simon Peter and the other disciple, the one whom Jesus loved, and said to them, "They have taken the Lord out of the tomb, and we do not know where they have laid him." Then Peter and the other disciple set out and went toward the tomb. The two were running together, but the other disciple outran Peter and reached the tomb first. He bent down to look in and saw the linen wrappings lying there, but he did not go in. Then Simon Peter came, following him, and went into the tomb. He saw the linen wrappings lying there, and the cloth that had been on Jesus' head, not lying with the linen wrappings but rolled up in a place by itself. Then the other disciple, who reached the tomb first, also went in, and he saw and believed; for as yet they did not understand the scripture, that he must rise from the dead. Then the disciples returned to their homes.

But Mary stood weeping outside the tomb. As she wept, she bent over to look into the tomb; and she saw two angels in white, sitting where the body of Jesus had been lying, one at the head and the other at the feet. They said to her, "Woman, why are you weeping?" She said to them, "They have taken away my Lord, and I do not know where they have laid him."

When she had said this, she turned around and saw Jesus standing there, but she did not know that it was Jesus. Jesus said to her, "Woman, why are you weeping? Whom are you looking for?" Supposing him to be the gardener, she said to him, "Sir, if you have carried him away, tell me where you have laid him, and I will take him away." Jesus said, "Mary!" She turned and said to him in Hebrew, "Rabbouni!" (which means Teacher). Jesus said to her, "Do not hold on to me, because I have not yet ascended to the Father. But go to my brothers and say to them, 'I am ascending to my Father and your Father, to my God and your God.'" Mary Magdalene went and announced to the disciples, "I have seen the Lord"; and she told them that Jesus had said these things to her.

John 20:1–18.

SECOND SUNDAY OF EASTER

JESUS APPEARS TO THE WOMEN

The lectionaries tell about Jesus appearing to his male disciples after the resurrection. This passage tells about the women disciples at the empty tomb. Ending the passage with a reference to the women's fear is a literary device that invites readers to witness to Jesus in their own time and place.

When the sabbath was over, Mary Magdalene, and Mary the mother of James, and Salome bought spices, so that they might go and anoint Jesus. And very early on the first day of the week, when the sun had risen, they went to the tomb. They had been saying to one another, "Who will roll away the stone for us from the entrance to the tomb?" When they looked up, they saw that the stone, which was very large, had already been rolled back. As they entered the tomb, they saw a youth, dressed in a white robe, sitting on the right side; and they were alarmed. But the youth said to them, "Do not be alarmed; you are looking for Jesus of Nazareth, who was crucified. He has been raised; he is not here. Look, there is the place they laid him. But go, tell his disciples and Peter that he is going ahead of you to Galilee; there you will see him, just as he told you." So they went out and fled from the tomb, for terror and amazement had seized them; and they said nothing to anyone, for they were afraid.

Mark 16:1 – 8

Song of Songs

THIRD SUNDAY OF EASTER

JESUS APPEARS TO MARY MAGDALENE

Women's experiences of God have often been discounted. Jesus scolds the eleven disciples for not believing the witness of the women.

Now after Jesus rose early on the first day of the week, he appeared first to Mary Magdalene, from whom he had cast out seven demons. She went out and told those who had been with him, while they were mourning and weeping. But when they heard that Jesus was alive and had been seen by her, they would not believe it.

After this Jesus appeared in another form to two of them, as they were walking into the country. And they went back and told the rest, but they did not believe them.

Later Jesus appeared to the eleven themselves as they were sitting at the table; and he upbraided them for their lack of faith and stubbornness, because they had not believed those who saw him after he had risen.

Mark 16:9 – 14

FOURTH SUNDAY OF EASTER

For the remainder of the Easter season, the lectionaries tell stories of the early church from the Acts of the Apostles. Stories of women in the life of the early church are offered here.

WOMEN BELIEVERS IN GREECE

When Paul and his co-workers travel to Greece, women are among those who join them. Many of these women believers are of high social standing. However, with the exception of Damaris, they are not named. Do we often think of the early church as being made up only of men?

After Paul and Silas had passed through Amphipolis and Apollonia, they came to Thessalonica, where there was a synagogue of the Jews. And Paul went in, as was his custom, and on three sabbath days argued with them from the scriptures, explaining and proving that it was necessary for the Christ to suffer and to rise from the dead, and saying, "This is the Christ, Jesus whom I am proclaiming to you." Some of them were persuaded and joined Paul and Silas, as did a great many of the devout Greeks and not a few of the leading women.

The believers sent Paul and Silas off to Beroea; and when they arrived, they went to the Jewish synagogue. These Jews were more receptive than those in Thessalonica, for they welcomed the message very eagerly and examined the scriptures every day to see whether these things were so. Many of them therefore believed, including not a few Greek women and men of high standing.

The believers immediately sent Paul away to the coast, but Silas and Timothy remained behind. Those who conducted Paul brought him as far as Athens; and after receiving instructions to have Silas and Timothy join him as soon as possible, they left him.

Paul stood in front of the Areopagus and said, "Athenians, I see how extremely religious you are in every way. While God has overlooked the times of human ignorance, now God commands all people everywhere to repent, because a day has been fixed on which God will have the world judged in righteousness by one whom God has appointed, and of this God has given assurance to all by raising him from the dead."

When they heard of the resurrection of the dead, some scoffed; but others said, "We will hear you again about this." At that point Paul left them. But some of them joined Paul and became believers, including Dionysius the Areopagite and a woman named Damaris, and others with them.

Acts of the Apostles 17:1 – 4, 10 – 12, 15, 22, 30 – 34

FIFTH SUNDAY OF EASTER

PRISCILLA AND AQUILA

Priscilla and Aquila are always named as a pair, genuine partners in ministry. They minister as teachers and missionaries in several cities.

Paul left Athens and went to Corinth. There he found a Jew named Aquila, a native of Pontus, who had recently come from Italy with his wife Priscilla, because Claudius had ordered all Jews to leave Rome. Paul went to see them, and, because he was of the same trade, he stayed with them, and they worked together — by trade they were tentmakers.

After saying in Corinth for a considerable time, Paul said farewell to the believers and sailed for Syria, accompanied by Priscilla and Aquila. At Cenchreae he had his hair cut, for he was under a vow. When they reached Ephesus, Paul left them there, but first he himself went into the synagogue and had a discussion with the Jews.

Now there came to Ephesus a Jew named Apollos, a native of Alexandria. He was an eloquent man, well-versed in the scriptures. He had been instructed in the Way of the Lord; and he spoke with burning enthusiasm and taught accurately the things concerning Jesus, though he knew only the baptism of John. Apollos began to speak boldly in the synagogue; but when Priscilla and Aquila heard him they took him aside and explained the Way of God to him more accurately.

Acts of the Apostles 18:1 – 3, 18 – 19, 24 – 26

SIXTH SUNDAY OF EASTER

PHOEBE AND PRISCA

Paul commends to the Romans the bearer of his letter, a woman named Phoebe, deacon and benefactor. As deacon, she exercised leadership in the church. As benefactor, she gave of her wealth and influence.

I commend to you our sister Phoebe, a deacon of the church at Cenchreae, so that you may welcome her in the Lord as is fitting for the saints, and help her in whatever she may require from you, for she has been a benefactor of many and of myself as well.

Greet Prisca and Aquila, who work with me in Christ Jesus, and who risked their necks for my life, to whom not only I give thanks, but also all the churches of the Gentiles. Greet also the church in their house. Greet my beloved Epaenetus, who was the first convert in Asia for Christ.

Romans 16:1 – 5

THE ASCENSION OF CHRIST

IN PRAISE OF WISDOM

Christ at his ascension can be interpreted in relation to the feminine figure of holy Wisdom. Her spirit filled Jesus at his baptism and will be poured out on the church at Pentecost.

I learned both what is secret and what is manifest,
for wisdom, the fashioner of all things, taught me.
There is in her a spirit that is intelligent, holy,
unique, manifold, subtle,
mobile, clear, unpolluted,
distinct, invulnerable, loving the good, keen,
irresistible, beneficent, humane,
steadfast, sure, free from anxiety,
all-powerful, overseeing all,
and penetrating through all spirits
that are intelligent, pure, and altogether subtle.
For wisdom is more mobile than any motion;
because of her pureness she pervades and penetrates all things.
For she is a breath of the power of God,
and a pure emanation of the glory of the Almighty;
therefore nothing defiled gains entrance into her.
For she is a reflection of eternal light,
a spotless mirror of the working of God
and an image of God's goodness.
Although she is but one, but can do all things,
and while remaining in herself, she renews all things;
in every generation she passes into holy souls
and makes them friends of God, and prophets;
for God loves nothing so much as the person who lives with wisdom.

Wisdom of Solomon 7:21 – 28

SEVENTH SUNDAY OF EASTER

When the Ascension is celebrated on the Seventh Sunday of Easter, the two sets of readings may be combined.

MARY, JUNIA, TRYPHAENA AND TRYPHOSA

Paul sends greetings to his partners in ministry in Rome, including a number of women: Prisca, Mary, Tryphaena, Tryphosa and Persis, and one who is called apostle, Junia.

Greet Mary, who has worked very hard among you. Greet Andronicus and Junia, my relatives who were in prison with me; they are prominent among the apostles, and they were in Christ before I was. Greet Ampliatus, my beloved in the Lord. Greet Urbanus, our co-worker in Christ, and my beloved Stachys. Greet Apelles, who is approved in Christ. Greet those who belong to the family of Aristobolus. Greet my relative Herodion. Greet those in the Lord who belong to the family of Narcissus.

Greet those workers in the Lord, Tryphaena and Tryphosa. Greet the beloved Persis, who has worked hard in the Lord. Greet Rufus, chosen in the Lord; and greet his mother — a mother to me also.

Romans 16:6 – 13

PENTECOST

DAUGHTERS AND MAIDSERVANTS SHALL PROPHESY
When the Holy Spirit descends on the church at Pentecost, women and men are empowered to prophesy, as had been foretold.

When the day of Pentecost had come, the twelve were all together in one place. And suddenly from heaven there came a sound like the rush of a violent wind, and it filled the entire house where they were sitting. Divided tongues, as of fire, appeared among them, and tongues rested on each of them. All of them were filled with the Holy Spirit and began to speak in other languages, as the Spirit gave them ability.

Peter, standing with the eleven, raised his voice and addressed the crowd, "O you Jewish people and all who live in Jerusalem, let this be known to you, and listen to what I say. Indeed, these are not drunk, as you suppose, for it is only nine o'clock in the morning. No, this is what was spoken through the prophet Joel:
'In the last days it will be, God declares,
that I will pour out my Spirit upon all flesh,
    and your sons and your daughters shall prophesy,
and your youth shall see visions,
    and your elders shall dream dreams.
Even upon my menservants and maidservants,
    in those days I will pour out my Spirit;
    and they shall prophesy.'"

Acts of the Apostles 2:1 – 4, 14 – 18

DAUGHTERS AND MAIDSERVANTS SHALL PROPHESY
In the reading included above, Peter quotes this passage from the book of the prophet Joel.

You shall eat in plenty and be satisfied,
    and praise the name of the LORD your God,
    who has dealt wondrously with you.
And my people shall never again be put to shame.
You shall know that I am in the midst of Israel,
    and that I, the LORD, am your God and there is no other.
And my people shall never again
    be put to shame.

Then afterward
    I will pour out my spirit on all flesh;
your sons and your daughters shall prophesy,
    your elders shall dream dreams,
    and your youth shall see visions.

Even on the menservants and maidservants
      in those days, I will pour out my spirit.

Joel 2:26–29

THE PROPHET DEBORAH
The first reading of the lectionary proclaims that daughters shall prophesy. This passage speaks of Deborah,
a prophet in Israel.

"Hear, O kings; give ear, O princes;
      to the LORD I will sing,
      I will make melody to the LORD, the God of Israel.

"Lord, when you sent out from Seir,
      when you marched from the region of Edom
the earth trembled,
      and the heavens poured,
      the clouds indeed poured water.
The mountains quaked before the LORD, the One of Sinai,
      before the Lord, the God of Israel.
In the days of Shamgar son of Anath,
      in the days of Jael, caravans ceased
      and travelers kept to the byways.
The peasantry prospered in Israel,
      they grew fat on plunder,
because you arose, Deborah,
      arose as a mother in Israel.
When new gods were chosen
      then war was in the gates.
Was shield or spear to be seen
      among forty thousand in Israel?
My heart goes out to the commanders of Israel
      who offered themselves willing among the people.
      Bless the Lord.

"Tell of it, you who ride on white donkeys,
      you who sit on rich carpets
      and you who walk by the way.
To the sound of musicans at the watering places,
      there they repeat the triumphs of the Lord,
      the triumphs of his peasantry in Israel.

"Then down to the gates marched the people of the Lord.

"Awake, awake, Deborah!
      Awake, awake, utter a song!

Arise, Barak, lead away your captives,
    O son of Abinoam."

Judges 5:3–12

THE SERVANT GIRL CHALLENGES PETER
This passage tells of a woman who spoke the truth to Peter.

While Peter was below in the courtyard, one of the servant girls of the high priest came by. When she saw Peter warming himself, she stared at him and said, "You also were with Jesus, the man from Nazareth." But he denied it, saying, "I do not know or understand what you are talking about." And he went out into the fore-court. Then the cock crowed.

And the servant-girl, on seeing him, began again to say to the bystanders, "This man is one of them." But again he denied it. Then after a little while the bystanders again said to Peter, "Certainly you are one of them; for you are a Galilean." But he began to curse, and he swore an oath, "I do not know this man you are talking about."

At that moment the cock crowed for the second time. Then Peter remembered that Jesus had said to him, "Before the cock crows twice, you will deny me three times." And he broke down and wept.

Mark 14:66–72

TRINITY SUNDAY

FIRST SUNDAY AFTER PENTECOST

GOD AS MOTHER
This passage considers God as a mother who gives birth and cares for her young and feeds them.

The Most High sustained you in a desert land,
      in a howling wilderness waste;
God shielded you, cared for you,
      guarded you as the apple of his eye.
As an eagle stirs up its nest,
      and hovers over its young;
as it speads its wings, takes them up,
      and bears them aloft on its pinions,
the LORD alone guided you;
      no sovereign God was with you.
The Most High set you atop the heights of the land,
      and fed you with produce of the field;
God nursed you with honey from the crags,
      with oil from flinty rock;
curds from the herd, and milk from the flock,
      with fat of lambs and rams;
Bashan bulls and goats,
      together with the choicest wheat —
      you drank fine wine from the blood of grapes.
Jacob ate its fill;
      Jerusalem grew fat, and kicked.
      You grew fat, bloated, and gorged!
You abandoned God who made you,
      and scoffed at the Rock of your salvation.
They made God jealous with strange gods,
      with abhorrent things they provoked him.
They sacrificed to demons, not God,
      to deities they have never known,
to new ones recently arrived,
      whom your ancestors had not feared.
You were unmindful of the Rock that bore you;
      you forget the God who gave your birth.

Deuteronomy 32:10 – 18

PRISCA AND CLAUDIA

The letters of the Christian scriptures often conclude with names of members of the church and a doxology or blessing. In this passage Prisca is named; all the sisters send greetings.

Greet Prisca and Aquila, and the household of Onesiphorus. Erastus remained in Corinth; Trophimus I left ill in Miletus. Do your best to come before winter. Eubulus sends greetings to you, as do Pudens and Linus and Claudia and all the brothers and sisters.

The Lord be with your spirit. Grace be with you.

2 Timothy 4:19–22

NINTH SUNDAY IN ORDINARY TIME

SECOND SUNDAY AFTER PENTECOST
PROPER 4: SUNDAY BETWEEN 29 MAY AND 4 JUNE

SABBATH REST FOR ALL

Sabbath rest is for all, including daughters and female slaves.

Observe the sabbath day and keep it holy, as the LORD your God commanded you. Six days you shall labor and do all your work. But the seventh day is a sabbath to the LORD your God; you shall not do any work — you, or your son or your daughter, or your male or female slave, or your ox or your donkey, or any of your livestock, or the resident alien in your towns, so that your male and female slave may rest as well as you. Remember that you were a slave in the land of Egypt, and the LORD your God brought you out from there with a mighty hand and an outstreched arm; therefore the LORD your God commanded you to keep the sabbath day.

Deuteronomy 5:12 – 15

Joseph and Mary

TENTH SUNDAY IN ORDINARY TIME

THIRD SUNDAY AFTER PENTECOST
PROPER 5: SUNDAY BETWEEN 5 AND 11 JUNE

THE WOMAN AND THE MAN IN THE GARDEN

The man blames the woman, and she blames the serpent; in fact they share the responsibility. With the eating come sorrow and fear, but also culture and social life, including—for good and for ill—gender roles. The woman will be the bearer of children, the mother of the living.

The LORD God called to the man, and said to him, "Where are you?" He said, "I heard the sound of you in the garden, and I was afraid, because I was naked; and I hid myself." God said, "Who told you that you were naked? Have you eaten from the tree of which I commanded you not to eat?" The man said, "The woman whom you gave to be with me, she gave me fruit from the tree, and I ate." Then the LORD God said to the woman, "What is this that you have done?" The woman said, "The serpent tricked me, and I ate." The LORD God said to the serpent,

> Because you have done this,
> > cursed are you among all animals
> > and among all wild creatures;
> upon your belly you shall go,
> > and dust you shall eat
> > all the days of your life.
> I will put enmity between you and the woman,
> > and between your offspring and hers;
> he will strike your head,
> > and you will strike his heel."

Genesis 3:9–15

JESUS' MOTHER AND SISTERS

Jesus' biological family finds it difficult to appreciate his ministry and his new identity. He establishes new relationships where all who do God's will are mothers and sisters to him and to one another.

The crowd came together again, so that Jesus and the disciples could not even eat. When his family heard it, they went out to restrain him, for people were saying, "He has gone out of his mind." And the scribes who came down from Jerusalem said, "He has Beelzebul, and by the ruler of the demons he casts out demons." And Jesus called them to him, and spoke to them in parables, "How can Satan cast out Satan? If a dominion is divided against itself, that dominion cannot stand. And if a house is divided against itself, that house will not be able to stand. And if Satan has risen up against himself and is divided, he cannot stand, but his end has come. But no one can enter a strong man's house and plunder his property without first tying up the strong man; then indeed the house can be plundered.

"Truly I tell you, people will be forgiven for their sins and whatever blasphemies they utter; but whoever blasphemes against the Holy Spirit can never have forgiveness, but is guilty of an eternal sin" — for they had said, "He has an unclean spirit."

Then the mother and the brothers of Jesus came; and standing outside, they sent to him and called him. A crowd was sitting around him; and they said to Jesus, "Your mother and your brothers and sisters are outside, asking for you." And Jesus replied, "Who are my mother and my brothers?" And looking at those who sat around him, Jesus said, "Here are my mother and my brothers! Whoever does the will of God is my brother and sister and mother."

Mark 3:20 – 35

ELEVENTH SUNDAY IN ORDINARY TIME

FOURTH SUNDAY AFTER PENTECOST
PROPER 6: SUNDAY BETWEEN 12 AND 18 JUNE

THE WIDOW'S OIL

Selling a child is a drastic remedy for debt. Elisha intervenes and the woman is empowered to provide for herself and her children.

The wife of a member of the company of prophets cried to Elisha, "Your servant my husband is dead; and you know that your servant feared the Lord, but a creditor has come to take my two children as slaves." Elisha said to her, "What shall I do for you? Tell me, what do you have in the house?" She answered, "Your servant has nothing in the house, except a jar of oil." He said, "Go outside, borrow vessels from all your neighbors, empty vessels and not just a few. Then go in, and shut the door behind you and your children, and start pouring into all these vessels; when each is full, set it aside." So she left him and shut the door behind her and her children; they kept bringing vessels to her, and she kept pouring. When the vessels were full, she said to her son, "Bring me another vessel." But he said to her, "There are no more." Then the oil stopped flowing. She came and told the man of God, and he said, "Go sell the oil and pay your debts, and you and your children can live on the rest."

2 Kings 4:1 – 7

TWELFTH SUNDAY IN ORDINARY TIME

FIFTH SUNDAY AFTER PENTECOST
PROPER 7: SUNDAY BETWEEN 19 AND 25 JUNE

THE WOMAN OF SHUMEN AND HER SON
The woman believes that the prophet can restore her child to life. Her determination brings Elisha to the child's assistance.

When the child of the Shunammite was older, he went out one day to his father among the reapers. He complained to his father, "Oh, my head, my head!" The father said to his servant, "Carry him to his mother." He carried him and brought him to his mother; the child sat on her lap until noon, and he died.

She went up and laid him on the bed of Elisha, the man of God, closed the door on him, and left. Then she called to her husband, and said, "Send me one of the servants and one of the donkeys, so that I may quickly go to the man of God and come back again." He said, "Why go to him today? It is neither new moon nor sabbath." She said, "It will be all right." Then she saddled the donkey and said to her servant, "Urge the animal on; do not hold back for me unless I tell you." So she set out, and came to the man of God at Mount Carmel.

When the man of God saw her coming, he said to Gehazi his servant, "Look, there is the Shunammite woman; run at once to meet her, and say to her, 'Are you all right? Is your husband all right? Is the child all right?'" She answered, "It is all right." When she came to the man of God at the mountain, she caught hold of his feet. Gehazi approached to push her away. But the man of God said, "Let her alone, for she is in bitter distress; the LORD has hidden it from me and has not told me."

Then she said, "Did I ask my lord for a son? Did I not say, 'Do not mislead me?'" He said to Gehazi, "Gird up your loins, and take my staff in your hand, and go. If you meet anyone, give no greeting, and if anyone greets you, do not answer; and lay my staff on the face of the child." Then the mother of the child said, "As the LORD lives, and as you yourself live, I will not leave without you." So he rose up and followed her. Gehazi went on ahead and laid the staff on the face of the child, but there was no sound or sign of life. He came back to meet Elisha and told him, "The child has not awakened."

When Elisha came into the house, he saw the child lying dead on his bed. So he went in and closed the door on the two of them, and prayed to the LORD. Then he got up on the bed and lay upon the child, putting his mouth upon his mouth, his eyes upon his eyes, and his hands upon his hands; and while he lay bent over him, the flesh of the child became warm. He got down, walked once to and fro in the room, and got up again and bent over him; the child sneezed seven times, and the child opened his eyes. Elisha summoned Gehazi and said, "Call the Shunammite woman." So he called her. When she came to him, he said, "Take your son." She came and fell at his feet, bowing to the ground; then she took her son and left.

2 Kings 4:18–37

THIRTEENTH SUNDAY IN ORDINARY TIME

SIXTH SUNDAY AFTER PENTECOST
PROPER 8: SUNDAY BETWEEN 26 JUNE AND 2 JULY

THE DAUGHTER OF JAIRUS AND THE WOMAN WITH A HEMORRHAGE
The story of the young girl who dies is joined to the story of the woman with a hemorrhage. In both cases,
confidence in Jesus leads to healing: The girl's father confidently seeks help from Jesus, and the woman takes
initiative on her own behalf. Jesus praises her faith.

When Jesus had crossed again in the boat to the other side, a great crowd gathered around him; and he was by the sea. Then one of the leaders of the synagogue named Jairus came and, when he saw Jesus, fell at his feet and begged him repeatedly, "My little daughter is at the point of death. Come and lay your hands on her, so that she may be made well, and live." So Jesus went with him.

And a large crowd followed Jesus and pressed in on him. Now there was a woman who had been suffering from hemorrhages for twelve years. She had endured much under many physicians, and had spent all that she had; and she was no better, but rather grew worse. She had heard about Jesus, and came up behind him in the crowd and touched his cloak, for she said, "If I but touch his clothes, I will be made well." Immediately her hemorrhage stopped; and she felt in her body that she was healed of her disease.

Immediately aware that power had gone forth from him, Jesus turned about in the crowd and said, "Who touched my clothes?" And his disciples said to him, "You see the crowd pressing in on you; how can you say, 'Who touched me?'" Jesus looked all around to see who had done it. But the woman, knowing what had happened to her, came in fear and trembling, fell down before him, and told him the whole truth. Jesus said to her, "Daughter, your faith has made you well; go in peace, and be healed of your disease."

While Jesus was still speaking, some people came from the leader's house to say, "Your daughter is dead. Why trouble the teacher any further?" But overhearing what they said, Jesus said to the leader of the synagogue, "Do not fear, only believe." Jesus allowed no one to follow him except Peter, James, and John, the brother of James. When they came to the house of the leader of the synagogue, Jesus saw a commotion, people weeping and wailing loudly. When he had entered, he said to them, "Why do you make a commotion and weep? The child is not dead but sleeping." And they laughed at him. Then Jesus put them all outside, and took the child's father and mother and those who were with him, and went in where the child was.

Jesus took her by the hand and said to her, "Talitha cum," which means, "Little girl, get up!" And immediately the girl got up and began to walk about (she was twelve years of age). At this they were overcome with amazement. Jesus strictly ordered them that no one should know this, and told them to give her something to eat.

Mark 5:21–43

FOURTEENTH SUNDAY IN ORDINARY TIME

SEVENTH SUNDAY AFTER PENTECOST
PROPER 9: SUNDAY BETWEEN 3 AND 9 JULY

MARY AND JESUS' SISTERS AND BROTHERS
How did Mary and Jesus' sisters feel at these words?

Jesus came to his hometown, and his disciples followed him. On the sabbath he began to teach in the synagogue, and many who heard him were astounded. They said, "Where did this man get all this? What is this wisdom that has been given to him? What deeds of power are being done by his hands! Is not this the carpenter, the son of Mary and brother of James and Joses and Judas and Simon, and are not his sisters here with us?" And they took offense at him. Then Jesus said to them, "Prophets are not without honor, except in their hometown, and among their own kin, and in their own house." And Jesus could not do deeds of power there, except that he laid his hands on a few sick people and cured them. And he was amazed at their unbelief.

Mark 6:1 – 6

FIFTEENTH SUNDAY IN ORDINARY TIME

EIGHTH SUNDAY AFTER PENTECOST
PROPER 10: SUNDAY BETWEEN 10 AND 16 JULY

HERODIAS AND HER DAUGHTER

How did the daughter of Herodias feel about being made a tool in her mother's plot and an accessory to John's murder? Notice how Herodias has the stomach to kill a prophet when her husband does not. Or is the author trying to get Herod off the hook for murdering John?

King Herod had heard of Jesus' name. Some were saying, "John the baptizer has been raised from the dead; and for this reason these powers are at work in him." But others said, "It is Elijah." And others said, "It is a prophet, like one of the prophets of old." But when Herod heard of it, he said, "John, whom I beheaded, has been raised."

For Herod himself had sent men who arrested John, bound him, and put him in prison on account of Herodias, his brother Philip's wife, because Herod had married her. For John had been telling Herod, "It is not lawful for you to have your brother's wife." And Herodias had a grudge against him, and wanted to kill him. But she could not, for Herod feared John, knowing that he was a righteous and holy man, and he protected him. When Herod heard John, he was greatly perplexed; and yet he liked to listen to him.

But an opportunity came when Herod on his birthday gave a banquet for his courtiers and officers and for the leaders of Galilee. When the daughter of Herodias came in and danced, she pleased Herod and his guests; and the king said to the girl, "Ask me for whatever you wish, and I will give it." And he solemnly swore to her, "Whatever you ask me, I will give you, even half of my dominion." She went out and said to her mother, "What should I ask for?" Herodias replied, "The head of John the baptizer." Immediately she rushed back to the king and requested, "I want you to give me at once the head of John the Baptist on a platter."

The king was deeply grieved; yet out of regard for his oaths and for the guests, he did not want to refuse her. Immediately the king sent a soldier of the guard with orders to bring John's head. He went and beheaded John in the prison, brought his head on a platter, and gave it to the girl. Then the girl gave it to her mother. When his disciples heard about it, they came and took John's body, and laid it in a tomb.

Mark 6:14–29

SIXTEENTH SUNDAY IN ORDINARY TIME

NINTH SUNDAY AFTER PENTECOST
PROPER 11: SUNDAY BETWEEN 17 AND 23 JULY

THE LOVER
A woman in love seeks her lover.

Upon my bed at night
> I sought the one whom my soul loves;
I sought, but did not find;
> I called, but there was no response.
"I will rise now and go about the city,
> in the streets and in the squares;
I will seek the one whom my soul loves."
> I sought, but did not find my love.
The sentinels found me,
> as they went about in the city.
"Have you seen the one whom my soul loves?"
Scarcely had I passed them,
> when I found the one whom my soul loves.
I held, and would not let go
> until I brought my beloved into my mother's house,
> and into the chamber of her that conceived me.

Song of Solomon 3:1 – 4

SEVENTEENTH SUNDAY IN ORDINARY TIME

TENTH SUNDAY AFTER PENTECOST
PROPER 12: SUNDAY BETWEEN 24 AND 30 JULY

DAVID MEETS BATHSHEBA AND PLOTS THE DEATH OF HER HUSBAND
What an abuse of power! David forces Bathsheba to commit adultery with him and then plots to kill her husband Uriah, the loyal soldier.

In the spring of the year, the time when kings go out to battle, David sent Joab with his officers and all Israel with him; they ravaged the Ammonites, and beseiged Rabbah. But David remained at Jerusalem.

It happened, late one afternoon, when David rose from his couch and was walking about on the roof of the king's house, that he saw from the roof a woman bathing; the woman was very beautiful. David sent someone to inquire about the woman. It was reported, "This is Bathsheba daughter of Eliam, the wife of Uriah the Hittite." So David sent messengers to get her, and she came to him, and he lay with her. (Now she was purifying herself after her period.) Then she returned to her house. The woman conceived; and she sent and told David, "I am pregnant."

So David sent word to Joab, "Send me Uriah the Hittite." And Joab sent Uriah to David. When Uriah came to him, David asked how Joab and the people fared, and how the war was going. Then David said to Uriah, "Go down to your house, and wash your feet." Uriah went out of the king's house, and there followed him a present from the king. But Uriah slept at the entrance of the king's house with all the servants of his lord, and did not go down to his house.

When they told David, "Uriah did not go down to his house," David said to Uriah, "You have just come from a journey. Why did you not go down to your house?" Uriah said to David, "The ark and Israel and Judah remain in booths; and my lord Joab and the servants of my lord are camping in the open field; shall I then go to my house, to eat and to drink, and to lie with my wife? As you live, and as your soul lives, I will not do such a thing."

Then David said to Uriah, "Remain here today also, and tomorrow I will send you back." So Uriah remained in Jerusalem that day. On the next day, David invited him to eat and drink in his presence and made him drunk; and in the evening he went out to lie on his couch with the servants of his lord, but he did not go down to his house.

In the morning David wrote a letter to Joab, and sent it by the hand of Uriah. In the letter he wrote, "Set Uriah in the forefront of the hardest fighting, and then draw back from him, so that he may be struck down and die."

2 Samuel 11:1–15

The gospel readings of the lectionaries for today and the next three Sundays are from the Gospel of John, interrupting the reading of the Gospel of Mark. The book of Ruth is a likely inspiration for John's story of the multiplication of loaves and fishes and the Bread of Life discourse.

RUTH GOES INTO THE FIELDS
Ruth benefits from the Mosaic law that grain should be left along the edges of fields after the harvest for widows such as herself.

Naomi had a kinsman on her husband's side, a prominent rich man, of the family of Elimelech, whose name was Boaz. And Ruth the Moabite said to Naomi, "Let me go to the field and glean among the ears of grain, behind someone in whose sight I may find favor." Naomi said to Ruth, "Go, my daughter." So Ruth went. She came and gleaned in the field behind the reapers. As it happened, she came to the part of the field belonging to Boaz, who was of the family of Elimelech. Just then Boaz came from Bethelehm. He said to the reapers, "The LORD be with you." They answered, "The LORD bless you." Then Boaz said to his servant who was in charge of the reapers, "To whom does this young woman belong?" The servant who was charge of the reapers answered, "She is the Moabite who came back with Naomi from the country of Moab. She said, 'Please, let me glean and gather among the sheaves behind the reapers.' So she came, and she has been on her feet from early this morning until now, without resting even for a moment."

Ruth 2:1–7

EIGHTEENTH SUNDAY IN ORDINARY TIME

ELEVENTH SUNDAY AFTER PENTECOST
PROPER 13: SUNDAY BETWEEN 31 JULY AND 6 AUGUST

BATHSHEBA MARRIES DAVID, AND DAVID REPENTS
After Bathsheba mourns Uriah's death she becomes David's wife. Nathan's prodding evokes David's brief confession. But it is Bathsheba's child who suffers.

When the wife of Uriah heard that her husband was dead, she made lamentation for him. When the mourning was over David sent and brought her to his house, and she became his wife, and bore him a son.

But the thing that David had done displeased the LORD, and the LORD sent Nathan to David. He came to him, and said to him, "There were two men in a certain city, the one rich and the other poor. The rich man had very many flocks and herds; but the poor man had nothing but one little ewe lamb, which he had bought. He brought it up, and it grew up with him and with his children; it used to eat of his meager fare, and drink from his cup, and lie in his bosom, and it was like a daughter to him.

"Now there came a traveler to the rich man, and the rich man was loath to take one of his own flock or herd to prepare for the wayfarer who had come to him, but he took the poor man's lamb, and prepared that for the guest who had come to him." Then David's anger was greatly kindled against the man. He said to Nathan, "As the LORD lives, the man who has done this deserves to die; he shall restore the lamb fourfold, because he did this thing, and because he had no pity."

Nathan said to David, "You are the man! Thus says the LORD, the God of Israel: I anointed you king over Israel, and I rescued you from the hand of Saul; I gave you your master's house, and your master's wives into your bosom, and gave you the house of Israel and of Judah; and if that had been too little, I would have added as much more. Why have you despised the word of the LORD, to do what is evil in God's sight? You have struck down Uriah the Hittite with the sword, and have taken his wife to be your wife, and have killed him with the sword of the Ammonites.

"Now therefore the sword shall never depart from your house, for you have despised me, and have taken the wife of Uriah the Hittite to be your wife. Thus says the LORD: I will raise up trouble against you from within your own house; and I will take your wives before your eyes, and give them to your neighbor, and he shall lie with your wives in the sight of this very sun. For you did it secretly; but I will do this thing before all Israel, and before the sun."

David said to Nathan, "I have sinned against the LORD." Nathan said to David, "Now the LORD has put away your sin; you shall not die. Nevertheless, because by this deed you have utterly scorned the LORD, the child that is born to you shall die." Then Nathan went to his house.

2 Samuel 11:26 — 12:15a

Boaz said to Ruth, "Now listen, my daughter, do not go to glean in another field or leave this one, but keep close to my young women. Keep your eyes on the field that is being reaped, and follow behind them. I have ordered the young men not to bother you. If you get thirsty, go to the vessels and drink from what the young men have drawn." Then Ruth fell prostrate, with her face to the ground, and said to him, "Why have I found favor in your sight, that you should take notice of me, when I am a foreigner?" But Boaz answered her, "All that you have done for your mother-in-law since the death of your husband has been fully told me, and how you left your father and mother and your native land and came to a people that you did not know before. May the LORD reward you for your deeds, and may you have a full reward from the LORD, the God of Israel, under whose wings you have come for refuge!" Then Ruth said, "May I continue to find favor in your sight, my lord, for you have comforted me and spoken kindly to your servant, even though I am not one of your servants."

Ruth 2:8 – 13

NINETEENTH SUNDAY IN ORDINARY TIME

TWELFTH SUNDAY AFTER PENTECOST
PROPER 14: SUNDAY BETWEEN 7 AND 13 AUGUST

BATHSHEBA BEARS SOLOMON
Bathsheba's child sickened and died as God's punishment of David. Later, however, she bore Solomon.

The LORD struck the child that Uriah's wife bore to David, and it became very ill. David therefore pleaded with God for the child; David fasted, and went in and lay all night on the ground. The elders of his house stood beside him, urging him to rise from the ground; but he would not, nor did he eat food with them. On the seventh day the child died. And the servants of David were afraid to tell him that the child was dead; for they said, "While the child was still alive, we spoke to him, and he did not listen to us; how then can we tell him the child is dead? He may do himself some harm." But when David saw that his servants were whispering together, he perceived that the child was dead; and David said to his servants, "Is the child dead?" They said, "He is dead."

Then David consoled his wife Bathsheba, and went to her, and lay with her; and she bore a son; and he named him Solomon. The LORD loved him, and sent a message by the prophet Nathan; so he named him Jedidiah [Beloved of the LORD], because of the LORD.

2 Samuel 12:15b – 19, 24 – 25

RUTH EATS OF THE BREAD
More than enough food, satisfaction and some left over: This is the abundance of messianic times. This image is important in the gospel story of the multiplication of loaves. Here the abundance arranged by Boaz is more than enough for Ruth; the leftovers are enough for Naomi.

At mealtime Boaz said to Ruth, "Come here, and eat some of this bread, and dip your morsel in the sour wine." So she sat beside the reapers, and he heaped up for her some parched grain. She ate until she was satisfied, and she had some left over.

When she got up to glean, Boaz instructed his young men, "Let her glean even among the standing sheaves, and do not reproach her. You must also pull out some handfuls for her from the bundles, and leave them for her to glean, and do not rebuke her."

So she gleaned in the field until evening. Then she beat out what she had gleaned, and it was about an ephah of barley. She picked it up and came into the town, and her mother-in-law saw how much she had gleaned. Then Ruth took out and gave Naomi what was left over after she herself had been satisfied.

Ruth 2:14 – 18

TWENTIETH SUNDAY IN ORDINARY TIME

THIRTEENTH SUNDAY AFTER PENTECOST
PROPER 15: SUNDAY BETWEEN 14 AND 20 AUGUST

WISDOM AS BANQUET-GIVER

Wisdom is depicted as a woman who gives a great banquet and invites the simple-hearted and ignorant to the feast.

Wisdom has built her house
and carved its seven pillars.
She has butchered the meat,
spiced the wine, and set her table.
She has dispatched her servant women.

She calls from the town heights,
"Let the simple-hearted come."
She tells the unschooled:
"Come, taste my bread,
drink my spiced wine.
Give up your ignorance and live,
walk the straight path of insight."

Canticle of Proverbs 9:1 – 6 ICEL

RUTH GLEANED UNTIL THE HARVESTS WERE DONE

As a widow without father or brothers to protect her, Ruth might be assaulted if she goes to glean in the fields of strangers. Boaz, a relative and honorable man, protects her.

Ruth's mother-in-law said to her, "Where did you glean today? And where have you worked? Blessed be the man who took notice of you." So she told her mother-in-law with whom she had worked, and said, "The name of the man with whom I worked today is Boaz." Then Naomi said to her daughter-in-law, "Blessed be he by the LORD, whose kindness has not forsaken the living or the dead!" Naomi also said to her, "The man is a relative of ours, one of our nearest kin." Then Ruth the Moabite said, "He even said to me, 'Stay close by my servants, until they have finished all my harvest.'" Naomi said to Ruth, her daughther-in-law, "It is better, my daughter, that you go out with his young women, otherwise you might be bothered in another field." So she stayed close to the young women of Boaz, gleaning until the end of the barley and wheat harvests; and she lived with her mother-in-law.

Ruth 2:19 – 23

Nativity

TWENTY-FIRST SUNDAY IN ORDINARY TIME

FOURTEENTH SUNDAY AFTER PENTECOST
PROPER 16: SUNDAY BETWEEN 21 AND 27 AUGUST

BATHSHEBA SECURES THE THRONE FOR SOLOMON
With Nathan's help, Bathsheba intercedes with David to ensure that her son Solomon will succeed to the throne rather than one of David's sons by another wife.

Nathan said to Bathsheba, Solomon's mother, "Have you not heard that Adonijah son of Haggith has become king and our lord David does not know it? Now therefore come, let me give you advice, so that you may save your own life and the life of your son Solomon. Go in at once to King David, and say to him, 'Did you not, my lord the king, swear to your servant, saying: Your son Solomon shall succeed me as king, and he shall sit on my throne? Why then is Adonijah king?' Then while you are still there speaking with the king, I will come in after you and confirm your words."

King David swore, saying, "As the LORD lives, who has saved my life from every adversity, as I swore to you by the LORD, the God of Israel, 'Your son Solomon shall succeed me as king, and he shall sit on my throne in my place'; so will I do this day." Then Bathsheba bowed with her face to the ground, and did obeisance to the king, and said, "May my lord King David live forever!"

1 Kings 1:11–19, 29–31

WISDOM AND THE HOLY SPIRIT
The feminine figure of holy Wisdom is likened to a holy spirit sent from God.

With you, O God, is wisdom, she who knows your works
and was present when you made the world;
she understands what is pleasing in your sight
and what is right according to your commandments.

Send her forth from the holy heavens,
and from the throne of your glory send her,
that she may labor at my side,
and that I may learn what is pleasing to you.
For she knows and understands all things,
and she will guide me wisely in my actions
and guard me with her glory.
Then my works will be acceptable,
and I shall judge your people justly,
and shall be worthy of the throne of my ancestor.

For who can learn the counsel of God?
Or who can discern what the Lord wills?

For the reasoning of mortals is worthless,
and our designs are likely to fail;
for a perishable body weighs down the soul,
and this earthly tent burdens the thoughtful mind.
We can hardly guess at what is on earth,
and what is at hand we find with labor;
but who has traced out what is in the heavens?
Who has learned your counsel,
unless you have given wisdom
and sent your holy spirit from on high?
And thus the paths of those on earth were set right,
and people were taught what pleases you
and were saved by wisdom.

Wisdom of Solomon 9:9 – 18

TWENTY-SECOND SUNDAY IN ORDINARY TIME

FIFTEENTH SUNDAY AFTER PENTECOST
PROPER 17: SUNDAY BETWEEN 28 AUGUST AND 3 SEPTEMBER

THE TWO MOTHERS IN DISTRESS

One woman is in anguish because her child has died, apparently in a way that would inspire guilt. The other woman shows great compassion for her child. God shows anguish for the suffering and compassion toward all.

Two women who were prostitutes came to the king and stood before him. The one woman said, "Please, my lord, this woman and I live in the same house; and I gave birth while she was in the house. Then on the third day after I gave birth, this woman also gave birth. We were together; there was no one else with us in the house, only the two of us were in the house.

"Then this woman's son died in the night, because she lay on him. She got up in the middle of the night and took my son from beside me while your servant slept. She laid him at her breast, and laid her dead son at my breast. When I rose in the morning to nurse my son, I saw that he was dead; but when I looked at him closely in the morning, clearly it was not the son I had borne."

But the other woman said, "No, the living son is mine, and the dead son is yours." The first said, "No, the dead son is yours, and the living son is mine." So they argued before the king.

Then the king said, "The one says, 'This is my son that is alive, and your son is dead'; while the other says, 'Not so! Your son is dead, and my son is the living one.'" So the king said, "Bring me a sword," and they brought a sword before the king. The king said, "Divide the living boy in two; then give half to the one, and half to the other."

But the woman whose son was alive said to the king—because compassion for her son burned within her—"Please, my lord, give her the living boy; certainly do not kill him!" The other said, "It shall be neither mine nor yours; divide it."

Then the king responded: "Give the first woman the living boy; do not kill him. She is his mother." All Israel heard of the judgment that the king had rendered; and they stood in awe of the king, because they perceived that the wisdom of God was in him, to execute justice.

1 Kings 3:16–28

TWENTY-THIRD SUNDAY IN ORDINARY TIME

SIXTEENTH SUNDAY AFTER PENTECOST
PROPER 18: SUNDAY BETWEEN 4 AND 10 SEPTEMBER

WISDOM BRINGS HER PEOPLE OUT OF EGYPT

The Exodus from Egypt is attributed to the action of holy Wisdom; it was she who brought about the deliverance of the people of Israel and led them through the desert.

A holy people and blameless race
wisdom delivered from a nation of oppressors.

She entered the soul of a servant of the Lord,
and withstood dread kings with wonders and signs.
She gave to holy people the reward of their labors;
she guided them along a marvelous way,
and became a shelter to them by day,
and a starry flame through the night.

She brought them over the Red Sea,
and led them through deep water;
but she drowned their enemies,
and cast them up from the depth of the sea.
Therefore the righteous plundered the ungodly;
they sang hymns, O Lord, to your holy name,
and praised with one accord your defending hand;
for wisdom opened the mouths of those who were mute,
and made the tongues of infants speak clearly.

Wisdom prospered their works by the hand of a holy prophet.
They journeyed through an uninhabited wilderness,
and pitched their tents in untrodden places.
They withstood their enemies and fought off their foes.

When they were thirsty, they called upon you
and water was given them out of flinty rock,
and from hard stone a remedy for their thirst.
For through the very things by which their enemies were punished,
they themselves received benefit in their need.

Wisdom of Solomon 10:15 – 21; 11:1 – 5

This Gentile woman is determined and seeks out Jesus in someone else's home. Her shrewd argument persuades Jesus to change his mind and heal her daughter.

Jesus set out and went away to the region of Tyre. He entered a house and did not want anyone to know he was there. Yet Jesus could not escape notice, but a woman whose little daughter had an unclean spirit immediately heard about him, and she came and bowed down at his feet. Now the woman was a Gentile, of Syrophoenician origin.

She begged Jesus to cast the demon out of her daughter. He said to her, "Let the children be fed first, for it is not fair to take the children's food and throw it to the dogs." But she answered him, "Sir, even the dogs under the table eat the children's crumbs." Then Jesus said to her, "For saying that, you may go — the demon has left your daughter." So she went home, found the child lying on the bed, and the demon gone.

Mark 7:24 – 30

TWENTY-FOURTH SUNDAY
IN ORDINARY TIME

SEVENTEENTH SUNDAY
AFTER PENTECOST
PROPER 19: SUNDAY BETWEEN 11 AND 17 SEPTEMBER

WISDOM SPEAKS
Holy Wisdom chides her people for ignoring her.

Wisdom cries out in the street;
       in the squares she raises her voice.
At the busiest corner she cries out;
       at the entrance of the city gates she speaks:
"How long, O simple ones, will you love being simple?
       How long will scoffers delight in their scoffing
       and fools hate knowledge?
Give heed to my reproof;
I will pour out my thoughts to you;
       I will make my words known to you."

Proverbs 1:20–23

THE WORKS OF ABRAHAM AND OF RAHAB
Rahab is linked with Abraham in this letter's argument that faith without works is barren.

Someone will say, "You have faith and I have works." Show me your faith apart from your works, and I by my works will show you my faith. You believe that God is one; you do well. Even the demons believe — and shudder. Do you want to be shown, you senseless person, that faith apart from works is barren?

Was not our ancestor Abraham justified by works when he offered his son Isaac on the altar? You see that faith was active along with his works, and faith was brought to completion by the works. Thus the scripture was fulfilled that says, "Abraham believed God, and it was reckoned to him as righteousness," and he was called the friend of God. You see that a person is justified by works and not by faith alone.

Likewise, was not Rahab the prostitute also justified by works when she welcomed the messengers and sent them out by another road? For just as the body without the spirit is dead, so faith without works is also dead.

James 2:18–26

TWENTY-FIFTH SUNDAY IN ORDINARY TIME

EIGHTEENTH SUNDAY AFTER PENTECOST
PROPER 20: SUNDAY BETWEEN 18 AND 24 SEPTEMBER

THE WOMAN OF WORTH

The capable woman is a competent businesswoman and provident householder. She carries out her responsibilities with wisdom and diligence, generosity and kindness. She is worthy of praise.

A capable wife who can find?
    She is far more precious than jewels.
The heart of her husband trusts in her,
    and he will have no lack of gain.
She does him good, and not harm,
    all the days of her life.
She seeks wool and flax,
    and works with willing hands.
She is like the ships of the merchant,
    she brings her food from far away.
She rises while it is still night
    and provides food for her household
    and tasks for her servant girls.
She considers a field and buys it;
    with the fruit of her hands she plants a vineyard.
She girds herself with strength,
    and makes her arms strong.
She perceives that her merchandise is profitable.
    Her lamp does not go out at night.
She puts her hands to the distaff,
    and her hands hold the spindle.
She opens her hand to the poor,
    and reaches out her hands to the needy.
She is not afraid for her household when it snows,
    for all her household are clothed in crimson.
She makes herself coverings;
    her clothing is fine linen and purple.
Her husband is known in the city gates,
    taking his seat among the elders of the land.
She makes linen garments and sells them;
    she supplies the merchant with sashes.
Strength and dignity are her clothing,
    and she laughs at the time to come.
She opens her mouth with wisdom,
    and the teaching of kindness is on her tongue.

She looks well to the ways of her household,
> and does not eat the bread of idleness.
Her children rise up and call her happy;
> her husband too, and he praises her:
"Many women have done excellently,
> but you surpass them all."
Charm is deceitful, and beauty is vain,
> but a woman who fears the LORD is to be praised.
Give her a share in the fruit of her hands,
> and let her works praise her in the city gates.

Proverbs 31:10–31

WISDOM FROM ABOVE
Early Christians retained and honored the tradition of holy Wisdom, though the feminine identity of wisdom was put aside.

Who is wise and understanding among you? Show by your good life that your works are done with gentleness born of wisdom. But if you have bitter envy and selfish ambition in your hearts, do not be boastful and false to the truth. Such wisdom does not come down from above, but is earthly, unspiritual, devilish. For where there is envy and selfish ambition, there will also be disorder and wickedness of every kind. But the wisdom from above is first pure, then peaceable, gentle, willing to yield, full of mercy and good fruits, without a trace of partiality or hypocrisy. And a harvest of righteousness is sown in peace for those who make peace.

Those conflicts and disputes among you, where do they come from? Do they not come from your cravings that are at war within you? You want something and do not have it; so you commit murder. And you covet something and cannot obtain it; so you engage in disputes and conflicts. You do not have, because you do not ask. You ask and do not receive, because you ask wrongly, in order to spend what you get on your pleasures.

Submit yourselves therefore to God. Resist the devil, and the devil will flee from you. Draw near to God, and God will draw near to you.

James 3:13 — 4:3, 7–8a

TWENTY-SIXTH SUNDAY IN ORDINARY TIME

NINTEENTH SUNDAY AFTER PENTECOST
PROPER 21: SUNDAY BETWEEN 25 SEPTEMBER AND 1 OCTOBER

ESTHER RESCUES HER PEOPLE

Esther exposes Haman's plot and justice is done. The Jewish people to this day celebrate Esther's triumph in the annual feast of Purim.

The king and Haman went in to feast with Queen Esther. On the second day, as they were drinking wine, the king again said to Esther, "What is your petition, Queen Esther? It shall be granted you. And what is your request? Even to the half of the kingdom, it shall be fulfilled." Then Queen Esther answered, "If I have won your favor, O king, and if it pleases the king, let my life be given me — that is my petition — and the lives of my people — that is my request. For we have been sold, I and my people, to be destroyed, to be killed, and to be annihilated. If we had been sold merely as slaves, men and women, I would have held my peace; but no enemy can compensate for this damage to the king."

Then King Ahasuerus said to Queen Esther, "Who is he, and where is he, who has presumed to do this?" Esther said, "A foe and enemy, this wicked Haman!" Then Haman was terrified before the king and the queen. The king rose from the feast in wrath and went into the palace garden, but Haman stayed to beg his life from Queen Esther, for he saw that the king had determined to destroy him. When the king returned from the palace garden to the banquet hall, Haman had thrown himself on the couch where Esther was reclining; and the king said, "Will he even assault the queen in my presence, in my own house?" As the words left the mouth of the king, they covered Haman's face.

Mordecai recorded these things, and sent letters to all the Jews who were in all the provinces of King Ahasuerus, both near and far, enjoining them that they should keep the fourteenth day of the month Adar and also the fifteenth day of the same month, year by year, as the days on which the Jews gained relief from their enemies, and as the month that had been turned for them from sorrow into gladness and from mourning into a holiday; that they should make them days of feasting and gladness, days for sending gifts of food to one another and presents to the poor. So the Jews adopted as a custom what they had begun to do, as Mordecai had written to them.

Esther 7:1 – 8; 9:20 – 23

TWENTY-SEVENTH SUNDAY IN ORDINARY TIME

TWENTIETH SUNDAY AFTER PENTECOST
PROPER 22: SUNDAY BETWEEN 2 AND 8 OCTOBER

THE CREATION OF WOMAN

As bone of bone and flesh of flesh, woman and man share their humanity equally and are companions fit for each other.

The LORD God said, "It is not good that the man should be alone; I will make him a companion fit for him." So out of the ground the LORD God formed every animal of the field and every bird of the air, and brought them to the man to see what he would call them; and whatever the man called every living creature, that was its name. The man gave names to all cattle, and to the birds of the air, and to every animal of the field; but for the man there was not found a companion fit for him.

So the LORD God caused a deep sleep to fall upon the man, and he slept; then God took one of his ribs and closed up its place with flesh. And the rib that the LORD God had taken from the man God made into a woman and brought her to the man. Then the man said,

"This at last is bone of my bones
    and flesh of my flesh;
she shall be called woman,
    for out of her man she was taken."

Therefore a man leaves his father and his mother and clings to his wife, and they become one flesh.

Genesis 2:18 – 24

THE WIFE OF JOB

This woman recognizes, long before Job does, what is at stake in the suffering of the innocent: the conflict between innocence and integrity on one hand, and the affirmation of the goodness of God in the face of suffering on the other hand.

There was once a man in the land of Uz whose name was Job. The man was blameless and upright, one who feared God and turned away from evil.

One day the heavenly beings came to present themselves before the LORD, and Satan also came among them to present himself before the LORD. The LORD said to Satan, "Where have you come from?" Satan answered the LORD, "From going to and fro on the earth, and from walking up and down on it." The LORD said to Satan, "Have you considered my servant Job? There is no one like him on the earth, a blameless and upright man who fears God and turns away from evil. He still persists in his integrity, although you incited me against him, to destroy him for no reason." Then Satan answered the LORD, "Skin for skin! All that people have they will give to save their lives. But stretch out your hand now and touch his bone and his flesh, and he will curse you to your face." The LORD said to Satan, "Very well, he is in your power; only spare his life."

So Satan went out from the presence of the LORD, and inflicted loathsome sores on Job from the sole of his foot to the crown of his head. Job took a potsherd with which to scrape himself, and sat among the ashes.

Then his wife said to him, "Do you still persist in your integrity? Curse God, and die." But he said to her, "You speak as any foolish woman would speak. Shall we receive the good at the hand of God, and not receive the bad?" In all this Job did not sin with his lips.

Job 1:1; 2:1–10

TWENTY-EIGHTH SUNDAY IN ORDINARY TIME

TWENTY-FIRST SUNDAY AFTER PENTECOST
PROPER 23: SUNDAY BETWEEN 9 AND 15 OCTOBER

WISDOM WAS GIVEN TO ME
Wisdom is precious. Cherishing her is the source of great benefit.

I prayed, and understanding was given me;
I called on God, and the spirit of wisdom came to me.
I preferred her to scepters and thrones,
and I accounted wealth as nothing in comparison with her.
Neither did I liken to her any priceless gem,
because all gold is but a little sand in her sight,
and silver will be accounted as clay before her.
I loved her more than health and beauty,
and I chose to have her rather than light,
because her radiance never ceases.
All good things came to me along with her,
and in her hands uncounted wealth.

Wisdom of Solomon 7:7 – 11

TWENTY-NINTH SUNDAY IN ORDINARY TIME

TWENTY-SECOND SUNDAY AFTER PENTECOST

PROPER 24: SUNDAY BETWEEN 16 AND 22 OCTOBER

THE DAUGHTERS OF JOB

Job's daughters are among the few women in the biblical narrative who receive an inheritance. It's also unusual that we are told their remarkable names.

The LORD restored the fortunes of Job when he had prayed for his friends; and the LORD gave Job twice as much as he had before. Then there came to him all his brothers and sisters and all who had known him before, and they ate bread with him in his house; they showed him sympathy and comforted him for all the evil that the LORD had brought upon him; and each of them gave him a piece of money and a gold ring. The LORD blessed the latter days of Job more than his beginning; and he had fourteen thousand sheep, six thousand camels, a thousand yoke of oxen, and a thousand donkeys.

He also had seven sons and three daughters. He named the first Jemimah [Dove], the second Keziah [Cinnamon], and the third Keren-happuch [Box of Eye Shadow]. In all the land there were no women so beautiful as Job's daughters; and their father gave them an inheritance along with their brothers. After this Job lived one hundred and forty years, and saw his children, and his children's children, four generations. And Job died, old and full of days.

Job 42:10–17

THIRTIETH SUNDAY IN ORDINARY TIME

TWENTY-THIRD SUNDAY
AFTER PENTECOST
PROPER 25: SUNDAY BETWEEN 23 AND 29 OCTOBER

THE LOVERS
Both the female and male voices in this love dialogue show reverence for the mother's role.

O that you were like a brother to me,
    who nursed at my mother's breast!
If I met you outside, I would kiss you,
    and no one would despise me.
I would lead you and bring you
    into the house of my mother,
    and into the chamber of the one who bore me.
I would give you spiced wine to drink
    the juice of my pomegranates.
O that his left hand were under my head,
    and that his right hand embraced me!
I adjure you, O daughters of Jerusalem,
    do not stir up or awaken love
    until it is ready.

Who is that coming up from the wilderness,
    leaning upon her beloved?
Under the apple tree I awakened you.
There your mother was in labor with you;
    there she who bore you was in labor.

Song of Solomon 8:1 – 5

Mary's Heart, Pierced in Sorrow

YEAR B

THIRTY-FIRST SUNDAY IN ORDINARY TIME

TWENTY-FOURTH SUNDAY AFTER PENTECOST
PROPER 26: SUNDAY BETWEEN 30 OCTOBER AND 5 NOVEMBER

RUTH, NAOMI AND ORPAH

Naomi, Ruth and Orpah show courage and a deep mutual bond. They care for one another in a society where widows are usually left in poverty, exposed to danger.

In the days when the judges ruled, there was a famine in the land, and a certain man of Bethlehem in Judah went to live in the country of Moab, he and his wife and two sons. The name of the man was Elimelech and the name of his wife Naomi, and the names of his two sons were Mahlon and Chilion; they were Ephrathites from Bethlehem in Judah. They went into the country of Moab and remained there. But Elimelech, the husband of Naomi, died, and she was left with her two sons. These took Moabite wives; the name of the one was Orpah and the name of the other Ruth. When they had lived there about ten years, both Mahlon and Chilion also died, so that Naomi was left without her two sons and her husband.

Then Naomi started to return with her daughters-in-law from the country of Moab, for she had heard in the country of Moab that the LORD had considered the chosen people and given them food. So she set out from the place where she had been living, she and her two daughters-in-law, and they went on their way to go back to the land of Judah. But Naomi said to her two daughters-in-law, "Go back each of you to your mother's house. May the LORD deal kindly with you, as you have dealt with the dead and with me. The LORD grant that you may find security, each of you in the house of your husband." Then she kissed them, and they wept aloud. They said to her, "No, we will return with you to your people." But Naomi said, "Turn back, my daughters, why will you go with me? Do I still have sons in my womb that they may become your husbands? Turn back, my daughters, go your way, for I am too old to have a husband. Even if I thought there was hope for me, even if I should have a husband tonight and bear sons, would you then wait until they were grown? No, my daughters, it has been far more bitter for me than for you, because the hand of the LORD has turned against me." Then they wept aloud again. Orpah kissed her mother-in-law, but Ruth clung to her.

So Naomi said, "See, your sister-in-law has gone back to her people and to her gods; return after your sister-in-law." But Ruth said,

"Do not press me to leave you
　or to turn back from following you!
Where you go, I will go;
where you lodge, I will lodge;
your people shall be my people,
　and your God my God.

225

Where you die, I will die —
    there will I be buried.
May the LORD do thus and so to me,
    and more as well,
if even death parts me from you!"

When Naomi saw that she was determined to go with her, she said no more to her.

So Naomi returned together with Ruth the Moabite, her daughter-in-law, who came back with her from the country of Moab. They came to Bethehem at the beginning of the barley harvest.

Ruth 1:1 – 18, 22

THIRTY-SECOND SUNDAY IN ORDINARY TIME

TWENTY-FIFTH SUNDAY AFTER PENTECOST

PROPER 27: SUNDAY BETWEEN 6 AND 12 NOVEMBER

THE WIDOW OF ZAREPHATH

Elijah brings God's grace to this poor woman, an outsider. Her generosity and God's favor bring abundance and new life to her and her son.

The word of the LORD came to Elijah, saying, "Go now to Zarephath, which belongs to Sidon, and live there; for I have commanded a widow there to feed you." So he set out and went to Zarephath. When he came to the gate of the town, a widow was there gathering sticks; he called to her and said, "Bring me a little water in a vessel, so that I may drink." As she was going to bring it, he called to her and said, "Bring me a morsel of bread in your hand." But she said, "As the LORD your God lives, I have nothing baked, only a handful of meal in a jar, and little oil in a jug; I am now gathering a couple of sticks, so that I may go home and prepare it for myself and my son, that we may eat it, and die."

Elijah said to her, "Do not be afraid; go and do as you have said; but first make me a little cake of it and bring it to me, and afterwards make something for yourself and your son. For thus says the LORD the God of Israel: The jar of meal will not be emptied and the jug of oil will not fail until the day that the LORD sends rain on the earth." She went and did as Elijah said, so that she as well as he and her household ate for many days. The jar of meal was not emptied, neither did the jug of oil fail, according to the word of the LORD that he spoke by Elijah.

1 Kings 17:8 – 16

RUTH MARRIES BOAZ

Naomi's wise plan leads to the marriage of Ruth and Boaz. The women rejoice with Naomi at the birth of the son of Boaz and Ruth; Naomi is no longer alone in the world.

Naomi, Ruth's mother-in-law said to her, "My daughter, I need to seek some security for you, so that it may be well with you. Now here is our kinsman Boaz, with whose young women you have been working. See, he is winnowing barley tonight at the threshing floor. Now wash and anoint yourself, and put on your best clothes and go down to the threshing floor; but do not make yourself known to the man until he has finished eating and drinking. When he lies down, observe the place where he lies; then, go and uncover his feet and lie down; and he will tell you what to do." Ruth said to Naomi, "All that you tell me I will do."

So Boaz took Ruth and she became his wife. When they came together, the LORD made her conceive, and she bore a son. Then the women said to Naomi,

"Blessed be the LORD, who has not left you this day without next-of-kin; and may God's name be renowned in Israel. The LORD shall be to you a restorer of life and nourisher of your old age; for your daughter-in-law who loves you, who is more to you than seven sons, has borne him." Then Naomi took the child and laid him in her bosom, and became his nurse. The women of the neighborhood gave him a name, saying, "A son has been born to Naomi." They named him Obed; he became the father of Jesse, the father of David.

Ruth 3:1 – 5; 4:13 – 17

THE POOR WIDOW
The widow's faith led her to give all she had to the temple. Her generosity, even in her poverty, indicts the vanity of the wealthy. Why should widows — even today — have to live in such poverty?

Jesus said, "Beware of the scribes, who like to walk around in long robes, and to be greeted with respect in the marketplaces, and to have the best seats in the synagogues and places of honor at banquets! They devour widows' houses and for the sake of appearance say long prayers. They will receive the greater condemnation."

Jesus sat down opposite the treasury, and watched the crowd putting money into the treasury. Many rich people put in large sums. A poor widow came and put in two small copper coins, which are worth a penny. Then Jesus called his disciples and said to them, "Truly I tell you, this poor widow has put in more than all those who are contributing to the treasury. For all of them have contributed out of their abundance; but she out of her poverty has put in everything she had, all she had to live on."

Mark 12:38 – 44

THIRTY-THIRD SUNDAY IN ORDINARY TIME

TWENTY-SIXTH SUNDAY AFTER PENTECOST
PROPER 28: SUNDAY BETWEEN 13 AND 19 NOVEMBER

HANNAH PRAYS AND HER PRAYER IS ANSWERED
Childless Hannah weeps as she prays. Eli interprets her fervent prayer as drunkenness; women's piety is often misinterpreted.

On the day when Elkanah sacrificed, he would give portions to his wife Peninnah and to all her sons and daughters; but to Hannah he gave a double portion, because he loved her, though the LORD had closed her womb. Her rival used to provoke her severely, to irritate her, because the LORD had closed her womb. So it went on year by year; as often as Hannah went up to the house of the LORD, Peninnah used to provoke her. Therefore Hannah wept and would not eat. Her husband Elkanah said to her, "Hannah, why do you weep? Why do you not eat? Why is your heart sad? Am I not more to you than ten sons?"

After they had eaten and drunk at Shiloh, Hannah rose and presented herself before the LORD. Now Eli the priest was sitting on the seat beside the doorpost of the temple of the LORD. She was deeply distressed and prayed to the LORD, and wept bitterly. She made this vow: "O LORD of hosts, if only you will look on the misery of your servant, and remember me, and not forget your servant, but will give to your servant a male child, then I will set him before you as a nazirite unto the day of his death. He shall drink neither wine nor intoxicants, and no razor shall touch his head."

As she continued praying before the LORD, Eli observed her mouth. Hannah was praying silently; only her lips moved but her voice was not heard; therefore Eli thought she was drunk. So Eli said to her, "How long will you make a drunken spectacle of yourself? Put away your wine." But Hannah answered, "No, my lord, I am a woman deeply troubled; I have drunk neither wine nor strong drink, but I have been pouring out my soul before the LORD. Do not regard your servant as a worthless woman, for I have been speaking out of my great anxiety and vexation all this time." Then Eli answered, "Go in peace, the God of Israel grant the petition you have made." And Hannah said, "Let your servant find favor in your sight." Then the woman went to her quarters, ate and drank with her husband, and her countenance was sad no longer.

They rose early in the morning and worshiped before the LORD; then they went back to their house at Ramah. Elkanah knew his wife Hannah, and the LORD remembered her. In due time Hannah conceived and bore a son. She named him Samuel, for she said, "I have asked him of the LORD."

1 Samuel 1:4–20

SONG OF HANNAH: Responsory

Hannah pours out her heart in joyful song. Her song is like the song of Mary. Their songs are placed at the end and the beginning of the liturgical year respectively.

I acclaim the LORD's greatness,
source of my strength.
I devour my foe,
I say to God with joy:
"You saved my life.
Only you are holy, LORD;
there is none but you,
no other rock like you."

God knows when deeds match words,
so make no arrogant claims.
The weapons of the strong are broken,
the defenseless gain strength.
The overfed now toil to eat,
while the hungry have their fill.

The childless bear many children,
but the fertile learn they are sterile.
The LORD commands death and life,
consigns to Sheol or raises up.

God deals out poverty and wealth,
casts down and lifts up,
raising the poor from squalor,
the needy from the trash heap,
to sit with the high and mighty,
taking their places of honor.

God owns the universe
and sets the earth within it.
God walks with the faithful
but silences the wicked in darkness;
their power does not prevail.

God's enemies will be broken,
heaven thunders against them.
The LORD will judge the earth,
and give power to the king,
victory to the anointed.

Canticle of 1 Samuel 2:1 – 10 ICEL

CHRIST THE KING

REIGN OF CHRIST
PROPER 29: SUNDAY BETWEEN 20 AND 26 NOVEMBER

EAT AND DRINK OF WISDOM
The ministry of Christ and the Spirit can be interpreted in terms of holy Wisdom. Hunger and thirst signify longing for the reign of Christ.

"I grew tall like a cedar in Lebanon,
    and like a cypress on the heights of Hermon.
I grew tall like a palm tree in En-gedi,
    and like rosebushes in Jericho;
like a fair olive tree in the field,
    and like a plane tree beside water I grew tall.
Like cassia and camel's thorn I gave forth perfume,
    and like choice myrrh I spread my fragrance,
like galbanum, onycha, and stacte,
    and like the odor of incense in the tent.
Like a terebinth I spread out my branches,
    and my branches are glorious and graceful.
Like the vine I bud forth delights,
    and my blossoms become glorious and abundant fruit.
"Come to me, you who desire me,
    and eat your fill of my fruits.
For the memory of me is sweeter than honey,
    and the possession of me sweeter than the honeycomb.
Those who eat of me will hunger for more,
    and those who drink of me will thirst for more."

Sirach 24:13–21

IN REMEMBRANCE OF HER

Jesus ministers to women and receives their ministry to him. One characteristic of Christ's reign is that the faith and love of women are remembered and honored by all.

While Jesus was at Bethany in the house of Simon the leper, as he sat at the table, a woman came with an alabaster jar of very costly ointment of nard, and she broke open the jar and poured the ointment on his head. But some were there who said to one another in anger, "Why was the ointment wasted in this way? For this ointment could have been sold for more than three hundred denarii, and the money given to the poor." And they scolded her.

But Jesus said, "Let her alone; why do you trouble her? She has performed a good service for me. For you always have the poor with you, and you can show kindness to them whenever you wish; but you will not always have me. She has done what she could; she has anointed my body beforehand for its burial. Truly I tell you, wherever the good news is proclaimed in the whole world, what she has done will be told in remembrance of her."

Mark 14:3 – 9

YEAR C

FIRST SUNDAY OF ADVENT

THE DAY OF THE LORD WILL COME LIKE LABOR PAINS
The second reading of the lectionaries speaks of the coming of our Lord Jesus Christ. This passage suggests that the coming of labor pains upon a pregnant woman is a fitting image for the future coming of Christ.

Concerning the times and the seasons, brothers and sisters, you do not need to have anything written to you. For you yourselves know very well that the day of the Lord will come like a thief in the night. When they say, "There is peace and security," then sudden destruction will come upon them, as labor pains come upon a pregnant woman, and there will be no escape! But you, beloved, are not in darkness, for that day to surprise you like a thief; for you are all children of light and children of the day; we are not of the night or of darkness. So then let us not fall asleep as others do, but let us keep awake and be sober; for those who sleep sleep at night, and those who are drunk get drunk at night. But since we belong to the day, let us be sober, and put on the breastplate of faith and love, and for a helmet the hope of salvation. For God has destined us not for wrath but for obtaining salvation through our Lord Jesus Christ, who died for us, so that whether we are awake or asleep we may live with him. Therefore encourage one another and build up each other, as indeed you are doing.

1 Thessalonians 5:1 – 11

SECOND SUNDAY OF ADVENT

BATHSHEBA: FOREMOTHER OF JESUS

The gospel reading in both lectionaries tells about John the Baptist and his preaching to prepare the way of the Lord. Bathsheba and her son Solomon are among those sent to prepare the way, centuries before. The way that leads to Solomon's birth is not easy for Bathsheba.

It happened, late one afternoon, when David rose from his couch and was walking about on the roof of the king's house, that he saw from the roof a woman bathing; the woman was very beautiful. David sent someone to inquire about the woman. It was reported, "This is Bathsheba daughter of Eliam, the wife of Uriah the Hittite." So David sent messengers to get her, and she came to him, and he lay with her. (Now she was purifying herself after her period.) Then she returned to her house. The woman conceived; and she sent and told David, "I am pregnant."

When the wife of Uriah heard that her husband was dead, she made lamentation for him. When the mourning was over, David sent and brought her into his house, and she became his wife, and bore him a son.

The Lord struck the child that Uriah's wife bore to David, and it became very ill. David therefore pleaded with God for the child; David fasted, and went in and lay all night on the ground. The elders of his house stood beside him, urging him to rise from the ground; but he would not, nor did he eat food with them. On the seventh day the child died.

Then David consoled his wife Bathsheba, and went to her, and lay with her; and she bore a son, and he named him Solomon. The Lord loved him, and sent a message by the prophet Nathan; so he named him Jedidiah [Beloved of the Lord] because of the Lord.

2 Samuel 11:2 – 5, 26 – 27; 12:15b – 18a, 24 – 25

Salome

THIRD SUNDAY OF ADVENT

RUTH: FOREMOTHER OF JESUS
The gospel reading in both lectionaries continues to tell of John the Baptist and the one who is coming. Ruth
and her son are among those who prepare the way, centuries before. Ruth is not an Israelite, but she is one
of the great women in the Davidic line.

Boaz said to the elders and all the people, "Today you are witnesses that I have acquired from the hand of Naomi all that belonged to Elimelech and all that belonged to Chilion and Mahlon. I have also acquired Ruth the Moabite, the wife of Mahlon, to be my wife, to maintain the dead man's name on his inheritance, in order that the name of the dead may not be cut off from his kindred and from the gate of his native place; today you are witnesses." Then all the people who were at the gate, along with the elders, said, "We are witnesses. May the LORD make the woman who is coming into your house like Rachel and Leah, who together built up the house of Israel. May you produce children in Ephrathah and bestow a name in Bethlehem, and, through the children that the LORD will give you by this young woman, may your house be like the house of Perez, whom Tamar bore to Judah."

So Boaz took Ruth and she became his wife. When they came together, the LORD made her conceive, and she bore a son. Then the women said to Naomi, "Blessed be the LORD, who has not left you this day without next-of-kin; and may God's name be renowned in Israel! The LORD shall be to you a restorer of life and a nourisher of your old age; for your daughter-in-law who loves you, who is more to you than seven sons, has borne him." Then Naomi took the child and laid him in her bosom, and became his nurse. The women of the neighborhood gave him a name, saying, "A son has been born to Naomi." They named him Obed; he became the father of Jesse, the father of David.

Now these are descendants of Perez: Perez became the father of Hezron, Hezron of Ram, Ram of Amminadab, Amminadab of Nahshon, Nahshon of Salmon, Salmon of Boaz, Boaz of Obed, Obed of Jesse, and Jesse of David.

Ruth 4:9–22

DAUGHTER ZION
Daughter Zion rejoices in anticipation of liberation.

Sing aloud, O daughter Zion;
    shout, O Israel!
Rejoice and exult with all your heart,
    O daughter Jerusalem!
The LORD has taken away the judgments against you,
    and has turned away your enemies.
The king of Israel, the LORD, is in your midst;
    you shall fear disaster no more.
On that day it shall be said to Jerusalem:

Do not fear, O Zion;
       do not let your hands grow weak.
The LORD, your God, is in your midst,
       a warrior who gives victory;
the LORD will rejoice over you with gladness
       and will renew you in love;
the LORD will exult over you with loud singing
       as on a day of festival.

Zephaniah 3:14 – 18a

FOURTH SUNDAY OF ADVENT

ELIZABETH SPEAKS PROPHETICALLY TO MARY
Elizabeth is filled with the Holy Spirit and speaks to Mary as a prophet would.

Mary set out and went with haste to a Judean town in the hill country, where she entered the house of Zechariah and greeted Elizabeth. When Elizabeth heard Mary's greeting, the child leaped in her womb. And Elizabeth was filled with the Holy Spirit and exclaimed with a loud cry, "Blessed are you among women, and blessed is the fruit of your womb. And why has this happened to me, that the mother of my Lord comes to me? For as soon as I heard the sound of your greeting, the child in my womb leaped for joy. And blessed is she who believed that there would be a fulfillment of what was spoken to her by the Lord."

Luke 1:39 – 45

SONG OF MARY: Responsory
Mary sings that God continues to rescue Israel.

I acclaim the greatness of the Lord,
I delight in God my savior,
who regarded my humble state.
Truly from this day on
all ages will call me blest.

For God, wonderful in power,
has used that strength for me.
Holy the name of the Lord!
whose mercy embraces the faithful,
one generation to the next.

The mighty arm of God
scatters the proud in their conceit,
pulls tyrants from their thrones,
and raises up the humble.
The Lord fills the starving
and lets the rich go hungry.

God rescues lowly Israel,
recalling the promise of mercy,
the promise made to our ancestors,
to Abraham's heirs for ever.

Canticle of Luke 1:46 – 55 ICEL

THE NATIVITY OF CHRIST: VIGIL

FOREMOTHERS AND FOREFATHERS OF JESUS
This list of Jesus' ancestors includes four women: Tamar, Rahab, Ruth and Bathsheba, the wife of David. The first three women (and the fourth's husband) acted in ways not understood by social convention in order to be faithful to God's purpose. They are models for Jesus in that way.

An account of the genealogy of Jesus the Christ, the son of David, the son of Abraham.

Abraham was the father of Isaac, Isaac of Jacob, Jacob of Judah and his brothers, Judah of Perez and Zerah by Tamar, Perez of Hezron, Hezron of Aram, Aram of Aminadab, Aminidab of Nahshon, Nahshon of Salmon, Salmon of Boaz by Rahab, Boaz of Obed by Ruth, Obed of Jesse, and Jesse the father of King David.

David was the father of Solomon by the wife of Uriah, Solomon of Rehoboam, Rehoboam of Abijah, Abijah of Asaph, Asaph of Jehoshaphat, Jehoshaphat of Joram, Joram of Uzziah, Uzziah of Jotham, Jotham of Ahaz, Ahaz of Hezekiah, Hezekiah of Manasseh, Manasseh of Amos, Amos of Josiah, and Josiah the father of Jechoniah and his brothers, at the time of the deportation to Babylon.

After the deportation to Babylon: Jechoniah was the father of Salathiel, Salathiel of Zerubbabel, Zerubbabel of Abiud, Abiud of Eliakim, Eliakim of Azor, Azor of Zadok, Zadok of Achim, Achim of Eliud, Eliud of Eleazar, Eleazar of Matthan, Matthan of Jacob, and Jacob of Joseph the husband of Mary, of whom Jesus was born, who is called the Christ.

So all the generations from Abraham to David are fourteen generations; and from David to the deportation to Babylon, fourteen generations; and from the deportation to Babylon to the Christ, fourteen generations.

Matthew 1:1 – 17

THE NATIVITY OF CHRIST: DURING THE NIGHT

MARY GIVES BIRTH TO JESUS

Giving birth in a stable is a sign of how insignificant this family is in its society. The true meaning of the event is first revealed to other outcasts, the shepherds. God works through people like these.

In those days a decree went out from Emperor Augustus that all the world should be registered. This was the first registration and was taken while Quirinius was governor of Syria. All went to their own towns to be registered.

Joseph also went from the town of Nazareth in Galilee to Judea, to the city of David called Bethlehem, because he was descended from the house and family of David. He went to be registered with Mary, to whom he was engaged and who was expecting a child.

While they were there, the time came for her to deliver her child. And she gave birth to her firstborn son and wrapped him in bands of cloth, and laid him in a manger, because there was no place for them in the inn.

In that region there were shepherds living in the fields, keeping watch over their flock by night. Then an angel of the Lord stood before them, and the glory of the Lord shone around them, and they were terrified. But the angel said to them, "Do not be afraid; for see — I am bringing you good news of great joy for all the people: to you is born this day in the city of David a Savior, who is the Christ, the Lord. This will be a sign for you: you will find a child wrapped in bands of cloth and lying in a manger." And suddenly there was with the angel a multitude of the heavenly host, praising God and saying,

"Glory to God in the highest heaven,
and peace to God's people on earth."

When the angels had left them and gone into heaven, the shepherds said to one another, "Let us go now to Bethlehem and see this thing that has taken place, which the Lord has made known to us." So they went with haste and found Mary and Joseph, and the child lying in the manger.

Luke 2:1 – 16

THE NATIVITY OF CHRIST: DAWN

DAUGHTER ZION

On one level, Mary herself is daughter Zion, who is sought out and not forsaken. On another level, Mary is the one who brings the promised salvation to daughter Zion, Jerusalem.

Upon your walls, O Jerusalem,
    I have posted sentinels;
    all day and all night
    they shall never be silent.
You who remind the LORD,
    take no rest,
    and give God no rest
    until Jerusalem is established
    and renowned throughout the earth.
The LORD has sworn by right hand
    and by mighty arm;
I will not again give your grain
    to be food for your enemies,
and foreigners shall not drink the wine
    for which you have labored;
but those who garner it shall eat it
    and praise the LORD,
and those who gather it shall drink it
    in my holy courts.

Go through, go through the gates,
    prepare the way for the people;
build up, build up the highway,
    clear it of stones,
    lift up an ensign over the peoples.
The LORD has proclaimed
    to the end of the earth:
Say to daughter Zion,
    "See, your salvation comes;
    behold, God comes bearing the reward,
    preceded by the recompense."
They shall be called, "The Holy People,
    The Redeemed of the Lord";
and you shall be called, "Sought Out,
    A City Not Forsaken."

Isaiah 62:6 – 12

MARY PONDERS THE SHEPHERDS' MESSAGE

Mary was a thoughtful and reflective woman. She did indeed have much to ponder. What did she think about all this?

When the angels had left them and gone into heaven, the shepherds said to one another, "Let us go now to Bethlehem and see this thing that has taken place, which the Lord has made known to us." So they went with haste and found Mary and Joseph, and the child lying in the manger. When they saw this, they made known what had been told them about this child; and all who heard it were amazed at what the shepherds told them. But Mary treasured all these words and pondered them in her heart. The shepherds returned, glorifying and praising God for all they had heard and seen, as it had been told them.

Luke 2:15–20

THE NATIVITY OF CHRIST: DURING THE DAY

WISDOM MAKES HER DWELLING AMONG GOD'S PEOPLE

The lectionaries offer the prologue to the Gospel of John: "In the beginning was the word . . . the word dwelled among us." In this passage, we hear of divine Wisdom, a feminine figure who is with God from the beginning, co-creator with God who pitches her tent in the midst of her people.

Wisdom praises herself,
> and tells of her glory in the midst of her people.
In the assembly of the Most High she opens her mouth,
> and in the presence of God's hosts she tells of her glory:

"I came forth from the mouth of the Most High,
> and covered the earth like a mist.
I dwelt in the highest heavens,
> and my throne was in a pillar of cloud.
Alone I compassed the vault of heaven
> and traversed the depths of the abyss.
Over waves of the sea, over all the earth,
> and over every people and nation I have held sway.
Among all these I sought a resting place;
> in whose territory should I abide?

"Then the Creator of all things gave me a command,
> and my Creator chose the place for my tent.
God said, 'Make your dwelling in Jacob,
> and in Israel receive your inheritance.'
Before the ages, in the beginning, God created me,
> and for all the ages I shall not cease to be.
In the holy tent I ministered before God,
> and so I was established in Zion.
Thus in the beloved city God gave me a resting place,
> and in Jerusalem was my domain.
I took root in an honored people,
> in the portion of the Lord's heritage."

Sirach 24:1 – 12

THE HOLY FAMILY

SUNDAY AFTER CHRISTMAS DAY

HANNAH'S PRAYER IS ANSWERED

In so many societies, a woman's worth is determined by her ability and willingness to bear children. Contrary to cultural expectations, Elkanah loves his wife, even though they are an infertile couple.

Hannah made this vow: "O LORD of hosts, if only you will look on the misery of your servant, and remember me, and not forget your servant, but will give to your servant a male child, then I will set him before you as a nazirite until the day of his death. He shall drink neither wine nor intoxicants, and no razor shall touch his head."

In due time Hannah conceived and bore a son. She named him Samuel, for she said, "I have asked him of the LORD."

The man Elkanah and all his household went up to offer to the LORD the yearly sacrifice, and to pay his vow. But Hannah did not go up, for she said to her husband, "As soon as the child is weaned, I will bring him, that he may appear in the presence of the LORD, and remain there forever; I will offer him as a nazarite for all time."

Her husband Elkanah said to her, "Do what seems best to you, wait until you have weaned him; only — may the LORD establish God's word." So the woman remained and nursed her son, until she weaned him. When she had weaned him, she took him up with her, along with a three-year-old bull, an ephah of flour, and a skin of wine. She brought him to the house of the LORD at Shiloh; and the child was young. Then they slaughtered the bull, and they brought the child to Eli. And she said, "Oh, my lord! As you live, my lord, I am the woman who was standing here in your presence, praying to the LORD. For this child I prayed; and the LORD has granted me the petition that I made. Therefore I have lent him to the LORD; as long as he lives, he is given to the LORD."

1 Samuel 1:11, 20 – 28

MARY QUESTIONS JESUS

Mary is anxious as she and Joseph search for Jesus. Her admonition brings a typical teenager's reply that also carries a deeper meaning: "Why were you worried?" This has theological meaning, too.

Every year the parents of Jesus went to Jerusalem for the festival of the Passover. And when Jesus was twelve years old, they went up as usual for the festival. When the festival was ended and they started to return, the boy Jesus stayed behind in Jerusalem, but his parents did not know it. Assuming that he was in the group of travelers, they went a day's journey. Then they started to look for him among their relatives and friends. When they did not find him, they returned to Jerusalem to search for him.

After three days they found Jesus in the temple, sitting among the teachers, listening to them and asking them questions. And all who heard Jesus were amazed at his understanding and his answers.

When his parents saw him they were astonished; and his mother said to him, "Child, why have you treated us like this? Look, your father and I have been searching for you in great anxiety." Jesus said to them, "Why were you searching for me? Did you not know that I must be in my Father's house?" But they did not understand what he said to them.

Then he went down with them and came to Nazareth, and was obedient to them. His mother treasured all these things in her heart. And Jesus increased in wisdom and in years, and in divine and human favor.

Luke 2:41 – 52

1 JANUARY: MARY, MOTHER OF JESUS

1 JANUARY: HOLY NAME OF JESUS

JESUS, BORN OF A WOMAN
Our adoption as children of God through Christ is effected through a woman, Mary.

When the fullness of time had come, God sent the Son, born of a woman, born under the law, in order to redeem those who were under the law, so that we might receive adoption as children. And because you are children, God has sent the Spirit of the Son into our hearts, crying, "Abba! Father!" So you are no longer a slave but a child, and if a child then also an heir, through God.

Galatians 4:4 – 7

MARY KNOWS JESUS' NAME
The name of Jesus was proclaimed to Mary by the angel before he was conceived. Mary is the bearer of this good news.

When the angels had left them and gone into heaven, the shepherds said to one another, "Let us go now to Bethlehem and see this thing that has taken place, which the Lord has made known to us." So they went with haste and found Mary and Joseph, and the child lying in the manger. When they saw this, they made known what had been told them about this child; and all who heard it were amazed at what the shepherds told them. But Mary treasured all these words and pondered them in her heart. The shepherds returned, glorifying and praising God for all they had heard and seen, as it had been told them.

After eight days had passed, it was time to circumcise the child; and he was called Jesus, the name given by the angel before he was conceived in the womb.

Luke 2:15 – 21

SECOND SUNDAY AFTER CHRISTMAS

WISDOM MAKES HER DWELLING AMONG GOD'S PEOPLE
*In this passage, we hear of divine Wisdom, a feminine figure who is with God from the beginning, co-creator
with God who pitches her tent in the midst of her people.*

Wisdom praises herself,
    and tells of her glory in the midst of her people.
In the assembly of the Most High she opens her mouth,
    and in the presence of God's hosts she tells of her glory:

"I came forth from the mouth of the Most High,
    and covered the earth like a mist.
I dwelt in the highest heavens,
    and my throne was in a pillar of cloud.
Alone I compassed the vault of heaven
    and traversed the depths of the abyss.
Over waves of the sea, over all the earth,
    and over every people and nation I have held sway.
Among all these I sought a resting place;
    in whose territory should I abide?

"Then the Creator of all things gave me a command,
    and my Creator chose the place for my tent.
God said, 'Make your dwelling in Jacob,
    and in Israel receive your inheritance.'
Before the ages, in the beginning, God created me,
    and for all the ages I shall not cease to be.
In the holy tent I ministered before God,
    and so I was established in Zion.
Thus in the beloved city God gave me a resting place,
    and in Jerusalem was my domain.
I took root in an honored people,
    in the portion of the Lord's heritage."

Sirach 24:1 – 12

THE EPIPHANY OF CHRIST

When the Epiphany is celebrated on the Second Sunday after Christmas, the two sets of readings may be combined.

THE QUEEN OF SHEBA GIVES AND RECEIVES GIFTS

In the lectionaries, the first reading tells that kings and ordinary people will bring homage and gifts; the gospel is about the magi. This passage tells about the Queen of Sheba, who brought gifts to King Solomon and received his gifts in return.

When the queen of Sheba heard of the fame of Solomon (fame due to the name of the LORD), she came to test him with hard questions. She came to Jerusalem with a very great retinue, with camels bearing spices, and very much gold, and precious stones; and when she came to Solomon, she told him all that was on her mind. Solomon answered all her questions; there was nothing hidden from the king that he could not explain to her. When the queen of Sheba had observed all the wisdom of Solomon, the house that he had built, the food of his table, the seating of his officials, and the attendance of his servants, their clothing, his valets, and his burnt offerings that he offered at the house of the LORD, there was no more spirit in her.

So she said to the king, "The report was true that I heard in my own land of your accomplishments and of your wisdom, but I did not believe the reports until I came and my own eyes had seen it. Not even half had been told me; your wisdom and prosperity far surpass the report that I had heard. Happy are your wives! Happy are these your servants, who continually attend you and hear your wisdom! Blessed be the LORD your God, who has delight in you and set you on the throne of Israel! Because the LORD loved Israel forever, you have been made king to execute justice and righteousness." Then she gave the king one hundred twenty talents of gold, a great quantity of spices, and precious stones; never again did spices come in such quantity as that which the queen of Sheba gave to King Solomon.

Moreover, the fleet of Hiram, which carried gold from Ophir, brought from Ophir a great quantity of almug wood and precious stones. From the almug wood the king made supports for the house of the LORD, and for the king's house, lyres also and harps for the singers; no such almug wood has come or been seen to this day.

Meanwhile King Solomon gave to the queen of Sheba every desire that she expressed, as well as what he gave her out of Solomon's royal bounty. Then she returned to her own land, with her servants.

1 Kings 10:1–13

THE MAGI SEE THE CHILD WITH MARY HIS MOTHER

Mary's motherhood is honored; the magi offer gifts and pay homage.

In the time of King Herod, after Jesus was born in Bethlehem of Judea, magi from the East came to Jerusalem, asking, "Where is the child who has been born king of the Jews? For we observed his star at its rising, and have come to pay him homage." When King Herod heard this, he was frightened, and all Jerusalem with him; and calling together all the chief priests and scribes of the people, he inquired of them where the Christ was to be born. They told him, "In Bethlehem of Judea; for so it has been written by the prophet:

'And you, Bethlehem, in the land of Judah,
are by no means least among the rulers of Judah;
for from you shall come a ruler
who is to shepherd my people Israel.'"

Then Herod secretly called for the magi and learned from them the exact time when the star had appeared. Then he sent them to Bethlehem, saying, "Go and search diligently for the child; and when you have found him, bring me word so that I may also go and pay him homage." When they had heard the king, they set out; and there, ahead of them, went the star that they had seen at its rising, until it stopped over the place where the child was. When they saw that the star had stopped, they were overwhelmed with joy. On entering the house, they saw the child with Mary his mother; and they knelt down and paid him homage. Then, opening their treasure chests, they offered him gifts of gold, frankincense, and myrrh. And having been warned in a dream not to return to Herod, they left for their own country by another road.

Matthew 2:1 – 12

The Woman at the Well

THE BAPTISM OF CHRIST

FIRST SUNDAY AFTER THE EPIPHANY

GOD IS BLESSED FOR ABIGAIL

In the gospel reading in the lectionaries, Jesus is described as God's beloved, with whom God is well pleased. In this story David blesses God for Abigail, who kept him from violence. Peace is her gift and her reward.

David said to Abigail, "Blessed be the LORD, the God of Israel, who sent you to meet me today! Blessed be your good sense, and blessed be you, who have kept me today from bloodguilt and from avenging myself by my own hand! For as surely as the LORD the God of Israel lives, who has restrained me from hurting you, unless you had hurried and come to meet me, truly by morning there would not have been left to Nabal so much as one male." Then David received from her hand what she had brought him; he said to Abigail, "Go up to your house in peace; see, I have heeded your voice, and I have granted your petition."

1 Samuel 25:32 – 35

SECOND SUNDAY IN ORDINARY TIME
SECOND SUNDAY AFTER THE EPIPHANY

ZION AS BRIDE
God and Israel are like a newly married couple, deeply in love.

For Zion's sake I will not keep silent,
    and for Jerusalem's sake I will not rest,
until her vindication shines out like the dawn
    and her salvation like a burning torch.
The nations shall see your vindication,
    and all the kings your glory;
and you shall be called by a new name
    that the mouth of the LORD will give.
You shall be a crown of beauty in the hand of the LORD,
    and a royal diadem in the hand of your God.

You shall no more be termed Forsaken,
    and your land shall no more be termed Desolate;
but you shall be called My Delight,
    and your land Married;
for the Lord delights in you,
    and your land shall be married.
For as a young man marries a young woman,
    so shall your builder marry you,
and as one rejoices in marrying the beloved,
    so shall your God rejoice over you.

Isaiah 62:1 – 5

THE WEDDING AT CANA
Mary knows that Jesus is ready to begin his public ministry, and that his objection is nominal.

There was a wedding in Cana of Galilee, and the mother of Jesus was there. Jesus and his disciples had also been invited to the wedding. When the wine gave out, the mother of Jesus said to him, "They have no wine." And Jesus said to her, "Woman, what concern is that to you and to me? My hour has not yet come." His mother said to the servants, "Do whatever he tells you." Now standing there were six stone water jars for the Jewish rites of purification, each holding twenty or thirty gallons. Jesus said to them, "Fill the jars with water." And they filled them up to the brim. Jesus said to them, "Now draw some out, and take it to the chief steward." So they took it. When the steward tasted the water that had become wine, and did not know where it came from (though the servants who had drawn the water knew), the steward called the bridegroom and said to him, "Everyone serves the good wine first, and then the inferior wine after the guests have become drunk. But you have kept the good wine until now." Jesus did this, the first of his signs, in Cana of Galilee, and revealed his glory; and his disciples believed in him.

John 2:1 – 11

THIRD SUNDAY IN ORDINARY TIME
THIRD SUNDAY AFTER THE EPIPHANY

THE MEDIUM OF ENDOR
Saul asks this woman to help him when he is unable to discern God's will. The medium listens to him, and later nourishes him.

When Saul saw the army of the Philistines, he was afraid, and his heart trembled greatly. When Saul inquired of the LORD, the LORD did not answer him, not by dreams, or by Urim, or by prophets. Then Saul said to his servants, "Seek out for me a woman who is a medium, so that I may go to her and inquire of her." His servants said to him, "There is a medium at Endor."

So Saul disguised himself and put on other clothes and went there, he and two men with him. They came to the woman by night. And he said, "Consult a spirit for me, and bring up for me the one whom I name to you." The woman said to him, "Surely you know what Saul has done, how he has cut off the mediums and the wizards from the land. Why then are you laying a snare for my life to bring about my death?" But Saul swore to her by the LORD, "As the LORD lives, no punishment shall come upon you for this thing."

Then the woman said, "Whom shall I bring up for you?" He answered, "Bring up Samuel for me." When the woman saw Samuel, she cried out with a loud voice; and the woman said to Saul, "Why have you deceived me? You are Saul!" The king said to her, "Have no fear; what do you see?" The woman said to Saul, "I see a divine being coming up out of the ground." He said to her, "What is his appearance?" She said, "An old man is coming up; he is wrapped in a robe." So Saul knew that it was Samuel, and he bowed with his face to the ground and did obeisance.

The woman came to Saul, and when she saw that he was terrified, she said to him, "Your servant has listened to you; I have taken my life in my hand, and have listened to what you have said to me. Now therefore, you also listen to your servant; let me set a morsel of bread before you. Eat, that you may have strength when you go on your way." He refused, and said, "I will not eat." But his servants, together with the woman, urged him; and he listened to their words. So he got up from the ground and sat on the bed. Now the woman had a fatted calf in the house. She quickly slaughtered it, and she took flour, kneaded it, and baked unleavened cakes. She put them before Saul and his servants, and they ate. Then they rose and went away that night.

1 Samuel 28:5 – 14, 20 – 25

FOURTH SUNDAY IN ORDINARY TIME
FOURTH SUNDAY AFTER THE EPIPHANY

THE MOTHER OF THE WIFE OF SIMON
Surely Simon's wife and women servants are also present, helping the older woman as she serves Jesus and the apostles and witnesses to Jesus' healing power.

After leaving the synagogue Jesus entered Simon's house. Now Simon's mother-in-law was suffering from a high fever, and they asked him about her. Then Jesus stood over her and rebuked the fever, and it left her. Immediately she got up and began to serve them.

As the sun was setting, all those who had any who were sick with various kinds of diseases brought them to Jesus; and he laid his hands on each of them and cured them. Demons also came out of many, shouting, "You are the Son of God!" But Jesus rebuked them and would not allow them to speak, because they knew that he was the Christ.

Luke 4:38 – 41

FIFTH SUNDAY IN ORDINARY TIME

FIFTH SUNDAY AFTER THE EPIPHANY

THE WOMAN OF SHUNEM LODGES A CLAIM WITH THE KING

The Shunnamite woman receives justice from the king. If she had not been a follower of Elisha, would the king have granted her request?

Elisha had said to the woman of Shunem whose son he had restored to life, "Get up and go with your household, and settle wherever you can; for the LORD has called for a famine, and it will come on the land for seven years." So the woman got up and did according to the word of the man of God; she went with her household and settled in the land of the Philistines seven years.

At the end of the seven years, when the woman returned from the land of the Philistines, she set out to appeal to the king for her house and her land. Now the king was talking with Gehazi the servant of the man of God, saying, "Tell me all the great things that Elisha has done." While he was telling the king how Elisha had restored a dead person to life, the woman whose son he had restored to life appealed to the king for her house and her land. Gehazi said, "My lord king, here is the woman, and here is her son whom Elisha restored to life." When the king questioned the woman, she told him. So the king appointed an official for her, saying, "Restore all that was hers, together with all the revenue of the fields from the day that she left the land until now."

2 Kings 8:1–6

SIXTH SUNDAY IN ORDINARY TIME

SIXTH SUNDAY AFTER THE EPIPHANY
PROPER 1: SUNDAY BETWEEN 11 AND 17 FEBRUARY

ESTHER BECOMES QUEEN
Esther and the other young women entered the king's harem. Did they feel privileged, or exploited, or both?

The servants who attended King Ahasuerus said, "Let beautiful young virgins be sought out for the king. And let the king appoint commissioners in all the provinces of his kingdom to gather all the beautiful young virgins to the harem in the citadel of Susa under custody of Hegai, the king's eunuch, who is in charge of the women; let their cosmetic treatments be given them. And let the girl who pleases the king be queen instead of Vashti." This pleased the king, and he did so.

Now there was a Jew in the citadel of Susa whose name was Mordecai son of Jair son of Shimei son of Kish, a Benjaminite. Kish had been carried away from Jerusalem along with the captives carried away with King Jeconiah of Judah, whom King Nebuchadnezzar of Babylon had carried away. Mordecai had brought up Hadassah, that is, Esther, his cousin, for she had neither father nor mother; and the girl was fair and beautiful, and when her father and her mother died, Mordecai adopted her as his own daughter. So when the king's order and his edict were proclaimed, and when many young women were gathered in the citadel of Susa in custody of Hegai, Esther also was taken into the king's palace and put in custody of Hegai, who had charge of the women. The girl pleased him and won his favor, and he quickly provided her with her cosmetic treatments and her portion of food, and with seven chosen maids from the king's palace, and advanced her and her maids to the best place in the harem. Esther did not reveal her people or kindred, for Mordecai had charged her not to tell. Every day Mordecai would walk around in front of the court of the harem, to learn how Esther was and how she fared.

Esther 2:2 – 11

SEVENTH SUNDAY IN ORDINARY TIME

SEVENTH SUNDAY AFTER THE EPIPHANY
PROPER 2: SUNDAY BETWEEN 18 AND 24 FEBRUARY

ESTHER SAVES THE KING'S LIFE
Esther and Mordecai are credited with saving the king from two conspirators.

In those days, while Mordecai was sitting at the king's gate, Bigthan and Teresh, two of the king's eunuchs, who guarded the threshhold, became angry and conspired to assassinate King Ahasuerus. But the matter came to the knowledge of Mordecai, and he told it to Queen Esther, and Esther told the king in the name of Mordecai. When the affair was investigated and found to be so, both the men were hanged on the gallows. It was recorded in the book of the annals in the presence of the king.

Esther 2:21 – 23

EIGHTH SUNDAY IN ORDINARY TIME

EIGHTH SUNDAY AFTER THE EPIPHANY
PROPER 3: SUNDAY BETWEEN 25 AND 29 FEBRUARY

ESTHER'S PRAYER

Esther prays for the deliverance of her people. She asks for courage and eloquent speech that she may do her part.

Queen Esther prayed to the Lord God of Israel, and said: "O my Lord, you only are our ruler; help me, who am alone and have no helper but you, for my danger is in my hand. Ever since I was born I have heard in the tribe of my family that you, O Lord, took Israel out of all the nations, and our ancestors from among all their fore-bears, for an everlasting inheritance, and that you did for them all that you promised. And now we have sinned before you, and you have handed us over to our enemies because we glorified their gods. You are righteous, O Lord! And now they are not satisfied that we are in bitter slavery, but they have covenanted with their idols to abolish what your mouth has ordained, and to destroy your inheri-tance, to stop the mouths of those who praise you and to quench your altar and the glory of your house, to open the mouths of the nations for the praise of vain idols, and to magnify forever a mortal ruler.

"O Lord, do not surrender your scepter to what has no being; and do not let them laugh at our downfall; but turn their plan against them, and make an example of him who began this against us. Remember, O Lord; make yourself known in this time of our affliction, and give me courage, O Ruler of the gods and Master of all dominion! Put eloquent speech in my mouth before the lion, and turn his heart to hate the man who is fighting against us, so that there may be an end of him and those who agree with him. But save us by your hand, and help me, who am alone and have no helper but you, O Lord."

Esther 14:3 – 14

YEAR C

TRANSFIGURATION SUNDAY

Some celebrate the Transfiguration on the Last Sunday after the Epiphany, and others on the Second Sunday of Lent.

GOD PROVIDES FOOD AND WIPES AWAY TEARS
In the gospel story of the Transfiguration, God is encountered atop a mountain as a voice from a bright cloud. This story provides another image: On a high mountain, God provides a feast of rich food and wipes away tears — roles often thought to belong to women.

On this mountain the LORD of hosts will make for all peoples
> a feast of rich food, a feast of well-aged wine,
> of rich food filled with marrow,
> of well-aged wines strained clear.
And God will destroy on this mountain
> the shroud that is cast over all peoples,
> the sheet that is spread over all nations;
> God will swallow up death forever.
Then the LORD God will wipe away the tears from all faces,
> and the disgrace of the people will be taken away from all the earth,
> for the LORD has spoken.
It will be said on that day,
> Lo, this is our God, we have waited for God so that we might be saved.
> This is the LORD for whom we have waited;
> let us be glad and rejoice in the salvation of the LORD.
> For the hand of the LORD will rest on this mountain.

Isaiah 25:6 – 10a

ASH WEDNESDAY

The lectionaries' readings call us to prayer, fasting and almsgiving; and to reconciliation with God and neighbor. The first three passages here tell how women in different circumstances were to be treated according to the ancient Law. They challenge all to do justice to and for women in contemporary society.

THE TREATMENT OF WOMEN SLAVES

When a man sells his daughter as a slave, she shall not go out as the male slaves do. If she does not please her master, who designated her for himself, then he shall let her be redeemed; he shall have no right to sell her to a foreign people, since he has dealt unfairly with her. If he designates her for his son, he shall deal with her as with a daughter. If he takes another wife to himself, he shall not diminish the food, clothing, or marital rights of the first wife. And if he does not do these three things for her, she shall go out without debt, without payment of money.

Exodus 21:7 – 11

SLAVES, WOMEN AND MEN, ARE SET FREE IN THE SABBATH YEAR

If a member of your community, whether a Hebrew man or a Hebrew woman, is sold to you and works for you six years, in the seventh year you shall set that person free. And when you send a male slave out from you a free person; you shall not send him out empty-handed. Provide liberally out of your flock, your threshing floor, and your wine press, thus giving to him some of the bounty with which the LORD your God has blessed you. Remember that you were a slave in the land of Egypt, and the LORD your God redeemed you; for this reason I lay this command upon you today. But if he says to you, "I will not go out from you," because he loves you and your household, since he is well off with you, then you shall take an awl and thrust it through his earlobe into the door, and he shall be your slave forever.

You shall do the same with regard to your female slave.

Deuteronomy 15:12 – 17

THE TREATMENT OF WOMEN TAKEN IN WAR

When you go out to war against your enemies, and the LORD your God hands them over to you and you take them captive, suppose you see among the captives a beautiful woman whom you desire and want to marry, and so you bring her home to your house; she shall shave her head, pare her nails, discard her captive's garb, and shall remain in your house a full month, mourning for her father and mother; after that you may go in to her and be her husband, and she shall be your wife.

But if you are not satisfied with her, you shall let her go free and not sell her for money. You must not treat her as a slave, since you have dishonored her.

Deuteronomy 21:10 – 14

PRIZE WISDOM!
Lent is interpreted as a journey toward Wisdom, the feminine figure of divine presence.

Get wisdom; get insight: do not forget, nor turn away
    from the words of my mouth.
Do not forsake her, and she will keep you;
    love her, and she will guard you.
The beginning of wisdom is this: Get wisdom
    and whatever else you get, get insight.
Prize her highly, and she will exalt you;
    she will honor you if you embrace her.
She will place on your head a fair garland;
    she will bestow on you a beautiful crown.

Hear, my child, and accept my words,
    that the years of your life may be many.
I have taught you the way of wisdom;
    I have led you in the paths of uprightness.
When you walk, your step will not be hampered;
    and if you run, you will not stumble.
Keep hold to instruction; do not let go;
    guard her, for she is your life.

Proverbs 4:5 – 13

Four other passages give us examples of women at prayer. Mary, Hannah, Judith and Esther can be models for Lent.

MARY, MODEL OF PRAYER
Mary sings that God continues to rescue Israel, a fact which gives her strength.

I acclaim the greatness of the Lord,
I delight in God my savior,
who regarded my humble state.
Truly from this day on
all ages will call me blest.

For God, wonderful in power,
has used that strength for me.
Holy the name of the Lord!

whose mercy embraces the faithful,
one generation to the next.

The mighty arm of God
scatters the proud in their conceit,
pulls tyrants from their thrones,
and raises up the humble.
The Lord fills the starving
and lets the rich go hungry.

God rescues lowly Israel,
recalling the promise of mercy,
the promise made to our ancestors,
to Abraham's heirs for ever.

Canticle of Luke 1:46–55 ICEL

HANNAH, MODEL OF PRAYER
Hannah pours out her heart in joyful song. Her song is like the song of Mary.

I acclaim the LORD's greatness,
source of my strength.
I devour my foe,
I say to God with joy:
"You saved my life.
Only you are holy, LORD;
there is none but you,
no other rock like you."

God knows when deeds match words,
so make no arrogant claims.
The weapons of the strong are broken,
the defenseless gain strength.
The overfed now toil to eat,
while the hungry have their fill.

The childless bear many children,
but the fertile learn they are sterile.
The LORD commands death and life,
consigns to Sheol or raises up.

God deals out poverty and wealth,
casts down and lifts up,
raising the poor from squalor,
the needy from the trash heap,

to sit with the high and mighty,
taking their places of honor.

God owns the universe
and sets the earth within it.
God walks with the faithful
but silences the wicked in darkness;
their power does not prevail.

God's enemies will be broken,
heaven thunders against them.
The LORD will judge the earth,
and give power to the king,
victory to the anointed.

> Canticle of 1 Samuel 2:1 – 10 ICEL

JUDITH, MODEL OF PRAYER
Judith prays that she can be the means by which God rescues the chosen people. God will protect the poor and downtrodden.

Judith cried out to the Lord with a loud voice, and said,

"O Lord God of my ancestor Simeon, to whom you gave a sword to take revenge on those strangers who had torn off a virgin's clothing to defile her, and exposed her thighs to put her to shame, and polluted her womb to disgrace her; for you said, 'It shall not be done' — yet they did it. So you gave up their rulers to be killed, and their bed, which was ashamed of the deceit they had practiced, was stained with blood, and you struck down slaves along with princes, and princes on their thrones. You gave up their wives for booty and their daughters to captivity, and all their booty to be divided among your beloved children who burned with zeal for you and abhorred the pollution of their blood and called on you for help — O God, my God, hear me also — a widow.

"For you have done these things and those that went before and those that followed. You have designed the things that are now, and those that are to come. What you had in mind has happened; the things you decided on presented themselves and said, 'Here we are!' For all your ways are prepared in advance, and your judgment is with foreknowledge.

"Here now are the Assyrians, a greatly increased force, priding themselves in their horses and riders, boasting in the strength of their foot soldiers, and trusting in shield and spear, in bow and sling. They do not know that you are the Lord who crushes wars; the Lord is your name. Break their strength by your might, and bring down their power in your anger; for they intend to defile your sanctuary, and to pollute the tabernacle where your glorious name resides, and to break off the horns of your altar with the sword. Look at their pride, and send your wrath upon their heads. Give to me, a widow, the strong hand to do what I plan. By the deceit of my lips strike down the slave with the prince and the prince with his servant; crush their arrogance by the hand of a woman.

"For your strength does not depend on numbers, nor your might on the powerful. But you are the God of the lowly, helper of the oppressed, upholder of the weak, protecter of the forsaken, savior of those without hope."

Judith 9:1 – 11

ESTHER, MODEL OF PRAYER
Esther prays for the deliverance of her people. She asks for courage and eloquent speech that she may do her part.

Queen Esther prayed to the Lord God of Israel, and said: "O my Lord, you only are our ruler; help me, who am alone and have no helper but you, for my danger is in my hand. Ever since I was born I have heard in the tribe of my family that you, O Lord, took Israel out of all the nations, and our ancestors from among all their forebears, for an everlasting inheritance, and that you did for them all that you promised. And now we have sinned before you, and you have handed us over to our enemies because we glorified their gods. You are righteous, O Lord! And now they are not satisfied that we are in bitter slavery, but they have covenanted with their idols to abolish what your mouth has ordained, and to destroy your inheritance, to stop the mouths of those who praise you and to quench your altar and the glory of your house, to open the mouths of the nations for the praise of vain idols, and to magnify forever a mortal ruler.

"O Lord, do not surrender your scepter to what has no being; and do not let them laugh at our downfall; but turn their plan against them, and make an example of him who began this against us. Remember, O Lord; make yourself known in this time of our affliction, and give me courage, O Ruler of the gods and Master of all dominion! Put eloquent speech in my mouth before the lion, and turn his heart to hate the man who is fighting against us, so that there may be an end of him and those who agree with him. But save us by your hand, and help me, who am alone and have no helper but you, O Lord."

Esther 14:3 – 14

Mary of Bethany, Gospel of John

FIRST SUNDAY OF LENT

MAKING PROVISION FOR WIDOWS

The lectionaries tell how Moses spoke the credal affirmation, "A wandering Aramean was my ancestor . . . The Lord brought us out of Egypt." The passages here list some of the obligations of justice that arise from the liberation of Israel, among them providing for widows.

When you reap your harvest in your field and forget a sheaf in the field, you shall not go back to get it; it shall be left for the lame, the orphan, and the widow, so that the LORD your God may bless you in all your undertakings. When you beat your olive trees, do not strip what is left; it shall be for the alien, the orphan, and the widow.

When you gather the grapes of your vineyard, do not glean what is left; it shall be for the lame, the orphan, and the widow. Remember that you were a slave in the land of Egypt; therefore I am commanding you to do this.

You, together with the Levites and the aliens who reside among you, shall celebrate with all the bounty that the LORD your God has given to you and to your house.

When you have finished paying all the tithe of your produce in the third year (which is the year of the tithe), giving it to the Levites, the aliens, the orphans, and the widows, so that they may eat their fill within your towns, then you shall say before the LORD your God: "I have removed the sacred portion from the house, and I have given it to the Levites, the resident aliens, the orphans, and the widows, in accordance with your entire commandment that you commanded me; I have neither transgressed nor forgotten any of your commandments: I have not eaten of it while in mourning; I have not removed any of it while I was unclean; and I have not offered any of it to the dead. I have obeyed the LORD my God, doing just as you commanded me. Look down from your holy habitation, from heaven, and bless your people Israel and the ground that you have given us, as you swore to our ancestors — a land flowing with milk and honey."

Deuteronomy 24:19 – 22; 26:11 – 15

SECOND SUNDAY OF LENT

HAGAR SEES GOD IN THE DESERT
The lectionaries tell how God made covenant with Abram. This passage tells of Hagar's encounter with God in the desert. God speaks to her and she apparently sees God.

Now Sarai, Abram's wife, bore him no children. She had an Egyptian slave-girl whose name was Hagar, and Sarai said to Abram, "You see that the Lord has prevented me from bearing children; go in to my slave-girl; it may be that I shall obtain children by her." And Abram listened to the voice of Sarai. So, after Abram had lived ten years in the land of Canaan, Sarai, Abram's wife, took Hagar the Egyptian her slave-girl, and gave her to her husband Abram as a wife.

Abram went into Hagar, and she conceived; and when she saw that she had conceived, Hagar looked with contempt on her mistress. Then Sarai said to Abram, "May the wrong done to me be on you! I gave my slave-girl to your embrace, and when she saw that she had conceived, she looked on me with contempt. May the LORD judge between you and me!" But Abram said to Sarai, "Your slave-girl is in your power; do to her as you please." Then Sarai dealt harshly with Hagar, and she ran away from her.

The angel of the LORD found Hagar by a spring of water in the wilderness, the spring on the way to Shur. And it said, "Hagar, slave-girl of Sarai, where have you come from and where are you going?" She said, "I am running away from my mistress Sarai." The angel of the LORD said to her, "Return to your mistress, and submit to her." The angel of the LORD also said to Hagar, "I will so greatly multiply your offspring that they cannot be counted for multitude." And the angel of the LORD said to Hagar,

"Now you have conceived and shall bear a son;
you shall call him Ishmael,
for the Lord has given heed to your affliction.
He shall be a wild ass of a man,
with his hand against everyone,
    and everyone's hand against him;
    and he shall live at odds with all his kin."

So Hagar named the LORD who spoke to her, "You are El-roi"; for she said, "Have I really seen God and remained alive after seeing the LORD?" Therefore the well was called Beer-lahai-roi; it lies between Kadesh and Bered.

Hagar bore Abram a son; and Abram named his son, whom Hagar bore, Ishmael. Abram was eighty-six years old when Hagar bore him Ishmael.

Genesis 16:1–16

JESUS AS MOTHER HEN

The Revised Common Lectionary provides this reading. Jesus speaks as a wisdom figure, and pictures himself as a mother hen, attentive and protective.

Some Pharisees came and said to him, "Get away from here, for Herod wants to kill you." He said to them, "Go and tell that fox for me, 'Listen, I am casting out demons and performing cures today and tomorrow, and on the third day I finish my work. Yet today, tomorrow, and the next day I must be on my way, because it is impossible for a prophet to be killed outside of Jerusalem. Jerusalem, Jerusalem, the city that kills prophets and stones those who are sent to it! How often have I desired to gather your children together as a hen gathers her brood under her wings, and you were not willing. See, your house is left to you. And I tell you, you will not see me until the time comes when you say, 'Blessed is the one who comes in the name of the Lord.'"

Luke 13:31 – 35

If the Transfiguration is celebrated on this Sunday:

GOD PROVIDES FOOD AND WIPES AWAY TEARS

In the gospel story of the Transfiguration, God is encountered atop a mountain as a voice from a bright cloud. This story provides another image: On a high mountain, God provides a feast of rich food and wipes away tears — roles often thought to belong to women.

On this mountain the LORD of hosts will make for all peoples
      a feast of rich food, a feast of well-aged wine,
      of rich food filled with marrow,
      of well-aged wines strained clear.
And God will destroy on this mountain
      the shroud that is cast over all peoples,
      the sheet that is spread over all nations;
      God will swallow up death forever.
Then the LORD God will wipe away the tears from all faces,
      and the disgrace of the people will be taken away from all the earth,
      for the LORD has spoken.
It will be said on that day,
      Lo, this is our God, we have waited for God so that we might be saved.
      This is the LORD for whom we have waited;
      let us be glad and rejoice in the salvation of the LORD.
      For the hand of the LORD will rest on this mountain.

Isaiah 25:6 – 10a

YEAR C | THIRD SUNDAY OF LENT

ZIPPORAH AND MOSES

The Roman lectionary tells how Moses experienced God in the burning bush. The first story here tells of Moses defending the seven women, after which their father gave Zipporah to be Moses' wife. In the second mysterious story, Zipporah not only shows medical skill, but also serves a priestly function.

One day, after Moses had grown up, he went out to his people and saw their forced labor. He saw an Egyptian beating a Hebrew, one of his kinsfolk. He looked this way and that, and seeing no one he killed the Egyptian and hid him in the sand. When he went out the next day, he saw two Hebrews fighting; and he said to the one who was in the wrong, "Why do you strike your fellow Hebrew?" He answered, "Who made you a ruler and judge over us? Do you mean to kill me as you killed the Egyptian?" Then Moses was afraid and thought, "Surely the thing is known." When Pharoah heard of it, he sought to kill Moses.

But Moses fled from Pharoah. He settled in the land of Midian, and sat down by a well. The priest of Midian had seven daughters. They came to draw water, and filled the troughs to water their father's flock. But some shepherds came and drove them away. Moses got up and came to their defense and watered their flock. When they returned to their father Reuel, he said, "How is it that you have come back so soon today?" They said, "An Egyptian helped us against the shepherds; he even drew water for us and watered the flock."

Reuel said to his daughters, "Where is he? Why did you leave the man? Invite him to break bread." Moses agreed to stay with the man, and Reuel gave Moses his daughter Zipporah in marriage. She bore a son, and he named him Gershom; for he said, "I have been an alien residing in a foreign land."

After a long time the king of Egypt died. The Israelites groaned under their slavery, and cried out. Out of the slavery their cry for help rose up to God. God heard their groaning, and God remembered the covenant with Abraham, Isaac, and Jacob. God looked upon the Israelites, and God took notice of them.

And the LORD said to Moses, "When you go back to Egypt, see that you perform before Pharoah all the wonders that I have put in your power; but I will harden his heart, so that he will not let the people go. Then you shall say to Pharoah, 'Thus says the LORD: Israel is my firstborn son. I said to you, "Let my son go that he may worship me." But you refused to let him go; now I will kill your firstborn son.'"

On the way, at a place where they spent the night, the LORD met Moses and tried to kill him. But Zipporah took a flint and cut off her son's foreskin, and touched Moses' feet with it, and said, "Truly you are a bridegroom of blood to me!" So God let Moses alone. It was then Zipporah said, "A bridegroom of blood by circumcision."

Exodus 2:11 – 21; 4:21 – 26

EAT AND DRINK OF WISDOM

The Revised Common Lectionary quotes Isaiah: "Come, buy wine and milk." This passage invites all to eat and drink of the feminine figure of holy Wisdom.

"I grew tall like a cedar in Lebanon,
  and like a cypress on the heights of Hermon.
I grew tall like a palm tree in En-gedi,
  and like rosebushes in Jericho;
like a fair olive tree in the field,
  and like a plane tree beside water I grew tall.
Like cassia and camel's thorn I gave forth perfume,
  and like choice myrrh I spread my fragrance,
like galbanum, onycha, and stacte,
  and like the odor of incense in the tent.
Like a terebinth I spread out my branches,
  and my branches are glorious and graceful.
Like the vine I bud forth delights,
  and my blossoms become glorious and abundant fruit.
"Come to me, you who desire me,
  and eat your fill of my fruits.
For the memory of me is sweeter than honey,
  and the possession of me sweeter than the honeycomb.
Those who eat of me will hunger for more,
  and those who drink of me will thirst for more."

Sirach 24:13–21

FOURTH SUNDAY OF LENT

THE MOTHER OF SAMSON

The lectionaries tell of the Israelites' first celebration of Passover in the Promised Land. This passage tells another story from the history of Israel: the miraculous conception of Samson. The angel prefers to deal directly with Samson's mother-to-be, but her husband keeps trying to be included in the conversation.

There was a certain man of Zorah, of the tribe of the Danites, whose name was Manoah. His wife was barren, having borne no children. And the angel of the LORD appeared to the woman and said to her, "Although you are barren, having borne no children, you shall conceive and bear a son. Now be careful not to drink wine or strong drink, or to eat anything unclean, for you shall conceive and bear a son. No razor is to come on his head, for the boy shall be a nazirite to God from birth. It is he who shall begin to deliver Israel from the hand of the Philistines."

Then the woman came and told her husband, "A man of God came to me, and his appearance was like that of an angel of God, most awe-inspiring; I did not ask him where he came from, and he did not tell me his name; but he said to me, 'You shall conceive and bear a son. So then drink no wine or strong drink, and eat nothing unclean, for the boy shall be a nazirite to God from birth to the day of his death.'"

Then Manoah entreated the LORD, and said, "O, LORD, I pray, let the man of God whom you sent come to us again and teach us what we are to do concerning the boy who will be born." God listened to Manoah, and the angel of God came again to the woman as she sat in the field; but her husband Manoah was not with her. So the woman ran quickly and told her husband, "The man who came to me the other day has appeared to me." Manoah got up and followed his wife, and came to the man and said to him, "Are you the man who spoke to this woman?" And he said, "I am." Then Manoah said, "Now when your words come true, what is to be the boy's rule of life; what is he to do?" The angel of the LORD said to Manoah, "Let the woman give heed to all that I said to her. She may not eat of anything that comes from the vine. She is not to drink wine or strong drink, or eat any unclean thing. She is to observe everything that I commanded her."

Manoah said to the angel of the LORD, "Allow us to detain you, and prepare a kid for you." The angel of the LORD said to Manoah, "If you detain me, I will not eat your food; but if you want to prepare a burnt offering, then offer it to the LORD." (For Manoah did not know that this was the angel of the LORD.) Then Manoah said to the angel of the LORD, "What is your name, so that we may honor you when your words come true?" But the angel of the LORD said to him, "Why do you ask my name? It is too wonderful."

So Manoah took the kid with the grain offering, and offered it on the rock to the LORD, to the one who works wonders. When the flame went up toward heaven from the altar, the angel of the LORD ascended in the flame of the altar while Manoah and his wife looked on; and they fell on their faces to the ground. The angel of the LORD did not appear again to Manoah and his wife. Then Manoah realized that it was the angel of the LORD. And Manoah said to his wife, "We shall surely die, for we have seen God." But his wife said to him, "If the LORD had meant to kill us, God would not have accepted a burnt offering and a grain offering at our hands, or shown us all these things, or now announced to us such things as these."

The woman bore a son, and named him Samson. The boy grew, and the LORD blessed him. The spirit of the LORD began to stir him in Mahaneh-dan, between Zorah and Eshtaol.

Judges 13:2–25

FIFTH SUNDAY OF LENT

The Roman lectionary and Revised Common Lectionary both provide women's stories, but use different passages from the Gospel of John. Any passage not read this Sunday may be used on the last Sunday of the liturgical year, page 343.

THE WOMAN WHOM JESUS DOES NOT CONDEMN
Jesus treats this woman as equal to the scribes and Pharisees and invites them all to enter a new way of life.

Jesus went to the Mount of Olives. Early in the morning he came again to the temple. All the people came to him and he sat down and began to teach them. The scribes and the Pharisees brought a woman who had been caught in adultery; and making her stand before all of them, they said to Jesus, "Teacher, this woman was caught in the very act of committing adultery. Now in the law Moses commanded us to stone such women. Now what do you say?" They said this to test Jesus, so that they might have some charge to bring against him.

Jesus bent down and wrote with his finger on the ground. When they kept on questioning him, he straightened up and said to them, "Let anyone among who who is without sin be the first to throw a stone at her." And once again he bent down and wrote on the ground. When they heard it, they went away, one by one, beginning with the elders.

And Jesus was left alone with the woman standing before him. Jesus straightened up and said to her, "Woman, where are they? Has no one condemned you?" She said, "No one, sir." And Jesus said, "Neither do I condemn you. Go your way, and from now on do not sin again."

John 8:1–11

MARY OF BETHANY ANOINTS JESUS
Though Jesus will later be anointed after being laid in the tomb, here Mary anoints him in front of all at the table. Mary's love and service are given to Jesus while he lives.

Six days before the Passover Jesus came to Bethany, the home of Lazarus, whom he had raised from the dead. There they gave a dinner for Jesus. Martha served, and Lazarus was one of those at the table with him. Mary took a pound of costly perfume made of pure nard, anointed Jesus' feet, and wiped them with her hair. The house was filled with the fragrance of the perfume. But Judas Iscariot, one of his disciples (the one who was about to betray him), said, "Why was this perfume not sold for three hundred denarii and the money given to the poor?" (He said this not because he cared about the poor, but because he was a thief; he kept the common purse and used to steal what was put into it.) Jesus said, "Leave her alone. She bought it so that she might keep it for the day of my burial. You always have the poor with you, but you do not always have me."

John 12:1–8

PASSION (PALM) SUNDAY

THE RAPE AND MURDER OF THE LEVITE'S WIFE
The lectionaries tell of the passion and death of Jesus. This passage tells of the suffering and death of a woman.
This woman is the Levite's wife, though the word concubine is used. Her broken body cries out to all Israel, yet
still the author gives her no voice.

At evening there was an old man coming from his work in the field. The man was from the hill country of Ephraim, and he was residing in Gibeah. (The people of the place were Benjaminites.) When the old man looked up and saw the wayfarer in the open square of the city, he said, "Where are you going and where do you come from?" He answered him, "We are passing from Bethlehem in Judah to the remote parts of the hill country of Ephraim, from which I come. I went to Bethlehem in Judah; and I am going to my home. Nobody has offered to take me in. We your servants have straw and water for our donkeys, with bread and wine for me and the woman and the young man along with us. We need nothing more." The old man said, "Peace be to you. I will care for all your wants; only do not spend the night in the square." So he brought him into his house, and fed the donkeys; they washed their feet, and ate and drank.

While they were enjoying themselves, the men of the city, a perverse lot, surrounded the house, and started pounding on the door. They said to the old man, the master of the house, "Bring out the man who came into your house, so that we may have intercourse with him." And the man, the master of the house, went out to them and said to them, "No, my brothers, do not act so wickedly. Since this man is my guest, do not do this vile thing. Here are my virgin daughter and his concubine; let me bring them out now. Ravish them and do whatever you want to them; but against this man do not do such a vile thing."

But the men would not listen to him. So the man seized his concubine, and put her out to them. They wantonly raped her, and abused her all through the night until the morning. And as the dawn began to break, they let her go. As morning appeared, the woman came and fell down at the door of the man's house where her master was, until it was light.

In the morning her master got up, opened the door of the house, and when he went out to go on his way, there was his concubine laying at the door of the house with her hands on the threshold. "Get up," he said to her, "We are going." But there was no answer. Then he put her on the donkey; and the man set out for his home. When he had entered his house, he took a knife, and grasping his concubine he cut her into twelve pieces, limb by limb, and sent her throughout all the territory of Israel. Then he commanded the men whom he sent, saying, "Thus shall you say to all the Israelites, 'Has such a thing ever happened since the day that the Israelites came up from the land of Egypt until this day? Consider it, take counsel, and speak out.'"

Judges 19:16–30

The story of the woman who anoints Jesus is not part of the gospel narrative in Year C of the lectionaries, but it is placed here to parallel its use in Years A and B. The woman's generous, self-giving love contrasts with the narrow self-righteousness of the dinner guests.

One of the Pharisees asked Jesus to eat with him, and Jesus went into the Pharisee's house and took his place at the table. And a woman in the city, who was a sinner, having learned that Jesus was eating in the Pharisee's house, brought an alabaster jar of ointment. She stood behind him at his feet, weeping, and began to bathe his feet with her tears and to dry them with her hair. Then she continued kissing his feet and anointing them with the ointment.

Now when the Pharisee who had invited Jesus saw it, he said to himself, "If this man were a prophet, he would have known who and what kind of woman this is who is touching him — that she is a sinner." Jesus spoke up and said to him, "Simon, I have something to say to you." "Teacher," he replied, "Speak."

"A certain creditor had two debtors; one owed five hundred denarii, and the other fifty. When they could not pay, he canceled the debts for both of them. Now which of them will love him more?" Simon answered, "I suppose the one for whom he canceled the greater debt." And Jesus said to him, "You have judged right."

Then turning toward the woman, he said to Simon, "Do you see this woman? I entered your house; you gave me no water for my feet, but she has bathed my feet with her tears and dried them with her hair. You gave me no kiss, but from the time I came in she has not stopped kissing my feet. You did not anoint my head with oil, but she has anointed my feet with ointment. Therefore, I tell you, her sins, which were many, have been forgiven; hence she has shown great love. But the one to whom little is forgiven, loves little."

Then Jesus said to her, "Your sins are forgiven." But those who were at the table with him began to say among themselves, "Who is this who even forgives sin?" And Jesus said to the woman, "Your faith has saved you; go in peace."

Luke 7:36 – 50

WOMEN IN THE PASSION ACCORDING TO LUKE

The Roman lectionary and Revised Common Lectionary appoint chapters 22 and 23 of Luke's gospel for this Sunday. Excerpts that tell women's stories are given here.

THE SERVANT GIRL CONFRONTS PETER

This woman must have been a follower of Jesus, as she knows Peter by sight. How scandalized she must have been by his denial.

The authorities seized Jesus and led him away, bringing him into the high priest's house. But Peter was following at a distance. When they had kindled a fire in the middle of the courtyard and sat down together, Peter sat among them. Then a servant-girl, seeing him in the firelight, stared at him and said, "This man also was with Jesus." But he denied it, saying, "Woman, I do not know him." A little later someone else, on seeing him, said, "You also are one of them." But Peter said, "I am not!" Then about an hour later still another kept insisting, "Surely this man also was with him; for he is a Galilean." But Peter said, "I do not know what you are talking about!" At that moment, while he was still speaking, the cock crowded. The Lord turned and looked at Peter. Then Peter remembered the word of the Lord, how he had said to him, "Before the cock crows today, you will deny me three times." And he went out and wept bitterly.

Luke 22:54 – 62

THE DAUGHTERS OF JERUSALEM
The compassion of the women is reciprocated by Jesus.

A great number of the people followed Jesus, and among them were women who were beating their breasts and wailing for him. But Jesus turned to them and said, "Daughters of Jerusalem, do not weep for me, but weep for yourselves and for your children. For the days are surely coming when they will say, 'Blessed are the barren, and the wombs that never bore, and the breasts that never nursed.'"

Luke 23:27 – 29

THE WOMEN WITNESS JESUS' DEATH
Faithful women prepare to care for the body of Jesus.

The women who had come with Jesus from Galilee followed, and they saw the tomb and how his body was laid. Then they returned, and prepared spices and ointments. On the sabbath they rested according to the commandment.

Luke 23:55 – 56

HOLY THURSDAY

MEMORIAL FEAST FOR THE DAUGHTER OF JEPHTHAH

In the lectionaries, the first reading tells of the establishment of the memorial feast of Passover, and the second reading tells of the institution of the eucharist as a memorial. This passage tells of the death of the daughter of Jephthah and the memorial feast kept by the women in her honor.

The spirit of the LORD came upon Jephthah, and he passed through Gilead and Manasseh. He passed on to Mizpah of Gilead, and from Mizpah of Gilead he passed on to the Ammonites. And Jephthah made a vow to the LORD, and said, "If you will give the Ammonites into my hand, then whoever comes out of the doors of my house to meet me, when I return victorious from the Ammonites, shall be the LORD's to be offered up by me as a burnt offering." So Jephthah crossed over to the Ammonites to fight against them; and the LORD gave them into his hand. Jephthah inflicted a massive defeat on them from Aroer to the neighborhood of Minnith, twenty towns, and as far as Abel-keramin. So the Ammonites were subdued before the people of Israel.

Then Jephthah came to his home at Mizpah; and there was his daughter coming out to meet him with timbrels and with dancing. She was his only child; he had no son or daughter except her. When he saw here, he tore his clothes, and said, "Alas, my daughter! You have brought me very low; you have become the cause of greater trouble to me. For I have opened my mouth to the LORD, and I cannot take back my vow."

She said to him, "My father, if you have opened your mouth to the LORD, do to me according to what has gone out of your mouth, now that the LORD has given you vengeance against your enemies, the Ammonites." And she said to her father, "Let this thing be done for me: Grant me two months, so that I may go and wander on the mountains, and bewail my virginity, my companions and I." "Go," he said and sent her away for two months.

So she departed, she and her companions, and bewailed her virginity on the mountains. At the end of two months, she returned to her father, who did with her according to the vow he had made. She had never slept with a man. So there arose an Israelite custom that for four days every year the daughters of Israel would go out to lament the daughter of Jephthah the Gileadite.

Judges 11:29–40

ABIGAIL, WASHER OF FEET

The gospel reading of the lectionaries tells how Jesus washed the feet of his disciples. This passage tells of Abigail, who washed the feet of David's servants as a gesture of hospitality and in response to being invited to marry King David.

David sent and wooed Abigail, to make her his wife. When David's servants came to Abigail at Carmel, they said to her, "David has sent us to you to take you to him as his wife." She rose and bowed down, with her face to the ground, and said,

"Behold your handmaiden is a servant to wash the feet of the servants of my lord." Abigail got up hurriedly and rode away on a donkey; her five maids attended her. She went after the messengers of David and became his wife.

1 Samuel 25:39c – 42

WIDOWS WHO WASH THE FEET OF THE SAINTS
The ministry of widows in the early church included prayer and service, such as washing the feet of the members of the community, as Jesus washed his disciples' feet. Widows probably washed other women's feet.

Let a widow be put on the list if she is not less than sixty years old and has been married only once; she must be well attested for her good works, as one who has brought up children, shown hospitality, washed the saints' feet, helped the afflicted, and devoted herself to doing good in every way.

1 Timothy 5:9 – 10

GOOD FRIDAY

The lectionaries tell of the passion and death of Jesus. Jesus' agony on the cross is a kind of childbirth, leading to new life. These passages tell of death in childbirth. The death of Jesus is also related here to Israel's loss of the ark, which in other writings is sometimes viewed as a fruitful womb.

THE DEATH OF RACHEL IN CHILDBIRTH

God appeared to Jacob again when he came from Paddan-aram, and he befriended Jacob. God said to him, "Your name is Jacob; no longer shall you be called Jacob, but Israel shall be your name." So he was called Israel. God said to him, "I am God Almighty; be fruitful and multiply; a nation and a company of nations shall come from you, and kings shall spring from you. The land that I gave to Abraham and Isaac I will give to you, and I will give the land to your offspring after you." Then God went up from him at the place where he had spoken with him. Jacob set up a pillar on the place where he had spoken with God, a pillar of stone; and Jacob poured out a drink offering on it, and poured oil on it. So Jacob called the place where God had spoken with him Bethel.

Then they journeyed from Bethel; and when they were still some distance from Ephrath, Rachel was in childbirth, and she had hard labor. When she was in her hard labor, the midwife said to her, "Do not be afraid; for now you will have another son." As her soul was departing (for she died), she named him Ben-oni; but his father called him Benjamin. So Rachel died, and she was buried on the way to Ephrath (that is, Bethlehem), and Jacob set up a pillar at her grave; it is the pillar of Rachel's tomb, which is there to this day.

Genesis 35:9 – 20

LOSS OF THE ARK AND THE DEATH OF THE WIFE OF PHINEHAS IN CHILDBIRTH

The ark of the covenant, Israel's symbol of Immanuel, God-with-us, is captured in battle. The story also shows that women, even when not engaged in violence, suffer the brunt of its consequences.

The word of Samuel came to all Israel.

In those days the Philistines mustered for war against Israel, and Israel went out to battle against them; they encamped at Ebenezer, and the Philistines encamped at Aphek. The Philistines drew up in line against Israel, and when the battle was joined, Israel was defeated by the Philistines, who killed about four thousand men on the field of battle.

When the troops came to the camp, the elders of Israel said, "Why has the LORD put us to rout today before the Philistines? Let us bring the ark of the covenant of the LORD here from Shiloh, so that God may come among us and save us from the power of our enemies." So the people sent to Shiloh, and brought from there the ark of the covenant of the LORD of hosts, who is enthroned on the cherubim. The two sons of Eli, Hophni and Phinehas, were there with the ark of the covenant of God.

When the ark of the covenant of the LORD came into the camp, all Israel gave a mighty shout, so that the earth resounded. When the Philistines heard the noise of the shouting, they said, "What does this great shouting in the camp of the Hebrews mean?" When they learned that the ark of the LORD had come to the camp, the Philistines were afraid; for they said, "Gods have come into the camp." They also said, "Woe to us! For nothing like this has happened before. Woe to us! Who can deliver us from the power of these mighty gods? These are the gods who struck the Egyptians with every sort of plague in the wilderness. Take courage, and be men, O Philistines, in order not to become slaves to the Hebrews as they have been to you; be men and fight."

So the Philistines fought; Israel was defeated, and they fled, everyone to his home. There was a very great slaughter, for there fell of Israel thirty thousand foot soldiers. The ark of God was captured, and the two sons of Eli, Hophni and Phinehas, died.

A man of Benjamin ran from the battle line, and came to Shiloh the same day, with his clothes torn and with earth upon his head. When he arrived, Eli was sitting upon his seat by the road watching, for his heart trembled for the ark of God. When the man came into the city and told the news, all the city cried out. When Eli heard the sound of the outcry, he said, "What is this uproar?" Then the man came quickly and told Eli. Now Eli was ninety-eight years old and his eyes were set, so that he could not see. The man said to Eli, "I have just come from the battle; I fled from the battle today." He said, "How did it go, my son?" The messenger replied, "Israel has fled before the Philistines, and there has also been a great slaughter among the troops; your two sons also, Hophni and Phinehas, are dead, and the ark of God has been captured." When he mentioned the ark of God, Eli fell over backward from his seat by the side of the gate; and his neck was broken and he died, for he was an old man, and heavy. He had judged Israel forty years.

Now his daughter-in-law, the wife of Phinehas, was pregnant, about to give birth. When she heard the news that the ark of God was captured, and that her father-in-law and her husband were dead, she bowed and gave birth; for her labor pains overwhelmed her. As she was about to die, the women attending her said to her, "Do not be afraid, for you have borne a son." But she did not answer or give heed. She named the child Ichabod, meaning, "The glory has departed from Israel," because the ark of God had been captured and because of her father-in-law and her husband. She said, "The glory has departed from Israel, for the ark of God has been captured."

1 Samuel 4:1 – 22

Six days before the Passover Jesus came to Bethany, the home of Lazarus, whom he had raised from the dead. There they gave a dinner for Jesus. Martha served, and Lazarus was one of those at the table with him. Mary took a pound of costly perfume made of pure nard, anointed Jesus' feet, and wiped them with her hair. The house was filled with the fragrance of the perfume. But Judas Iscariot, one of his disciples (the one who was about to betray him), said, "Why was this perfume not sold for three hundred denarii and the money given to the poor." (He said this not because he cared about the poor, but because he was a thief; he kept the common purse and used to steal what was put into it.) Jesus said, "Leave her alone. She bought it so that she might keep it for the day of my burial. You always have the poor with you, but you do not always have me."

John 12:1–8

WOMEN IN THE PASSION ACCORDING TO JOHN
Both the Roman lectionary and Revised Common Lectionary assign chapters 18 and 19 of John's gospel to this day. Excerpts that tell women's stories are given here.

THE SERVANT WOMAN CONFRONTS PETER
While Jesus affirms his identity to the high priest, Peter denies his connection to Jesus after being challenged by a woman who knows the truth.

Simon Peter and another disciple followed Jesus. Since that disciple was known to the high priest, he went with Jesus into the courtyard of the high priest, but Peter was standing outside at the gate. So the other disciple, who was known to the high priest, went out, spoke to the woman who guarded the gate, and brought Peter in. The woman said to Peter, "You are not also one of this man's disciples, are you?" He said, "I am not."

Now Simon Peter was standing and warming himself. They asked him, "You are not also one of his disciples, are you?" He denied it and said, "I am not." One of the slaves of the high priest, a relative of the man whose ear Peter had cut off, asked, "Did I not see you in the garden with him?" Again Peter denied it, and at that moment the cock crowed.

John 18:15–17, 25–27

Jesus' death is witnessed by his mother and other faithful women followers. Jesus' creation of a new family of God is symbolized when the disciple takes Jesus' mother into his own home.

Standing near the cross of Jesus were his mother, and his mother's sister, Mary the wife of Clopas, and Mary Magdalene. When Jesus saw his mother and the disciple whom he loved standing beside her, he said to his mother, "Woman, here is your son." Then Jesus said to the disciple, "Here is your mother." And from that hour the disciple took her into his own home.

John 19:25 – 27

Forgotten Woman of Bethany, Gospel of Mark

EASTER VIGIL

JESUS APPEARS TO THE WOMEN

The lectionaries tell of Jesus appearing to his male disciples after the resurrection. This passage tells of the risen Christ and his women disciples. They run to tell the men, but are not believed.

On the first day of the week, at early dawn, the women came to the tomb, taking the spices that they had prepared. They found the stone rolled away from the tomb, but when they went in, they did not find the body. While they were perplexed about this, suddenly two men in dazzling clothes stood beside them. The women were terrified and bowed their faces to the ground, but the men said to them, "Why do you look for the living among the dead? He is not here, but has risen. Remember how he told you, while he was still in Galilee, that the Son of Man must be handed over to sinners, and be crucified, and on the third day rise again."

Then the women remembered his words, and returning from the tomb, they told all this to the eleven and to all the rest. Now it was Mary Magdalene, Joanna, Mary the mother of James, and the other women with them who told this to the apostles. But these words seemed to them an idle tale, and they did not believe the women. But Peter got up and ran to the tomb; stopping and looking in, he saw the linen cloths by themselves; then he went home, amazed at what had happened.

Luke 24:1 – 12

Further readings for the Easter Vigil appear on pages 52 – 70, Easter Vigil, Year A.

EASTER SUNDAY

JESUS APPEARS TO MARY MAGDALENE

Mary Magdalene, the first witness of the empty tomb, runs to report the news. She is unable to fully communicate what has happened: It is a novel and earth-shattering event. Her sorrow is soon transformed to joy. The risen Christ commissions the faithful disciple Mary Magdalene as "apostle to the apostles."

Early on the first day of the week, while it was still dark, Mary Magdalene came to the tomb and saw that the stone had been removed from the tomb. So she ran and went to Simon Peter and the other disciple, the one whom Jesus loved, and said to them, "They have taken the Lord out of the tomb, and we do not know where they have laid him." Then Peter and the other disciple set out and went toward the tomb. The two were running together, but the other disciple outran Peter and reached the tomb first. He bent down to look in and saw the linen wrappings lying there, but he did not go in. Then Simon Peter came, following him, and went into the tomb. He saw the linen wrappings lying there, and the cloth that had been on Jesus' head, not lying with the linen wrappings but rolled up in a place by itself. Then the other disciple, who reached the tomb first, also went in, and he saw and believed; for as yet they did not understand the scripture, that he must rise from the dead. Then the disciples returned to their homes.

But Mary stood weeping outside the tomb. As she wept, she bent over to look into the tomb; and she saw two angels in white, sitting where the body of Jesus had been lying, one at the head and the other at the feet. They said to her, "Woman, why are you weeping?" She said to them, "They have taken away my Lord, and I do not know where they have laid him."

When she had said this, she turned around and saw Jesus standing there, but she did not know that it was Jesus. Jesus said to her, "Woman, why are you weeping? Whom are you looking for?" Supposing him to be the gardener, she said to him, "Sir, if you have carried him away, tell me where you have laid him, and I will take him away." Jesus said, "Mary!" She turned and said to him in Hebrew, "Rabbouni!" (which means Teacher). Jesus said to her, "Do not hold on to me, because I have not yet ascended to the Father. But go to my brothers and say to them, 'I am ascending to my Father and your Father, to my God and your God.'" Mary Magdalene went and announced to the disciples, "I have seen the Lord"; and she told them that Jesus had said these things to her.

John 20:1–18

SECOND SUNDAY OF EASTER

JESUS APPEARS TO THE WOMEN

The lectionaries tell of Jesus appearing to his male disciples after the resurrection. This passage tells of the risen Christ and his women disciples. They run to tell the men, but the men do not believe them.

On the first day of the week, at early dawn, the women came to the tomb, taking the spices that they had prepared. They found the stone rolled away from the tomb, but when they went in, they did not find the body. While they were perplexed about this, suddenly two men in dazzling clothes stood beside them. The women were terrified and bowed their faces to the ground, but the men said to them, "Why do you look for the living among the dead? He is not here, but has risen. Remember how he told you, while he was still in Galilee, that the Son of Man must be handed over to sinners, and be crucified, and on the third day rise again."

Then the women remembered his words, and returning from the tomb, they told all this to the eleven and to all the rest. Now it was Mary Magdalene, Joanna, Mary the mother of James, and the other women with them who told this to the apostles. But these words seemed to them an idle tale, and they did not believe the women. But Peter got up and ran to the tomb; stopping and looking in, he saw the linen cloths by themselves; then he went home, amazed at what had happened.

Luke 24:1 – 12

THIRD SUNDAY OF EASTER

JESUS APPEARS TO MARY MAGDALENE
Jesus speaks to Mary and she speaks to him. Mary boldly reports, "I have seen the Lord."

Mary stood weeping outside the tomb. As she wept, she bent over to look into the tomb; and she saw two angels in white, sitting where the body of Jesus had been lying, one at the head and the other at the feet. They said to her, "Woman, why are you weeping?" She said to them, "They have taken away my Lord, and I do not know where they have laid him."

When she had said this, she turned around and saw Jesus standing there, but she did not know that it was Jesus. Jesus said to her, "Woman, why are you weeping? Whom are you looking for?" Supposing him to be the gardener, she said to him, "Sir, if you have carried him away, tell me where you have laid him, and I will take him away." Jesus said to her, "Mary!" She turned and said to him in Hebrew, "Rabbouni!" (which means Teacher). Jesus said to her, "Do not hold on to me, because I have not yet ascended to the Father. But go to my brothers and say to them, 'I am ascending to my Father and your Father, to my God and your God.'" Mary Magdalene went and announced to the disciples, "I have seen the Lord"; and she told them that Jesus had said these things to her.

John 20:11 – 18

FOURTH SUNDAY OF EASTER

For the rest of the Easter season, the lectionaries tell stories of the early church from the Acts of the Apostles. Here stories of women in the life of the early church are presented, also taken from Acts.

TABITHA, DEVOTED TO GOOD WORKS

Tabitha is important in the Christian community at Joppa. She is the only woman explicitly named in Acts as a disciple. She takes care of the widows in Joppa out of her own resources, and her death affects the community so much that they send for Peter's help.

In Joppa there was a disciple whose name was Tabitha, which in Greek is Dorcas. She was devoted to good works and acts of charity. At that time she became ill and died. When they had washed her, they laid her in a room upstairs. Since Lydda was near Joppa, the disciples, who heard that Peter was there, sent two men to him with the request, "Please come to us without delay." So Peter got up and went with them; and when he arrived, they took him to the room upstairs. All the widows stood beside him, weeping and showing tunics and other clothing that Dorcas had made while she was with them. Peter put all of them outside, and then he knelt down and prayed. He turned to the body and said, "Tabitha, get up." Then she opened her eyes, and seeing Peter, she sat up. He gave her his hand and helped her up. Then calling the saints and widows, he showed her to be alive. This became known throughout Joppa, and many believed in the Lord. Meanwhile Peter stayed in Joppa for some time with a certain Simon, a tanner.

Acts of the Apostles 9:36 – 43

FIFTH SUNDAY OF EASTER

ANANIAS AND SAPPHIRA

Sapphira and her husband Ananias conspire to lie to the church and therefore to God. Their dishonesty has consequences. This is a difficult story that offends modern sensibilities, but notice that the woman and man are treated equally.

A man named Ananias, with the consent of his wife Sapphira, sold a piece of property. With his wife's knowledge, he kept back some of the proceeds, and brought only a part and laid it at the apostles' feet. "Ananias," Peter asked, "why has Satan filled your heart to lie to the Holy Spirit and to keep back part of the proceeds of the land? While it remained unsold, did it not remain your own? And after it was sold, were not the proceeds at your disposal? How is it that you have contrived this deed in your heart? You did not lie to us but to God!" Now when Ananias heard these words, he fell down and died. And great fear seized all who heard of it. The young men came and wrapped up his body, then carried him out and buried him.

After an interval of about three hours his wife came in, not knowing what had happened. Peter said to her, "Tell me whether you and your husband sold the land for such and such a price." And she said, "Yes, that was the price." Then Peter said to her, "How is it that you have agreed together to put the Spirit of the Lord to the test? Look, the feet of those who have buried your husband are at the door, and they will carry you out." Immediately she fell down at his feet and died. When the young men came in they found her dead, so they carried her out and buried her beside her husband. And great fear seized the whole church and all who heard of these things.

Acts of the Apostles 5:1–11

SIXTH SUNDAY OF EASTER

LYDIA, WORSHIPER OF GOD

Paul's first experience of the Philippian church is a Sabbath gathering of women. Lydia is the first convert in Europe. She opens her home and it becomes a house church.

Paul and Timothy went down to Troas. During the night Paul had a vision: there stood a man of Macedonia pleading with him and saying, "Come over to Macedonia and help us." When Paul had seen the vision, we immediately tried to cross over to Macedonia, being convinced that God had called us to proclaim the good news to them.

We set sail from Troas and took a straight course to Samothrace, the following day to Neapolis, and from there to Philippi, which is a leading city of the distrinct of Macedonia and a Roman colony. We remained in this city for some days.

On the sabbath day we went outside the gate by the river, where we supposed there was a place of prayer; and we sat down and spoke to the women who had gathered there. A certain woman named Lydia, a worshiper of God, was listening to us; she was from the city of Thyatira and a dealer in purple cloth. The Lord opened her heart to listen eagerly to what was said by Paul. When she and her household were baptized, she urged us, saying, "If you have judged me to be faithful to the Lord, come and stay at my home." And she prevailed upon us.

Acts of the Apostles 16:9 – 15

ASCENSION OF CHRIST

THE JOYS OF WISDOM

Christ at his ascension is interpreted in relation to the feminine figure of holy Wisdom.

Happy are those who find wisdom,
    and those who get understanding,
for her income is better than silver,
    and her revenue better than gold.
She is more precious than jewels,
    and nothing you desire can compare with her.
Long life is in her right hand;
    in her left hand are riches and honor.
Her ways are ways of pleasantness,
    and all her paths are peace.
She is a tree of life to those who lay hold of her;
    those who hold her fast are called happy.

Proverbs 3:13–18

SEVENTH SUNDAY OF EASTER

When the Ascension is celebrated on the Seventh Sunday of Easter, the two sets of readings may be combined.

THE SLAVE GIRL, THE JAILER'S FAMILY, LYDIA
The perceptive slave girl recognizes Paul as a man of God. The jailer's household and family who are baptized certainly include women. Lydia's home is a meeting place for the local church.

One day, as we were going to the place of prayer, we met a slave girl who had a spirit of divination and brought her owners a great deal of money by fortune-telling. While she followed Paul and us, she would cry out, "These men are slaves of the Most High God, who proclaim to you a way of salvation." She kept doing this for many days. But Paul, very much annoyed, turned and said to the spirit, "I order you in the name of Jesus Christ to come out of her." And it came out that very hour.

But when her owners saw that their hope of making money was gone, they seized Paul and Silas and dragged them into the marketplace before the authorities. When they had brought them before the magistrates, they said, "These men are disturbing our city; they are Jews and are advocating customs that are not lawful for us as Romans to adopt or observe." The crowd joined in attacking them, and the magistrates had them stripped of their clothing and ordered them to be beaten with rods. After they had given them a severe flogging, they threw them into prison and ordered the jailer to keep them securely. Following these instructions, he put them in the innermost cell and fastened their feet in the stocks.

About midnight Paul and Silas were praying and singing hymns to God, and the prisoners were listening to them. Suddenly there was an earthquake, so violent that the foundations of the prison were shaken; and immediately all the doors were opened and everyone's chains were unfastened. When the jailer woke up and saw the prison doors wide open, he drew his sword and was about to kill himself, since he supposed that the prisoners had escaped. But Paul shouted in a loud voice, "Do not harm yourself, for we are all here." The jailer called for lights, and coming in, he fell down trembling before Paul and Silas.

Then he brought them outside and said, "Sirs, what must I do to be saved?" They answered, "Believe on the Lord Jesus, and you will be saved, you and your household." They spoke the word of the Lord to him and to all who were in his house. At the same hour of the night he took them and washed their wounds; then he and his entire family were baptized without delay. He brought them up into the house and set food before them; and he and his entire household rejoiced that he had become a believer in God.

When morning came, the magistrates sent the police, saying, "Let those men go." And the jailer reported the message to Paul, saying, "The magistrates sent word to let you go; therefore come out now and go in peace." But Paul replied, "They have beaten us in public, uncondemned, men who are Roman citizens, and have thrown us into prison; and now are they going to discharge us in secret? Certainly not! Let them come and take us out themselves." The police reported these words to the magistrates, and they were afraid when they heard that they were Roman citizens; so they came and apologized to them. And they took them out and asked them to leave the city.

After leaving the prison they went to Lydia's home; and when they had seen and encouraged the brothers and sisters there, they departed.

Acts of the Apostles 16:16 – 40

PENTECOST

DAUGHTERS AND MAIDSERVANTS SHALL PROPHESY
When the Holy Spirit descends on the church at Pentecost, women and men are empowered to prophesy, as had been foretold.

When the day of Pentecost had come, the twelve were all together in one place. And suddenly from heaven there came a sound like the rush of a violent wind, and it filled the entire house where they were sitting. Divided tongues, as of fire, appeared among them, and tongues rested on each of them. All of them were filled with the Holy Spirit and began to speak in other languages, as the Spirit gave them ability.

Peter, standing with the eleven, raised his voice and addressed the crowd, "O you Jewish people and all who live in Jerusalem, let this be known to you, and listen to what I say. Indeed, these are not drunk, as you suppose, for it is only nine o'clock in the morning. No, this is what was spoken through the prophet Joel:

'In the last days it will be, God declares,
that I will pour out my Spirit upon all flesh,
 and your sons and your daughters shall prophesy,
and your youth shall see visions,
 and your elders shall dream dreams.
Even upon my menservants and maidservants,
 in those days I will pour out my Spirit;
 and they shall prophesy.'"

Acts of the Apostles 2:1 – 4, 14 – 18

DAUGHTERS AND MAIDSERVANTS SHALL PROPHESY
In the first reading of the lectionaries, included above, Peter quotes this passage from the book of the prophet Joel.

You shall eat in plenty and be satisfied,
 and praise the name of the LORD your God,
 who has dealt wondrously with you.
And my people shall never again be put to shame.
You shall know that I am in the midst of Israel,
 and that I, the LORD, am your God and there is no other.
And my people shall never again
 be put to shame.
Then afterward
 I will pour out my spirit on all flesh;
your sons and your daughters shall prophesy,
 your elders shall dream dreams,
 and your youth shall see visions.
Even on the menservants and maidservants
 in those days, I will pour out my spirit.

Joel 2:26 – 29

THE PROPHET HULDAH

The first reading of the lectionaries proclaims that daughters shall prophesy. This story tells of Huldah, prophet in Israel. She authenticates the newly rediscovered book of the Law and the community believes.

The priest Hilkiah, Akikam, Achbor, Shaphan, and Asaiah went to the prophetess Huldah the wife of Shullum son of Tikvah, son of Harhas, keeper of the wardrobe; she resided in Jerusalem in the Second Quarter, where they consulted her. She declared to them, "Thus says the LORD, the God of Israel: Tell the man who sent you to me, Thus says the LORD, I will indeed bring disaster on this place and on its inhabitants—all the words of the book that the king of Judah has read. Because they have abandoned me and have made offerings to other gods, so that they have provoked me to anger with all the work of their hands, therefore my wrath will be kindled against this place and it will not be quenched.

"But as to the king of Judah, who sent you to inquire of the LORD, thus shall you say to him, Thus says the LORD, the God of Israel: Regarding the words that you have heard, because your heart was penitent, and you humbled yourself before the LORD, when you heard how I spoke against this place, and against its inhabitants, that they should become a desolation and a curse, and because you have torn your clothes and wept before me, I also have heard you, says the LORD. Therefore, I will gather you to your ancestors, and you shall be gathered to your place in peace; your eyes shall not see all the disasters that I will bring on this place." They took the message back to the king.

2 Kings 22:14 – 20

THE SERVANT GIRL QUESTIONS PETER

This passage tells of a woman who spoke prophetically to Peter.

The authorities seized Jesus and led him away, bringing him into the high priest's house. But Peter was following at a distance. When they had kindled a fire in the middle of the courtyard and sat down together, Peter sat among them. Then a servant-girl, seeing him in the firelight, stared at him and said, "This man also was with Jesus." But he denied it, saying, "Woman, I do not know him." A little later someone else, on seeing him, said, "You also are one of them." But Peter said, "I am not!" Then about an hour later still another kept insisting, "Surely this man also was with him; for he is a Galilean." But Peter said, "I do not know what you are talking about!" At that moment, while he was still speaking, the cock crowded. The Lord turned and looked at Peter. Then Peter remembered the word of the Lord, how he had said, to him, "Before the cock crows today, you will deny me three times." And he went out and wept bitterly.

Luke 22:54 – 62

TRINITY SUNDAY

FIRST SUNDAY AFTER PENTECOST

WISDOM AS CREATOR
The feminine figure of holy Wisdom is involved in the creation of the world. She is a model for Jesus in the prologue of the Gospel of John.

Does not wisdom call,
    and does not understanding raise her voice?
On the heights, beside the way,
    at the crossroads she takes her stand;
beside the gates in front of the town,
    at the entrance of the portals she cries out:
"To you, O people, I call,
    and my cry is to all that live.
The LORD created me at the beginning of the divine work,
    the first of God's acts of long ago.
Ages ago I was set up,
    at the first, before the beginning of the earth.
When there were no depths I was brought forth,
    when there were no springs abounding with water.
Before the mountains had been shaped,
    before the hills, I was brought forth —
when God had not yet made earth and fields,
    or the world's first bits of soil.
When the heavens were established,
    when God drew a circle on the face of the deep,
when the skies above were made firm,
    when the foundations of the deeps were established,
when God assigned to the sea its limit,
    so that the waters might not transgress God's command,
when the foundations of the earth were marked out,
    then I was beside God, like a master worker,
and I was daily God's delight,
    rejoicing before God always,
rejoicing in the inhabited world
    and delighting in the human race."

Proverbs 8:1 – 4, 22 – 31

Paul's letters often conclude with the names of members of the church and a blessing. Here Paul greets many women, including Julia and the unnamed sister of Nereus.

Greet Asyncritus, Phlegon, Hermes, Patrobas, Hermas, and the brothers and sisters who are with them. Greet Philologus, Julia, Nereus and his sister, and Olympas, and all the saints who are with them. Greet one another with a holy kiss. All the churches of Christ greet you.

Now to God who is able to strengthen you according to my gospel and the proclamation of Jesus Christ, according to the revelation of the mystery that was kept secret for long ages but is now disclosed, and through the prophetic writings is made known to all the Gentiles, according to the command of the eternal God, to bring about the obedience of faith — to the only wise God, through Jesus Christ, to whom be the glory forever! Amen.

Romans 16:14 – 16, 25 – 27

NINTH SUNDAY IN ORDINARY TIME

SECOND SUNDAY AFTER PENTECOST
PROPER 4: SUNDAY BETWEEN 29 MAY AND 4 JUNE

GOD WASHES IN FRESH WATER
God cleans and refreshes the chosen people, tasks thought to belong to women.

I will draw you from the nations,
gather you from exile
and bring you home.

I will wash you in fresh water,
rid you from the filth of idols
and make you clean again.

I will make you a new heart,
breathe new spirit into you.
I will remove your heart of stone,
give you back a heart of flesh.

I will give you my own spirit
to lead you in my ways,
faithful to what I command.

Then you will live in the land,
the land I gave your ancestors.
You will be my people
and I will be your God.

Canticle of Ezekiel 36:24 – 28 ICEL

GOD AS PROVIDER OF FOOD

Feeding children is thought to be women's work. Here God feeds the people by hand with heaven's bread, like a mother who feeds her child.

You hand-fed your people
with food for angels,
heaven's bread:
ready to eat,
richly satisfying,
pleasing to every taste.

Eating this bread,
they tasted your sweetness,
the perfect meal
for their deepest hunger and hope.

Canticle of the Wisdom of Solomon 16:20 – 21 ICEL

Mary Magdalene

TENTH SUNDAY IN ORDINARY TIME

THIRD SUNDAY AFTER PENTECOST
PROPER 5: SUNDAY BETWEEN 5 AND 11 JUNE

THE WIDOW OF ZAREPHATH

Elijah brings God's grace to this poor woman, an outsider. Her generosity and God's favor bring abundance and new life to her and her son. In the second story, the woman professes faith. This foreign woman is a sign to God's chosen people.

The word of the LORD came to Elijah, saying, "Go now to Zarephath, which belongs to Sidon, and live there; for I have commanded a widow there to feed you." So he set out and went to Zarephath. When he came to the gate of the town, a widow was there gathering sticks; he called to her and said, "Bring me a little water in a vessel, so that I may drink." As she was going to bring it, he called to her and said, "Bring me a morsel of bread in your hand." But she said, "As the LORD your God lives, I have nothing baked, only a handful of meal in a jar, and little oil in a jug; I am now gathering a couple of sticks, so that I may go home and prepare it for myself and my son, that we may eat it, and die."

Elijah said to her, "Do not be afraid; go and do as you have said; but first make me a little cake of it and bring it to me, and afterwards make something for yourself and your son. For thus says the LORD the God of Israel: The jar of meal will not be emptied and the jug of oil will not fail until the day that the LORD sends rain on the earth." She went and did as Elijah said, so that she as well as he and her household ate for many days. The jar of meal was not emptied, neither did the jug of oil fail, according to the word of the LORD that he spoke by Elijah.

The child of the widow of Zarephath became ill; his illness was so severe that there was no breath left in him. She then said to Elijah, "What have you against me, O man of God? You have come to me to bring my sin to remembrance, and to cause the death of my son." But he said to her, "Give me your son." He took him from her bosom, carried him up into the upper chamber where he was lodging, and laid him on his own bed. He cried out to the LORD, "O LORD my God, have you brought calamity even upon the widow with whom I am staying, by killing her son?" Then he stretched himself upon the child three times, and cried out to the LORD, "O LORD my God, let this child's life come into him again." The LORD listened to the voice of Elijah; the life of the child came into him again, and he revived. Elijah took the child, brought him down from the upper chamber into the house, and gave him to his mother; then Elijah said, "See, your son is alive." So the woman said to Elijah, "Now I know that you are a man of God, and that the word of the LORD in your mouth is truth."

1 Kings 17:8 – 24

Being a widow without a son is still a dangerous situation today. Jesus gives this widow back her son. Why should widows live in poverty and fear?

Jesus went to a town called Nain, and his disciples and a large crowd went with him. As Jesus approached the gate of the town, a man who had died was being carried out. He was his mother's only son; and she was a widow; and with her was a large crowd from the town. When the Lord saw her, he had compassion for her and said to her, "Do not weep." Then he came forward and touched the bier, and the bearers stood still. And Jesus said, "Young man, I say to you, rise!" The dead man sat up and began to speak, and Jesus gave him to his mother. Fear seized all of them; and they glorified God, saying, "A great prophet has risen among us!" and "God has looked favorably on the chosen people!" This word about him spread throughout Judea and all the surrounding country.

Luke 7:11–17

ELEVENTH SUNDAY IN ORDINARY TIME

FOURTH SUNDAY AFTER PENTECOST
PROPER 6: SUNDAY BETWEEN 12 AND 18 JUNE

BATHSHEBA MARRIES DAVID, AND DAVID REPENTS
After Bathsheba mourns Uriah's death she becomes David's wife. Nathan's prodding evokes David's brief confession. But it is Bathsheba's child who suffers.

When the wife of Uriah heard that her husband was dead, she made lamentation for him. When the mourning was over David sent and brought her to his house, and she became his wife, and bore him a son.

But the thing that David had done displeased the LORD, and the LORD sent Nathan to David. He came to him, and said to him, "There were two men in a certain city, the one rich and the other poor. The rich man had very many flocks and herds; but the poor man had nothing but one little ewe lamb, which he had bought. He brought it up, and it grew up with him and with his children; it used to eat of his meager fare, and drink from his cup, and lie in his bosom, and it was like a daughter to him.

"Now there came a traveler to the rich man, and the rich man was loath to take one of his own flock or herd to prepare for the wayfarer who had come to him, but he took the poor man's lamb, and prepared that for the guest who had come to him." Then David's anger was greatly kindled against the man. He said to Nathan, "As the LORD lives, the man who has done this deserves to die; he shall restore the lamb fourfold, because he did this thing, and because he had no pity."

Nathan said to David, "You are the man! Thus says the LORD, the God of Israel: I anointed you king over Israel, and I rescued you from the hand of Saul; I gave you your master's house, and your master's wives into your bosom, and gave you the house of Israel and of Judah; and if that had been too little, I would have added as much more. Why have you despised the word of the LORD, to do what is evil in God's sight? You have struck down Uriah the Hittite with the sword, and have taken his wife to be your wife, and have killed him with the sword of the Ammonites.

"Now therefore the sword shall never depart from your house, for you have despised me, and have taken the wife of Uriah the Hittite to be your wife. Thus says the LORD: I will raise up trouble against you from within your own house; and I will take your wives before your eyes, and give them to your neighbor, and he shall lie with your wives in the sight of this very sun. For you did it secretly; but I will do this thing before all Israel, and before the sun."

David said to Nathan, "I have sinned against the Lord." Nathan said to David, "Now the Lord has put away your sin; you shall not die. Nevertheless, because by this deed you have utterly scorned the Lord, the child that is born to you shall die." Then Nathan went to his house.

2 Samuel 11:26 — 12:15a

Naboth the Jezreelite had a vineyard in Jezreel, beside the palace of King Ahab of Samaria. And Ahab said to Naboth, "Give me your vineyard, so that I may have it for a vegetable garden, because it is near my house; I will give you a better vineyard for it; or, if it seems good to you, I will give you its value in money." But Naboth said to Ahab, "The Lord forbid that I should give you my ancestral inheritance." Ahab went home resentful and sullen because of what Naboth the Jezreelite had said to him; for he had said, "I will not give you my ancestral inheritance." He lay down on his bed, turned away his face, and would not eat.

Ahab's wife Jezebel came to him and said, "Why are you so depressed that you will not eat?" He said to her, "Because I spoke to Naboth the Jezreelite and said to him, 'Give me your vineyard for money; or else, if you prefer, I will give you another vineyard for it'; but he answered, 'I will not give you my vineyard.'" His wife Jezebel said to him, "Do you not govern Israel? Get up, eat some food, and be cheerful; I will give you the vineyard of Naboth the Jezreelite."

So she wrote letters in Ahab's name and sealed them with his seal; she sent the letters to the elders and the nobles who lived with Naboth in his city. She wrote in the letters, "Proclaim a fast, and seat Naboth at the head of the assembly; seat two scoundrels opposite him, and have them bring a charge against him, saying, 'You have cursed God and the king.' Then take him out, and stone him to death."

The men of his city, the elders and the nobles who lived in his city, did as Jezebel had sent word to them. Just as it was written in the letters that she had sent to them, they proclaimed a fast and seated Naboth at the head of the assembly. The two scoundrels came in and sat opposite him; and the scoundrels brought a charge aginst Naboth, in the presence of the people, saying, "Naboth cursed God and the king." So they took him outside the city, and stoned him to death. Then they sent to Jezebel, saying, "Naboth has been stoned; he is dead."

As soon as Jezebel heard that Naboth had been stoned and was dead, Jezebel said to Ahab, "Go, take possession of the vineyard of Naboth the Jezreelite, which he refused to give you for money; for Naboth is not alive, but dead." As soon as Ahab heard that Naboth was dead, Ahab set out to go down to the vineyard of Naboth the Jezreelite, to take possession of it.

Then the word of the LORD came to Elijah the Tishbite, saying: Go down to meet King Ahab of Israel, who rules in Samaria; he is now in the vineyard of Naboth, where he has gone to take possession. You shall say to him, "Thus says the LORD: Have you killed, and also taken possession?" You shall say to him, "Thus says the LORD: In the place where dogs licked up the blood of Naboth, dogs will also lick up your blood."

Ahab said to Elijah, "Have you found me, O my enemy?" He answered, "I have found you. Because you have sold yourself to do what is evil in the sight of the LORD, I will bring disaster on you."

1 Kings 21:1–21a

It takes courage on the woman's part to act in this wondrously generous manner, barging into someone else's home, a dinner gathering of all men. She probably expected the negative reaction of the other men, but what did she expect of Jesus?

One of the Pharisees asked Jesus to eat with him, and Jesus went into the Pharisee's house and took his place at the table. And a woman in the city, who was a sinner, having learned that Jesus was eating in the Pharisee's house, brought an alabaster jar of ointment. She stood behind him at his feet, weeping, and began to bathe his feet with her tears and to dry them with her hair. Then she continued kissing his feet and anointing them with the ointment.

Now when the Pharisee who had invited Jesus saw it, he said to himself, "If this man were a prophet, he would have known who and what kind of woman this is who is touching him — that she is a sinner."

Jesus spoke up and said to him, "Simon, I have something to say to you." "Teacher," he replied, "Speak." "A certain creditor had two debtors; one owed five hundred denarii, and the other fifty. When they could not pay, he canceled the debts for both of them. Now which of them will love him more?" Simon answered, "I suppose the one for whom he canceled the greater debt." And Jesus said to him, "You have judged rightly."

Then turning toward the woman, he said to Simon, "Do you see this woman? I entered your house; you gave me no water for my feet, but she has bathed my feet with her tears and dried them with her hair. You gave me no kiss, but from the time I came in she has not stopped kissing my feet. You did not anoint my head with oil, but she has anointed my feet with ointment. Therefore, I tell you, her sins, which were many, have been forgiven; hence she has shown great love. But the one to whom little is forgiven, loves little." Then Jesus said to her, "Your sins are forgiven."

But those who were at the table with him began to say among themselves, "Who is this who even forgives sins?" And Jesus said to the woman, "Your faith has saved you; go in peace."

Soon afterwards Jesus went on through cities and villages, proclaiming and bringing the good news of the dominion of God. The twelve were with Jesus, as well as some women who had been cured of evil spirits and infirmities: Mary, called Magdalene, from whom seven demons had gone out, and Joanna, the wife of Herod's steward Chuza, and Susanna, and many others, who provided for them out of their resources.

Luke 7:36 — 8:3

TWELFTH SUNDAY IN ORDINARY TIME

FIFTH SUNDAY AFTER PENTECOST
PROPER 7: SUNDAY BETWEEN 19 AND 25 JUNE

NO LONGER MALE OR FEMALE
Is this a vision of the time of salvation, or of the garden of Eden, when the man and the woman were equal? Equality of women and men in Christ remains to be realized.

In Christ Jesus you are all children of God through faith. As many of you as were baptized into Christ have clothed yourselves with Christ. There is no longer Jew or Greek, there is no longer slave or free, there is no longer male and female; for all of you are one in Christ Jesus.

Galatians 3:26 – 28

THIRTEENTH SUNDAY IN ORDINARY TIME

SIXTH SUNDAY AFTER PENTECOST

PROPER 8: SUNDAY BETWEEN 26 JUNE AND 2 JULY

HAGAR AND SARAH AS ALLEGORY

The stories of Sarah and Hagar provide the basis for Paul's complex allegory. Does he do justice to their stories? Hagar remains rejected in Paul's letter as in Genesis, but Jesus reached out to such oppressed and forgotten persons.

It is written that Abraham had two sons, one by a slave woman and the other by a free woman. One, the child of the slave, was born according to the flesh; the other, the child of the free woman, was born through the promise.

Now this is an allegory: These women are two covenants. One woman, in fact, is Hagar, from Mount Sinai, bearing children for slavery. Now Hagar is Mount Sinai in Arabia, and corresponds to the present Jerusalem, for she is in slavery with her children.

But the other woman, Sarah, corresponds to the Jerusalem above; she is free, and she is our mother. For it is written,

"Rejoice, you childless one, you who bear no children,
burst into song and shout, you who endure no birthpangs;
for the children of the desolate woman are more numerous
than the children of the one who is married."

Now you, my friends, are children of the promise, like Isaac. But just as at that time the child who was born according to the flesh persecuted the child who was born according to the Spirit, so it is now also. But what does the scripture say? "Drive out the slave and her child; for the child of the slave will not share the inheritance with the child of the free woman." So then, friends, we are children, not of the slave but of the free woman. For freedom Christ has set us free. Stand firm, therefore, and do not submit again to a yoke of slavery.

Galatians 4:22 — 5:1

FOURTEENTH SUNDAY IN ORDINARY TIME

SEVENTH SUNDAY AFTER PENTECOST
PROPER 9: SUNDAY BETWEEN 3 AND 9 JULY

GOD AS NURSING MOTHER
God is described as a nursing mother and as a mother who carries and cuddles her child.

Rejoice with Jerusalem!
Be glad for her,
all who love her.
Share her great joy,
all who know her sadness.

Now drink your fill
from her comforting breast,
enjoy her plentiful milk.

For this is what the Lord says:
"Look! to her I extend
peace like a river,
the wealth of the nations
like a stream in full flood.
And you will drink!

"I will carry you on my shoulders,
cuddle you on my lap.
I will comfort you
as a mother nurses her child.

"Jerusalem will be your joy.
Your heart will rejoice to see it.
You will flourish like grass in spring."

Canticle of Isaiah 66:10–14a ICEL

THE ISRAELITE SLAVE GIRL ADVISES NAAMAN
The Israelite slave girl who serves Naaman's wife does not rejoice at Naaman's ailment, but in mercy brings the good news of the prophet Elisha who can heal him.

Naaman, commander of the army of the king of Aram, was a great man and in high favor with his master, because by him the LORD had given victory to Aram. The man, though a mighty warrior, suffered from leprosy. Now the Arameans on one of their raids had taken a young girl captive from the land of Israel, and she served Naaman's wife. She said to her mistress, "If only my lord were with the prophet who is in Samaria! He would cure him of his leprosy." So Naaman went in and told his lord just what the girl from the land of Israel had said. And the king of Aram said, "Go then, and I will send along a letter to the king of Israel."

Naaman went, taking with him ten talents of silver, six thousand shekels of gold, and ten sets of garments. He brought the letter to the king of Israel, which read, "When this letter reaches you, know that I have sent to you my servant Naaman, that you may cure him of his leprosy." When the king of Israel read the letter, he tore his clothes and said, "Am I God, to give death or life, that this man sends word to me to cure a man of his leprosy. Just look and see how he is trying to pick a quarrel with me."

But when Elisha the man of God heard that the king of Israel had torn his clothes, he sent a message to the king, "Why have you torn your clothes? Let him come to me, that he may learn that there is a prophet in Israel." So Naaman came with his horses and chariots, and halted at the entrance of Elisha's house.

Elisha sent a messenger to him, saying, "Go, wash in the Jordan seven times, and your flesh shall be restored and you shall be clean." But Naaman became angry and went away, saying, "I thought that for me he would surely come out, and stand and call on the name of the LORD his God, and would wave his hand over the spot, and cure the leprosy! Are not Abana and Pharpar, the rivers of Damascus, better than all the waters of Israel? Could I not wash in them, and be clean?" He turned and went away in a rage. But his servants approached and said to him, "Dear master, if the prophet had commanded you to do something difficult, would you not have done it? How much more, when all he said to you was, 'Wash, and be clean'?" So he went down and immersed himself seven times in the Jordan, according to the word of the man of God; his flesh was restored like the flesh of a young boy, and he was clean.

2 Kings 5:1–14

JESUS' MOTHER

All disciples of Jesus become his new family, and members of his biological family are called to become disciples.

The mother and brothers of Jesus came to him, but they could not reach him because of the crowd. And Jesus was told, "Your mother and your brothers are standing outside, wanting to see you." But he said to them, "My mother and my brothers are those who hear the word of God and do it."

Luke 8:19–21

FIFTEENTH SUNDAY IN ORDINARY TIME

EIGHTH SUNDAY AFTER PENTECOST
PROPER 10: SUNDAY BETWEEN 10 AND 16 JULY

THE WOMAN WITH A HEMORRHAGE AND THE DAUGHTER OF JAIRUS
Jesus directs his healing ministry to the twelve-year-old girl and to the woman who had sought healing for many years. Her state of ritual impurity was of no concern to him.

The crowd welcomed Jesus, for they were all waiting for him. Just then there came a man named Jairus, a leader of the synagogue. He fell at Jesus' feet and begged him to come to his house, for he had an only daughter, about twelve years old, who was dying.

As he went, the crowds pressed in on Jesus. Now there was a woman who had been suffering from hemorrhages for twelve years; and though she had spent all she had on physicians, no one could cure her. She came up behind him and touched the fringe of his clothes, and immediately her hemorrhage stopped. Then Jesus asked, "Who touched me?" When all denied it, Peter said, "Master, the crowds surround you and press in on you." But Jesus said, "Someone touched me; for I noticed that power had gone out from me."

When the woman saw that she could not remain hidden, she came trembling; and falling down before him, she declared in the presence of all the people why she had touched him, and how she had been immediately healed. Jesus said to her, "Daughter, your faith has made you well; go in peace."

While Jesus was still speaking, someone came from the leader's house to say, "Your daughter is dead; do not trouble the teacher any longer." When Jesus heard this, he replied, "Do not fear. Only believe, and she will be saved."

When he came to the house, he did not allow anyone to enter with him, except Peter, John, and James, and the child's father and mother. They were all weeping and wailing for her; but Jesus said, "Do not weep; for she is not dead but sleeping." And they laughed at him, knowing that she was dead. But Jesus took her by the hand and called out, "Child, get up!" Her spirit returned, and she got up at once. Then he directed them to give her something to eat. Her parents were astounded; but Jesus ordered them to tell no one what had happened.

Luke 8:40−56

SIXTEENTH SUNDAY IN ORDINARY TIME

NINTH SUNDAY AFTER PENTECOST
PROPER 11: SUNDAY BETWEEN 17 AND 23 JULY

SARAH WILL BEAR A SON

Sarah's laughs, first with wry humor when the visitors promise her a child and later with joy when she gives birth to Isaac. Her laughter and her child are gifts from God.

The LORD appeared to Abraham by the oaks of Mamre, as he sat at the entrance of his tent in the heat of the day. Abraham looked up and saw three men standing near him. When he saw them, he ran from the tent entrance to meet them, and bowed down to the ground. He said, "My lord, if I find favor with you, do not pass by your servant. Let a little water be brought, and wash your feet, and rest yourselves under the tree. Let me bring a little bread, that you may refresh yourselves, and after that you may pass on — since you have come to your servant." So they said, "Do as you have said."

And Abraham hastened into the tent to Sarah, and said, "Make ready quickly three measures of choice flour, knead it, and make cakes." Abraham ran to the herd, and took a calf, tender and good, and gave it to the servant, who hastened to prepare it. Then he took curds and milk and the calf that he had prepared, and set it before them; and he stood by them under the tree while they ate.

They said to him, "Where is your wife Sarah?" And Abraham said, "There, in the tent." Then one said, "I will surely return to you in due season, and your wife Sarah shall have a son." And Sarah was listening at the tent entrance behind him. Now Abraham and Sarah were old, advanced in age; it had ceased to be with Sarah after the manner of women.

So Sarah laughed to herself, saying, "After I have grown old and my husband is old, shall I have pleasure?" The LORD said to Abraham, "Why did Sarah laugh, and say, 'Shall I indeed bear a child, now that I am old?' Is anything too wonderful for the LORD? At the set time I will return to you, in due season, and Sarah shall have a son." But Sarah denied, saying, "I did not laugh"; for she was afraid. God said, "Oh yes, you did laugh."

Genesis 18:1 – 15

MARTHA AND MARY

Like Sarah, Martha does household chores. She and Mary have different gifts and distinct personalities. Yet Jesus calls them both.

As Jesus and his disciples went on their way, Jesus entered a certain village, where a woman named Martha welcomed him into her home. She had a sister named Mary, who sat at the Lord's feet and listened to what he was saying. But Martha was distracted by her many tasks; so she came to him and asked, "Lord, do you not care that my sister has left me to do all the work by myself? Tell her then to help me."

313

But the Lord answered her, "Martha, Martha, you are worried and distracted by many things; there is need of only one thing. Mary has chosen the better part, which will not be taken away from her."

Luke 10:38–42

Junia, Mistaken as Junius

SEVENTEENTH SUNDAY IN ORDINARY TIME

TENTH SUNDAY AFTER PENTECOST
PROPER 12: SUNDAY BETWEEN 24 AND 30 JULY

GOMER, WIFE OF HOSEA
To the prophet, Gomer and their children were symbols of the troubled relationship between the people and God. What did Gomer think?

When the LORD first spoke through Hosea, the LORD said to Hosea, "Go, take for yourself a wife of whoredom and have children of whoredom, for the land commits great whoredom by forsaking the LORD." So he went and took Gomer daughter of Diblaim, and she conceived and bore him a son.

And the LORD said to Hosea, "Name him Jezreel; for in a little while I will punish the house of Jehu for the blood of Jezreel, and I will put an end to the kingdom of the house of Israel. On that day I will break the bow of Israel in the valley of Jezreel."

Gomer conceived again and bore a daughter. Then the LORD said to Hosea, "Name her Lo-ruhamah, for I will no longer have pity on the house of Israel or forgive them. But I will have pity on the house of Judah, and I will save them by the LORD their God; I will not save them by bow, or by sword, or by war, or by horses, or by horsemen."

When Gomer had weaned Lo-ruhamah, she conceived and bore a son. Then the LORD said, "Name him Lo-ammi, for you are not my people and I am not your God."

Yet the number of the people of Israel shall be like the sand of the sea, which can be neither measured nor numbered; and in the place where it was said to them, "You are not my people," it shall be said to them, "Children of the living God."

Hosea 1:2–10

HAPPY THE WOMB THAT BORE YOU
Jesus emphasizes that faithful discipleship is the way to intimate relationship with him.

While Jesus was speaking, a woman in the crowd raised her voice and said to him, "Blessed is the womb that bore you and the breasts that nursed you!" But Jesus said, "Blessed rather are those who hear the word of God and obey it!"

Luke 11:27–28

EIGHTEENTH SUNDAY IN ORDINARY TIME

ELEVENTH SUNDAY AFTER PENTECOST
PROPER 13: SUNDAY BETWEEN 31 JULY AND 6 AUGUST

GOD'S MOTHER-LOVE
God's love of Israel is the love of a mother for her children.

When Israel was a child, I loved him,
     and out of Egypt I called my son.
The more I called them,
     the more they went from me,
they kept sacrificing to the Baals,
     and offering incense to idols.

Yet it was I who taught Ephraim to walk,
     I took them up in my arms;
     but they did not know that I healed them.
I led them with cords of human kindness,
     with bands of love.
I was to them like those
     who lift infants to their cheeks.
     I bent down to them and fed them.
How can I give you up, Ephraim?
     How can I hand you over, O Israel?
How can I make you like Admah?
     How can I treat you like Zeboiim?
My heart recoils within me;
     my compassion grows warm and tender.
     I will not execute my fierce anger;
I will not again destroy Ephraim;
for I am God and no mortal,
     the Holy One in your midst,
     and I will not come in wrath.

They shall go after the LORD,
     who roars like a lion;
when God roars,
     the children shall come trembling from the west.
They shall come trembling like birds from Egypt,
     and like doves from the land of Assyria;
     and I will return them to their homes, says the LORD.

Hosea 11:1 – 11

NINETEENTH SUNDAY IN ORDINARY TIME

TWELFTH SUNDAY AFTER PENTECOST
PROPER 14: SUNDAY BETWEEN 7 AND 13 AUGUST

GOD AS PROVIDER OF FOOD, GOD AS MOTHER BEAR
God feeds her children in the wilderness. Like a mother bear, God defends her cubs tenaciously and fiercely.

I have been the LORD your God
>   ever since the land of Egypt;
you know no God but me,
>   and besides me there is no savior.
It was I who fed you in the wilderness,
>   in the land of drought.
When I fed them, they were satisfied;
>   they were satisfied, and their heart was proud;
>   therefore they forgot me.
So I will become like a lion to them,
>   like a leopard I will lurk beside the way.
I will fall upon them like a bear robbed of her cubs,
>   and will tear open the covering of their heart;
there I will devour them like a lion,
>   as a wild animal would mangle them.

Hosea 13:4–8

TWENTIETH SUNDAY IN ORDINARY TIME

THIRTEENTH SUNDAY AFTER PENTECOST
PROPER 15: SUNDAY BETWEEN 14 AND 20 AUGUST

ESTHER AND THE FEAST OF PURIM
Esther is perhaps the only biblical woman who makes laws regarding liturgical celebration. She promulgates the regulations of the feast of Purim.

Haman son of Hammedatha the Agagite, the enemy of all the Jews, had plotted against the Jews to destroy them, and had cast Pur — that is "the lot" — to crush and destroy them; but when Esther came before the king, he gave orders in writing that the wicked plot that he had devised against the Jews should come upon his own head, and that he and his sons should be hanged on the gallows. Therefore these days are called Purim, from the word Pur. Thus because of all that was written in this letter, and of what they had faced in this matter, and of what had happened to them, the Jews established and accepted as a custom for themselves and their descendants and all who joined them, that without fail they would continue to observe these two days every year, as it was written and at the time appointed. These days should be remembered and kept throughout every generation, in every family, province, and city; and these days of Purim should never fall into disuse among the Jews, nor should the commemoration of these days cease among their descendants.

Queen Esther daughter of Abihail, along with the Jew Mordecai, gave full written authority, confirming this second letter about Purim. Letters were sent wishing peace and security to all the Jews, to the one hundred twenty-seven provinces of the kingdom of Ahasuerus, and giving orders that these days of Purim should be observed at their appointed seasons, as the Jew Mordecai and Queen Esther enjoined on the Jews, just as they had laid down for themselves and for their descendants regulations concerning their fasts and their lamentations. The command of Queen Esther fixed these practices of Purim, and it was recorded in writing.

Esther 9:24 – 32

TWENTY-FIRST SUNDAY IN ORDINARY TIME

FOURTEENTH SUNDAY AFTER PENTECOST
PROPER 16: SUNDAY BETWEEN 21 AND 27 AUGUST

THE BENT-OVER WOMAN
Jesus freed the woman from her infirmity after eighteen years of suffering. What laws or traditions have prevented the liberation of women over the centuries?

Jesus was teaching in one of the synagogues on the sabbath. And just then there appeared a woman with a spirit that had crippled her for eighteen years. She was bent over and was quite unable to stand up straight. When Jesus saw her, he called her over and said, "Woman, you are set free from your ailment." When he laid his hands on her, immediately she stood up straight and began praising God.

But the leader of the synagogue, indignant because Jesus had cured on the sabbath, kept saying to the crowd, "There are six days on which work ought to be done; come on those days and be cured, and not on the sabbath day." But the Lord answered him and said, "You hypocrites! Does not each of you on the sabbath untie his ox or his donkey from the manger, and lead it away to give it water? And ought not this woman, a daughter of Abraham whom Satan bound for eighteen long years, be set free from this bondage on the sabbath day?"

When Jesus said this, all his opponents were put to shame; and the entire crowd was rejoicing at all the wonderful things that he was doing.

Luke 13:10–17

TWENTY-SECOND SUNDAY IN ORDINARY TIME

FIFTEENTH SUNDAY AFTER PENTECOST
PROPER 17: SUNDAY BETWEEN 28 AUGUST AND 3 SEPTEMBER

COME TO WISDOM
Putting on the yoke of the feminine figure of holy Wisdom gives rest and joy.

My child, from your youth choose discipline,
    and when you have gray hair you will still find wisdom.
Come to her like one who plows and sows,
    and wait for her good harvest.
For when you cultivate her you will toil but little,
    and soon you will eat of her produce.
She seems very harsh to the undisciplined;
    fools cannot remain with her.
She will be like a heavy stone to test them,
    and they will not delay in casting her aside.
For wisdom is like her name;
    she is not readily perceived by many.
Listen, my child, and accept my judgment;
    do not reject my counsel.
Put your feet into her fetters,
    and your neck into her collar.
Bend your shoulders and carry her,
    and do not fret under her bonds.
Come to her with all your soul,
    and keep her ways with all your might.
Search out and seek, and she will become known to you;
    and when you get hold of her, do not let her go.
For at last you will find the rest she gives,
    and she will be changed into joy for you.
Then her fetters will become for you a strong defense,
    and her collar a glorious robe.
Her yoke is a golden ornament,
    and her bonds a purple cord.
You will wear her like a glorious robe,
    and put her on like a splendid crown.

Sirach 6:18–31

THE WOMAN WHO MIXES LEAVEN

In baking to feed others, women are co-creators with God.

Again Jesus said, "To what should I compare the dominion of God? It is like yeast that a woman took and mixed in with three measures of flour until all of it was leavened."

Luke 13:20–21

TWENTY-THIRD SUNDAY IN ORDINARY TIME

SIXTEENTH SUNDAY AFTER PENTECOST
PROPER 18: SUNDAY BETWEEN 4 AND 10 SEPTEMBER

OUR SISTER APPHIA

Apphia is one of many women in the early church about whom we know little beyond her name. She is important in the household or circle of Philemon.

Paul, a prisoner of Christ Jesus, and Timothy our brother,

To Philemon our dear friend and co-worker, and Apphia our sister, to Archippus our fellow soldier, and to the church in your house:

Grace to you and peace from God, our Father, and the Lord Jesus Christ.

When I remember you in my prayers, I always thank my God because I hear of your love for all the saints and your faith toward the Lord Jesus. I pray that the sharing of your faith may become effective when you perceive all the good that we may do for Christ. I have indeed received much joy and encouragement from your love, because the hearts of the saints have been refreshed through you, my brother.

Philemon 1–7

TWENTY-FOURTH SUNDAY IN ORDINARY TIME

SEVENTEENTH SUNDAY AFTER PENTECOST
PROPER 19: SUNDAY BETWEEN 11 AND 17 SEPTEMBER

THE ONE WHO KNOWS ALL THINGS KNOWS HER

Holy Wisdom — a feminine figure in the Bible — here is identified with strength, understanding, riches and the word of God.

Hear the commandments of life, O Israel;
>give ear, and learn wisdom!

Why is it, O Israel, why is it that you are in the land of your enemies,
>that you are growing old in a foreign country,

that you are defiled with the dead,
>that you are counted among those in Hades?

You have forsaken the fountain of wisdom.

If you had walked in the way of God,
>you would be living in peace forever.

Learn where there is wisdom,
>where there is strength,
>where there is understanding,

so that you may at the same time discern
>where there is length of days, and life,

where there is light for the eyes, and peace.

Who has found her place?
>And who has entered her storehouses?

The one who knows all things knows her,
>she was found by God's understanding.

The one who prepared the earth for all time

filled it with four-footed creatures;

the one who sends forth the light, and it goes;
>it was called, and it obeyed God, trembling;

the stars shone in their watches and were glad;
>they were called, and they said, "Here we are!"
>They shone with gladness for God who made them.

This is our God;
>no other can be compared to our God,

who found the whole way to knowledge,
>   and gave her to servant Jacob
>   and to beloved Israel.
Afterward she appeared on earth and lived with humankind.

She is the book of the commandments of God,
>   the law that endures forever.
All who hold her fast will live,
>   and those who forsake her will die.
Turn, O Jacob, and take her;
>   walk toward the shining of her light.
Do not give your glory to another,
>   or your advantages to an alien people.
Happy are we, O Israel,
>   for we know what is pleasing to God.

Baruch 3:9 – 15, 32 — 4:4

THE WOMAN AND THE LOST COIN
Parallel stories about a man and a woman provide images of God's love for sinners.

All the tax collectors and sinners were coming near to listen to Jesus. And the Pharisees and the scribes were grumbling and saying, "This fellow welcomes sinners and eats with them."

So Jesus told them this parable: "Which one of you, having a hundred sheep and losing one of them, does not leave the ninety-nine in the wilderness and go after the one that is lost until he finds it? When he has found it, he lays it on his shoulders and rejoices. And when he comes home, he calls together his friends and neighbors, saying to them, 'Rejoice with me, for I have found my sheep that was lost.' Just so, I tell you, there will be more joy in heaven over one sinner who repents than over ninety-nine righteous persons who need no repentance.

"Or what woman having ten silver coins, if she loses one of them, does not light a lamp, sweep the house, and search carefully until she finds it? When she has found it, she calls together her friends and neighbors, saying, 'Rejoice with me, for I have found the coin that I had lost.' Just so, I tell you, there is joy in the presence of the angels of God over one sinner who repents."

Luke 15:1 – 10

TWENTY-FIFTH SUNDAY IN ORDINARY TIME

EIGHTEENTH SUNDAY AFTER PENTECOST
PROPER 20: SUNDAY BETWEEN 18 AND 24 SEPTEMBER

THE WIDOW JUDITH

Judith, a wealthy widow, is devout and observant. She hears about the misery of her people, and prepares for her ministry of liberation.

In those days, Judith heard about the misery of her people; she was the daughter of Merari son of Ox son of Joseph son of Oziel son of Elkiah son of Ananias son of Gideon son of Raphain son of Ahitub son of Elijah son of Hilkiah son of Eliab son of Nathanael son of Salamiel son of Sarasadi son of Israel.

Her husband Manasseh, who belonged to her tribe and family, had died during the barley harvest. For as he stood overseeing those who were binding sheaves in the field, he was overcome by the burning heat, and took to his bed and died in his town Bethulia. So they buried him with his ancestors in the field between Dothan and Balamon.

Judith remained as a widow for three years and four months at home where she set up a tent for herself on the roof of her house. She put sackcloth around her waist and dressed in widow's clothing. She fasted all the days of her widowhood, except the day before the sabbath and the sabbath itself, the day before the new moon and the day of the new moon, and the festivals and days of rejoicing of the house of Israel.

She was beautiful in appearance, and was very lovely to behold. Her husband Manasseh had left her gold and silver, men and women slaves, livestock, and fields; and she maintained this estate. No one spoke ill of her, for she feared God with great devotion.

Judith 8:1–8

WIDOWS IN THE EARLY CHURCH

Widows on the list were supported by the local church; other widows would have been cared for by relatives or wealthy women. Widows had a significant ministry in the early church. The details are not known, except that this ministry was soon severely restricted.

Honor widows who are really widows. If a widow has children or grandchildren, they should first learn their religious duty to their own family and make some repayment to their parents; for this is pleasing in God's sight. The real widow, left alone, has set her hope on God and continues in supplications and prayers night and day; but the widow who lives for pleasure is dead even while she lives. Give these commands as well, so that they may be above reproach. And whoever does not provide for relatives, and especially for family members, has denied the faith and is worse than an unbeliever.

Let a widow be put on the list if she is not less than sixty years old and has been married only once; she must be well attested for her good works, as one who has brought up children, shown hospitality, washed the saints' feet, helped the afflicted, and devoted herself to doing good in every way. But refuse to put younger widows on the list; for when their sensual desires alienate them from Christ, they want to marry, and so they incur condemnation for having violated their first pledge. Besides that, they learn to be idle, gadding about from house to house; and they are not merely idle, but also gossips and busybodies, saying what they should not say. So I would have younger widows marry, bear children, and manage their households, so as to give the adversary no occasion to revile us. For some have already turned away to follow Satan. If any believing woman has relatives who are really widows, let her assist them; let the church not be burdened, so that it can assist those who are real widows.

1 Timothy 5:3 – 16

TWENTY-SIXTH SUNDAY IN ORDINARY TIME

NINETEENTH SUNDAY AFTER PENTECOST
PROPER 21: SUNDAY BETWEEN 25 SEPTEMBER AND 1 OCTOBER

THE PRAYER OF JUDITH

Judith — a widow — prays that she can be the means by which God rescues the chosen people. As a God of the powerless and marginalized, God especially cares for and with women.

Judith cried out to the Lord with a loud voice, and said,

"O Lord God of my ancestor Simeon, to whom you gave a sword to take revenge on those strangers who had torn off a virgin's clothing to defile her, and exposed her thighs to put her to shame, and polluted her womb to disgrace her; for you said, 'It shall not be done' — yet they did it. So you gave up their rulers to be killed, and their bed, which was ashamed of the deceit they had practiced, was stained with blood, and you struck down slaves along with princes, and princes on their thrones. You gave up their wives for booty and their daughters to captivity, and all their booty to be divided among your beloved children who burned with zeal for you and abhorred the pollution of their blood and called on you for help — O God, my God, hear me also — a widow.

"For you have done these things and those that went before and those that followed. You have designed the things that are now, and those that are to come. What you had in mind has happened; the things you decided on presented themselves and said, 'Here we are!' For all your ways are prepared in advance, and your judgment is with foreknowledge.

"Here now are the Assyrians, a greatly increased force, priding themselves in their horses and riders, boasting in the strength of their foot soldiers, and trusting in shield and spear, in bow and sling. They do not know that you are the Lord who crushes wars; the Lord is your name. Break their strength by your might, and bring down their power in your anger; for they intend to defile your sanctuary, and to pollute the tabernacle where your glorious name resides, and to break off the horns of your altar with the sword. Look at their pride, and send your wrath upon their heads. Give to me, a widow, the strong hand to do what I plan. By the deceit of my lips strike down the slave with the prince and the prince with his servant; crush their arrogance by the hand of a woman.

"For your strength does not depend on numbers, nor your might on the powerful. But you are the God of the lowly, helper of the oppressed, upholder of the weak, protecter of the forsaken, savior of those without hope."

Judith 9:1 – 11

TWENTY-SEVENTH SUNDAY IN ORDINARY TIME

TWENTIETH SUNDAY AFTER PENTECOST
PROPER 22: SUNDAY BETWEEN 2 AND 8 OCTOBER

DAUGHTER ZION AS A WIDOW
Daughter Zion is seen as a widow, lonely and friendless.

How lonely sits the city
   that once was full of people!
How like a widow she has become,
   she that was great among the nations!
She that was a princess among the provinces
   has become a vassal.

She weeps bitterly in the night,
   with tears on her cheeks;
among all her lovers
   she has no one to comfort her;
all her friends have dealt treacherously with her,
   they have become her enemies.

Judah has gone into exile with suffering
   and hard servitude;
she lives now among the nations,
   and finds no resting place;
her pursuers have all overtaken her
   in the midst of her distress.

The roads to Zion mourn,
   for no one comes to the festivals;
all her gates are desolate,
   her priests groan;
her young girls grieve,
   and her lot is bitter.

Her foes have become the masters,
   her enemies prosper,
because the Lord has made her suffer
   for the multitude of her transgressions;
her children have gone away,
   captives before the foe.

From daughter Zion has departed all her majesty.
Her princes have become like stags
    that find no pasture;
they fled without strength
    before the pursuer.

Lamentations 1:1 – 6

.

LOIS AND EUNICE

Lois and Eunice are models of faith for Timothy. Sincere and prayerful, they too share in the power of the Holy Spirit.

Paul, an apostle of Christ Jesus by the will of God, for the sake of the promise of life that is in Christ Jesus,

    To Timothy, my beloved child:

    Grace, mercy, and peace from God, the father, and Christ Jesus our Lord.

    I am grateful to God — whom I worship with a clear conscience, as my ancestors did — when I remember you constantly in my prayers night and day. Recalling your tears, I long to see you so that I may be filled with joy. I am reminded of your sincere faith, a faith that lived first in your grandmother Lois and your mother Eunice and now, I am sure, lives in you. For this reason I remind you to rekindle the gift of God that is within you through the laying on of my hands; for God did not give us a spirit of cowardice, but rather a spirit of power and of love and of self-discipline.

2 Timothy 1:1 – 7

TWENTY-EIGHTH SUNDAY
IN ORDINARY TIME

TWENTY-FIRST SUNDAY
AFTER PENTECOST
PROPER 23: SUNDAY BETWEEN 9 AND 15 OCTOBER

THE ISRAELITE SLAVE GIRL ADVISES NAAMAN

The Israelite slave girl who serves Naaman's wife does not rejoice at Naaman's ailment, but in mercy brings the good news of the prophet Elisha who can heal him.

Naaman, commander of the army of the king of Aram, was a great man and in high favor with his master, because by him the LORD had given victory to Aram. The man, though a mighty warrior, suffered from leprosy. Now the Arameans on one of their raids had taken a young girl captive from the land of Israel, and she served Naaman's wife. She said to her mistress, "If only my lord were with the prophet who is in Samaria! He would cure him of his leprosy." So Naaman went in and told his lord just what the girl from the land of Israel had said. And the king of Aram said, "Go then, and I will send along a letter to the king of Israel."

Naaman went, taking with him ten talents of silver, six thousand shekels of gold, and ten sets of garments. He brought the letter to the king of Israel, which read, "When this letter reaches you, know that I have sent to you my servant Naaman, that you may cure him of his leprosy." When the king of Israel read the letter, he tore his clothes and said, "Am I God, to give death or life, that this man sends word to me to cure a man of his leprosy. Just look and see how he is trying to pick a quarrel with me."

But when Elisha the man of God heard that the king of Israel had torn his clothes, he sent a message to the king, "Why have you torn your clothes? Let him come to me, that he may learn that there is a prophet in Israel." So Naaman came with his horses and chariots, and halted at the entrance of Elisha's house.

Elisha sent a messenger to him, saying, "Go, wash in the Jordan seven times, and your flesh shall be restored and you shall be clean." But Naaman became angry and went away, saying, "I thought that for me he would surely come out, and stand and call on the name of the LORD his God, and would wave his hand over the spot, and cure the leprosy! Are not Abana and Pharpar, the rivers of Damascus, better than all the waters of Israel? Could I not wash in them, and be clean?" He turned and went away in a rage. But his servants approached and said to him, "Dear master, if the prophet had commanded you to do something difficult, would you not have done it? How much more, when all he said to you was, 'Wash, and be clean'?" So he went down and immersed himself seven times in the Jordan, according to the word of the man of God; his flesh was restored like the flesh of a young boy, and he was clean.

2 Kings 5:1–14

JUDITH DINES WITH HOLOFERNES

Judith is resourceful and courageous, and prays to God for strength as she works for the freedom of her people.
She proclaims like the prophets, "God is with us."

Holofernes commanded his servants to bring Judith in where his silver dinnerware was kept, and ordered them to set a table for her with some of his own delicacies, and with some of his own wine to drink. But Judith said, "I cannot partake of them, or it will be an offense, but I will have enough with the things I brought with me." Holofernes said to her, "If your supply runs out, where can we get you more of the same? For none of your people are here with us." Judith replied, "As surely as you live, my lord, your servant will not use up the supplies I have with me before the Lord carries out by my hand what God has determined."

Then the servants of Holofernes brought her into the tent, and she slept until midnight. Toward the morning watch she got up and sent this message to Holofernes: "Let my lord now give orders to allow your servant to go out and pray." So Holofernes commanded his guards not to hinder her. She remained in the camp three days. She went out each night to the valley of Bethulia, and bathed at the spring in the camp. After bathing, she prayed the Lord God of Israel to direct her way for the triumph of the chosen people. Then she returned purified and stayed in the tent until she ate her food toward evening.

Now Judith had told her maid to stand outside the bedchamber and to wait for her to come out, as she did on the other days; for she said she would be going out for her prayers. She had said the same things to Bagoas. So everyone went out, and no one, either small or great, was left in the bedchamber. Then Judith, standing beside Holofernes' bed, said in her heart, "O Lord God of all might, look in this hour on the work of my hands for the exaltation of Jerusalem. Now indeed is the time to help your heritage and to carry out my design to destroy the enemies who have risen up against us."

She went up to the bedpost near Holofernes' head, and took down his sword that hung there. She came close to his bed, took hold of the hair of his head, and said, "Give me strength today, O Lord God of Israel!" Then she struck his neck twice with all her might, and cut off his head. Next she rolled his body off the bed and pulled down the canopy from the posts. Soon afterward she went out and gave Holofernes' head to her maid, who placed it in her food bag.

Then the two of them went out together, as they were accustomed to do for prayer. They passed through the camp, circled around the valley, and went up the mountain to Bethulia, and came to its gates. From a distance Judith called out to the sentries at the gates. "Open, open the gate! God, our God, is with us, still showing power in Israel and strength against our enemies, as God has done today!"

Judith 12:1 – 9; 13:3 – 11

Lydia, Leader of the Church at Philippi

TWENTY-NINTH SUNDAY IN ORDINARY TIME

TWENTY-SECOND SUNDAY AFTER PENTECOST
PROPER 24: SUNDAY BETWEEN 16 AND 22 OCTOBER

THE SONG OF JUDITH
Judith sings a song of triumph, for God has foiled the enemy through her hand.

Judith began this thanksgiving before all Israel, and all the people loudly sang this song of praise. And Judith said:

Begin a song to my God with tambourines,
      sing to my Lord with cymbals.
Raise a new psalm;
      exalt and call upon God's name.
For the Lord is a God who crushes wars
      and sets up camp among the chosen people;
      God delivered me from the hands of my pursuers.
The Assyrian came down from the mountains of the north;
      they came with myriads of warriors;
their numbers blocked up the wadis,
      and their cavalry covered the hills.
The boasted that they would burn up my territory,
      and kill my youth with the sword,
and dash my infants to the ground,
      and seize my children as booty,
      and take my virgins as spoil.

But the Lord Almighty has foiled them
      by the hand of a woman.
For their mighty one did not fall by the hands of the young men,
      nor did the sons of the Titans strike him down,
      nor did tall giants set upon him;
but Judith daughter of Merari
      with the beauty of her countenance undid them.

For Judith put away her widow's clothing
      to exalt the oppressed in Israel.
She anointed her face with perfume;
      she fastened her hair with a tiara
      and put on a linen gown to beguile him.

Her sandal ravished his eyes,
>her beauty captivated his mind,
>and the sword severed his neck.

The Persians trembled at her boldness,
>the Medes were daunted at her daring.

Then my oppressed people shouted;
>my weak people cried out, and the enemy trembled;
>they lifted up their voices, and the enemy were turned back.

Sons of slave girls pierced them through
>and wounded them like the children of fugitives;
>they perished before the army of my Lord.

I will sing to my God a new song.
O Lord, you are great and glorious,
>wonderful in strength, invincible.

Let all your creatures serve you,
>for you spoke, and they were made.

You sent forth your spirit, and it formed them;
>there is none that can resist your voice.

For the mountains shall be shaken to their foundations with the waters;
>before your glance the rocks shall melt like wax.

But to those who fear you
>you show mercy

Judith 15:14 — 16:15

THE PERSISTENT WIDOW

Jesus endorses the actions of women in persistently seeking justice. This story also confirms women's experience: Legal systems often ignore them.

Jesus told them a parable about their need to pray always and not to lose heart. He said, "In a certain city there was a judge who neither feared God nor had respect for people. In that city there was a widow who kept coming to him and saying, 'Grant me justice against my opponent.' For a while he refused; but later he said to himself, 'Though I have no fear of God and no respect for anyone, yet because this widow keeps bothering me, I will grant her justice, so that she may not wear me out by continually coming.'" And the Lord said, "Listen to what the unjust judge says. And will not God grant justice to God's chosen ones who cry out day and night? Will God delay long in helping them? I tell you, God will quickly grant justice to them. And yet, when the Son of Man comes, will he find faith on earth?"

Luke 18:1 — 8

THIRTIETH SUNDAY IN ORDINARY TIME

TWENTY-THIRD SUNDAY
AFTER PENTECOST
PROPER 25: SUNDAY BETWEEN 23 AND 29 OCTOBER

GOD LISTENS TO WIDOWS
Widows who have been wronged have God's ear.

The Most High will not show partiality to the poor;
　　but God will listen to the prayer of one who is wronged.
God will not ignore the supplication of the orphan
　　or the widow when she pours out her complaint.
Do not the tears of the widow run down her cheek
　　as she cries out against the one who causes them to fall?

Sirach 35:16–19

SUSANNA IS THREATENED
Two lustful and wicked judges try to trap Susanna, a righteous woman who trusts in God and defends herself.

There was a man living in Babylon whose name was Joakim. He married the daughter of Hilkiah, named Susanna, a very beautiful woman and one who feared the Lord. Her parents were righteous, and had trained their daughter according to the law of Moses. Joakim was very rich, and had a fine garden adjoining his house; the Jews used to come to him because he was the most honored of them all.

That year two elders from the people were appointed as judges. Concerning them the Lord has said, "Wickedness came forth from Babylon, from elders who were judges, who were supposed to govern the people." These men were frequently at Joakim's house, and all who had a case to be tried came to them there.

When the people left at noon, Susanna would go into her husband's garden to walk. Every day the two elders used to see her, going in and walking about, and they began to lust for her. They suppressed their consciences and turned away their eyes from looking to heaven or remembering their duty to administer justice. Both were overwhelmed with passion for her, but they did not tell each other of their distress, for they were ashamed to disclose their lustful desire to seduce her. Day after day they watched eagerly to see her.

One day they said to each other, "Let us go home, for it is time for lunch." So they both left and parted from each other. But turning back, they met again, and when each pressed the other for the reason, they confessed their lust. Then together they arranged for a time when they could find her alone.

Once, while they were watching for an opportune day, she went in as before with only two maids, and wished to bathe in the garden, for it was a hot day. No one was there except the two elders, who had hidden themselves and were watching her. She said to her maids, "Bring me olive oil and ointments, and shut the garden doors so that I can bathe." They did as she told them; they shut the doors of the garden and went out by the side doors to bring what they had been commanded; they did not see the elders, because they were hiding.

When the maids had gone out, the two elders got up and ran to her. They said, "Look, the garden doors are shut, and no one can see us. We are burning with desire for you; so give your consent, and lie with us. If you refuse, we will testify against you that a young man was with you, and this was why you sent your maids away."

Susanna groaned and said, "I am completely trapped. For if I do this, it will mean death for me; if I do not, I cannot escape your hands. I choose not to do it; I will fall into your hands, rather than sin in the sight of the Lord."

Then Susanna cried out with a loud voice, and the two elders shouted against her. And one of them ran and opened the garden doors. When the people in the house heard the shouting in the garden, they rushed in at the side door to see what had happened to her. And when the leaders told their story, the servants felt very much ashamed, for nothing like this had ever been said about Susanna.

Daniel 13:1 – 27

THIRTY-FIRST SUNDAY IN ORDINARY TIME

TWENTY-FOURTH SUNDAY AFTER PENTECOST
PROPER 26: SUNDAY BETWEEN 30 OCTOBER AND 5 NOVEMBER

SUSANNA IS FALSELY ACCUSED

When Susanna does not submit, the wicked judges falsely accuse her and she is wrongly convicted. Steadfast in her innocence, she calls upon God.

The next day, when the people gathered at the house of her husband Joakim, the two elders came, full of their wicked plot to have Susanna put to death. In the presence of the people they said, "Send for Susanna daughter of Hilkiah, the wife of Joakim." So they sent for her. And she came with her parents, her children, and all her relatives.

Now Susanna was a woman of great refinement and beautiful in appearance. As she was veiled, the scoundrels ordered her to be unveiled, so that they might feast their eyes on her beauty. Those who were with her and all who saw her were weeping.

Then the two elders stood up before the people and laid their hands on her head. Through her tears she looked up toward heaven, for her heart trusted in the Lord. The elders said, "While we were walking in the garden alone, this woman came in with two maids, shut the garden doors, and dismissed the maids. Then a young man, who was hiding there, came to her and lay with her. We were in a corner of the garden, and when we saw this wickedness we ran to them. Although we saw them embracing, we could not hold the man, because he was stronger than we, and he opened the doors and got away. We did, however, seize this woman and asked who the young man was, but she would not tell us. These things we testify."

Because they were elders of the people and judges, the assembly believed them and condemned her to death.

Then Susanna cried out with a loud voice, and said, "O eternal God, you know what is secret and are aware of all things before they come to be; you know that these men have given false evidence against me. And now I am to die, though I have done none of the wicked things that they have charged against me."

Daniel 13:28 – 43

YEAR C

THIRTY-SECOND SUNDAY
IN ORDINARY TIME

TWENTY-FIFTH SUNDAY
AFTER PENTECOST
PROPER 27: SUNDAY BETWEEN 6 AND 12 NOVEMBER

THE WIDOW'S MITE

The widow is commended for her faith and generosity in her poverty. Why do social systems perpetuate poverty among women anyway?

Jesus looked up and saw rich people putting their gifts into the treasury; he also saw a poor widow put in two small copper coins. Jesus said, "Truly I tell you, this poor widow has put in more than all of them; for all of them have contributed out of their abundance, but she out of her poverty has put in all she had to live on."

Luke 21:1–4

Nympha and Her House Church

THIRTY-THIRD SUNDAY IN ORDINARY TIME

TWENTY-SIXTH SUNDAY AFTER PENTECOST

PROPER 28: SUNDAY BETWEEN 13 AND 19 NOVEMBER

SUSANNA IS VINDICATED

Susanna's innocence is proven and her trust in God confirmed. Justice triumphs, due to Susanna's faith. But why is the community and Susanna's family silent about the unjust actions of these men over the years?

The Lord heard Susanna's cry. Just as she was being led off to execution, God stirred up the holy spirit of a young lad named Daniel, and he shouted with a loud voice, "I want no part in shedding this woman's blood!"

All the people turned to him and asked, "What is this you are saying?" Taking his stand among them he said, "Are you such fools, O Israelites, as to condemn a daughter of Israel without examination and without learning the facts? Return to court, for these men have given false evidence against her."

So all the people hurried back. And the rest of the elders said to Daniel, "Come, sit among us and inform us, for God has given you the standing of an elder." Daniel said to them, "Separate them far from each other, and I will examine them."

When they were separated from each other, he summoned one of them and said to him, "You old relic of wicked days, your sins have now come home, which you have committed in the past, pronouncing unjust judgments, condemning the innocent and acquitting the guilty, though the Lord said, 'You shall not put an innocent and righteous person to death.' Now then, if you really saw this woman, tell me this: Under what tree did you see them being intimate with each other?" He answered, "Under a mastic tree." And Daniel said, "Very well! This lie has cost you your head, for the angel of God has received the sentence from God and will immediately cut you in two."

Then, putting him to one side, he ordered them to bring the other. And he said to him, "You offspring of Canaan and not of Judah, beauty has beguiled you and lust has perverted your heart. This is how you have been treating the daughters of Israel, and they were intimate with you through fear; but a daughter of Judah would not tolerate your wickedness. Now then, tell me: Under what tree did you catch them being intimate with each other?" He answered, "Under an evergreen oak." Daniel said to him, "Very well! This lie has cost you also your heart, for the angel of God is waiting with the sword to split you in two, so as to destroy you both."

Then the whole assembly raised a great shout and blessed God, who saves those who hope in God. And they took action against the two elders, because out of their own mouths Daniel had convicted them of bearing false witness; they did to them as they had wickedly planned to do to their neighbor. Acting in accordance with the law of Moses, they put them to death. Thus innocent blood was spared that day.

Hilkiah and his wife praised God for their daughter Susanna, and so did her husband Joakim and all her relatives, because she was found innocent of a shameful deed. And from that day onward Daniel had a great reputation among the people.

Daniel 13:44 – 64

CHRIST THE KING

REIGN OF CHRIST
PROPER 29: SUNDAY BETWEEN 20 AND 26 NOVEMBER

LIVE ACCORDING TO WISDOM
Those who seek Wisdom and follow her path are an image of Christ's reign.

I thank you and praise you,
    and I bless the name of the Lord.

While I was still young, before I went on my travels,
    I sought wisdom openly in my prayer.
Before the temple I asked for her,
    and I will search for her until the end.

From the first blossom to the ripening grape
    my heart delighted in her;
my foot walked on the straight path;
    from my youth I followed her steps.

I inclined my ear a little and received her,
    and I found for myself much instruction.
I made progress in her;
    to the one who gives wisdom I will give glory.

For I resolved to live according to wisdom,
    and I was zealous for the good,
    and I shall never be disappointed.
My soul grappled with wisdom,
    and in my conduct I was strict.
I spread out my hands to the heavens,
    and lamented my ignorance of her.
I directed my soul to her,
    and in purity I found her.

Sirach 51:12b – 20

Whichever gospel passage was not used on the Fifth Sunday of Lent may be used here.

LEAVE HER ALONE
In Christ's reign the loving service of women is not scorned or forbidden by men.

Six days before the Passover Jesus came to Bethany, the home of Lazarus, whom he had raised from the dead. There they gave a dinner for Jesus. Martha served, and Lazarus was one of those at the table with him. Mary took a pound of costly perfume made of pure nard, anointed Jesus' feet, and wiped them with her hair. The house was filled with the fragrance of the perfume. But Judas Iscariot, one of his disciples (the one who was about to betray him), said, "Why was this perfume not sold for three hundred denarii and the money given to the poor?" (He said this not because he cared about the poor, but because he was a thief; he kept the common purse and used to steal what was put into it.) Jesus said, "Leave her alone. She bought it so that she might keep it for the day of my burial. You always have the poor with you, but you do not always have me."

John 12:1–8

THE WOMAN WHOM JESUS DOES NOT CONDEMN
This gospel passage gives a vision of Christ's reign in which women and men equally are invited and enabled to live anew.

Jesus went to the Mount of Olives. Early in the morning he came again to the temple. All the people came to him and he sat down and began to teach them. The scribes and the Pharisees brought a woman who had been caught in adultery; and making her stand before all of them, they said to Jesus, "Teacher, this woman was caught in the very act of committing adultery. Now in the law Moses commanded us to stone such women. Now what do you say?" They said this to test Jesus, so that they might have some charge to bring against him.

Jesus bent down and wrote with his finger on the ground. When they kept on questioning him, he straightened up and said to them, "Let anyone among you who is without sin be the first to throw a stone at her." And once again he bent down and wrote on the ground. When they heard it, they went away, one by one, beginning with the elders.

And Jesus was left alone with the woman standing before him. Jesus straightened up and said to her, "Woman, where are they? Has no one condemned you?" She said, "No one, sir." And Jesus said, "Neither do I condemn you. Go your way, and from now on do not sin again."

John 8:1–11

APPENDIX 1

Psalms

PSALMS

Excerpts from some psalms that include feminine images of God are offered here. They may be used as responsories following other readings.

GOD AS SHELTERING MOTHER

Hear my just claim, God,
give me your full attention.
My prayer deserves an answer,
for I speak the truth.
Decide in my favor,
you always see what is right.

I call to you, God,
for you answer me.
Give me your attention,
hear me out.

Show me your wonderful love,
save the victims
of those who resist you.

Keep a loving eye on me.
Guard me under your wings,
hide me from those who attack,
from predators who surround me.
They close their heart,
they mouth contempt.

Psalm 17:1 – 2, 6 – 7, 8 – 10

GOD AS MIDWIFE

You are the Holy One enthroned,
the Praise of Israel.
Our people trusted, they trusted you;
you rescued them.
To you they cried, and they were saved;
they trusted and were not shamed.

But you, God, took me from the womb,
you kept me safe at my mother's breast.

I belonged to you from the time of birth,
you are my God from my mother's womb.

I will sing of you in the great assembly,
make good my promise before your faithful.
The poor shall eat all they want.
Seekers of God shall give praise.
"May your hearts live for ever!"

Psalm 22:4 – 6, 10 – 11, 26 – 27

GOD AS MOTHER WHO WASHES HER CHILDREN

Have mercy, tender God,
forget that I defied you.
Wash away my sin,
cleanse me from my guilt.

You love those centered in truth;
teach me your hidden wisdom.
Wash me with fresh water,
wash me bright as snow.

Creator, reshape my heart,
God, steady my spirit.
Do not cast me aside
stripped of your holy spirit.

Help me, stop my tears,
and I will sing your goodness.
Lord, give me words
and I will shout your praise.

Psalm 51:3 – 4, 8 – 9, 12 – 13, 16 – 17

GOD AS SHELTERING MOTHER

Care for me, God, take care of me,
I have nowhere else to hide.
Shadow me with your wings
until all danger passes.

I have decided, O God,
my decision is firm:

to you I will sing my praise.
Awake, my soul, to song!

Awake, my harp and lyre,
so I can wake up the dawn!
I will lift my voice in praise,
sing of you, Lord, to all nations.
For your love reaches heaven's edge,
your unfailing love, the skies.

O God, rise high above the heavens!
Spread your glory across the earth!

Psalm 57:2, 8 – 9, 10 – 12

GOD AS SHELTERING MOTHER

Hear me, God! I cry out,
listen to my prayer.
I call from far away,
for my courage fails.
Lead me to a mountain height
where I can be safe.

You are my refuge,
a tower of strength against my foes.
Welcome me into your home,
under your wings for ever.

God, you surely hear my vows;
give me the blessings of those who honor your name.

I sing your name always,
each day fulfilling my vows.

Psalm 61:2 – 3, 4 – 5, 6, 9

GOD AS SHELTERING MOTHER

All you sheltered by the Most High,
who live in Almighty God's shadow,
say to the Lord, "My refuge, my fortress,
my God in whom I trust!"

God will free you from hunters' snares,
will save you from deadly plague,
will cover you like a nesting bird.
God's wings will shelter you.

"I deliver all who cling to me,
raise the ones who know my name,
answer those who call me,
stand with those in trouble.
These I rescue and honor,
satisfy with long life,
and show my power to save."

Psalm 91:1 – 2, 3 – 4, 14 – 16

Mary and the Dragon

APPENDIX 2

Essays

The Feminine as Omitted, Optional, or Alternative Story: A Feminist Review of the Episcopal Eucharistic Lectionary

Jean Campbell, OSH

Over the past few years, feminists have focused attention upon recovering feminine images of God and the role of women in the scriptural account of salvation history. The work of Elisabeth Schüssler Fiorenza, Phyllis Trible, Elisabeth Moltmann-Wendel, and others have shown that the scriptures, although heavily influenced by patriarchal and hierarchical structures, contain a significant account of women in relationship to salvation history and the understanding of God in both masculine and feminine images and metaphors. Yet, the fact that these scriptural images, metaphors and stories are part of the Christian tradition is largely unknown. A letter to the editor of *The Living Church* responding to the suggestion that feminine images of God should be included in the liturgy, raised the question, "When and by whom was this information [feminine images of God] disclosed in history?"[1]

The ways in which we understand and know God are formed within the liturgy of the church. What we pray and sing as well as the stories we re-tell in public worship form and shape what we believe about God and about ourselves in relationship to God and to each other.

> When Christians gather for worship, their identity as Christians is established or reinforced: the common heritage is recalled and celebrated; their heroes, founders, and holy people are commemorated; and the work of God in human history and in the life of the community is recognized.[2]

If we do not know when and by whom the feminine images of God and the story of women in salvation history are disclosed, we need to begin to reexamine what stories we tell within our liturgy.

It is my contention that feminine images and stories of women are to be found in the Bible, but they have been ignored, designated as optional, or have been assigned as alternative scripture readings within the eucharistic lectionary of the Episcopal Church. Feminine images of God and the stories of faithful women have not been recognized as a significant part of the story of the people of God by those responsible for appointing the lections. Thus, when feminists speak of reclaiming the feminine aspects of salvation history, the common reaction is that one is somehow changing either scripture or the tradition. In fact many feminists are merely asking that the fullness of the scriptures and tradition be recognized within the public prayer of the church.

This study focuses upon the Sunday eucharistic lectionary of *The Book of Common Prayer* and includes the portions of scripture appointed for every Sunday in the three-year cycle, along with those lessons appointed for Christmas and Ascension Day. The *Revised Standard Version* of the Bible was used for the translation of the scriptures. This is the most commonly used version of the Bible in parish churches and therefore would most accurately reflect the texts that are heard at a normal parish eucharist. In those instances where some verses are optional, they were included in the readings appointed. Where alternative readings are given, all the lections appointed were included in the study.

Marjorie Procter-Smith identifies several levels of interpretation which are operable when one begins to look at the lectionary. First, the lectionary is selective: it chooses to use certain texts and exclude others; hence it operates on a hermeneutical principle. The lessons appointed for Sundays imply that they are important to nourish and sustain the ongoing life of the community. A second level of interpretation is defining what verses of a given selection shall be read: the lectionary defines the limits of the text, its beginning and end. The third level is the relationship between the first and second lesson, and the Gospel reading: how the lessons interact will interpret certain texts.[3]

I would suggest a fourth level of interpretation: where the text is placed in regard to the calendar of the church year. The lectionary is rooted in the cycle of the church year and as such will determine what stories are remembered within significant festal cycles, as well as how often a particular passage will be read.

In her article, Procter-Smith establishes two categories, "significant" and "peripheral," to designate biblical passages which include references either to feminine images of God or to women. For the purposes of this study, pericopes in which women played a prominent role, or the image of God was feminine, are regarded as "significant." For instance, God as mother, Isaiah 66:13; the woman anointing the feet of Jesus, Matthew 26:1 – 13; the parable of the lost coin, Luke 15:1 – 10; or wives being subject to their husbands, Ephesians 5:21 – 33, are identified as "significant" passages. Where there is passing reference to the feminine, these were regarded as peripheral, such as the metaphorical references to Jerusalem, Isaiah 65:18; reference to a hen gathering her brood, Luke 13:34; the "women of our company," Luke 24:22; or "Apphia our sister" in Philemon. The categories of significant and peripheral do not judge the text as being negative or positive in reference to females or feminine images of God.[4]

The following chart shows the total number of pericopes included in the study and the numbers of significant and peripheral passages:

	O.T.	Gospel	Epistles	Acts
Total	175	182	164	24
References to Women	48	47	9	6
(Percent of Total)	(23%)	(21%)	(5%)	(25%)
Significant	12	23	1	0
Peripheral	36	24	8	6

There are also six pericopes from the Book of the Revelation, one of which makes reference to the "Bride" (22:17). The lessons from Acts are appointed for the Easter season, and in each case alternatives are appointed.

Given the patriarchal nature of scripture, the lections, on the whole, are positive in regard to women and seem to be numerous. However, when one begins to examine the lectionary and the various levels through which the scripture is interpreted one begins to discern a pattern in which the feminine metaphors for God and the experience of women are omitted, or are assigned as optional or alternative readings. For instance, of the forty-seven gospel pericopes eleven passages are designated as optional readings.

For the principal service of Easter, year A, John 20:1 – 18 is appointed with verses 11 – 18 optional. An alternative gospel is also appointed, Matthew 28:1 – 10. The optional verses from John contain the encounter between Mary Magdalene and the risen Lord with her subsequent proclamation to the disciples: "I have seen the Lord." John 20:11 – 18 is the gospel appointed for Tuesday in Easter week in all three years. However, the fact that it is an optional passage in an alternative gospel reading on the principal service of Easter once every three years will diminish the possibility of the community hearing the story of the appearance of Jesus to Mary Magdalene and of her proclamation of the resurrection.

There is an interesting comparison to be found in the reading for Easter year C where Luke 24:1 – 10 omits v. 11, which recounts the disbelief of the disciples to the proclamation of the women that they had experienced the empty tomb and were given a message. To include the Marcan account of the fear of the women, Mark 16:1 – 8 in year B, and to leave out the incredulity of the male disciples in Luke (24:11) causes one to ask what the underlying assumptions were in selecting the verses.

The story of the Samaritan woman at the well is read on Lent 3A. Again the portion of the story which is optional, John 4:27 – 38, contains the questioning of the disciples and also relates the evangelism of the woman to those in the city to "come and see" (v. 28). Both the amazement that Jesus would be revealed to a woman and her activity in bringing others to Jesus are not considered significant enough to be included in the pericope.

The story of the annunciation to Abraham and Sarah [Proper 11C, Genesis 18:1 – 10a (10b – 14)] also provides for optional verses. Sarah's response of confusion and laughter to the promise that she would bear a child is contained in the optional verses. The gospel for this Sunday is the story of Mary and Martha, Luke 10:38 – 42. The cluster of stories on this Sunday provides a rare opportunity of exploring the human encounter with the divine as experienced in the lives of women.

On the 5th Sunday of Lent year A, John 11:1 – 44 is appointed, with verses 1 – 16 as optional. The optional verses identify the relationship between Mary, Martha, Lazarus, and Jesus, along with the discussion between Jesus and the disciples concerning the raising of Lazarus. Verse 45 is not included in the lection which speaks of those "who had come with Mary," who saw and believed. There appears to be a pattern, consciously or unconsciously determined, in which the stories of women are considered optional or are omitted in the portions of scripture read in our Sunday eucharistic gatherings.

The role of women is also ignored or diminished in the passion gospels through both omissions and the use of optional passages. The passion gospel appointed for Palm Sunday in all cases provides for portions of the story to be deleted. While recognizing that the passion gospel is the longest reading of the church year, the fact remains that those verses which recount the role of women in the salvific mission of Jesus are considered optional by the church. Often on the parochial level, the optional portions are omitted in order to "shorten" the liturgy.

In the three synoptic accounts of the passion appointed on Palm Sunday, in all cases, the optional passages relate the involvement of women in the passion of Jesus Christ. In both the long and short form of the Matthean account, 27:55−66 are optional. "There were also many women there, looking on from afar, who had followed Jesus from Galilee, ministering to him; among whom were Mary Magdalene, and Mary the mother of James and Joseph, and the mother of the sons of Zebedee" (vv. 55−56). The remaining verses recount the burial of Jesus and the watchfulness of Mary Magdalene and the other Mary at the sepulcher after Joseph of Arimathea had left.

The Marcan account of the passion appointed for year B allows for the omission of 15:40−47. Again, this is the account of the women who followed, ministered, and saw where Jesus was laid in the tomb.

Year C [Luke (22:39−72), 23:1−49 (50−56)] does include Luke 23:49, which states that the women who were with Jesus from Galilee "stood at a distance and saw these things." However, the optional passage, 23:50−56, recounts the ministry of the women who followed, saw, and prepared spices and ointments for the burial of Jesus.

The ministry of women is to be found at the beginning and the end of the passion narrative in both the gospel of Matthew and Mark. Yet, the stories of the woman anointing the feet of Jesus at Bethany, Matthew 26:6−13 and Mark 14:3−9, are omitted from the Sunday eucharistic lectionary.

Mark 14:3−9 is separated from the passion narrative and appointed for the Monday in Holy Week as an alternative to the Johannine account of the anointing of Jesus' feet by Mary of Bethany (John 12:1−11). The Johannine account shifts the emphasis from the service of the woman to the dialogue between Judas and Jesus and the concern for the poor. Matthew 26:1−5, 14−25 is appointed for the Wednesday in Holy Week; however, the anointing of the feet of Jesus at the house of Simon the leper is deleted. One must raise the question as to why the one gospel story which is identified as the one to be remembered wherever the gospel is preached should be deleted from the Sunday lectionary. Matthew states: "Truly, I say to you, wherever this gospel is preached in the whole world what she had done will be told in memory of her" (Matthew 14:13), or again, in the gospel of Mark: "Wherever the gospel is preached in the whole world, what she has done will be told in memory of her" (Mark 14:9).

The compilers of the lectionary did include the story of the woman anointing the feet of Jesus in the gospel of Luke. Luke 7:36−50 is appointed for Proper 6C. Luke does not include it as part of the passion narrative, but places it earlier in the gospel account. There are some notable differences in the story as recounted by Luke in comparison with the story in either Matthew or Mark. In Luke, the focus is on forgiveness and the teaching to Simon. Only in Luke is the woman identified as a sinner: "And behold, a woman of the city, who was a sinner" (Luke 8:37). The first lesson appointed with this gospel is that of II Samuel 11:26 — 12:10, 13−15. It is the story of Nathan's confrontation with David who had slept with the "wife of Uriah." The sin of David and the woman who is a sinner are paralleled in the choosing of the propers for this day. The fullness of the faithful witness of the woman anointing the feet of Jesus is thus further diminished.

It should be noted that the lectionary of *The Book of Common Prayer* also omits the verses which follow after the story of the woman anointing the feet of Jesus in the gospel of Luke. Luke, chapter 8, concerns discipleship, yet verses 1–3 are omitted from the reading, which identifies those who followed Jesus. The twelve are mentioned as being with Jesus in his preaching and "also some women who had been healed . . . Mary, called Magdalene, . . . and Joanna, . . . and Susanna, and many others, who provided for them out of their means."

The story of the Shunammite woman and Elisha is appointed for the fifth Sunday after Epiphany in year B, II Kings 4:(8–17), 18–21, (22–31), 32–37. The optional passages tell the story of the recognition, hospitality, persistence, and assertiveness of the Shunammite woman: she is a wealthy woman who offers Elisha hospitality (v. 8): "I perceive that this is a holy man of God" (v. 9). She asks for nothing in return, yet Elisha promises her a child as she has none and her husband is old. In vv. 22–25 she is certain that the man of God can help her son who is ill so she takes the initiative and seeks out Elisha. This is a story of a woman who is strong, perceptive, and faithful, but again, those portions which portray the fullness of the woman's experience of faithfulness are optional. The lectionary also links this story with the healing of Simon's mother-in-law, which gives an emphasis upon the healing aspect of the story.[6]

Another omission from the proclamation of the story of salvation is the woman with the issue of blood. The story of Jairus' daughter and the woman who has faith are intricately interwoven stories found in the synoptic gospels. Yet when they are to be appointed for proclamation in the Sunday liturgy there is a curious twist: only the Marcan story of Jairus' daughter is told (Proper 8B), and the faithfulness of the woman with the "flow of blood" (Mark 25–34) is omitted from the hearing of the community. The parallel stories, Matthew 9:18–26 and Luke 8:40–53, are not included in the eucharistic lectionary.

In reviewing the lections, one begins to notice that some of the most prominent feminine passages in scripture fall on days which can be replaced with other propers. A major attempt was made in the calendar of the church year to maintain the primacy of Sunday, yet if a feast day falls on a Sunday, "when desired," "the Collect, Preface, and one or more of the Lessons appointed" of feasts of our Lord and all other major feasts may be used instead of the Sunday propers, except on Sundays "from the Last Sunday after Pentecost through the First Sunday after the Epiphany, or from the Last Sunday after the Epiphany through Trinity Sunday."[7]

The only passage in the gospels which provides a feminine metaphor for God is the story of the woman with the lost coin, found in Luke 15:1–10, which is appointed for Proper 19C. Proper 19 falls on the Sunday closest to September fourteenth, Holy Cross Day, a feast of our Lord.[8] Therefore, when Holy Cross Day falls on a Sunday, "when desired," the propers for Holy Cross Day can be substituted for those appointed. Some parishes, contrary to the rubrics of the BCP, continue to transfer a major feast to a Sunday, thus further diluting the Sunday lectionary. The woman with the lost coin is a complementary story to the parable of the shepherd with the lost sheep in Luke. It will be read once every three years, if it is not supplanted by the festal propers.

Another explicitly feminine metaphor for God, Isaiah 66:10–16, occurs in Proper 9 of year C on the Sunday closest to July sixth, hence on the Sunday closest to Independence Day, a day listed as a major feast.[9] A number of parishes use the propers appointed for July fourth instead of the Sunday propers appointed. In the practice of the normal parish, one would question how often people will hear: "Behold, I will extend prosperity to her like a river and the wealth of the nations like an overflowing stream; and you shall suck, you shall be carried upon her hip and dandled upon her knees. As one whom his mother comforts, so I will comfort you; you shall be comforted in Jerusalem" (Isaiah 66:12 – 13).

Isaiah 49:8 – 18 contains the passage: "Can a woman forget her suckling child, that she should have no compassion on the son of her womb? Even these may forget, yet I will not forget you" (v. 15). It is appointed for the eighth Sunday after Epiphany in year A and also for Proper 3A. One might assume that in a forty-year period, one will hear a given proper twelve times or more. Yet, the fourth to the ninth Sundays after Epiphany and Propers 1 – 4 are dependent upon the movable date of Easter. From 1985 to 2025, this passage will be read five times on the eighth Sunday after the Epiphany in year A, and as Proper 3A once, a total of six times in forty years.[10]

This paper has not attempted to include an extensive account of the omissions of the stories of women in salvation history, or to provide an exhaustive list of the feminine images of God contained in the scriptures. Noticeably absent from the lectionary are selections from the books of Ruth, Judith, Esther, and Judges, along with maternal metaphors from the Old Testament, such as Deuteronomy 32:18 and Psalm 131. The Acts and the epistles recount the stories of women who (such as Lydia, Tabitha, and Priscilla) supported and sustained the missionary activities of Peter and Paul. Yet, these too are excluded from the public retelling of the story of the church.

I have focused on the Sunday eucharistic lectionary of *The Book of Common Prayer* and how the scriptures appointed are used in the parochial setting. There is a whole facet of work in the lectionary revisions that are currently going on which needs to identify more fully the remembering of women in the proclamation of the story of salvation.

I have shown that those stories which are included are all too often designated as optional readings, appointed as an alternative text, displaced by the cycle of feasts, or omitted altogether. The letter quoted in the opening paragraphs of this paper is, I believe, typical of many people in the church. We do not know the stories of women contained in scripture nor are we aware of the rich feminine metaphors of God in the Hebrew Scriptures because they have not been part of the story proclaimed within our Sunday eucharistic worship. The fullness of the compassionate, merciful, and loving God, as well as the history of the women who have been faithful, have not been considered of value to be heard publicly in the gathering of the community of faith.

One can only hope that those who are empowered to make the decisions of what is proclaimed in the eucharist will allow the fullness of the story to be retold. At the same time the church needs to revise the lectionary so that the story of the whole people of God may be proclaimed in the Body of Christ.

Notes

1. Braxton H. Tabb, Jr., letter to the editor, "Disclosed by Whom?" *The Living Church* 196, no. 13 (March 27, 1988): 4.
2. Majorie Procter-Smith, "Images of Women in the Lectionary," in Elisabeth Schüssler Fiorenza and Mary Collins, eds., *Women – Invisible in Church and Theology, Concilium* 182 (Edinburgh: T. & T. Clark, Ltd., 1985): 51.
3. Procter-Smith, 52.
4. Procter-Smith, 54 – 5.
5. *The Common Lectionary* has John 20:1 – 18 as the first option for the principal Easter reading in all three years, with synoptic lections as alternatives.
6. In *The Common Lectionary,* this passage from II Kings is linked with Luke 10:38 – 42, the hospitality of Mary and Martha.
7. *The Book of Common Prayer,* 1979, 16.
8. Ibid., 16.
9. Ibid., 17.
10. Computations made from "Tables for Finding Holy Days," *The Book of Common Prayer,* 880 – 85.

Bibliography

Fuller, Reginald. *Preaching the New Lectionary.* Collegeville, Minnesota: The Liturgical Press, 1974.

Moltmann-Wendel, Elisabeth. *The Women Around Jesus.* New York: Crossroad, 1982.

Schneiders, Sandra M. *Women and the Word.* New York: Paulist Press, 1986.

Schüssler Fiorenza, Elisabeth. *Bread Not Stone.* Boston: Beacon Press, 1984.

Schüssler Fiorenza, Elisabeth. *In Memory of Her.* New York: Crossroad, 1984.

Schüssler Fiorenza, Elisabeth and Mary Collins, eds. *Women – Invisible in Church and Theology, Concilium,* Vol. 182. Edinburgh: T. & T. Clark Ltd., 1985.

Jean Campbell is a member of the North American Academy of Liturgy, to which she delivered this paper in 1990.

Women in the Bible and the Lectionary

Ruth Fox, OSB

At the conclusion of a four-hour presentation I once gave on "Women of the Bible," one of the participants exclaimed, "I never knew Jesus had women disciples." She was puzzled why she had never heard this before, since she had been a devout church-going Catholic for all her 35 years. She heard the Sunday scripture readings and listened to homilies week after week. Yet, her admission confirmed once again that the revisions of the lectionary mandated by the Second Vatican Council suffer a serious flaw.

The revision of the lectionary was mandated by the *Constitution on the Sacred Liturgy:* "The treasures of the Bible are to be opened up more lavishly, so that richer fare may be provided for the faithful at the table of God's word." (#51) On May 25, 1969, the Sacred Congregation for Divine Worship promulgated a new order of readings for use at Mass. From this directive, the National Conference of Catholic Bishops in the United States authorized the publishing of a new lectionary for use in our churches, effective Palm Sunday, 1970. Thus many more books and passages of the Bible were made available to Catholics through the scripture readings at Sunday and daily Mass. Homilies based on the readings were to illustrate the relevance of these passages to the daily life of Christians. For over 25 years, pastors and liturgists, as well as Catholics in the pew, have been rejoicing at this increased exposure to the word of God. The assumption was widely made that the new lectionary faithfully presented the essence of the Bible, with omissions of only some few troubling or gory passages.

This satisfying assumption has recently been controverted by shocking evidence to the contrary. A careful analysis of the lectionary reveals that a disproportionate number of passages about the women of the Bible have been omitted. Women's books, women's experiences, women's accomplishments have been largely overlooked in the assigned scripture readings that are proclaimed in our churches on Sundays and weekdays. In this article I will first point out some of the significant biblical passages about women that are omitted altogether, are relegated to weekdays, or are designated as optional. I hope to illustrate how some readings are used to reinforce what some believe to be the weaknesses or proper role of women. Then I will make a cursory review of the imbalance of the saints recognized in the lectionary. Finally, I will offer some suggestions for liturgists and presiders to rectify the deficiencies.

FIRST TESTAMENT WOMEN

A survey of the lectionary reveals that the account of the two brave midwives, Shiphrah and Puah of the book of Exodus, is omitted entirely from the lectionary. The weekday reading of Exodus 1:8 – 22 (lectionary #389, Monday of the 15th Week in Ordinary Time, Year I) skips from verse 14 to 22, thus excising the story of these valiant women who put their own lives at risk by defying pharaoh's law of death to uphold God's law of life.

Deborah, named a prophet and judge of Israel and recognized as a mother of Israel, is also passed over in the lectionary. As prophet and judge, Deborah advised her people, planned a military strategy against the Canaanites, appointed a general, and then led the victorious battle. Deborah's song of victory in Judges 5:1–31 is considered to be one of the most ancient extant compositions of the Bible, but it is not used in the lectionary. Although Gideon, Jotham, and Jephthah from the Book of Judges find their way into the weekday lectionary, Deborah is left standing outside the gate.

The Book of Ruth gains only two weekday readings (#423, Friday of the 20th Week in Ordinary Time, Year I, and #424, Saturday of the 20th Week in Ordinary Time, Year I), the famous "Wherever you go" passage showing her devotion to her mother-in-law, and the passage exalting her bearing of a son for her husband Boaz.

Huldah the prophet, who made history in 2 Kings 22, is excised from weekday reading #373 (Wednesday of the 12th Week in Ordinary Time, Year II). This woman, a seventh-century BCE contemporary of Jeremiah and one of the few women or men literally labeled a prophet, was consulted by King Josiah, the reformer. When an old scroll (now thought to be probably the original form of Deuteronomy) was found in the temple by the priest Hilkiah, the king ordered, "Go, consult the LORD for me, for the people, for all Judah, about the stipulations of this book that has been found . . ." (2 Kings 22:13). The royal delegation took the scroll not to Jeremiah, but to Huldah, who verified the authenticity of the scroll and, as a prophet, spoke God's warnings to the king. The verses referring to Huldah (verses 15–19) are neatly sliced out of the middle of the lectionary passage (2 Kings 22:8–13; 23:1–3).

Esther, a great heroine in a time of oppression, is proclaimed only in a Lenten weekday reading (#228), in which is recorded her prayer appealing to God for strength. No account of the bravery with which she saved her people from annihilation is given anywhere in the lectionary. Three other passages from the Book of Esther are found in the lectionary (in the Common of Saints, #737; and in Masses for Various Occasions, #821, #876). But not only might these passages never be used in the parish, all three are accounts of the prayer of Esther's uncle, Mordecai.

Judith, another heroine who jeopardizes her life for her people, is recalled in just two passages: Judith 13:18, 19, 20 (lectionary #709) is an optional responsorial psalm for the Common of the Blessed Virgin ("You are the highest honor of our race"). And lectionary #737, in the Common of Saints (Judith 8:2–8) praises the recluse Judith's asceticism and physical beauty; it is recommended for proclamation on the memorials of saints who were widows. Judith's initiative, determination, and great courage in saving her nation are nowhere presented in the lectionary.

The heroism of the Maccabee brothers is recounted on 32nd Sunday of Ordinary Time in Year C (#157), but the passage stops short of the tribute paid to their mother, who encouraged their bravery. Although the mother's valor is recognized in the Bible as "most admirable and worthy of everlasting remembrance" (2 Maccabees 7:20), she is actually remembered by the church only on Wednesday of 33rd Week in Ordinary Time (#499) — and then only in Year I! The sons and their mother are again separated in the Common of Martyrs (lectionary #713.2 and 713.3 deal with the sons, while 713.4 deals with the mother).

SECOND TESTAMENT WOMEN

Two of the most obvious exclusions of women from Second Testament scriptures are found in different readings from the daily lectionary. In the continuous reading from Romans, verses 1 and 2 of chapter 16 are omitted from lectionary #490 (Saturday of the 31st Week in Ordinary Time, Year I): "I commend to you our sister Phoebe, who is a deaconess [the Greek word is "deacon"; the revised NAB uses "minister"] of the church of Cenchrae. Please welcome her in the Lord, as saints should. If she needs help in anything, give it to her, for she herself has been of help to many, including myself." Thus church-goers will never hear in our liturgy of Phoebe, a woman who was a deacon.

Another overt omission of a verse about women's spiritual influence is made from 2 Timothy 1:1 – 12, assigned to Wednesday of the 9th Week in Ordinary Time, Year II, which as lectionary #355 neatly excises verses 4 and 5, including: "I find myself thinking of your sincere faith — faith which first belonged to your grandmother Lois and to your mother Eunice."

There are also noteworthy omissions of women from the assigned gospel passages. It seems incredible that the Magnificat, the beautiful and revolutionary song of Mary in Luke 1:46 – 56, is never proclaimed on a Sunday. It is found on a weekday before Christmas (#199) and on two feast days of Mary, the Visitation (#572) and Assumption (#622). By not assigning it to a Sunday, though, the lectionary seems willing to risk that not many Catholics will hear this marvelous song of praise attributed to Mary.

The Gospel of Luke is the only one that narrates Jesus' healing of a woman who had been crippled for eighteen years (Luke 13:10 – 17); yet, this pericope is assigned to Saturday of the 29th Week in Ordinary Time (#479). Although Jesus recognizes her with the unusual status of "daughter of Abraham," this touching story of her faith and Jesus' breaking of the Sabbath law in the synagogue to heal a woman is not proclaimed on any Sunday.

It is well known that Jesus' women disciples, led by Mary Magdalene, were the first witnesses to the resurrection, according to all the gospels. However, Easter Sunday's gospel (#43) stops just at the point of the beautiful story of Jesus' appearance to Mary Magdalene in the garden and his important commission to her: "Go to my brothers and tell them . . ." (John 20:17; the newer Canadian lectionary rectifies this problem by adding verses 10 – 18). In fact this appearance of Jesus to Mary Magdalene does not rate any Sunday of the Easter season but is assigned to Easter Tuesday (#262) and used again on the saint's memorial (always a weekday, never a Sunday) in July (#603). However, Peter and John's race to the tomb in John 20:1 – 9 (#43) is retold every Easter Sunday and Jesus' appearance to Thomas in John 20:19 – 31 (#44) is read on the Second Sunday of Easter every year.

While it is only natural that the gospels for the Sundays of Easter should proclaim the appearances of the risen Lord, the gospels assigned to the fourth through the seventh Sundays of Easter use excerpts from the prayer of Christ at the Last Supper, ignoring Christ's appearance to and dialogue with Mary Magdalene in John 20:11 – 18 for Sunday proclamation. Similarly, the gospel for Easter Monday (#261) gives Matthew's account of the women finding Christ risen (Matthew 28:8 – 15). While Matthew 28:1 – 10 is read at the Easter Vigil in Year A, Matthew 28:8 – 15 would make an excellent follow-up Sunday gospel, yet it is relegated to Monday.

The first reading for each of the Sundays of Easter is taken from the Acts of the Apostles. The selections focus on the sermons and activities of Peter, Paul, Barnabas and Stephen. The women leaders found in the Acts of the Apostles — Tabitha, Lydia and Priscilla — are given second place in the weekday readings of the Easter Season.

MAKING WOMEN OPTIONAL

Throughout the lectionary, some of the assigned gospel passages that are quite lengthy have optional cut-off points to make the readings shorter and supposedly more acceptable to the Sunday assembly. The presider is authorized to read the whole passage or to cut it short. Several of the passages set aside by parentheses as optional and expendable relate the experiences of women.

February 2, the feast of the Presentation of the Lord in the Temple, is assigned the gospel of Luke 2:22 – 40. When Mary and Joseph presented Jesus in the Temple, they were met by Simeon and the prophet Anna, both of whom recognized the infant as the Savior. In the lectionary (#524), the verses about the prophet Anna may be omitted. This same gospel is read on the Sunday after Christmas in Year B (#17) but both Simeon and Anna are considered optional here. The prophet Anna might never appear to witness to Jesus in our churches.

Jesus' healing of a woman with a hemorrhage is significant for Jesus' disregard for the taboos against women (speaking to a woman in public, being touched by a woman, being made unclean by the touch of a bleeding woman). Yet this miracle with its implications may be sliced out of the gospel (Mark 5:21 – 43) in the optional short reading for the 13th Sunday in Ordinary Time in Year B (#99). If the presider decides not to read it in Year B it is never heard by the Sunday assembly. Matthew's and Mark's complete version of this story may be heard on a weekday (Tuesday of the 4th Week in Ordinary Time, every year, #324; and Monday of the 14th Week in Ordinary Time, every year, #383), but Luke's version is omitted altogether in Year C.

The Gospel of Matthew is used for the passion reading on Palm Sunday, Year A (#38). Although Matthew's passion account begins with the anointing of Jesus on the head by a woman, the lectionary omits these verses, 26:6 – 13. The optional short version of this same reading also concludes just before the mention of the faithful women who had followed Jesus to Jerusalem from Galilee. The gospel reading for Wednesday of Holy Week (#260) begins again with Matthew 26:14, repeating the story from Sunday of the betrayal by Judas, and excluding again the anointing by a woman.

For Year B, the Palm Sunday passion reading from Mark (#38), only the optional long version includes the anointing of Jesus on the head by a woman and the witness of the women at the cross. Thus the role of Jesus' women disciples is again excluded for those who might hear only the short version.

In the Gospel of John the anointing of Jesus is performed by Mary of Bethany at a banquet served by her sister Martha. This version of the anointing story (John 12:1 – 8) is read only on a weekday, Monday of Holy Week (#258). It is not included in the reading of the passion on Good Friday, taken each year from the Gospel of John.

One might ask if any account of the anointing of Jesus by a woman is familiar to Catholics. Of course, the sinful and penitent woman of Luke 7:36–50, who washes Jesus' feet with her tears, is presented on the 11th Sunday in Ordinary Time in Year C (#94) and every year on Thursday of the 24th Week in Ordinary Time (#446). The lectionary does not give us the same familiarity with Mark's and Matthew's versions where a woman, not identified as a sinner, assumes the role of a prophet in anointing Jesus on the head. It is of this woman that Jesus promised (in vain?) "I assure you, wherever the good news is proclaimed throughout the world, what she did will be spoken of as her memorial." (Matthew 26:13)

The gospel of Luke also includes a passage (8:1–3) that makes note of some of Jesus' women disciples: Mary Magdalene, Joanna, Susanna and others unnamed. These three short verses are attached to Luke 7:36–50 when read on the 11th Sunday in Ordinary Time in Year C (#94). Why? By association with the woman in Luke 7:37, are the women named in Luke 8:2–4 also assumed to be sinful? However, these verses are marked as optional. But if they are omitted, Joanna and Susanna may go unknown except for a weekday mention (Friday of the 24th Week in Ordinary Time, every year, #447).

One of the few feminine images of God in the gospels, "the reign of God is like yeast which a woman took . . . ," (Matthew 13:33) is optional on the only Sunday it appears (16th Sunday in Ordinary Time, Year A, #107). Matthew's and Luke's parables with this image along with the mustard seed are found on weekdays (Monday of the 17th Week in Ordinary Time, #401; and Tuesday of the 30th Week in Ordinary Time, #480). Probably few Sunday homilies present the image of baker-woman God to balance the image of farmer God.

MAKING WOMEN STEREOTYPES

Sometimes in the lectionary when women are not overlooked or rendered optional, passages containing positive references to a woman are left out, while those containing negative ones are retained. For example, Exodus 15:20–21, in which Miriam (sister of Moses and Aaron) is identified as a prophet and leads a liturgy of thanksgiving after the crossing of the sea, is omitted from the lectionary. These verses could easily have been attached to the Easter Vigil reading (#42) that exalts the role of Moses, particularly since modern scholarship has pretty much proven that the older scriptural tradition is that of Miriam leading the liturgy of thanksgiving; the account of Moses leading the song of victory was added later, borrowing from the Miriam story. However, Miriam's weaker side is revealed in the story of her envy and punishment with leprosy (Numbers 12:1–13) in a weekday reading (Tuesday of the 18th Week in Ordinary Time, Year I, #408).

Another disturbing tendency is the editing of texts according to gender stereotypes. One of the most convincing examples is the lectionary's editing of Proverbs 31 for the 33rd Sunday in Ordinary Time, Year A (#158). The lectionary omits the verses (31:14–18, 21–29) that praise the woman's initiative, business acumen, dignity and wisdom: "Like merchant ships she secures her provisions from afar. . . . She picks out a field to purchase; out of her earnings she plants a vineyard. She is girt about with strength. . . . She makes garments and sells them. . . . She is clothed with strength and dignity." However, the lectionary does include the passages praising the woman for serving her husband and being his "unfailing prize." The gospel for this day is Matthew 25:14 – 30, the story about the three servants who are given silver pieces. Only with the reading of the complete passage of the industrious woman will listeners be able to find a connection to the industrious male servant of the gospel.

The tragedy of the sacrifice of the daughter of Jephthah is read on Thursday of the 20th Week in Ordinary Time, Year I (#422). Her father, having made a rash vow to sacrifice "whoever comes out of the doors of my house to me when I return in triumph" (Judges 11:31), felt obligated to fulfill his brazen promise. The lectionary augments the tragedy by succeeding this reading with the response "Here am I, Lord; I come to do your will" and Psalm 40. Does this imply that God approved Jephthah's impulsive vow or that parents have unlimited, life-threatening authority over their children? Victims of violence should surely never be expected to sing "Here am I, Lord" on the table of sacrifice. Those who sing this song may well ask, "Where is the God who rescued the son Isaac from his father, but did not rescue the daughter from her father?"

On Holy Family Sunday, the Sunday after Christmas, one would hope to find readings portraying the family of Mary, Joseph, and Jesus as a model for contemporary families. The first reading from Sirach does refer to respect for mothers as well as fathers (Sirach 3:4, see lectionary #17). But the responsorial psalm that follows, Psalm 128, addressed to men, portrays the psalmist's ideal role of women: "Your wife shall be like a fruitful vine in the recesses of your home." The second reading clearly puts the family relationships in similar perspective, "You who are wives, be submissive to your husbands" (Colossians 3:18). Credit must be given to the U.S. bishops who requested and received permission from the Vatican in June 1992 to omit that verse and the following three verses from public reading. A similar permission was requested and received to shorten Ephesians 5:21 – 32 to omit "Wives should be submissive to their husbands . . ." on the 21st Sunday in Ordinary Time, Year B (lectionary #123), on Tuesday of the 30th Week in Ordinary Time, Year II (lectionary #480), and at weddings (lectionary #775). One wonders if liturgists and pastors are aware of these permissions: See the *Newsletter of the Bishops' Committee on the Liturgy,* June 1992.

The first reading on Pentecost Sunday (#64) is from Acts 2:1 – 11. The opening verse as given in the Bible (NAB) reads: "When the day of Pentecost came it found *them* gathered in one place" (emphasis mine). Those who were gathered are named in Acts 1 as the eleven and "some women in their company, and Mary the mother of Jesus, and his brothers." In the lectionary, the opening sentence is interpreted and modified to read "When the day of Pentecost came it found the *brethren* gathered in one place" (emphasis mine). Now "brethren" theoretically may be an inclusive noun, but it is not heard as such in this selection. Have homilies revealed that Mary and other women received the Holy Spirit on Pentecost along with the Twelve and other men?

An important part of our Catholic liturgical experience is the remembrance and celebration of the holy men and women who have been faithful to Christ unto death. From the time of the early martyrs, liturgical tradition has brought the saints to our attention for veneration, inspiration, and encouragement. The 1970 lectionary, of course, follows the revised calendar. But the revised sanctoral cycle indicates an unbalanced ratio of 144 male saints to 28 female saints. (The U.S. bishops have since added 10 men and 7 women to the roster.) The month of June alone brings 19 men before the church for veneration, and no women!

Days in the sanctoral cycle are ranked in the descending order of solemnity, feast, memorial and optional memorial. Celebrations in honor of Mary, Joseph, John the Baptist, Peter and Paul are given the status of solemnities. Feasts also are assigned to these 5 again, as well as 14 more men. The highest rank in the calendar that any woman besides Mary has achieved is that of memorial. Even though Mary Magdalene has been recognized through the centuries as "apostle to the apostles" (see John Paul II, "On The Dignity and Vocation of Women," 16), she ranks below the Twelve in the liturgy.

Further study of the lectionary reveals that 42 of the male saints have at least one proper reading assigned for their day, while only 8 female saints (not counting Mary) have a special reading. Of these 8 women, only Mary Magdalene, Theresa of the Child Jesus, and Anne (who shares a memorial with Joachim) are assigned a proper first reading and gospel. Memorials without proper readings may use readings from the appropriate set of "common" readings (Common of Martyrs, Common of Saints and so on). However, for days ranked below feasts, which includes all the memorials of women, liturgical guidelines recommend the use of the daily continuous readings from the lectionary.

Memorials of both men and women saints use both the Common of Martyrs and the Common of Saints, but only memorials of men use the Common of Pastors and the Common of Doctors. Furthermore, only memorials of women are assigned to the Common of Virgins, even though many of the male saints are in fact virgins (i.e., celibate or vowed religious), too.

The memorials of the only two women ever named "doctors" of the church—Catherine of Siena and Teresa of Avila—each do have proper first readings, but the gospel is not chosen from the Common of Doctors, but from the Common of Virgins (for both Catherine and Teresa) or the Common of Saints/Religious (for Teresa)!

Women and men who are looking for spiritual nourishment from the stories of our ancestors both male and female are discovering that the diet is very meager at the table of the liturgy.

SUGGESTIONS

A revised lectionary was recently approved by the National Conference of Catholic Bishops and sent to Rome for confirmation. However, the Vatican withdrew its initial confirmation of one translation (the New Revised Standard Version) and ordered a reworking of another (the Revised New American Bible) because of the use of inclusive language. There are no substantial changes in the selections of readings in the lectionary. There are, however, some actions that presiders and liturgists can take to use the lectionary to its maximum potential and correct some of the deficiencies noted above.

1. Choose to read the long versions of the gospel whenever a short version is provided. If that will seem to make Mass too long, perhaps something else could be shortened, such as the homily.

2. At the beginning of Mass have the commentator or presider call attention to verses that have been omitted from the lectionary readings. This information also can be supplied in the bulletin.

3. Preach on the full biblical text, especially the omitted verses.

4. Include the omitted verses in the assigned reading, either by retyping the full passage and inserting it in the lectionary, or by reading the complete passage from the Bible itself; the Bible was used for proclamation before the lectionary ever came into being. (For more on the legality of adding verses to the lections, see the book by canonist John Huels, *More Disputed Questions on the Liturgy,* published by Liturgy Training Publications.)

5. Use scripture passages about women that are neglected by the lectionary on other occasions in parish life, on evenings of formation or reflection, or the commissioning of ministers, for example. For catechists: Anna the prophet, Priscilla and Aquila, Lydia, Lois, and Eunice; for musicians: Miriam or Judith leading the singing with tambourines; for lectors: Huldah, the prophet; for ministers of hospitality: the women who welcome prophets in 1 Kings 17 or 2 Kings 4; for ministers of communion: Martha's confession in John 11.

6. Use the Magnificat or portions of Esther's and Judith's prayers to open or close parish meetings until people come to learn them by heart.

7. For communal anointings of the sick, add an extra reading from Mark or Matthew on the woman anointing Jesus on the head to prepare him for his passion; or refer to it in the homily.

8. At funeral vigils for women, use the full reading from Proverbs 31.

9. For pro-life rallies use Exodus 1:8–22, including the omitted verses 14–21 on the midwives.

10. Celebrate all optional memorials of women saints throughout the year.

INVALUABLE MANIFESTATIONS

The rationale used for the choosing of the scripture texts for the lectionary is found in the introduction to the lectionary, especially #7 and #8. Omitted passages are those of lesser importance; they contain serious literary, critical, or exegetical problems; they will not be understood by the faithful; they are not essential to the meaning of the text; they have lesser spiritual value; they have little pastoral worth; they contain truly difficult questions. Certainly all of us would agree that not all passages of the Bible are suitable for public reading in the liturgy. And an analysis of the lectionary similar to mine would reveal that many stories of men also are omitted. But given the already limited focus on women in the Bible, it would seem that lectionary editors would choose to be more inclusive of women — if they wished the liturgy to speak to women. But it is not just a matter of speaking to women. Just as men are held up as spiritual models for women (how many sermons have we heard on the faith of Peter?), so, too, men's spirituality is enriched and aided with feminine patterns of holiness.

Since Vatican II we have been reminded again and again that "the liturgy is the summit toward which the activity of the Church is directed; at the same time it is the fountain from which all her power flows" (*Constitution on the Sacred Liturgy*, 10). The liturgy is meant to be a source of holiness and a celebration of union with God for all God's people. If liturgy is to be authentic, then, it must speak to the experience of women as well as to men. Since "Sacred Scripture is of paramount importance in the celebration of the liturgy" (CSL, 24) then the scripture readings should represent the totality of salvation history and human experience. Because the homily is to be drawn mainly from the scripture readings, it follows that if the readings overlook women or present negative stereotypes, homilies will also. The full history of God's intervention in the lives of women and men needs to be made known, if the celebration of the liturgy is to "pertain to the whole body of the church" (CSL, 26).

Pope John Paul II has himself called for the recognition and appreciation of the historical gifts of women: "The church asks at the same time that these invaluable 'manifestations of the Spirit,' which with great generosity are poured forth upon the 'daughters' of the eternal Jerusalem, may be attentively recognized and appreciated so that they may return for the common good of the church and of humanity, especially in our times." (*On the Dignity and Vocation of Women*, 31)

(The original and much shorter version of this article first appeared as "Strange Omission of Key Women in Lectionary" in *National Catholic Reporter*, May 13, 1994, 13 – 14.)

Ruth Fox is the liturgy director at Sacred Heart Monastery in Richardton, North Dakota, and president of the Federation of St. Gertrude, a canonical association of 18 monasteries in the United States and Canada. She writes and gives retreats on the women of the Bible.

Women in the Lectionary

Eileen Schuller, OSU

The Canadian church has been using the new edition of the Sunday lectionary for just over one year now. In the past year, I have been asked on more than one occasion whether the lectionary is "favorable" to women and whether the new edition of the lectionary is "better or worse" for women in comparison with what we were using previously. While this might not be the precise way I would choose to formulate the question, the concern expressed is valid: there is something of real importance at stake for women and for the church as a whole in the choice of scripture passages which are heard in the regular Sunday morning assembly.

In offering some reflections on this issue, I would want to situate the question within a somewhat broader perspective. On the one hand, the lectionary introduced in Advent 1969 has been widely acclaimed as one of the most successful achievements of the liturgical reform; it fulfils the mandate of the Second Vatican Council that in our Sunday assemblies we have "more reading from Holy Scripture and it is to be more varied and suitable" (*Constitution on the Sacred Liturgy*, 35), arranged so as to focus on the paschal mystery of Jesus Christ. This does not mean, however, that over the last twenty years, no questions have been raised about specific aspects of lectionary structure and selection. There has been, for example, considerable critique of the choice of the Old Testament passages in Ordinary Time, particularly insofar as they are selected to "harmonize" (*Introduction to the Lectionary*, 67) with the New Testament in a more-or-less typological way.

More recently, serious questions have been asked about what our congregations hear about women as the lectionary is read over the three-year cycle. Do the passages read on Sunday morning help or hinder us in dealing with what it means for women to have a full and equal role in both church and society? Are the stories about women which are in the Bible adequately represented in the lectionary, or does the choice of Sunday readings give the impression that the Bible is even more male-centered than one would find if one sat down and read it through as a whole? Are there some passages which, even though they are in the Bible, need not or should not necessarily be read in the Sunday assembly? When we recall that a lectionary is, by definition, selective (that is, certain biblical passages are read, and others are omitted) it is appropriate to ask if concern about women was given adequate or even explicit consideration in the choices of passages made in the late 1960s. The question becomes even more important when we admit that for many Catholics the Sunday readings become "the Bible"; these are virtually the only scripture passages which they read or know.

Before attempting to survey briefly both what we do find in the lectionary and what is omitted, I would want to make two brief asides. I am interested specifically in the choice of passages, rather than the related (and also important) issue of the specific translation from Greek or Hebrew which is used. The new edition of the lectionary adopts the New Revised Standard Version translation which strives to avoid masculine-orientated language in passages which refer to both men and women. Thus, for language about people, the new edition of the lectionary is more inclusive than the previous edition (though the NRSV is by no means the "last word" on this point, and there is need for much further study of principles of translation, particularly for use in a liturgical context).

Secondly, it needs to be emphasized that the new edition of the lectionary is not a revision or a re-doing of the lectionary per se. The choice of readings follows the lectionary of the universal church, as promulgated in 1969, with minor supplements added in 1981. Occasionally a reading was slightly expanded by the addition of a few verses, but any major rethinking of the choice of readings remains a project for the future.

WOMEN IN THE OLD TESTAMENT READINGS

Though traditional study of the Bible has tended to put the emphasis on leading male figures, there are many more women mentioned in the Old Testament than has often been realized. Of these, Sarah appears in two Old Testament readings in the Sunday lectionary (Genesis 18:1 – 10, 16th Sunday C; and Genesis 17:15 – 26, 21:1 – 7, Holy Family B) as well as in the second reading from Hebrews 11 (Holy Family B and 19th Sunday C). We also are introduced to Hannah (1 Samuel 1:20 – 28, Holy Family C), the widow of Zarephath (1 Kings 17:10 – 16, 32nd Sunday B; 1 Kings 17:8 – 24, 10th Sunday C), the "wealthy woman of Shunem" (2 Samuel 12:7 – 13, 11th Sunday C). With the addition of a verse in the new edition, Miriam "and all the women [who] went out with her with tambourines and with dancing" (Exodus 15:20) are part of the Exodus reading at the Easter Vigil.

However, many women of the Old Testament receive no mention in the Sunday lectionary. We do not hear the stories of the matriarchs, Rebekah and Rachel, nor of Hagar, Deborah, or Huldah, the prophet to whom King Josiah turned in order to authenticate the law code found in the temple (2 Kings 22:14 – 15). Although the opening chapters of the book of Exodus are filled with women whose acts of courage and initiative saved the life of Moses and made possible the divine plan of deliverance (the midwives Shiphrah and Puah, the mother of Moses, his sister, his wife Zipporah), none of these are in the lectionary.

There are no readings at all from the books of Ruth, Judith, or Esther. Nor do we ever hear the stories of three of the women whom Matthew includes in the genealogy of Jesus (Matthew 1:3 – 6): Tamar, Rahab, and Ruth. And even in many of the examples given above, the "harmonization" with the gospel shifts the perspective away from the women in the Old Testament passage (for example, the reading from Genesis 18 highlights Abraham's hospitality to his guests and the gospel tells of Mary and Martha's hospitality to Jesus; Sarah's presence and even the promise that she shall have a son become secondary).

It is especially instructive to see how the creation narratives in Genesis 1 – 3 are treated in the lectionary, given that these chapters have been so formative in our understanding of male/female relationships and roles. The Priestly version in Genesis 1 which speaks of God creating men and women together in the divine image is read at the Easter Vigil, and thus is heard only on this one occasion by that segment of the community who attend this service. Instead, on Sunday mornings on three separate occasions (Lent 1 A, 10 and 27 Sundays B) the assembly hears parts of the creation story from Genesis 2 – 3, a text which is much more problematic in that it can be interpreted to imply that women are subordinate and to be blamed for sin coming into the world. However, some passages which have been very influential in the past in shaping attitudes are not included at all (for example, Genesis 3:16, "I will greatly increase your pangs in childbearing . . . and your husband shall rule over you").

The biblical passages which speak with rich female imagery in praise of Lady Wisdom are well represented in the lectionary: Proverbs 8:22 – 31, Trinity Sunday C; Proverbs 9:1 – 6, 20th Sunday B; Wisdom 6:12 – 16, 32nd Sunday A; Wisdom 7:7 – 11, 28th Sunday B; Sirach 24:1 – 12, 2nd Sunday after Christmas; Baruch 3:9 – 15, 32 — 4:4, Easter Vigil). The wisdom texts from Proverbs and Ben Sira which speak most harshly and negatively about wives, daughters and the "foreign woman" are omitted. The lectionary does include the praise of the "capable wife" from Proverbs 31 (33rd Sunday A), paralleling her to the man with five talents in the gospel of the day; in the new edition of the lectionary, some verses are added to include her qualities of business acumen and wisdom. The reading from Sirach 3:2 – 16 on the obligation to parents (Holy Family A) is, for the most part, explicit in speaking of both fathers and mothers.

Another type of passage draws upon female imagery and language in speaking of God. A few of these are found in the lectionary, including Isaiah 49:14 – 15 (8th Sunday A), "Does a woman forget her nursing child . . ." and Isaiah 66:13 (14th Sunday C), "As a mother comforts her child, so I will comfort you," although many others are never read in the context of the Sunday assembly.

WOMEN IN THE GOSPEL READINGS

Since the intent of extending the Sunday lectionary to a three-year cycle was to read the gospels in the entirety, we can rightly expect that all the gospel material about women would be included. Thus over the three years, we hear of:

- The Canaanite woman who challenges Jesus (Matthew 15:21 – 28, 20th Sunday A);
- Simon's mother-in-law who is cured and "began to serve them" (Mark 1:29 – 31, 5th Sunday B);
- The healing of Jairus' daughter (Mark 5:21 – 43, 13th Sunday B);
- The widow with her offering (Mark 12:41 – 44, 32nd Sunday B);
- The woman who anoints Jesus (Luke 7:36 – 50, 11th Sunday C);
- The raising of the son of the widow of Nain (Luke 7:11 – 17, 10th Sunday C);
- Mary and Martha who welcome Jesus into their home (Luke 10:38 – 42, 16th Sunday C);
- Martha's confession of faith, "I believe that you are the Messiah, the son of God" (John 11:1 – 44, Lent 5 A);
- The Samaritan woman at whose testimony many come to believe (John 4:5 – 42, Lent 3 A);
- The woman taken in adultery (John 8:1 – 11, Lent 5 C);
- The women who go to the tomb on Easter morning (Matthew 28:1 – 10, Mark 16:1 – 8, Luke 24:1 – 12, Easter Vigil).

In addition, we read a number of stories which involve Mary:
- The Annunciation (Luke 1:26 – 38, Advent 4 B);
- The visit to Elizabeth (Luke 1:39 – 45, Advent 4 C);
- The Christmas story;
- The wedding feast of Cana (John 2:1 – 12, 2nd Sunday C);
- Mary at the foot of the Cross (John 19:25 – 27, Good Friday);
- Mary in the upper room at Pentecost (Act 1:12 – 14, Easter 7 A).

In the earlier edition of the lectionary, a number of passages about women only appeared in the long version of a gospel reading, and so were omitted when a community chose the shorter reading. In the new edition, a few of these passages are now always read, e.g.:
- The women who traveled with Jesus and "provided for them out of their own resources" (Luke 8:1 – 3, 11th Sunday C);
- The parable of the woman who mixes yeast in the dough (Matthew 13:33, 16th Sunday A).

But there are still a number of occasions when, if the shorter reading is chosen, stories about women are what is omitted, e.g.:
- The women who stand by the cross and prepare the body for burial in Mark 15:40 – 47 and Matthew 27:55, 61, Passion Sunday;
- The woman with a hemorrhage in Mark 5:25 – 34, 13th Sunday B;
- The woman who anoints Jesus before his passion (Mark 14:3 – 9, Passion Sunday B;
- The prophet Anna in Luke 2:36 – 40, Holy Family B.

A few stories are absent totally from the lectionary. Most odd is the omission of Luke's account of the "daughter of Abraham" cured by Jesus on the Sabbath (Luke 13:10 – 17). Previously, neither of the two post-resurrection appearances to Mary Magdalene was included (Mark 16:9 – 11 and John 20:11 – 18); the new edition now gives these verses from John as an optional addition on Easter Sunday and as an optional gospel when November 2 falls on a Sunday.

The lectionary also includes parables and stories in which women feature as the main character:
- The widow and the unjust judge (Luke 18:1 – 8, 29th Sunday C);
- The woman searching for her lost coin, paralleling the shepherd searching for his lost sheep (Luke 15:8 – 9, 24th Sunday C);
- The woman mixing in the yeast, paralleling the man sowing the mustard seed (Matthew 13:31 – 33, 16th Sunday A).

WOMEN IN THE EPISTLES

We know from both the Acts of the Apostles and the epistles the names of a number of women in the early church, some of whom held positions of leadership and engaged in missionary work; yet almost none of these appear in the Sunday lectionary. For example, there is no mention of:
- Tabitha, "devoted to good works and acts of charity" (Acts 9:36 – 42);
- Lydia, a dealer in purple cloth, the first European convert and head of the household where Paul stayed in Philippi (Acts 16:14 – 15, 40);
- The four daughters of Philip "who had the gift of prophecy" (Acts 21:10);

- Prisca, whom Paul considers "a co-worker in Christ Jesus" (Romans 16:3 – 4);
- Junia, "prominent among the apostles" (Romans 16:7);
- Euodia and Syntyche, co-workers of Paul who "struggled beside me in the work of the gospel" (Philippians 4:2 – 3);
- Eunice and Lois, mother and grandmother who passed the faith on to Timothy (2 Timothy 1:5).

One of the places where a woman is named is the passing reference to Chloe (1 Corinthians 1:11, 3rd Sunday A), unfortunately not a name which many people today even recognize as female.

In addition to specific women, the epistles include a number of statements about women and their place in the Christian community. We read Paul's declaration of the profound and radical effect of baptism: "there is no longer Jew or Greek, there is no longer slave or free, there is no longer male and female, for all of you are one in Christ Jesus" (Galatians 3:28, 12th Sunday C). Those passages which give more concrete directions for roles and role distinction between men and women have not been included in the Sunday lectionary, probably because their problematic and time-bound nature was recognized: for example, the injunction that women veil their heads (1 Corinthians 11:1 – 16) or keep silent (1 Corinthians 14:34 – 35) or 1 Timothy 2:15, "she will be saved through childbearing."

If there is any single text which has generated discussion about whether or not it should be included in the lectionary it is the passage, "wives, be subject to your husbands as you are to the Lord" (Ephesians 5:22, 21st Sunday B); the comparable text from Colossians 3:18 – 19 is optional for Holy Family A. Both passages belong to the category of "household codes," which in the Greco-Roman world was an established genre of writing which outlined right conduct in hierarchical relations: children/parents, masters/slaves, husbands/wives. The lectionary chooses not to read the sections on slaves and masters. In the most recent revision of the lectionary in the United States, the American bishops allowed the option of omitting Ephesians 5:22 – 24, though this creates a rather odd passage in which husbands are addressed, but not wives. In the new Canadian edition of the lectionary, the Episcopal Commission for Liturgy made the judgment that the passage as a whole with its marriage imagery of the relationship between Christ and the church is important enough that sections should not be omitted; some verses were added (Ephesians 4:32, 5:1 – 2, 5:21) which place the admonition to wives in a broader context in which all Christians are exhorted to "be subject to one another out of reverence for Christ."

CONCLUSION

What then do we conclude about how the passages chosen for the Sunday lectionary deal with women? This brief survey has tried to survey the main texts, though clearly not every passage could be examined in detail in this short space. Certainly there is no systematic plot to eliminate women from the lectionary. The congregation on Sunday morning is introduced to a number of biblical women, especially from the gospels, and many of the most negative passages in the Bible are not read.

However, there is still much room for improvement and revision. The choice of scripture passages in the lectionary in the Roman tradition is based on a number of principles which need to be held in balance (e.g., a focus on the paschal mystery, use of the "most important" readings on Sundays, the tradition that links certain biblical books to seasons of the church year) and it is not a "given" that every biblical passage about women necessarily belongs in the Sunday lectionary traditions which have been part of the church's life throughout history, and with ever-deepening understanding of and sensitivity to the life of women in society today, we will come to a time when a major revision of the lectionary will be undertaken.

Yet, even within the traditional framework, the lectionary could make room for the stories of more women, especially women of the Old Testament and women who exercised leadership in the early Christian community. Some commentators have suggested that the "texts of terror," biblical stories of violence and abuse of women (for example, Jephthah's daughter, the unnamed concubine of Judges 19) do need to be heard, as readings which give voice to similar stories in the lives of women today. Furthermore, given the well-established principle of not choosing "texts which present real difficulties . . . for pastoral reasons" (*Introduction of the Lectionary,* 76), a strong case can be made for the omission to any passages which can serve to reinforce and give scriptural sanction to the subordination of women.

And perhaps, at times, we ask too much of the lectionary. The Sunday readings at Mass can never be the only context in which we experience the Bible. There is a real need for small group Bible study, catechetical and adult-learning programs to provide an arena for people to explore the full scope of what the Bible says about women; here we can bring our own experiences to interact with the text in ways which are not possible within the parameters of the Sunday eucharist.

Notes

1. For a discussion of the new edition as well as basic information about the lectionary, see *National Bulletin on Liturgy,* Winter 1992, 199 – 220.

2. For a study of women in the Common Lectionary, see Marjorie Procter-Smith, "Images of Women in the Lectionary," in Mary Collins and Elisabeth Schüssler Fiorenza, eds., *Women – Invisible in Theology and Church, Concilium* 182 (Edinburgh: T. & T. Clark, 1985): 51 – 62. A similar study has looked at the lectionary of the Book of Common Prayer: Jean Campbell, "The Feminine as Omitted, Optional or Alternative Story: A Feminist Review of the Episcopal Eucharistic Lectionary," *Proceedings of the North American Academy of Liturgy* (1990): 59 – 67. The only detailed study of the Roman lectionary which I have found is in German: Birgit Janetzy, "Ihre Names sind im Buch des Lebens: Frauengeschichte und ernauertes Lectionar," in Teresa Berger and Albert Gerhards, eds., *Liturgie und Frauenfrage* (Erzabtei St. Ottilien: EOS Verlag, 1990): 415 – 430.

3. For a brief statement of both the principles of translation and some of the broader issues, see the introduction by the NRSV Committee at the beginning of any edition of the NRSV.

4. Many of these passages are the focus of discussion in *The Women's Bible Commentary,* Carol A. Newsom and Sharon H. Ringe, eds. (Knoxville: Westminster/John Knox Press, 1992).

5. There has been much discussion among biblical scholars in recent years about whether the problems are with how Genesis 2 – 3 has been interpreted through the centuries or whether the text itself is fundamentally androcentric. For two opposing views, compare Phyllis Trible, "A Love Story Gone Awry," in *God and the Rhetoric of Sexuality* (Philadelphia: Fortress Press, 1978): 72 – 143; and David

Clines, "What Does Eve Do to Help? And Other Irredeemably Androcentric Orientations in Genesis 1–3," in *What Does Eve Do to Help?* (Sheffield: Sheffield Academic Press, 1990): 9–24.

6. This does not mean that every verse in all the gospels is read. In general, where the same incident occurs in two or three gospels only one version is included.

7. The Matthean version of this story is not read at all (Matthew 26:6–13) which is somewhat ironic given that the pericope ends, "Truly, I tell you, wherever this good news is proclaimed in the whole world, what she has done will be told in remembrance of her."

8. [Editor's note: it also needs to be remembered that Ordinary Sundays 6 through 13 are sometimes omitted because of variation in the date of Easter. Ordinary Sundays 9 through 11 are omitted half the time or more. These omissions are not evenly divided among cycles A, B and C, at least within the span of, for example, the six complete three-year cycles between 1972 and 1989. In that period Ordinary Sunday 7 A was omitted 3 times, 7 B was omitted twice, and 7 C was omitted 4 times. Readings that involve women that are scheduled for Ordinary Sundays 6 through 13 will actually be used only occasionally, therefore.]

9. In a comparable household code in 1 Peter, part of the injunction to slaves is read but without the verses which establish the context and thus the passage becomes a general admonition of all Christians (1 Peter 2:10b–25; Easter 4 A).

10. For the term and a collection of biblical stories, see Phyllis Trible, *Texts of Terror* (Philadelphia: Fortress Press, 1984).

11. For a study of how this principle is applied in the lectionary as a whole, see Eileen Schuller, "Some Criteria for the Choice of Scripture Texts in the Roman Lectionary," in Peter C. Finn and James M. Schellman, eds., *Shaping English Liturgy* (Washington: Pastoral Press, 1990): 385–404.

Eileen Schuller is an Ursuline Sister of Chatham, Ontario. She is a recognized expert on the Dead Sea Scrolls. Sister Schuller is a member of the subcommittee on the liturgical psalter of ICEL, and was a member of the advisory committee on the new Canadian edition of the lectionary. Formerly on the faculty of Atlantic School of Theology in Halifax, she is now associate professor of religious studies at McMaster University in Hamilton.

INDEX OF SCRIPTURE READINGS

Column one: The scripture passages used in this book are listed in the order in which they appear in the Bible. For instance, in the third row we see Genesis 2:18–24, the story of the creation of the first woman.

Column two: The Sunday or festival on which this book has suggested using the passage is given. A, B and C signify which year of the three-year cycle. OT represents Ordinary Time. For example, in this table we see that the story of the creation of the first woman is suggested for proclamation on OT 27B, that is, the Twenty-Seventh Sunday of Ordinary Time in year B.

Column three: The relationship of the passage to the lectionaries is shown here.

The abbreviations RL and RCL indicate that the passage is used in the Roman lectionary or the Revised Common Lectionary. The abbreviation Alt, for alternative, signifies that the passage is used in neither lectionary.

Superscript 1 and 2 designate the first and second series of the Revised Common Lectionary for first readings on the ninth to last Sundays of the year. In the first series passages from the Hebrew scriptures are read semi-continuously; in the second series passages from the Hebrew scriptures have been selected in light of the gospel reading.

If the abbreviations RL or RCL appear without elaboration, the verses included here are exactly the same as in the lectionary. When the passage used in this book is not precisely the same in the lectionary, the complete citation of the passage as it appears in the 1992 Canadian edition of the Roman lectionary is given.

Genesis 1:26 — 2:3	Easter Vigil ABC	RL 1:1 — 2:2
		RCL 1:1 — 2:4a
	Trinity A	RCL 1:1 — 2:4a
Genesis 2:18–24	OT 27B	RL 2:7ab, 8b, 18–24
		RCL[2]
Genesis 2:15–17; 3:1–7	Lent 1A	RL 2:7–9, 16–18, 2–5; 3:1–7
		RCL
Genesis 3:9–15	OT 10B	RL 3:8–15
		RCL[2] 3:8–15
Genesis 6:9–22; 7:24; 8:14–19	OT 9A	RCL[1]
Genesis 8:15–21	Lent 1B	Alt
Genesis 11:27–32; 12:10–20	Lent 2A	Alt
Genesis 12:1–9	OT 10A	RCL[1]
Genesis 15:1–6; 17:3b–5, 15–16; 21:1–7	Holy Family B	RL
Genesis 16:1–16	Lent 2C	Alt
Genesis 17:1–7, 15–16	Lent 2B	RCL

Genesis 17:15 – 22	Lent 2B	Alt
	Easter Vigil ABC	Alt
Genesis 18:1 – 15	OT 16C	RL 18:1 – 10a
		RCL² 18:1 – 10a
Genesis 18:1 – 15; 21:1 – 7	OT 11A	RCL¹ 18:1 – 15, (21:1 – 7)
Genesis 19:1 – 11	OT 6A	Alt
Genesis 19:15 – 26	OT 7A	Alt
Genesis 21:8 – 21	Easter Vigil ABC	Alt
	OT 12A	Alt
Genesis 23:1 – 6, 17 – 20	OT 19A	Alt
Genesis 24:34 – 38, 42 – 49, 58 – 67	OT 14A	RCL¹
Genesis 24:53 – 61	Baptism of Christ B	Alt
Genesis 25:19 – 34	OT 15A	RCL¹
Genesis 27:1 – 17	OT 16A	Alt
Genesis 29:15 – 28	OT 17A	Alt
Genesis 29:31 – 35	OT 22A	Alt
Genesis 30:1 – 13	OT 23A	Alt
Genesis 30:14 – 24	OT 24A	Alt
Genesis 31:19 – 35	OT 26A	Alt
Genesis 34:1 – 7, 25 – 31	Passion A	Alt
Genesis 35:9 – 20	Good Friday ABC	Alt
Genesis 38:6 – 19	Advent 2A	Alt
Genesis 38:20 – 30	Advent 3A	Alt
Genesis 39:6c – 20	OT 18A	Alt
Genesis 41:38 – 45	OT 20A	Alt
Exodus 1:8 — 2:10	Easter Vigil ABC	Alt
	OT 21A	RCL¹
Exodus 2:11 – 21; 4:21 – 26	Lent 3C	Alt
Exodus 15:19 – 21	Easter Vigil ABC	Alt
	Pentecost A	Alt
Exodus 20:1 – 4, 7 – 9, 12 – 20	OT 27A	RCL¹
	Lent 3B	RL 20:1 – 17
		RCL 20:1 – 17
Exodus 21:7 – 11	Ash Wednesday ABC	Alt
Exodus 22:21 – 27	OT 30A	RL
Exodus 35:20 – 29	Lent 4B	Alt
Numbers 11:10 – 15	Transfiguration A	Alt
	Lent 2A	Alt
Numbers 12:1 – 16; 20:1	OT 5A	Alt
Numbers 27:1 – 11	Easter Vigil ABC	Alt
	OT 29A	Alt

Deuteronomy 5:12–15	OT 9B	RL RCL²
Deuteronomy 15:12–17	Ash Wednesday ABC	Alt
Deuteronomy 21:10–14	Ash Wednesday ABC	Alt
Deuteronomy 24:19–22; 26:11–15	Lent 1C	Alt
Deuteronomy 32:10–18	Trinity B	Alt
Joshua 2:1–21	Advent 2B	Alt
Joshua 6:17–25	Advent 3B	Alt
Joshua 15:16–19	OT 30A	Alt
Judges 4:1–7	OT 33A	RCL¹
Judges 4:17–22; 5:1, 24–27, 31	OT 27A	Alt
Judges 5:3–4, 7–9	Easter Vigil ABC	Alt
Judges 5:10–12	Easter Vigil ABC	Alt
Judges 5:3–12	Pentecost B	Alt
Judges 11:29–40	Holy Thursday ABC	Alt
Judges 13:2–25	Lent 4C	Alt
Judges 16:4–22	OT 31A	Alt
Judges 19:16–30	Passion C	Alt
Ruth 1:1–18, 22	OT 31B	RCL¹ 1:1–18
Ruth 2:1–7	OT 17B	Alt
Ruth 2:8–13	OT 18B	Alt
Ruth 2:14–18	OT 19B	Alt
Ruth 2:19–23	OT 20B	Alt
Ruth 3:1–5; 4:13–17	OT 32B	RCL¹
Ruth 4:9–22	Advent 3C	Alt
1 Samuel 1:11, 20–28	Holy Family C	RL 1:11, 20–22, 24–28
1 Samuel 1:4–20	OT 33B	RCL¹
1 Samuel 2:1–10	Ash Wednesday ABC OT 33B	Alt RCL¹
1 Samuel 2:1–5	Easter Vigil ABC	Alt
1 Samuel 2:6–10	Easter Vigil ABC	Alt
1 Samuel 4:1–22	Good Friday ABC	Alt
1 Samuel 18:20–22, 27–29; 19:11–17	Lent 4A	Alt
1 Samuel 25:14–31	OT 7B	Alt
1 Samuel 25:32–35	Baptism of Christ C	Alt
1 Samuel 25:39c–42	Holy Thursday ABC	Alt
1 Samuel 28:5–14, 20–25	OT 3C	Alt
2 Samuel 11:1–15	OT 17B	RCL¹
2 Samuel 11:2–5, 26–27; 12:15b–18a, 24-25	Advent 2C	Alt

2 Samuel 11:26 — 12:15a	OT 18B	RCL[1] 11:26 — 12:13a
	OT 11C	RCL[2] 11:26 — 12:10, 13 – 15
2 Samuel 12:15b – 19, 24 – 25	OT 19B	Alt
2 Samuel 13:1 – 22	Passion B	Alt
2 Samuel 14:1 – 21	OT 2A	Alt
2 Samuel 20:1 – 2, 14 – 22	OT 2B	Alt
1 Kings 1:11 – 19, 29 – 31	OT 21B	Alt
1 Kings 3:16 – 28	OT 22B	Alt
1 Kings 10:1 – 13	Epiphany ABC	Alt
1 Kings 17:8 – 16	OT 32B	RL 17:10 – 16 RCL[2]
1 Kings 17:8 – 24	OT 10C	RL 17:8 – 9, 17 – 21a 22 – 24 RCL[1] 17:8 – 16, (17 – 24) RCL[2] 17:17 – 24
1 Kings 21:1 – 21a	OT 11C	RCL[1] 21:1 – 10, (11 – 14), 15 – 21a
2 Kings 4:1 – 7	OT 11B	Alt
2 Kings 4:8 – 17	OT 13A	RL 4:8 – 12a, 14 – 17
2 Kings 4:18 – 37	OT 12B	Alt
2 Kings 5:1 – 14	OT 6B	RCL
	OT 14C	RCL[1]
	OT 28C	RL RCL[2] 5:1 – 3, 7 – 15c
2 Kings 8:1 – 6	OT 5C	Alt
2 Kings 22:14 – 20	Easter Vigil ABC	Alt
	Pentecost C	Alt
Nehemiah 9:13 – 21	Transfiguration B	Alt
	Lent 2B	Alt
Judith 8:1 – 8	OT 25C	Alt
Judith 9:1 – 11	Ash Wednesday ABC	Alt
	OT 26C	Alt
Judith 12:1 – 9; 13:3 – 11	OT 28C	Alt
Judith 13:18 – 20	Baptism of Christ A	Alt
Judith 15:14 — 16:15	OT 29C	Alt
Judith 15:14 — 16:5	Easter Vigil ABC	Alt
Judith 16:5 – 16:15	Easter Vigil ABC	Alt
Esther 2:2 – 11	OT 6C	Alt
Esther 2:21 – 23	OT 7C	Alt
Esther 7:1 – 8; 9:20 – 23	OT 26B	RCL[1]

Esther 8:1 – 8	Lent 4B	Alt
Esther 9:24 – 32	OT 20C	Alt
Esther 14:3 – 14	Ash Wedneday ABC	Alt
	OT 8C	Alt
Job 1:1; 2:1 – 10	OT 27B	RCL[1]
Job 42:10 – 17	OT 29B	Alt
Psalm 17:1 – 2, 6 – 7, 8 – 10	Easter Vigil ABC	Alt
Psalm 51:3 – 4, 8 – 9, 12 – 13, 16 – 17	Easter Vigil ABC	Alt
Psalm 57:2, 8 – 9, 10 – 12	Easter Vigil ABC	Alt
Psalm 61:2 – 3, 4 – 5, 6, 9	Easter Vigil ABC	Alt
Psalm 91:1 – 2, 3 – 4, 14 – 16	Easter Vigil ABC	Alt
Proverbs 1:20 – 23	OT 24B	RCL[1] 1:20 – 33
Proverbs 3:13 – 18	Ascension C	Alt
Proverbs 4:5 – 13	Ash Wednesday ABC	Alt
Proverbs 8:1 – 4, 22 – 31	Trinity C	RL 8:22 – 31 RCL
Proverbs 9:1 – 6	OT 20B	RL RCL[2]
Proverbs 31:10 – 31	OT 33A	RL 31:10 – 13, 16 – 18, 20, 26, 28 – 31
	OT 25B	RCL[1]
Song of Solomon 3:1 – 4	OT 16B	Alt
Song of Solomon 8:1 – 5	OT 30B	Alt
Wisdom of Solomon 6:12 – 16	OT 32A	RL RCL[2]
Wisdom of Solomon 7:7 – 11	OT 28B	RL
Wisdom of Solomon 7:21 – 28	Ascension B	Alt
Wisdom of Solomon 9:9 – 18	OT 21B	Alt
Wisdom of Solomon 10:15 – 21; 11:1 – 5	Easter Vigil ABC OT 23B	Alt Alt
Wisdom of Solomon 16:20 – 21	OT 9C	Alt
Sirach 1:1 – 10	Ascension A	Alt
Sirach 3:2 – 7	Holy Family A	RL 3:2 – 6, 12 – 14
Sirach 4:11 – 18	Christ the King A	Alt
Sirach 6:18 – 31	OT 22C	Alt
Sirach 24:1 – 12	Christmas Day ABC Christmas 2 ABC	Alt RL 24:1 – 4, 8 – 12
Sirach 24:13 – 21	Lent 3C Christ the King B	Alt Alt

Sirach 35:16–19	OT 30C	RL 35:15–17, 20–22
		RCL[2] 35:12–17
Sirach 51:12b–20	Christ the King C	Alt
Isaiah 25:6–10a	Transfiguration C	Alt
	Lent 2C	Alt
Isaiah 42:10–16	OT 3B	Alt
Isaiah 46:3–4	Trinity A	Alt
Isaiah 49:13–16a	Easter Vigil ABC	Alt
	OT 8A	RCL 49:8–16a
Isaiah 51:1–6	OT 21A	RCL[2]
Isaiah 54:5–14	Easter Vigil ABC	RL
	OT 5B	Alt
Isaiah 62:1–5	OT 2C	RL
		RCL
Isaiah 62:6–12	Christmas Dawn ABC	RL
		RCL
Isaiah 66:5–9	OT 4B	Alt
Isaiah 66:10–14a	OT 14C	RL
		RCL[2]
Jeremiah 31:15–17	Lent 5B	Alt
Lamentations 1:1–6	OT 27C	RCL[1]
Baruch 3:9–15, 32—4:4	Easter Vigil ABC	RL
	OT 24C	Alt
Ezekiel 36:24–28	OT 9C	Alt
Susanna/Daniel 13:1–64	Easter Vigil ABC	Alt
Susanna/Daniel 13:1–27	OT 30C	Alt
Susanna/Daniel 13:28–43	OT 31C	Alt
Susanna/Daniel 13:44–64	OT 33C	Alt
Hosea 1:2–10	OT 17C	RCL[1]
Hosea 2:14–20	OT 8B	RL 2:14, 15, 19–20
		RCL
Hosea 11:1–11	OT 18C	RCL[1]
Hosea 13:4–8	OT 19C	Alt
Joel 2:26–29	Pentecost ABC	Alt
Micah 6:1–8	Easter Vigil ABC	Alt
	OT 4A	RCL
Zephaniah 3:14–18a	Advent 3C	RCL 3:14–20
Zechariah 9:9–12	OT 14A	RL 9:9–10
		RCL[2]
Matthew 1:1–17	Christmas Vigil ABC	RL 1:1–25
Matthew 1:18–25	Advent 4A	RL 1:18–24
		RCL

Matthew 2:1 – 12	Epiphany ABC	RL
		RCL
Matthew 2:13 – 23	Holy Family A	RL 2:13 – 15, 19 – 33
		RCL
Matthew 8:14 – 17	OT 9A	Alt
Matthew 9:18 – 26	OT 10A	RCL 9:9 – 13, 18 – 26
Matthew 11:16 – 19, 25 – 30	OT 14A	RCL
Matthew 13:31 – 33	OT 16A	RL 13:24 – 43
	OT 17A	RCL 13:31 – 33, 44 – 52
Matthew 13:54 – 58	OT 16A	Alt
	OT 17A	Alt
Matthew 14:1 – 12	OT 18A	Alt
Mathew 15:21 – 28	OT 20A	RL
		RCL 15:(10 – 20), 21 – 28
Matthew 20:17 – 28	OT 25A	Alt
Matthew 23:37 – 39	OT 26A	Alt
Matthew 25:1 – 13	OT 32A	RL
		RCL
Matthew 26:6 – 13	Passion A	Alt
	Christ the King A	Alt
Matthew 26:69 – 75	Passion A	RL 26:14 — 27:66
		RCL 26:14 — 27:66
	Pentecost A	Alt
Matthew 27:15 – 22	Passion A	RL 26:14 — 27:66
		RCL 26:14 — 27:66
Matthew 27:55 – 61	Passion A	RL 26:14 — 27:66
		RCL 26:14 — 27:66
Matthew 27:55 – 56	OT 2A	Alt
Matthew 28:1 – 10	Easter Vigil A	RL
		RCL
	Easter 2A	Alt
Mark 1:29 – 34	OT 5B	RL
		RCL
Mark 3:20 – 35	OT 10B	RL
		RCL
Mark 5:21 – 43	OT 13B	RL
		RCL
Mark 6:1 – 6	OT 14B	RL
		RCL 6:1 – 13
Mark 6:14 – 29	OT 15B	RCL
Mark 7:24 – 30	OT 23B	RCL 7:24 – 37

Mark 12:38–44	OT 32B	RL
		RCL
Mark 14:3–9	Passion B	RL 14:1 — 15:47
		RCL 14:1 — 15:47
	Christ the King B	Alt
Mark 14:66–72	Passion B	RL 14:1 — 15:47
		RCL 14:1 — 15:47
	Pentecost B	Alt
Mark 15:40–41	Passion B	RL 14:1 — 15:47
		RCL 14:1 — 15:47
	OT 2B	Alt
Mark 16:1–8	Easter Vigil B	RL
		RCL
	Easter 2B	Alt
Mark 16:9–14	Easter 3B	Alt
Luke 1:26–38	Advent 4B	RL
		RCL
Luke 1:39–45	Advent 4C	RL
		RCL 1:39–45,
		(46–55)
Luke 1:46–55	Advent 3A, 3B, 4C	RCL 1:47–55
		RL
		RCL 1:47–55
	Ash Wednesday ABC	Alt
Luke 2:1–16	Christmas Night ABC	RL
		RCL 2:1–14
		(15–20)
Luke 2:15–20	Christmas Dawn ABC	RL
		RCL[2]:(1–17), 8–20
Luke 2:15–21	1 January ABC	RL 2:16–21
		RCL 2:15–21
Luke 2:22–40	Holy Family B	RL
Luke 2:41–52	Holy Family C	RL
		RCL
Luke 4:38–41	OT 4C	Alt
Luke 7:11–17	OT 10C	RL
		RCL
Luke 7:36–50	Passion C	Alt
Luke 7:36 — 8:3	OT 11C	RL
		RCL
Luke 8:1–3	OT 2B	Alt
Luke 8:19–21	OT 14C	Alt
Luke 8:40–56	OT 15C	Alt

Luke 10:38 – 42	OT 16C	RL
		RCL
Luke 11:27 – 28	OT 17C	Alt
Luke 13:10 – 17	OT 21C	RCL
Luke 13:20 – 21	OT 22C	Alt
Luke 13:31 – 35	Lent 2C	RCL
Luke 15:1 – 10	OT 24C	RL 15:1 – 32
		RCL
Luke 18:1 – 8	OT 29C	RL
		RCL
Luke 21:1-4	OT 32C	Alt
Luke 22:54 – 62	Passion C	RL 22:14 — 23:56
		RCL 22:14 — 23:56
	Pentecost C	Alt
Luke 23:27 – 29	Passion C	RL 22:14 — 23:56
		RCL 22:14 — 23:56
Luke 23:55 – 56	Passion C	RL 22:14 — 23:56
		RCL 22:14 — 23:56
Luke 24:1 – 12	Easter Vigil C	RL
		RCL
	Easter 2C	Alt
John 2:1 – 11	OT 2C	RL 2:1 – 12
		RCL
John 4:5 – 30, 39 – 42	Lent 3A	RL 4:5 – 42
		RCL 4:5 – 42
John 8:1 – 11	Lent 5C	RL
	Christ the King C	Alt
John 11:1 – 45	Lent 5A	RL
		RCL
John 12:1 – 8	Lent 5C	RCL
	Good Friday ABC	Alt
	Christ the King C	Alt
John 18:15 – 17, 25 – 27	Good Friday ABC	RL 18:1 — 19:42
		RCL 18:1 — 19:42
John 19:25 – 27	Good Friday ABC	RL 18:1 — 19:42
		RCL 18:1 — 19:42
John 20:1 – 18	Easter Sunday ABC	RL
		RCL
John 20:1 – 2	Easter 3A	Alt
John 20:11 – 18	Easter 3C	Alt
Acts of the Apostles 1:6 – 14	Easter 7A	RL
Acts of the Apostles 2:1 – 4, 14 – 18	Pentecost ABC	RCL 2:1 – 21
Acts of the Apostles 5:1 – 11	Easter 5C	Alt

Acts of the Apostles 9:36–43	Easter 4C	RCL
Acts of the Apostles 12:1–17	Easter 4A	Alt
Acts of the Apostles 16:9–15	Easter 6C	RCL
Acts of the Apostles 16:16–40	Easter 7C	RCL 16:16–34
Acts of the Apostles 17:1–4, 10–12, 15, 22, 30–34	Easter 4B	Alt
Acts of the Apostles 18:1–3, 18–19, 24–26	Easter 5B	Alt
Acts 21:4–14	Easter 5A	Alt
Romans 4:13–25	OT 10A	RL 4:18–25 RCL
Romans 8:18-26	Advent 1A	Alt
Romans 16:1–5	Easter 6B	Alt
Romans 16:6–13	Easter 7B	Alt
Romans 16:14–16, 25–27	Trinity C	Alt
1 Corinthians 1:10–18	OT 3A	RL 1:10–13, 17–18 RCL
1 Corinthians 16:19–24	Trinity A	Alt
Galatians 3:26–28	Easter Vigil ABC OT 12C	Alt RL 3:26–29 RCL 3:26–29
Galatians 4:4–7	1 January ABC	RL RCL
Galatians 4:22 — 5:1	OT 13C	Alt
Philippians 4:1–7	OT 28A	RCL 4:1–9
Colossians 4:15–18	Easter 6A	Alt
1 Thessalonians 5:1–11	Advent 1C	Alt
1 Timothy 5:3–16	OT 25C	Alt
1 Timothy 5:9–10	Holy Thursday ABC	Alt
2 Timothy 1:1–7	OT 27C	RCL 1:1–14
2 Timothy 4:19–22	Trinity B	Alt
Philemon 1–7	OT 23C	RCL 1–21
Hebrews 11:8, 11–12, 31	Holy Family B	RL 11:8, 11–12, 17–19
James 2:18–26	OT 24B	Alt
James 3:13 — 4:3, 7–8a	OT 25B	RL 3:16 — 4:3 RCL
Revelation 12:1–5a	Advent 1B	Alt